WALKIN
WOUNDED

THE LIFE AND POETRY OF
VERNON SCANNELL

ANDREW TAYLOR

OXFORD
UNIVERSITY PRESS

OXFORD
UNIVERSITY PRESS

Great Clarendon Street, Oxford, OX2 6DP,
United Kingdom

Oxford University Press is a department of the University of Oxford.
It furthers the University's objective of excellence in research, scholarship,
and education by publishing worldwide. Oxford is a registered trade mark of
Oxford University Press in the UK and in certain other countries

© Andrew Taylor 2013

The moral rights of the author have been asserted

First Edition published in 2013

Impression: 1

British Library Cataloguing in Publication Data

Data available

ISBN 978-0-19-960318-3

Printed in Great Britain by
Clays Ltd, St Ives plc

For Sam, Abi, and Bec,
and Lucy, Sophie, and Tom.

Contents

Foreword

by John Carey

People who like poetry tend to have particular poems that they remember
at particular times of the year. Browning's 'It is the first mild day of March'
always comes into my head as the days start to grow warmer, and Hopkins's
'Summer ends now' as they cool. But for years now my most regularly
remembered seasonal poem has been Vernon Scannell's 'Autumn':

> It is the football season once more
> And the back pages of the Sunday papers
> Again show the blurred anguish of goalkeepers.
>
> In Maida Vale, Golders Green and Hampstead
> Lamps ripen early in the surprising dusk;
> They are blurred like stale rinds with a fuzz of mist...

A poet as big as Scannell cannot be summed up in a single quotation, of course.
All the same, these lines show some of his key traits. There is the wry wit,
twinned with an equally wry despondency. There is the gritty urban milieu,
and the eye for beauty that lights it up, turning the streetlamps into ripening
fruit. Most of all there are the human depths seen beneath the surface of things.
The goalkeepers' anguish, which seems comic at first, is truly anguish and does
not belong just to goalkeepers. It signifies our common failure and loss, including the loss of another year of life as winter approaches.

Scannell nearly always works at two levels, one realistic and external, the
other imaginative, metaphorical, haunted by memory and desire. Already in
his early poems he shows his facility for slipping into dream or nightmare
or fantasy as he looks at ordinary things:

> Policemen hard as ebony
> Hold heavy bruises in gloved hands

Rows of houses are 'stern as soldiers'; rain falls 'as though the sky has been
bereaved'; on washing lines 'the white sheets puff their chests towards the

sun'. These are all from his 1957 collection *A Mortal Pitch*, but the ability to transform the ordinary with a single word never deserts him, and for the reader it always brings a thrill of surprise, especially when the word comes from some quite unexpected context—the gravestones in 'War Cemetery: Ranville', for example, 'White as aspirin'.

Starting to read a Scannell poem is, on this level, a little like waiting for the curtain to go up at the theatre. You know something exciting is going to happen, but you don't know what. He is the only poet, so far as I know, who has written a whole poem about a fish and chip shop ('Frying Tonight'). It is a triumph of succulence and sensuousness, and it is serious. It has none of the amused condescension a more uppity poet would resort to. For a cultured, little-magazine poet a Parisian café would seem an acceptable poetic subject, but a fish and chip shop would deserve mention only in some effortful bid for social realism. But Scannell is not like that. He writes as someone who sees the beauty of fish and chip shops and loves their smells, sights, and sounds, from the dumpy, dark vinegar bottles, 'Like little holy sisters in white caps', to the fresh peeled chips that 'spit and sizzle like a thousand cats' as they cascade into the hot oil.

Scannell is also the only poet I know of who dares to use the English language as the English language is really used—'What slaps you in the eyeballs is her tits', for example, from 'Dreamgirl'. It is true that Philip Larkin, whom Scannell remembers admiringly in 'In Memoriam PAL, 2.12.85', might just have written that line. But Larkin, lacking Scannell's military experience, could never have managed the poetic equivalent of an ordinary British other-ranker's speech that Scannell reproduces in 'What a fucking awful mob' ('Swearing In') or 'Not a bad old bastard, Captain Treve' ('Varieties of Bastard').

How other people talk is very important to Scannell. Like Browning, he is a master of the dramatic monologue and, like Browning, he uses it to make his speakers give themselves away. This calls for great psychological acuity, for we must believe, if the monologue is to work, in the emotional tangle that we are allowed to glimpse. The suspicious husband in 'A Simple Need', tormenting himself with his imaginings ('That's all I want. Just to see them at it once'), inevitably brings Shakespeare's Othello to mind, and Scannell achieves this in a poem not thirty lines long, every phrase of which could be heard in a pub any night of the week. The hardest thing for a male poet is to write a successful dramatic monologue in which the speaker is female and (in so far as a male critic can judge) I should say that Scannell does this with complete conviction in, for example 'The Defrauded Woman Speaks' or 'The Widow's Complaint'. To write such poems requires what psychologists call empathy, the ability to enter another person's feelings, and it is Scannell's great gift. Some of his finest poems are powered by it, delving into lives wholly unlike his own, pained by their pains, fearing their fears—a bride dreading her husband's approach (in 'A Victorian Honeymoon'), a grandmother visiting her children's graves ('Grandma in Winter'), a child arsonist ('Incendiary'), a boy killing a cat ('A Case of Murder'). Sometimes the empathy is so keen that the poem is almost unbearable to reread, as in 'Incident at West Bay', about two children drowned in a car accident.

Children are a natural subject for Scannell because they live in fantasy and metaphor, as poets do. He does not sentimentalize them, but he sees what they lose by growing up. In 'Jane at Play' he notices that the doll the little girl likes best is the one that would, to other eyes, seem the ugliest, and this leads him to compare her spontaneous love with our adult artificiality:

> It is only later that we choose
> To favour things which publish our good taste.

Of his poems about children my favourite is 'Growing Pain'.

> The boy was barely five years old.
> We sent him to the little school
> And left him there to learn the names
> Of flowers in jam jars on the sill
> And learn to do as he was told.
> He seemed quite happy there until
> Three weeks afterwards, at night,
> The darkness whimpered in his room.
> I went upstairs, switched on his light,
> And found him wide awake, distraught,
> Sheets mangled, and his eiderdown
> Untidy carpet on the floor.
> I said, 'Why can't you sleep? A Pain?
> He snuffled, gave a little moan,
> And then he spoke a single word:
> 'Jessica.' The sound was blurred.
> 'Jessica? What do you mean?'
> 'A girl at school called Jessica,
> She hurts – ' he touched himself between
> The heart and stomach ' – she has been
> Aching here and I can see her.'

> Nothing I had read or heard
> Instructed me in what to do.
> I covered him and stroked his head.
> 'The pain will go in time,' I said.

I do not think that anyone but Scannell could have written this poem. Both in subject and treatment it is far beyond Larkin's scope. It is wise, sad, tender, and funny all at once. It is also technically meticulous, its rhythms adjusted to its meanings, so that the sing-song lilt of the first five lines imitates the carefree infant life, and with the arrival of love's first pang the rhythms and line-breaks grown jagged.

Like many of Scannell's poems it makes you want to know more about his life—more, that is, than you can get from the usual websites and reference books. He is not the sort of poet whose work remains iconic and remote. It is drenched in humanity. It resounds with memories.

> In a French orchard lies whatever is left
> Of my friend Gordon Rennie ...

Who was he? In what combat did he fall? Scannell's life as a boxer comes indistinctly into sight, too, in a poem like 'Comeback', but what was it really like? Then there is 'My Father's Face', a poem of memory and forgiveness—but of what and for what? With some of the most poignant poems you feel your ignorance excluding you from something of profound importance to the poet:

> And often some small thing will summon the memory
> Of my small son Benjamin. A smile is his sweet ghost.
> But behind, in the dark the white twigs of his bones
> Form a pattern of guilt and waste.

Guilt for what? Is Benjamin real or imagined? Such questions are raised by all the poems about failed love, alienation, and painful parting. If Scannell did not make us care so much, it would not matter. But he does, and it does. That is why a biography is needed—not by Scannell but by us. The poems, as personal as a fingerprint, make us want to know the m`an who wrote them, and who had those thoughts, and experienced so much, and lived through convulsions of history that we escaped.

Acknowledgements

My first thanks are due to the people who shared Vernon Scannell's life—to his widow, Jo Scannell; to Angela Beese; to Jo Peters; and to his four children, Jane, Nancy, John, and Jacob. They have allowed me unrestricted access to his letters, diaries, and private papers, and to their own thoughts and memories, in the interests of producing as full and honest account of his life as possible. I hope they will feel that this book repays their trust.

I visited Stella (Ella Cope) at her care home, and in spite of her age and fading memory, she was able to recall her feelings about the failure of her relationship with Vernon. Her cousin Elizabeth Whitmore was also generous with her time and her encouragement. Scannell's sister-in-law, Jenny Bain, and his two half-sisters, Pat Cornford and Tina Daubney, have also been most helpful. In Otley, Stephen Phillips kindly invited me to look over Vernon Scannell's house in North Street, where he now lives. To all of them, my thanks.

I owe a considerable debt to Scannell's two literary executors, his good friends Martin Reed and Jeremy Robson. They have been unfailingly supportive, supplying me with letters and cuttings from their private collections, talking to me at length about their own recollections of Scannell, and answering what must have seemed to be an endless stream of questions. Martin also generously allowed me to 'borrow' his collection of signed first editions of Scannell's poetry and novels for some three years. He must have been relieved to see them again.

Both Martin and Jeremy have also been occasionally challenging and critical when they have disagreed with any of my conclusions or interpretations, while accepting that the ultimate responsibility for what appears in the book is my own. Martin Reed's wife, Ruth, who sadly died while the book was in preparation, also shared her memories of Scannell and gave me access to her private diaries. In addition, she gave me and my wife magnificent lunches whenever we visited, and became a dear friend to both of us. We will miss her.

Professor John Carey, who wrote the foreword to the book, has been a source of advice and encouragement not just from the very earliest days of the book, but for the last forty years. I've also valued the support of my friend and agent Mandy Little, who is a mixture, like all good agents, of diplomat, union negotiator, agony aunt and—just occasionally—workhouse master. My old friend Julian Bene has argued with me over every chapter as he argues over everything, and the book is better as a result.

At Oxford University Press, Jacqueline Baker and Rachel Platt have been enthusiastic and encouraging from the start. Every writer needs a good copy-editor to keep him honest and stop him being self-indulgent, and I have had one of the best in Jeremy Langworthy.

Scannell's friends and fellow poets have been generous with their time and their encouragement: Dannie Abse, David Annwn, Alan Brownjohn, Christopher Hampton, Seamus Heaney, Laurence Lerner, Alexis Lykiard, Peter Reading, Anne Stevenson, Anthony Thwaite, and Kit Wright.

My efforts to explain the damage that was done to Scannell by his war service have leaned heavily on the help and advice of Dr Felicity de Zulueta, Consultant Psychiatrist in Psychotherapy at the South London and Maudsley NHS Trust, Honorary Senior Lecturer in Traumatic Studies at Kings College London, and author of *From Pain to Violence: The Traumatic Roots of Destructiveness*. The conclusions I draw, of course, are my own, but without her generous help I would have been lost in a vast and complex field.

The vast majority of Scannell's personal papers, including his diaries, notebooks, manuscripts, and letters, are held in the Special Collections Department at Leeds University's Brotherton Library. Ownership of the archive was transferred from the family to the Library while I was working on the book, so the items were largely un-catalogued, which added considerably to the task of the team of librarians there, under the leadership first of Chris Sheppard and then of Katy Goodrum. In some three years, there surely should have been at least one misunderstanding, one complaint, or one failure of good humour—but there wasn't.

I am also grateful for the help of librarians in the British Library, Oxford University's Bodleian Library, and the London Library, and also in the Study Centre of Aylesbury Library, Buckinghamshire. Annie Scott, Cultural Co-ordinator with Aberdeenshire Council, helped me with information about Duff House in the war years, Isobel Alexander of Banff shared some of her knowledge of local families, and the local historian David Hallam gave me valuable information about Beeston, Nottinghamshire, in the 1920s. Mark Hiles helped to fill out Scannell's memories of Berinsfield for me, and Harold Alderman gave me the benefit of his encyclopaedic knowledge of the history of boxing.

On military matters, the Gordon Highlanders Museum in Aberdeen and the Argyll and Sutherland Highlanders Museum in Stirling have been very helpful with the background to Scannell's war years, and the Army Personnel Centre in Glasgow located his personal army records. In particular, Charles Reid at the Gordon Highlanders Museum agreed to read the relevant chapters of the book before publication. Any errors or omissions that remain, of course, are mine alone.

In addition, I have received valuable help and advice from Dr Niall Barr, Reader in Military History at the Defence Academy of the UK, from Professor Ashley Jackson and Dr Jonathan Fennell of the Defence Studies Department of King's College, London, and from Lieutenant-Colonel Tom Ridgway, former President of Courts Martial for the British Army, who was most helpful in interpreting the Army records, and who gave me considerable help in understanding the procedures of military courts.

Among other individuals who have helped with specific aspects of Scannell's story are Bob and Inge Ball; Natalie Bartington; Bob Barton, formerly of the BBC, who knows more than anyone I've ever met about how to track people down and get them to talk to you, and has taught me a little of it; Ivy Benson, who generously allowed me to use photographs of Vernon Scannell taken by her late husband, Alan Benson; Jean Bourne; Andy Boyd; Don Brown; Tom Bruggen; Derek Caseley; John Coggrave; Penny Crick; David Couper; Robert Crick; Jack Dalglish; June Emerson; Peter Fanning; Richard Field; Simon Funnell; Jim Greenhalf; Anne Harvey; Peter Henderson, Archivist of The King's School, Canterbury; Cliff Holden; Joseph Hone; Simon Jenkins; Emma Kilcoyne; Alan Millard; Mike Morrogh, Archivist of Shrewsbury School; Betty Mulcahy; Michael Parkinson; Martin Priestley; Tony Scull; David Smith; Rob Todd; Dudley Treffry; and Paul Trewelha.

Most of all, of course, I want to thank my wife, Penny. She has shared in this whole project from its start; working with me in Leeds University library; travelling to Sweden, Dorset, Otley, and everywhere else; reading the book chapter by chapter as it grew; and arguing over ideas, phrases, and individual words. In this, as in everything, I could not have wished for a more generous and enthusiastic partner.

And finally, Dr Tim Littlewood and his NHS team in the Haematology Department of Oxford Radcliffe Hospitals. They may not have not been directly involved with my research and writing, but without their care and skill over the past years, there would not have been a book at all, or indeed anything else. I don't forget.

Sources

Apart from the conversations and interviews noted above with Vernon Scannell's family and friends, this book is based almost entirely on his own published and unpublished writings. His four volumes of memoirs, *The Tiger and the Rose* (1971), *A Proper Gentleman* (1977), *Argument of Kings* (1987), and *Drums of Morning* (1992) have been a valuable source. The most useful information has been gleaned from Scannell's personal papers in the Special Collections Department at Leeds University's Brotherton Library.

Other letters and documents are held by the Special Collections Department of Reading University; the Archives and Special Collections Department of Calgary University; the Special Collections Department of Pennsylvania State University; the Special Collections and University Archives Department of the McFarlin Library at the University of Tulsa, Oklahoma; and the BBC Archive at Caversham. To all of them I owe my thanks for the friendliness, speed, and efficiency with which they answered all my queries. The documents they supplied are acknowledged in the text.

Vernon Scannell's main published writings are listed below:

- *Graves and Resurrections* (The Fortune Press, 1948).
- *The Fight* (Peter Nevill, 1953).
- *The Wound and The Scar* (Peter Nevill, 1953).
- *A Mortal Pitch* (Villiers, 1957).
- *The Big Chance* (John Long, 1960).
- *The Masks of Love* (Putnam, 1960).
- *The Face of the Enemy* (Putnam, 1961).
- *The Shadowed Place* (John Long, 1961).
- *A Sense of Danger* (Putnam, 1962).
- *New Poems 1962: A P. E. N. Anthology* (Hutchinson, 1962), editor with Patricia Beer and Ted Hughes.
- *The Dividing Night* (Putnam, 1962).
- *Edward Thomas*, Writers and their Work series (British Council, 1963).

- *The Big Time* (Longmans, 1965).
- *The Loving Game* (Robson Books, 1965).
- *Walking Wounded: Poems 1962–65* (Eyre and Spottiswoode, 1965).
- *Epithets of War: Poems 1965–69* (Eyre and Spottiswoode, 1969).
- *The Dangerous Ones* (Pergamon Press, 1970).
- *Mastering the Craft* (Pergamon Press, 1970).
- *Selected Poems* (Allison & Busby, 1971).
- *Company of Women* (Sceptre Press, 1971).
- *The Tiger and the Rose* (Hamish Hamilton, 1971).
- *The Winter Man* (Allison & Busby, 1973).
- *The Apple-Raid and Other Poems* (Chatto & Windus, 1974).
- *The Loving Game: Poems* (Robson Books, 1975).
- *A Morden Tower Reading* (Morden Tower Publications, 1976), with Alexis Lykiard.
- *Not Without Glory: Poets of the Second World War* (Woburn Press, 1976).
- *A Proper Gentleman* (Robson Books, 1977).
- *Of Love And Music* (Mapletree Press, 1979).
- *New and Collected Poems 1950–1980* (Robson Books, 1980).
- *Winterlude* (Robson Books, 1982).
- *How To Enjoy Poetry* (Piatkus Books, 1983).
- *Ring of Truth* (Robson Books, 1983).
- *How to Enjoy Novels* (Piatkus Books, 1984).
- *Argument of Kings* (Robson Books, 1987).
- *Funeral Games and Other Poems* (Robson Books, 1987).
- *Sporting Literature* (Oxford University Press, 1987), editor.
- *The Clever Potato* (London: Hutchinson, 1988).
- *Soldiering On* (Robson Books, 1989).
- *Love Shouts and Whispers* (Hutchinson, 1990).
- *A Time for Fires* (Robson Books, 1991).
- *Travelling Light* (Bodley Head, 1991).
- *Drums of Morning—Growing up in the Thirties* (Robson Books, 1992).
- *On Your Cycle, Michael* (Red Fox, 1992).
- *Collected Poems, 1950–93* (Robson Books, 1993).
- *The Black and White Days* (Robson Books, 1996).
- *Feminine Endings* (Enitharmon Press, 2000).
- *Views and Distances* (Enitharmon Press, 2000).
- *Of Love and War: New and Selected Poems* (Robson Books, 2002).

- *Behind the Lines* (Shoestring Press, 2004).
- *A Place to Live* (The Happy Dragons Press, 2007).
- *Last Post* (Shoestring Press, 2007).

SELECTED BOOKS

Abse, Dannie and Howard Sergeant (eds.), *Mavericks* (London: Poetry and Poverty Editions, 1957).

Anand, Mulk Raj, *Conversations in Bloomsbury* (London: Wildwood House, 1981).

Badham-Thornhill, Desmond (ed.), *Three Poets, Two Children* (London: Thornhill Press, 1975).

Barker, Felix, *Gordon Highlanders in North Africa and Sicily* (Sidcup: Bydand Press, 1944).

Beevor, Antony, *D Day: The Battle for Normandy* (London: Viking, 2009).

Bierman, John and Colin Smith, *Alamein: War Without Hate* (London: Viking, 2002).

Borthwick, Alastair, *Battalion* (London: Baton Wicks, 2001).

Bryant, Arthur, *The Turn of the Tide* (London: Grafton, 1986).

Caccia-Dominioni, Paolo, *Alamein 1933–1962* (London: Allen and Unwin, 1966).

Carver, Field Marshal Lord, *El Alamein* (London: B. T. Batsford, 1982).

Church, Richard, *The Voyage Home* (London: Heinemann, 1964).

Cramer, James, *Gone for a Soldier* (London: Privately published, 2004).

Douglas, Keith, *Alamein to Zem Zem* (London: Faber and Faber, 1946).

Fergusson, Bernard, *The Black Watch and the King's Enemies* (London: Collins, 1950).

Fothergill, Stephen, *The Last Lamplighter* (London: London Magazine Editions, 2000).

Harvey, Anne (ed.), *Elected Friends* (London: Enitharmon Press, 1991).

Hastings, Max, *Overlord, D Day and the Battle for Normandy* (London: Michael Joseph, 1984).

——, *All Hell Let Loose* (London, HarperCollins, 2011).

Howarth, Patrick, *My God, Soldiers* (London: Hutchinson, 1989).

Jeffrey, Keith, *MI6, The History of the Secret Intelligence Service* (London: Bloomsbury, 2011).

Knightley, Philip, *Philby: The Spy Who Betrayed a Generation* (London: Doubleday, 1968).

Miles, Wilfrid, *Life of a Regiment*, V: *Gordon Highlanders 1939–1945* (London: Frederick Warne, 1961).

Morrison, Blake, *The Movement* (Oxford: Oxford University Press, 1980).

Robson, Jeremy (ed.), *Poems from Poetry and Jazz in Concert* (London: Souvenir Press, 1969).

Salmond, J. B., *History of the 51st Highland Division* (Bishop Aukland: Pentland Press, 1994).

Thomas, Donald, *An Underworld at War* (London: John Murray, 2003).

Webb, Barry, *Edmund Blunden, a Biography* (New Haven and London: Yale University Press, 1990).

Willetts, Paul, *Fear and Loathing in Fitzrovia* (London: Dewi Lewis, 2003).

Woolf, Cecil and Jean Moorcroft Wilson, *Authors Take Sides on the Falklands* (London: Cecil Woolf, 1982).

List of Illustrations

List of Plates

No one is really interesting until
To love him has become no longer easy
A Note for Biographers, from *Walking Wounded*

I

Beginnings

Over sixty years ago
A boy of five would walk to school…

'The Clever Potato', from *The Clever Potato* (1988)

Looking back on his early life from the relative safety of his mid-forties, Vernon Scannell observed blithely and unconvincingly that most people have a broadly similar experience of childhood:

> …Where infants crawl
> Is much the same for every baby born,
> And later, when the subject walks erect,
> In private park or back street of a town,
> The difference is much less than you'd expect.[1]

In fact, Scannell struggled all his life to escape from the shadow of his miserable early years—not least by abandoning the name Bain, inherited from his father, in favour of Scannell, one found for him by chance in a Soho brothel. Perhaps he really thought that everyone shared his experiences, which would suggest that he had a particularly bleak view of humanity. More likely, in this poem as in his change of name, he was shrugging off painful memories of his own past. In suggesting that his childhood was just like anyone else's, the middle-aged Vernon Scannell seems to be trying to shake the experiences of the young Vernon Bain out of his soul.

I

Just above the tobacconist's shop in the little Irish farming town of Ballaghaderreen, County Roscommon, were a couple of rooms to rent—small, slightly shabby, but definitely respectable. That was where James Bain made some sort of home for his family in the lean years of the mid-1920s. Downstairs, behind the tobacconist's, he had set up a photographic studio which he hoped would provide enough business to support his wife and the two boys: upstairs, life was tough and often brutal.

Anyone from outside the family would have thought the leather strap in the sitting room looked bizarrely out of place. Presumably Bain honed his cut-throat razor on it every morning when he shaved—but in that case, surely it should have been stored conveniently in the bathroom, not hanging by a loop from a hook beside the fireplace.

For four-year-old Vernon and his six-year-old brother Kenneth though, there was no confusion—it would be several years before they discovered that there was a gentler, less painful use than they knew for the thick, pliable, strip of dark brown leather that hung menacingly there throughout their childhood. For them, it was the instrument with which their father would thrash them until they screamed. On one occasion, Vernon remembered long afterwards, he was stretched out and beaten repeatedly on the bare buttocks because he was believed to have stolen a piece of sugared fruit. He hadn't, but his angry father would not believe his denials, and hit him all the harder until he confessed anyway.[2]

Kenneth was regularly beaten as well by the Irish Christian Brothers who ran the local school in Ballaghaderreen, although he thought nothing of their punishments compared with the violence regularly meted out by his father;[3] Vernon, being younger, enjoyed the rather more tender care of Sister Martin and the other Sisters of Charity at the infant school which they ran in the nearby convent. There was, of course, nothing particularly unusual about a harsh teaching regime in the early 1920s: all over Britain, not just in the rural Ireland where they lived, 'Spare the rod and spoil the child' was almost universally acknowledged as a proper prescription for bringing up young boys, and often girls too.

For James Bain, though, the beatings were more than parental punishment: they certainly didn't hurt him more than they hurt the boys. As adults, Kenneth and Vernon would frequently reminisce about their mistreatment at the hands of the Old Man—a term they used without any affection. 'My father was a sadistic man and his sadism took both physical and mental forms', Vernon recalled in his diary in 1954:

> I remember beatings I received when I would have been no more than three
> or four years—not slaps with the hand, but strokes with a leather strap on the

bare flesh. I remember too being held over the top banister of spiral flights of stairs, my screams of terror at being allowed to drop affording him, no doubt, delirious excitement. This may or may not account for the fear of heights which has troubled me seriously in adult life.[4]

There were more bizarre attempts at discipline than the leather strap. At the age of eight, he was taken with the ten-year-old Kenneth into his grandmother's room, where she lay, close to death. She had been in a coma for two days, and gave no response when the boys' father whispered their names in her ear. For the Old Man, perhaps, it was a moving last meeting between his sons and his dying mother, but Vernon remembered only a terrifying sense of imminent death and decay:

> I don't think I was afraid, but I was certainly repelled. She lay quite still on her back, and her flesh was yellow and waxy. It seemed that the heat of the room might melt the waxen features and show the skull beneath.

Infinitely worse than that, though, was the incident a few days later, after the old woman had died:

> My brother and I were playing in an upstairs room, and in some way we incurred my father's wrath. For a punishment, he said, we should sleep that night in grandmother's deathbed. Of course he had no intention of fulfilling that threat, but we believed him, and the rest of that day was spent in such a fever of horror as I have not since experienced.[5]

Sometimes the bullying would be dressed up as a joke: as the family had travelled to Ireland, the Old Man had held the tiny Vernon out over the rail of the Dublin ferry, high above the black waves, laughing at his uncontrollable shrieks of terror. Another time, he watched in excited amusement as Kenneth ripped the silver paper off a huge bar of Cadbury's chocolate—an unprecedented treat—only to find that the bar was made of wood, a shop window display model. Neither Kenneth nor Vernon, who had been watching in eager anticipation, ever forgot.[6]

Perhaps such incidents were ill-conceived jokes, emotional clumsiness rather than deliberate cruelty, but they took place against a background of constant, deliberate violence and the infliction of pain. As the boys grew a little older, their father would forget the strap—although Kenneth and Vernon never did—and he would resort to his fists, punching them to the ground. No one, in those days of closed curtains and stiff upper lips, would ask too many questions about why boys were arriving at school covered in cuts, welts, and bruises.

Almost worse though, when they were young, was the emotional cold-ness of the household—there were no hugs and kisses, no expressions of love or affection. The closest bond in the family was that between Kenneth and Vernon, united in their fear and dislike of their father. Their mother, Elsie, never interfered in the beatings, and often took the lead in the abuse and mockery of the two small boys. At the root of her cruelty in Ballaghaderreen, perhaps, was a silent and terrible resentment—for the first few years of his life, Vernon was dressed in girl's clothes and treated as the daughter she had longed for and never had.[7] Shortly before the family left England, she had given birth to a third son, Philip, who had died soon after he was born. It must have seemed then that her yearning was never going to be satisfied.

Whatever the reason, the verbal and emotional attacks to which the boys were subjected were unrelenting. Kenneth was constantly derided as clumsy and disgusting, an 'ugly ape', while Vernon got off perhaps more lightly with 'young pup'. Praise and encouragement were things neither of them ever knew. Perhaps it is possible to trace the chronic lack of self-confidence which plagued both of them throughout their lives back to these spiteful tirades from their parents—certainly Kenneth's widow, Jenny Bain, believes so, some eighty years later. 'The boys were both seriously damaged for much of their lives. Their mother and father were an evil pair', she says.[8]

It was a hard life for the parents too. Things were tough all over Britain in 1926—the year of the General Strike—and Bain had brought his family to Ireland from Nottinghamshire, where they had been living with his wife's parents, in the forlorn hope of finding something better. He was a photog-rapher by trade, but the business he had tried to set up in Spilsby, Lincolnshire—where Vernon was born in 1922—had failed. The family had moved in with Elsie's parents before making the optimistic move to Ballaghaderreen, where Bain set up his makeshift studio and waited for the orders to come in. But he was disappointed: Ballaghaderreen was as poor a little town as Spilsby had been, and there was no money to spare for modern fripperies like photography. The family struggled by on soda bread, potatoes, and porridge, huddled in the winter before a smoky, smouldering peat fire. Occasional dishes of herrings, mutton stew, or black pudding were a rare treat.

If there had been money to spend in the town, it is unlikely anyway that much of it would have gone to James Bain and his family, even if people had wanted photographs. It was only four years since the Anglo-Irish Treaty had ended the shootings, killings, and bloody reprisals of the Irish Revolution and established the Irish Free State: many of the townspeople would still have known their home by its Irish name, Bealach an Doirin, the way of the little oak wood, rather than the Anglicized version. The English accents of a family of incomers from across the Irish Sea would have been unlikely to win many friends.

Children, of course, live in several worlds at once. As an old man, Vernon could still bring to mind a daytime, picture-postcard image of the town:

> A time of horse-lugged wagons, vans and carts
> On cobbled streets[9]

but he also had vague memories of the secret children's world of fights, taunts, and teasing, in which his English vowels were ridiculed and his tears mocked as he was beaten up and pushed into the village pond. And at night there were fresh and even more private terrors—he liked to hear stories of the malign 'Little People', who had apparently threatened to steal away a neighbour, but there was also Shaggery-Bags, an old woman who lived a mile or so away in Castlemore and was rumoured to make castor oil out of little boys. Somewhere between these night-time imaginings and the real world of the day lurked the tramps and tinkers who would come to the door with knick-knacks and strings of mushrooms for sale, and who would leave with muttered curses and threats of the evil eye when they were turned away. Thrilling stories of fights, blood, beatings, and injuries filtered down from their camp to the boys—one more terrifying world just over the horizon.

Inside or outside the house, it was a bleak, frightening, and unfriendly existence.

II

James Bain struggled on for a few months, but within a year he had to admit defeat, and pack up his photographic equipment again. The family was on the move once more, back to live with Elsie's parents in Chilwell Road, Beeston in their small terraced house with its outside lavatory at the end of the little back garden. For Vernon, with his keen child's eye for specific events, there were two aspects of the journey back that stood out. First,

Figure 1. Elsie, Vernon, and Kenneth. A family holiday in 1924, probably in Skegness, shortly before the move to Ballaghadereen. (Photo: Not known. Scannell family collection)

there was the shame of being dressed in a toddler's pom-pom bonnet and carried in his father's arms to convince the ticket-clerk that he was under four years old, and thus young enough for free travel—an indignity for the five-year-old boy, but a useful money-saving trick for his hard-up father. And second, as the ferry chugged back across the Irish Sea towards Liverpool—with Vernon this time presumably keeping well away from his father and the rail—he remembered the shock of watching an old man, unsteady on his feet, pitch headfirst down a flight of steps and lie motionless at the bottom, a pool of liquid spreading out alarmingly from his prone body. It was only years later, remembering the smell, that he realized that it was whisky.[10]

But arriving in Beeston was more than worth the journey. For the boys, this was a return to a remembered world of happiness and luxury—'tinned peaches and marzipan-cake for tea', as Vernon put it[11]—and it did not disappoint them. There was still little enough money to spend, but they got to share a bed in their own attic room, far away from the grown-ups; their grandfather made them wooden scooters, and for a twopenny ticket there were the occasional silent and captioned delights of the Saturday afternoon cinema.

Figure 2. 'Miss Steeples', later Mrs Ella Reeves, was Vernon's favourite teacher at Nether Street Infants' School in Beeston. 'Whatever conquests [she] might have made,' he wrote later, 'none was more complete than her domination of my small heart.' (Photo: Not known. Scannell family collection)

Vernon walked each morning to Nether Street Infants' School, where his teacher, Miss Steeples, thrilled him. 'She had beautiful finger-nails and smelled like Boots Cash Chemists', he recalled fondly.[12] He would watch her longingly from a distance, like a tiny John Betjeman pining for Miss Joan Hunter Dunn, as she made her way home, swinging a bag of tennis balls, from the club where she played in the long summer evenings. 'Whatever conquests Miss Steeples might have made,' he wrote wistfully in his late forties, 'none was more complete than her domination of my small heart.'[13]

In winter, Nether Street was memorable too for the hot baked potato which first kept his hands warm on the way to school and later provided a welcome and nourishing lunch—an ingenious piece of energy-efficiency which he later memorialized in his children's poem 'The Clever Potato'.[14] Perhaps his mother may have been happier in herself than she had been at Ballaghaderreen—while she was living at Beeston she gave birth to Sylvie, the daughter she had always wanted.

But it was in Beeston that the young Vernon saw another frightening manifestation of his father's bullying sadism—this time involving the father of a friend when Vernon was about seven years old. The Old Man and Elsie had got to know a couple in Nottingham who had a young son, Ivan, of about Vernon's age. The incident happened one Sunday afternoon, when they were visiting the house in Chilwell Road, and both Vernon and Kenneth remembered it with horror all their lives.

They had been given cheap pairs of children's boxing gloves for Christmas, and the Old Man was trying unsuccessfully to persuade Vernon and Ivan to put them on and fight. Then he turned to Ivan's father, Bob, and pressed him to box. Unwillingly, Bob squeezed his hands into the gloves, which were much too small for an adult's fists:

> My father was waiting, shirt sleeves rolled up, eager eyes bulging with antici-
> patory pleasure, his mouth fixed in the peculiar half-grin, half-snarl, that
> Kenneth and I had come to recognize as a danger signal . . . He knocked Bob's
> gloves to one side with his left hand and drove his right into Bob's face and
> followed up with three or four blows delivered with full force, and all the time
> that snarling and self-congratulatory grin was unchanged but his eyes grew
> wider with delight and satisfaction.[15]

Vernon would never forget that cruel half-grin, which would haunt his imagination. Bob was terrified and humiliated, his nose bleeding, as he tried to protect himself; the two women were crying out in protest. The children, shocked and frightened, could recognize something like the playground bullying that they had witnessed at school, but were dimly aware of some dark undertone that they did not quite understand. 'Just a bit of fun', the Old Man protested, still with the bizarre, threatening leer on his face.

Vernon would recount the story later in *Drums of Morning*, and both he and Kenneth told it to their families. It marked a watershed in the seven-year-old Vernon's feelings for his father: before then, he said, he had felt simply fear of the Old Man, but from that day on, he hated him even more than he feared him.

Perhaps the shock and fear were even greater because generally the Old Man seems to have been less of a terror in Beeston than he had been before: it was harder to be openly violent in a household that included his wife's parents as well as his own immediate family. Vernon's memories of this time have his mother picking out the tunes of the popular sentimental songs of the time on the piano, while her father played the violin and the Old Man sang along in his 'stern baritone'.[16] At other times, he would tell his sons stories of the Great War, in which he had served with the King's Own Scottish Borderers. Although they learned to discount the more unlikely accounts of his own heroism, the roll call of names—the Somme, Loos, and Passchendaele—and evocative words and phrases like Very lights, whizz-bangs, and dug-outs all blended with the images of combat they had gleaned from the 'twopenny weeklies' to help create a fascination with the First World War that stayed with Vernon and would resurface in his poetry years later.

For all his apparent mellowing, James Bain's relationship with his sons remained rather an armed truce than a declaration of peace, and perhaps the most significant contribution that he made to their happiness while they were at Beeston was simply by not being there. For weeks at a time during the summer, he would go to Skegness, a good 80 miles away, where he would try to make a few pounds working as a photographer on the beach.[17] With the Depression beginning, times were hard.

This, then, was the childhood that was 'much the same' as everybody else's. Throughout their lives, Kenneth and Vernon could never forget the harshness and brutality with which their father had treated them. Vernon, certainly, never said a good word about him, to his own children or to anyone else. And yet, for all his faults, James Bain seems to have struggled manfully to provide for his family at a time when jobs and money were hard to find. Somehow—probably with the help of Elsie's parents—he scrabbled together enough money to enable him to set himself up in yet another small photographic business, this time in Derby. Now, the plan was to leave the boys behind while James and Elsie left to get the business started, taking the baby, christened Sylvie but called Sylvia throughout her life, with them.

Elsie would get some time alone with the baby daughter she had longed for, and the boys had little enough objection to being separated from their parents for a while. The only disadvantage for them was that they would be apart from each other as well: Ken was to stay at Beeston, while Vernon was to go to live with his father's parents in Eccles, near Manchester.

(iii)

The house in Beeston had been small enough, but Bardsley Street in Eccles already had four adults crammed into its two bedrooms before the arrival of the shy and nervous nine-year-old Vernon. He was to sleep with his grandparents in one room—which, he remembered vividly 'smelled strongly of piss from the pot which they kept under their bed'[18]—while his two uncles, James's brothers John and Percy, shared the other. Downstairs, they all huddled for warmth around the open fire in the kitchen, which was where they cooked, ate, washed, and relaxed. The only other room, the parlour, was strictly reserved for visitors.

Neither set of grandparents had much money but, however tight money had been in Beeston because of the Depression, Eccles was definitely a step down. Elsie's father owned his own small lace factory, while the men at Bardsley Street were all manual labourers: Vernon's father, it was generally acknowledged, had married 'above himself'.

The street consisted of two identical terraces of drab brick built houses facing each other across the road; down at the end, beyond a fence, was the black, stagnant water of the reservoir; and beyond that, looming mysteriously over the water, were the dark windows of the sanatorium, which was spoken about in hushed tones as the place where people went to die. There were traders and even occasional street entertainers hustling for pennies in the cobbled market square, but there was not the same easy access to open country to play in as there had been in Nottinghamshire, and the reservoir was a poor substitute for the River Trent, with its barges, punts, and houseboats. For Vernon, though, none of that mattered. To make up for everything, there was his grandmother, 'a plump and lovable Lancashire woman who cooked magnificent meat and potato pie and was imperturbably goodnatured'.[19] She had left school at twelve and spent her life working in a mill—but she would take him with her to the Regent Cinema where, miraculously, the characters in the films could now speak, and on the way home she would buy fish and chips for him, and a bottle of stout for herself. Among Vernon's papers after his death, dog-eared and fragile, in spidery, uncertain, old lady's writing, was a treasured letter from her, recalling the months he had spent in Eccles. 'Do you remember when you used to go to school through the churchyard?' she wrote. 'You used to cry when you walk [sic] over the graves. Them was nice times then.'[20]

Then there was his grandfather, blind in one eye and as good as blind in the other, but still prepared to take his young grandson on the tram to watch rugby league matches, or to sit by the fire singing songs and telling him stories in his gentle, rumbling bass voice.[21] In return, Vernon sat and read to him: where Beeston had offered little more appealing than *The Pilgrim's Progress* or *Popular Educators*, in Bardsley Street the young boy discovered

Kidnapped, the adventures of Sexton Blake or Huckleberry Finn, and—a particular favourite—the antics of Billy Bunter. He could lose himself in a book and feel safe and independent; books never let him down in the way that people all too often had done.

Vernon's lifelong love affair with books, reading, and the world of the imagination had started earlier, during the bleak days in Ballaghaderreen, sparked by his brother as they huddled away from their father:

> We were both able to read fairly unusually young. I can't remember exactly the age, but I was certainly reading fairly comfortably by five, and I know my brother was too. It was Kenneth who taught me to read.
>
> Television had not been dreamed about, and in fact I was about 14 before we had a radio in the house, so there was no canned entertainment. If you wanted an imaginative experience or escape you had to do it through reading. It was the only thing available. There were movies, but they cost money, and money was in pretty short supply when I was a child.[22]

His two uncles seemed to have the strength and independence of demigods, with Percy's gramophone and John's motorbike—though they were still capable of being awed into silence by their father's raised voice. They had different attitudes towards Vernon's love of reading—John, like Vernon's father, saw it as a waste of time, while Percy could be relied on to produce seemingly endless supplies of twopenny magazines like *The Wizard* and *The Hotspur.*

There were a few problems—Vernon found it hard to make friends, and while he had all but fallen in love with his teacher at Beeston, he felt at Clarendon Road Council School, Eccles, that neither teachers nor pupils liked him. He was an outsider; his accent, now an uneasy mixture of English Midlands and Irish burr, was the subject of incessant mockery; and he was a serious child and a keen reader. All these factors set him apart, and children do not like difference.

But nothing could destroy the simple magic of Bardsley Street. For a boy who had been used to cuffs, blows, and beatings in a house where the only emotions on display were anger and contempt, the relaxed, gentle atmosphere must have been heaven, and Vernon remembered his year in Eccles as the best of his childhood.[23] He felt wanted.

He must have known, though, that it could not last. Just a year after his arrival, the news came that his father was on the move again, this time to Aylesbury in Buckinghamshire. He was planning to rent another photographic studio and try once more to get a business off the ground, and the family was going to be together again. For most children, it would have been wonderful news, but Vernon left Eccles with a heavy heart.

He was still only nine years old, and it was Aylesbury that he would remember as the town where he grew up. Spilsby, the little market town on the southern edge of the Lincolnshire Wolds where he was born and which he left before he was three years old, was nothing more than a name. Even Ballaghaderreen, Beeston, and Eccles survived only as patchy and uncertain memories, vague images that he would occasionally bring to mind, and sometimes even write about. His poem 'A Small Hunger', for instance, describes the incident with the chocolate bar, and 'A Dead Dog' tells the story of how, as a child, he took home the body of a dog after finding it in the streets of Ballaghaderreen.

More than the memories, though, those first nine years had established patterns that would last through his life—a lack of self-confidence that would be reflected in his misgivings as an adult and a poet about the quality of his work, an anxiety about affection, and a belief that he would always be let down. Perhaps, too, as he remembered those journeys by tram to watch the Salford rugby league team with his grandfather, he felt the first stirrings of his lifelong love of sport. Most of all, though, his childhood had fixed in him a fear of his parents, and an awareness of the grim pleasure his father took in inflicting pain. That fear would only grow stronger, and develop during his years in Aylesbury into a deep and passionate loathing.

2

Aylesbury

Not foreign stamps or hollow eggs in beds
Of cotton wool, not model aeroplanes
Or rolling stock, not hoarded coins or cards,
But articles of apparatus, kit
And clothing of a special usefulness,
The paraphernalia of the fighter's craft.
It seems unlikely now that all that gear,
Which came to be the tackle and the tools
Of my life's trade, could thrill me in those days
As later only women's secrets could.

'Comeback', from *The Winter Man* (1973)

I

Aylesbury was a place where the Bain family at last found relative prosperity: a small inheritance from Elsie's mother had enabled them to take over the rent of an existing photographic studio and a small flat in the town's Market Square. The nearby RAF base at Halton Camp, filled with young airmen wanting photographs to send home for their proud parents, provided enough potential business to offer James Bain's latest venture at least a chance of success.

Aylesbury was a small market town—only four years before the family arrived, the livestock and sheep had been driven out of Market Square at the end of the last regular cattle fair to be held in the town, and the local hunt still met there each month, horses stamping and steaming as their riders were plied with stirrup-cups from the Bull's Head pub close by the photographic studio. There would be summer walks in the Chilterns for the young Vernon and Kenneth, cricket at Hartwell just outside the town when

Figure 3. Kingsbury Square, Aylesbury. The Bain family moved here in 1933, to the flat above James Bain's eshop where Vernon would spend his adolescence. (Photo: Not known. Postcard from Scannell family collection)

they were a little older, and pints of beer when they were older still, either in the Bull's Head or one of the many other pubs in the town.

It sounds like a rural idyll. And yet, like many of England's small towns, 1930s Aylesbury was almost certainly far more comfortable in the rosy glow of nostalgia than it was as a place to live. The Bains' flat was somewhere the family could be together again, but it does not sound like a particularly roomy or welcoming home. A dark and narrow flight of stairs led up from the street to the studio, with James Bain's darkroom above it on the second floor; another flight led to the poky little flat on the next floor up. One tiny bedroom just had room for the three-quarter sized bed shared by Vernon and Kenneth, while their parents and the four-year-old Sylvia were crammed into the other. There was one other room, with a cooker, a table, and, of course, James Bain's 'evil leather strap'[1] hanging by the wall.[2] There was also, incongruously, an old upright piano which had been brought from Elsie's parents' house in Beeston, and which she used to play occasionally and without any great skill. Vernon always felt that—at least until Kenneth started to teach himself to play it a couple of years later—it was there more to remind the family and any infrequent visitors that his mother had been used to a slightly higher status than she currently enjoyed.

But piano or not, Vernon later remembered his first home in Aylesbury with little affection. It was, he said, 'a dingy and musty flat which was always redolent of cats' piss'.[3]

School for the two boys was a half-mile walk away, down by the canal. Their names appear together in the school roll for 1931 at Queen's Park Boys' Council School, where Kenneth would stay for the next three years, Vernon for just over five—a time he later described, like many men looking back on their schooldays, as 'bearable but not inspiring'.[4] It was here that he received the rudiments of an education—a skimpy introduction to the basic subjects that was designed to fit the boys for the low-paid jobs they could expect to move into when they reached the age of fourteen. For Kenneth and Vernon, used to the Old Man's fists and leather strap, the threat of the schoolteacher's cane at least held few terrors.

Later, Vernon wrote about some of the teachers he had known there—the headmaster, Mr Little, but universally known as Nap, or Napoleon, because of his short stature and boundless self-importance; the elderly 'Pete' Dawson, who was rumoured to weep in school assembly each Armistice Day as he thought of the son he had lost in the First World War; 'Toss' Plested, who basked in the adulation that playing soccer and cricket for Aylesbury brought him; and the unfortunate Mr Gunstone, who had no affectionate nickname and no known first name, and who could never control the class despite wielding the cane more frequently and more enthusiastically than any of his colleagues.[5]

At Queen's Road—a far cry, incidentally, from Billy Bunter and the serene stone dignity of Greyfriars School that had fascinated the young Vernon at Bardsley Street—he was introduced to poetry, under the bored and apparently uninterested tutelage of 'Pete' Dawson. Plenty of parents in today's less testing times might be glad if their ten-year-olds could study Gray, Wordsworth, Keats, and Tennyson—though Mr Dawson's technique of using the class anthology as a useful source of material for badly behaved pupils to copy out page by page was maybe not the most inspirational way to encourage a love of literature. But Vernon, at least by his own account, was hooked anyway—not just by the straightforward narrative force of poems such as Tennyson's 'The Charge of the Light Brigade', John Masefield's 'Cargoes', or Henry Newbolt's 'He Fell Among Thieves', but also, he claimed, by the mysterious and haunting beauty of the language that he found in poems scattered through the anthology:

The poem which cast a real spell over me was, apart from the first five lines, quite incomprehensible; and years later, when I first came across T. S. Eliot's observation that poetry can communicate before it is understood, I remembered my finding Wordsworth's sonnet, "It is a beauteous evening, calm and free," as perplexing as it was haunting.[6]

Well, maybe. At home, when he was not looking after his little sister, he was reading voraciously, despite a shortage of books and the determined lack of interest, even outright opposition, of his father—*Ivanhoe*, Edgar Wallace, *Tom Brown's Schooldays*, and, whenever he could get hold of weekly copies of *The Magnet*, more Billy Bunter stories. At the same time, like many boys of his age, he was writing stories of his own—'The Green Army', the tale of a band of outlaws who sound suspiciously like Robin Hood and his merry men, filled an exercise book, followed by a series of Edgar Wallace-style detective adventures. There was also 'The Tale of the Illnesses', which sounds like an early version of *The Goon Show*, 'full of butter-brained puns on the names of ailments, with characters called Monia ("Is this dress new, Monia?") Geddit? Or Enza ("The door opened and in flew Enza")', he remembered later. 'Poor Kenneth was the only person who had the patience and good nature to read the stuff.'[7]

A couple of years later, urged on by this patient older brother, he would infuriate his father with his half-stifled laughter as he revelled in the adventures of P. G. Wodehouse's Jeeves and Bertie Wooster, or with his intense immersion in the adventure novels of John Buchan. There was Dickens, too, and a fascination for *David Copperfield*—not just the story, he would say later, but 'the weight and taste and texture of the words…the poetic quality in Dickens's prose'.[8]

But picking up any book was an act of rebellion. Books, the Old Man believed, were the mark of a sissy:

My father had never read a book in his life. In fact he was hostile to books. When he saw us, the boys, reading, he'd say 'Always got your head in a book— no wonder you've got spots. Put it away—go out, go for a run! Chop some trees down!' Absurd things of that kind. I think he partly hated our reading because it took us into a place where he couldn't follow, and he liked to dominate us.[9]

Even to a twelve-year-old boy, chopping trees down seemed a slightly strange pastime to suggest in the middle of a town, but that wasn't the only oddity about Bain's behaviour with his children. Underpants, he told them frequently, were an effete affectation that no real man would ever dream of wearing; he never wore them, and neither should they. Underpants, in the Old Man's view, would sap the manliness out of his sons as effectively as turning the pages of a book.[10] It was only when, puzzled and slightly embarrassed, they were issued with standard regulation army underpants when they signed up at the beginning of the War, that they realized that wearing them was not just permissible but actually normal.

Generally, Vernon's reading was that of any moderately intelligent boy of his time: it is not *what* he read that is surprising, but the fact that, bombarded by contempt and criticism from his father, he read at all.

(ii)

James Bain's photography business seems at last to have been prospering, because after a couple of years the family moved again, this time the short distance to a new shop in nearby Kingsbury Square. Instead of the constant smell of cat that hung over their home in Market Square, the flat above this shop seemed 'excitingly clean and well-lit and comparatively roomy'.[11] The living accommodation was still limited to a single sitting room and two bedrooms, but now there was a double shop window with Bain's photographs on display, and a studio that customers could walk straight into off the street. The Old Man's darkroom was out in the back yard in a converted brick shed, reached by a wooden outdoor flight of stairs down from the first floor into the yard below. An extra room upstairs was also given over to the business—but for Kenneth and Vernon, the most important change was in the size of their bedroom.

Unlike the room in Market Square, which had barely had space for the bed they still had to share, this one had a small chest of drawers and a cane chair over which they could throw their clothes at night. It gave them a refuge, somewhere they could retreat to and avoid their father's contemptuous and angry abuse every time they wanted to pick up a book. Elsie seems still to have been at best a distant and wintry presence in the house, rarely raising her voice, but never defending her children either, and still less showing any affection for them. She seldom did anything more ambitious in the kitchen than open a tin, and the boys were usually left to fend for themselves. An apple would be a treat to be shared—something they remembered as adults, when one would hold out a piece of fruit, and the other would reply, 'You cut, I'll choose.' When clashes with their father came, even when he hit the young boys with his fists, her response was to blame them for provoking him. Sylvia was treated more gently, but this, it seemed to the two boys, was the way life was—bad-tempered and frequently violent disapproval from their father, and a bland, slightly brittle lack of emotion from their mother. Elsie was a Christian Scientist, and just about the only influence she had on the lives of her children was to pack them off to a Christian Science Sunday School each week, and to refuse to send them to a doctor when they were ill. Sickness, pain, and even poverty itself, were the result of 'error', and to seek to evade them through professional intervention would be sinful.[12]

Presumably because she was a woman, the Old Man seemed to tolerate her liking for books, and she read popular novels avidly, taking refuge in them from bleak reality. Whenever they could, the boys, too, quietly ignored their father's complaints, avoiding trouble by slipping away to their room to settle down and read in private. Certainly, neither of them was affected by his dislike of reading—although he did begin to influence them in a different way.

Although, as far as his two sons knew, James Bain had never so much as entered a boxing ring himself, he was passionately interested in the sport—the only reading that he tolerated was of magazines such as *The Ring* and *Fight Stories*. This was the passion that he passed on to his two young sons. Books and boxing would compete for their attention through their lives.

(iii)

Vernon would have been about twelve when, accompanied as always by his older brother, he turned up for the first time at the Aylesbury and District Boxing Club training night at the Castle Street Hall, five minutes' walk from Kingsbury Square. The interest of the two boys had been aroused by their father's boxing magazines, and Bain had encouraged them—presumably as the next best thing to chopping down trees—to take up the sport.

The gymnasium in the hall had been specially set up for the night, with two rings for sparring marked off with single ropes, and punch bags hanging from the ceiling. The two boys, dressed in shorts, vest, and gym shoes, skipped with ropes, punched the bags, and did exercises on the floor designed to build up their muscles and turn them into muscular and implacable fighting machines.[13] Then they finally put on the gloves and sparred for three ninety-second rounds. For weeks, Vernon had been secretly practising feints, blows, and footwork, dancing around on his toes in the space between the bed and the windows in his room: tonight, it was all coming true. It was not exactly love at first punch—to begin with, he said later, he felt only 'a queer mixture of fear and fascination',[14] and being big for his age, he was regularly put in the ring with older and stronger boys who dealt out frequent lambastings—but that night was the start of a lifelong fascination for the sport and everything to do with it:

> The place was pungent with the mingled scents of sweat and massage liniment and loud with the sound of thudding fists on punchball and bag, the swish and rhythmic slapping of skipping ropes, the grunts and snorts of physical effort. This, or something like it, was where those heroic figures of the ring, whose lives I had read about in the pulp magazines, had started.[15]

Looking back on his days as a young amateur, he was realistic about his abilities: 'I don't think I could have been an exciting boxer to watch, but, at that level of the amateur game, I was a difficult one to beat.'[16] At times in his adult life, notably after the death of the boxer Johnny Owen during a bout in 1980, he would worry about the dangers of professional boxing[17]—his novel *Ring of Truth* concludes with a graphic description of a boxer killed in the ring. Frequently, too, he would become wearied by the constant fascination of journalists for the well-worn clichés of the 'pugilist-poet'. But the passion that was sparked that night never left him. He would boast later in his life of having been paid £1 a round to spar with Freddie Mills, who became world light-heavyweight champion. 'I must have sparred with him about ten times', he said. 'One such time was before his fight with Gus Lesnevich for the light-heavyweight championship of the world, which Freddie won. I liked him very much. When I published my first novel in 1952, *The Fight*, he came along to the publication party and helped to promote the book.'[18]

Vernon boxed as a schoolboy, as a student, as a successful amateur, and briefly as a less successful professional. When he needed money later in his life, he even boxed in a fairground booth, and it was to boxing that he instinctively turned when he was seeking subjects for his novels later in his life. He taught his sons to box, and he also taught the son of one of his lovers. Even in the last, bed-ridden days of his long life, he was following the boxing avidly on the television that had been brought into his room.

Despite the occasional sneers of the literary journalists, he came to believe that there was no incompatibility between boxing and poetry—in fact, he would claim, the writer and the boxer shared important qualities. In his poem 'Mastering the Craft', for instance, the craft in question is that of both boxing and literature. The successful fighter, he says, should learn the basic moves, and then achieve a subtle mastery of different styles and manoeuvres:

> The same with poets: they must train,
> Practise metre's footwork, learn
> The old iambic left and right,
> To change the pace and how to hold
> The big punch till the proper time,
> Jab away with accurate rhyme;
> Adapt the style or be knocked cold...

Figure 4. Vernon as a boxer at around 14 years of age. This highly posed shot, taken a couple of years after he first took up the sport, gives little indication of the tough, determined fighter that he was to become. (Photo: Not known. Scannell family collection)

Although he adds wryly, no amount of training or preparation can defeat raw, untutored, brilliant inspiration:

> Yet here comes one,
> No style at all, untrained and fat,
> Who still contrives to knock you flat. [19]

It is hard, in fact, to think of another poet who has written so cogently about a sport, and certainly not about boxing—poets, whatever he claimed, tend to use parts of the brain that don't respond well to being rattled around in the skull like ice in a cocktail shaker. Housman enthuses about strong-limbed young athletes crowned with bays, but there is always the feeling that he is more interested in the strong limbs than the athletics; Sir Henry Newbolt may write about 'ten to make and the match to win', but his subject is the glory of Empire rather than the glory of cricket. Although *Vitaï Lampada* was a schoolboy favourite of his, if it had been Vernon on whose shoulder his Captain's hand smote, it seems likely that he might have ended up on a charge and the Captain nursing a split lip and a few loose teeth.

Scannell, by contrast, wrote about boxing with the detailed knowledge and feeling of someone who had indeed mastered the craft:

> I moved away,
> Stepped in and jabbed and jolted back his head;
> I saw my chance and threw a big right hand.
> I felt the jar to elbow as my fist
> Connected with his jaw. He should have gone . . . [20]

Only a poet who had been in the ring could have known about the shock to the puncher's elbow of a heavy blow, or about the ominous sag of disappointment when such a blow fails to knock his opponent down. But more importantly, Scannell uses this intimate knowledge of boxing to enlarge on observations that he has to make about life, literature, love, ambition, ageing, disappointment—a whole range of disparate themes. Sometimes, as in 'Last Attack', he uses it with a sort of bawdy schoolboy humour: the poem is evidently about a cynical old manager, urging his battered and past-it boxer on for one last bout:

> A last campaign for old time's sake.
> Stick up for me tonight old buddy,
> Just one more big attack; I'll never
> Send you in to fight again. [21]

But all is not what it seems. Vernon professed to be surprised and puzzled when a schoolteacher told him that a poem of his about a boxer being bullied into the ring had been read out in a school assembly. He had written no such poem, he protested—until she pointed out 'Last Attack' in a volume of his work. Embarrassed, he noted in his diary: 'It's not about a boxer's manager exhorting his fighter to go into the ring. It's about an old lecher exhorting his cock to "stick up for me, old buddy". Those assembled children must have been a bit puzzled.' [22]

But the most important aspect of boxing is its discipline and control, and it is here that its relevance to Scannell's poetry is most marked. Boxing is essentially *controlled* violence, and Scannell believed that poetry was, in the same way, *controlled* emotion. Successful poets, like boxers, need to work to understand the structure of their craft—in their case, metre, prosody, versification, rhyme—but they also need the instinct to bend and adapt the rules when necessary:

> Prescribed forms, adapted to carry a particular and individual voice, are the best way of tackling the job...I don't necessarily mean iambic pentameters, heroic couplets, sonnets, villanelles and so on—though I would not preclude any of these—but taking a more or less regular measure on which to build, composing some kind of tune, while remembering that a too facile or too beguiling one can distract as well as attract. [23]

Without some appreciation of the rules and discipline, in other words, a would-be poet is just a versifier, a would-be boxer just a thug.

(iv)

On that magical first night at the church hall in Castle Street in early 1934, however, all that was in the future. That night and in the succeeding weeks, the two boys trained separately, Vernon as a junior and Kenneth, two years older and at that age, much bigger, as a senior, but the lasting passion for boxing was a shared one, and five years later they would be boxing together for the Aylesbury Club. 'By the time I was sixteen, I was the star representative of the club', Vernon noted proudly in his diary later, [24] and newspaper reports of the time seem to confirm the brothers' ability. 'K. Bain (Aylesbury) beat W. J. Cole (Vauxhall Motors) on points', reads the *Bucks Herald* report of 3 December 1937, while the next column notes 'V. Bain (Aylesbury) beat J. Ford (St Pancras) on points. Bain appeared to have the physical advantages in this contest, and his counter of a straight left to Ford's face was the chief scoring blow seen.'

Their father must have been delighted that his two namby-pamby sons had put aside their books and taken up a man's sport. He paid their subscriptions for the Aylesbury Boxing Club, turned up each week to watch them train, and later travelled to see their bouts—the only aspect of their lives, according to Vernon, in which he showed any positive interest at all. In any case, far from welcoming his support, the two boys bitterly resented his constant presence—'watching us with an expression that we knew so well but could never confidently interpret, a faint smirk, almost a sneer, entirely humourless and obscurely menacing'.[25]

Later, looking back on his childhood from an Egyptian military prison, he would remember returning to Aylesbury with the rest of the team from boxing matches in London and around the south-east. Bruised and weary, often with split lips and black eyes, they would be singing happily in the back of the coach:

> At least the old man couldn't spoil those moments nor, for that matter, those times when you were actually in the ring and the fight was going just the way you wanted it to go, you were on target with the jab, you felt it connecting cleanly, with the knuckles, and you saw his head jerk back as if on an invisible puppet-wire and you slipped or blocked the counter and jabbed again until the opening offered itself and you threw the big right hand or whipped in the left-hook and he faded away and he was on the floor and the crowd in the darkness beyond the white brilliance of the arc-lamps was just a grey tidal wave of noise sweeping over you, warm and exalting.[26]

By their early teens, the violence of their young childhood and the constant abuse and criticism had alienated both boys completely from their father. And, for all his pleasure at their interest in boxing, the violence at home had never stopped.

Even as a young boy, Vernon was fascinated by the history of boxing, by the great names of both the past and the present. He knew their life stories, he could rattle off the statistics that marked out their careers, and he knew the names of every current national and international boxing champion at every weight. So when in September 1935 the Scottish flyweight champion, Benny Lynch, a rough, tough fighter from Glasgow's Gorbals, was challenging for the world title, it was natural that Vernon should have a view. Lynch had already fought the champion, Jackie Brown, to a draw, and the September meeting was a return bout. Vernon, with all the passion of a thirteen-year-old boy, was rooting for the challenger.

Brown, like Vernon's father, came from Manchester, and as a result the Old Man was a passionate supporter. When Vernon declared that he thought that Lynch would win, his father was dismissive: the champion would thrash him in a couple of rounds, he declared. In any other household it might have been an enjoyable argument, the sort of dispute that fathers and sons have had since sport began. But the next morning, when Vernon appeared for breakfast, his father was sitting smoking with Elsie over a cup of tea, in an angry, surly, sulky mood. He had listened to the fight on the radio he had recently bought, a fresh mark of the continuing success of his business. When his son asked excitedly who had won, he said nothing for a moment. Then, as if the words were being dragged from his mouth on chains, he muttered: 'Lynch. Knock-out. Second round. It was a fluke.'

The young boy, of course, was cock-a-hoop. His favourite had won, he had been right, what he had predicted had happened. For most people, it would have been a time for some light-hearted teasing, good-natured banter, maybe an argument about the respective merits of the two fighters. But not here. Bain said nothing for a moment, then suddenly got up, stepped over to his happy, excited thirteen-year-old son, and punched him, once, as hard as he could in the face.

He walked out of the room without a word, and Elsie looked down at her son, lying dazed on the floor with blood dripping from his mouth. 'You shouldn't have taunted him. You might have known', she said.[27]

(v)

The only source for all these stories of bullying and brutality, of course, is Vernon himself, years later, in the memoirs he wrote about his early life, and in the stories he told to his friends, his lovers, and his family. All the other people who would know the truth—Kenneth, Sylvia, Elsie, and Bain himself—are dead. Like many men, Scannell enjoyed telling his children about the hard times he had known as a child, and he wrote about them in memoirs such as *The Tiger and the Rose* and *Drums of Morning*: perhaps he exaggerated, misunderstood, even made stories up for effect? A brutalized childhood, after all, impresses children and sells books.

Writing privately, in his unpublished diaries, he expresses very ambivalent views about the reliability of autobiography. 'All writing is autobiographical; and I might go further and say that formal autobiography is the least reliable',[28] he says at one point, and at another: 'The novelist will almost certainly reveal far more of his true self in his stories than in his avowedly autobiographical writings. I think it was Frederic Raphael who said, "Truth is stranger than fiction, but fiction is truer".'[29]

So is Vernon Scannell the author telling the truth about Vernon Bain the boy? The first piece of evidence is that the stories he told were consistent—he made no secret, at any time of his life, of his loathing for his parents, and of the physical beatings he had suffered at the Old Man's hands. Neither did Kenneth, as his widow, Jenny Bain, makes clear:

> They both hated their father. Although Kenneth came to terms with it later, Vernon never did. They would both reminisce about how awful the Old Man was. Their mother never showed any affection for either of them—no hugs, no kisses, and certainly never any praise.[30]

When Elsie Bain read *The Tiger and the Rose*, she protested at the reference in it to her 'girlish greed for sweets'. A letter to him from Australia, where she was living with Sylvia, declared: 'The sweet-eating is a figment of your imagination—quite false.'[31] About the surely more hurtful accusations that her husband abused the boys, that she did nothing, and that she was cold and unfeeling, she was silent.

Vernon's two half-sisters—James Bain's daughters from a later marriage—also remembered beatings from their father with a leather strap or occasionally a dog chain around their legs. Towards the end of his life, suffering from Parkinson's disease and confined to a wheelchair, the Old Man would listen to Vernon's programmes on the radio and boast proudly to them about his son's achievements, and about how early Vernon had started reading as a child.[32] There was too much history for the two men ever to be reconciled, but he could say to his daughters some of the things he had never managed to say to his son.

(vi)

Vernon himself—reversing Philip Larkin's melancholy view of life as 'first boredom, then fear'[33]—said of his years in Aylesbury, 'I remember chiefly

boredom and frustration which increased as I grew older.'[34] For him, the
fear had come earlier, and as he passed through his teenage years, it hardened into a cold, hard dislike.

Boxing remained a passion—not even a half-understood and fumbled
sexual assault at the age of twelve, carried out by one of his trainers who
was supposedly 'fitting him for a jockstrap', could put him off—and he
grew into a broad-shouldered youth with an imposing presence. By sixteen, regularly taken for three or four years older, he had started drinking
in the local pubs, and he boxed with increasing success, taking part in the
National Schoolboy Championships and club bouts, often facing boys
older than himself. His increasing strength and skill helped to build his
confidence, sparked the grudging approval of the Old Man, and also made
him a less attractive target for the physical bullying that had been such a
big part of his childhood. James Bain's tongue still lashed the two boys, but
his fists flew less frequently, and when they did, the target was more likely
to be his wife and her cold, cutting sarcasm—it was not only the boys
who found neither warmth nor affection in the Kingsbury Square flat.
They still came in for the occasional full-hearted, clenched-fist blow in
the face, but by now they were beginning to be capable of defending
themselves—and there was an increasing danger for the Old Man that one
day they might hit back.

They were growing away from their father in other ways, too—going to
more places where he could not follow. Kenneth—adored by Vernon—was
starting to find poems to encourage his younger brother to read. An old
Methuen *Anthology of Modern Verse*, first published in 1921, included the
work of Thomas Hardy, Edward Thomas, Wilfred Owen, Walter de la Mare,
and Charlotte Mew, and revived the stirrings of interest that Vernon had felt
a couple of years before, in 'Pete' Dawson's class at Queen's Park School.
And this time, there was no one to tell him to copy out pages of it as a
punishment.

Over the next few years, Kenneth would continue to guide his younger
brother's reading, forging an emotional closeness between the two that
would last through their lives. From Aylesbury's County Non-Fiction
Library, they borrowed Siegfried Sassoon's *Memoirs of an Infantry Officer*,
Edmund Blunden's *Undertones of War*, and Robert Graves's *Goodbye to All
That*—all reinforcing the early interest they had shared in the terrors and
suffering of the First World War. There was Hemingway too, E. M. Forster's
Howard's End, and Henry Fielding's *Tom Jones*—all smuggled discreetly up to

the tiny bedroom overlooking the back yard of the flat, and pored over intently in defiance of the Old Man's muscular contempt.

While Kenneth branched out into Milton, Pope, Keats, Shelley, and Wordsworth, Vernon remained entranced by the lyrical verse of the late nineteenth and early twentieth centuries, treasuring his battered Methuen *Anthology* and losing himself in the rhythms and the language of Hardy, Thomas, and de la Mare. Looking back as an established poet, he sounds dismissive about his teenage self:

> The conscious, analytical part of my response was often lulled into a kind of stupor by the rhythms and the richness of the imagery of the poetry I was reading. I had not yet arrived at the point where I would understand that the pleasures of poetry could be far more various and invigorating than the languors I was then content to experience, that the proper reading of a poem was not an act of passive submission but one of collaboration with its author.[35]

It seems a harsh judgement on a boy in his mid-teens who was bravely teaching himself about poetry and literature—but in any case, the young Vernon was branching out beyond merely reading other people's poetry. He was starting to write his own, imitating as best he could the lush Georgian language of his Methuen models—his efforts, he said later, were 'like parodies of the worst poems in the anthology'.[36] He learned quickly not to show them to his parents—his mother would not be interested, and his father's only response to a carefully worked-out epic in the style of Sir Walter Scott's *Marmion* was an angry accusation of plagiarism. 'The Day That Summer Died' was another piece that he wrote as an adolescent and remembered as an adult. The poem—admittedly later polished by Scannell—still appears in anthologies:

> From everywhere the mourners came
> The day that Summer died,
> From shores of sleep and dreamland,
> From vale and mountainside...
> The trees all stood in silent grief,
> The wind lay down and cried;
> And Beauty came in sombre robes
> The day that Summer died.[37]

If, as the older Vernon seems to imply, there was something self-indulgent about the literary tastes of the teenager, that is surely no more than any young boy is entitled to. Perhaps there was something similarly self-regarding about

the long walks he and Kenneth used to take in the Chilterns, consciously
following in the footsteps of Rupert Brooke more than twenty years before
them. Like him, they tramped through the country lanes and the beech
woods, before stopping at a Chiltern pub for beer and bread and cheese,
revelling in the role of young, romantic, carefree, gifted poets. From the age
of fourteen, Vernon later recalled, he was 'not quite sure whether I wanted
to be a romantic poet like Rupert Brooke, or a tough boxer with scar tissue
on the eyebrows and a cauliflower ear'.[38]

Instead of either he became—for a few years—an accounts clerk.

(vii)

Vernon was just fifteen when he left school early in 1937. He answered an
advertisement in the *Bucks Herald* for a junior accounts clerk at the local
office of the British Equitable and General Assurance Company in the
Market House, just a couple of minutes' walk from his home. The advertisement asked for a candidate 'preferably with matriculation', which meant
they were looking for a boy from a grammar school, rather than a humble
elementary school, like Queen's Park—but Vernon applied anyway, off his
own bat, delivering his letter by hand to the office. He knew better than to
hope for encouragement at home, and his father's reaction was predictable:
'You don't stand a chance. You're wasting your time.'[39] But, after an interview with one of the partners, he was taken on at fifteen shillings[40] for a
48-hour, five and a half day week with a half day on Thursdays.[41] His job
was answering the telephone, filing letters, and checking the lengthy columns of pounds, shillings, and pence compiled by the manager and his
assistant.

It was a lowly role, and all but four shillings[42] of his weekly pay packet
went to supplement the family finances in Kingsbury Square, but the job
took him away from school and into the world of work—a tough transition
to make in 1930s Britain. Two of his evenings were to be given up to evening
classes in book-keeping but even so, the job gave him a sort of freedom,
with a small amount of his own money and the opportunity to try out new
skills such as smoking a sixpenny pipe which he bought from Woolworth's
(he remained a smoker until the last few years of his life). He also spent
several hours a week sitting at his desk either secretly scribbling 'shapeless
stories and poem-shaped pieces of nonsense'[43] or, equally secretly, fantasiz-

ing hopelessly about the office typist, a slightly flirtatious woman in her thirties who probably never even noticed him. He even showed her the scruffy exercise book with 'The Day That Summer Died' written out in his best handwriting. To his delight, she pronounced it 'Lovely'.[44]

Less innocently, perhaps, his role as keeper of the office petty cash and handler of stamps and postage provided the temptation to cream off an occasional shilling or so to supplement his pay. But best of all, the job gave him one over on the Old Man who, far from being proud of his son's success in finding a job, continued to sneer at his supposed incompetence.

In fact, he seems to have been quite good at it. 'Casting the figures', as his daily check on the accounts was called, left him forever with the ability to calculate a running total with speed and accuracy, and, for all its repetitiveness and tedium, he looked back on his start in office life with a degree of nostalgia. Nearly thirty years later, he imagined an elderly clerk shaking his head at the disrespectful young tyros who have followed him into the company:

> They were beautiful, the old books, beautiful I tell you.
> You've no idea, you young ones, with all those machines...
> You should have seen them, my day-book and sales ledger:
> The unused lines were always cancelled in red ink.
> You wouldn't find better kept books in the city.
> But it's no good talking: I know what you all think.[45]

It is in no sense an autobiographical poem, but it is significant that, when he is seeking for an image to express the significance of a cherished skill that defines the character and self-worth of an individual, the 43-year-old Vernon Scannell should light upon the office environment of his youth.

(viii)

Meanwhile, far away from Aylesbury, and unnoticed by Vernon or his brother, Europe was stumbling towards war. In 1933, as the Bain family were settling into their flat in Kingsbury Square, an unknown Adolf Hitler was coming to power as Chancellor of Germany; while Vernon was going through school and starting work, Germany was re-arming; but neither Vernon nor his brother, like most of the rest of the population, took much

notice. For them, the Great War—the First World War—was safely consigned
to history, and it was impossible to believe that there could ever be a Second.
Their father, in the unlikely event that they might have listened to him,
would have left them in no doubt: there would be no war, since Hitler
knew that the British army would be too much for him.

The Munich Crisis of 1938 brought 'a feeling of mild excitement followed by an equally mild sense of anti-climax',[46] but the teenage Vernon
had more important things on his mind—girls, for instance, who had recently
begun to enter his consciousness with a series of nervous encounters and
ardent fumblings beneath the canal bridge close to the Queen's Road School,
or the bottles of brown ale that he and Kenneth had started sampling enthusiastically in the local pubs.

There were still books, too—he had just lit upon D. H. Lawrence[47]—and
he and Kenneth were beginning to discover music with the aid of a cheap
gramophone they had pooled their meagre earnings to buy—Debussy, Liszt,
Schubert, and Beethoven. There was boxing, and the continuing need to
avoid the Old Man's fists and tantrums. All or any of these seemed more
interesting and more urgent than the political twists and turns in Europe.

The war memorial in Market Square had been there as long as Vernon had
been alive, its long columns of names of the First World War dead little more
than a frisson of excitement to a boy brought up on 'It's a Long Way to Tipperary'
and unlikely tales of his father's bravery and derring-do in the trenches. And if
the darkening news from Europe did ever catch his attention, there was, after all
the reassurance of Neville Chamberlain, the Prime Minister: there would, he
told a cheering crowd on 30 September 1938, be peace for our time.

It was, of course, a peace that lasted less than twelve months. The stumble
towards war turned into a brisk walk, then a trot, and finally a full-blown
gallop. The day after Chamberlain's promise, German troops marched into
what had been Czechoslovakia's Sudetenland; in August of the following year a non-aggression pact between Nazi Germany and Russia was
announced; and on 1 September 1939, after weeks of diplomatic wrangling,
deceptions, prevarications, and border skirmishes, German troops invaded
Poland. Two days later, war was declared, a war that was to cost the world
some 60 million lives, lay waste to cities, and reshape Europe and the world.
A new list of names—many of them present alongside Vernon Bain's on the
old Queen's Street School entry roll, or familiar to him from his training
nights at the boxing club—would eventually be added to the war memorial.

And alongside those soldiers, sailors, airmen and civilians who died, countless numbers of others had their lives irrevocably changed by the conflict. Some were bereaved; some lost limbs or suffered other terrible wounds; others were mentally scarred and never recovered. Among these last would be Vernon Bain.

3

The Long and Lovely Summer

Marauding engines grumbled
As we played
With high explosives
Of primed limbs and lips;
Incendiary kisses fell...

'Kathleen', from *Of Love and War* (2002)

I

It was 7.40 p.m. on 3 September 1939, just eight hours and twenty-five minutes after Neville Chamberlain's broadcast announcing the declaration of war on Germany, and passengers in the third-class dining room on the SS *Athenia* were just finishing their evening meals. The ship, a 13,500-ton British passenger cruiser carrying 1,418 passengers and crew from Liverpool to Montreal, was some 250 miles north-west of Ireland and making good time. Then there was a loud explosion—some passengers said two, very close together—from the stern, and all the lights went out. The ship lurched violently to port, sending dishes, cutlery, food and passengers careering across the floor in the darkness. Some 117 people died in what was the war's first German submarine attack—the U-Boat captain said later that the *Athenia* was zig-zagging violently, and he had believed it to be a military vessel.

The ship's sinking marked the start of the Battle of the Atlantic, and was instrumental in sparking terror of the U-Boat threat that would nearly strangle British resistance—but elsewhere, the declaration of war was largely followed by a widespread anticlimax, an uneasy feeling that something dreadful was in prospect, but that nothing was happening. Preparations for war had been in hand for more than two years, with instructions issued for anti-gas measures and arrangements for air-raid shelters and emergency services to deal with bombing casualties but, now that the moment had arrived, little seemed to have changed. There were lurid accounts of the brutal Nazi conquest of Poland, reports of minor skirmishing in the west between the French and German armies, and a few months later, a short-lived and ineffective British expedition to Norway, but otherwise there was little news of fighting or military action.

All that changed, of course, after some eight months, when German forces thundered through the Ardennes into Belgium in the Battle of France, introducing a new word, *blitzkrieg*, into the vocabulary of the British press, forcing France out of the war and leading to the mass evacuation that would become known as Dunkirk. The growling defiance of Winston Churchill was heard on the radio instead of the more emollient tones of the shattered and defeated Neville Chamberlain; Britain knew by then, with the reports of the bizarre 'triumph' of the little ships, the news

Figure 5. Vernon at age 17. Less than two years after this photograph was taken, probably by his father, he was married with a child, and had left his new wife to join the Army. (Photo: Not known. Scannell family collection)

of the Fall of France, and the return of the remnants of a beaten and
bedraggled army, that it was in a war.

Or at least, many people did. But for some, Vernon Bain among them, the
phoney war continued for several more months, with cloudless blue skies
and blazing sunshine stretching one of the best summers anyone had ever
known well into October. Of course he knew that the war had started, and
he occasionally discussed with Kenneth what it might mean for them—but
it seemed a long way off. Vernon was young and strong, fighting in boxing
matches and occasionally in pubs as well, and winning most of the time, and
those dreamy months brought him love, sex, poetry, booze, and the beginnings of a degree of independence. For a young man of eighteen, it sounds
very much like Paradise.

II

For the Bain family, February 1940 was memorable not for any news of the
war, but for another house move, this time away from the Kingsbury Square
flat, which James Bain kept on to use as his studio and maybe for other
secret purposes which would become clear later. Their new home was a
Victorian four-bedroom semi-detached house that he had rented in Manor
Road, a short walk from the town centre. One room was kept as a refuge
for Elsie's sister, Aunt Clarice, who might have to flee London if the bombing should start, so the two boys—now eighteen and twenty—still shared a
bedroom, although at last each one had a bed to himself. The house had a
garage, a garden, even a small orchard with peach, pear, and cherry trees—
for the Old Man, it was a mark of the success that he had dreamed of. He
had also bought himself a new car, and agreed reluctantly to send twelve-
year-old Sylvia to a small fee-paying school: the photographic business was
paying well.

He was rubbing his hands with glee at the thought of the imminent
conflict. With tens of thousands of young men being called up, he reasoned,
there would be huge demands for photographs, whether for wives, families,
and sweethearts to give to the men who were marching away, or for the
young men themselves, resplendent in their new uniforms. His business had
been gradually expanding for the last few years, but he expected the war to
transform his fortunes.

The town was dark at night now, blackout curtains drawn tightly, street lamps extinguished for fear of German bombers, and cars nosing their way cautiously through the streets with their headlamps covered apart from a narrow slit that allowed a feeble glimmer through onto the road immediately ahead.

Vernon had already been building on his earlier canal-side adventures and making a few tentative but more ambitious excursions into the intriguing if rather frightening territory of sex—a place that where he was to find fascination, excitement, and also trouble, all his life. (As was famously said about George Best, Vernon's problem with women was that he didn't have a problem with women.) But this was different. Since just before Christmas, he had been going out with a slim, dark-haired girl whom he names in *Drums of Morning* as Sally Herbert and in *The Tiger and the Rose* as Angela, but whose real name was Barbara Phillips. It was she, he revealed in *The Tiger and the Rose*, who 'had the very doubtful pleasure of taking my reluctantly preserved virginity. She was small, nubile and promiscuously passionate.'[1] Barbara came from Buckingham, but lived during the week in a boarding house in Aylesbury and working in a hairdresser's shop close to the Kingsbury Square flat. One of the last poems of Scannell's life, 'Black-Out', seems to contain a nostalgic memory of their night-time meetings:

> And still he waits, this lad of eighteen years,
> and still she does not come. A car slides past,
> its headlamps masked, so just the merest smear
> of pallid yellow trickles on the road;
> and then, as his anxiety swells, he hears
> the distant clicking of her heels at last . . .[2]

Like the young Vernon and Barbara, the couple in the poem are lost in each other, unaware of the horror that is building for their future:

> from far away, deep growl of guns
> begins its low and unrelenting threat,
> which neither he nor she can hear as yet.[3]

For the time being, Barbara did not know either that she was eight years older than Vernon—now eighteen, he looked several years older than his age, although he was still being paid only £1 5s.[4] a week. He didn't realize that the age gap was so big, but, with the self-conscious insecurity of that treacherous terrain between boyhood and being a man, he was quite sure that she would never agree to go out with someone as young as he was. He pawned some of his boxing prizes so that he could pay, as a man should, when they went out together in the evening, supplementing the proceeds whenever they slipped away for an illicit night together in a hotel with the few shillings he was by now regularly filching from the petty cash at the office. At home, like a small boy sneaking away to try a forbidden cigarette, he fibbed and dodged to keep the secret of the developing relationship from the Old Man, and in the hotel he would clench his pipe between his teeth to convince the receptionist that he was mature, staid, and—crucially—married. But his age was about to be revealed in an embarrassingly public way.

For both Kenneth and Vernon, the war offered a way out of Aylesbury. They had been talking vaguely for some time about which branch of the Armed Forces they would join, but continuing unenthusiastically in their jobs, Kenneth in a nearby photograph studio, and Vernon still totting up his figures at the life assurance offices. However, when Vernon thought of fighting, he still thought of tying on boxing gloves, not picking up a gun; the training he was interested in was the twice-weekly skipping and sparring at the boxing club rather than the basic training that the army would inflict on him.

But this particular night, in late March 1940, they were aware that the need to make a decision about their futures was getting more pressing. At twenty, Kenneth was likely to be called up soon, and Vernon would not far behind him. The brothers agreed that, rather than waiting to be summoned separately, it would be better to volunteer and hope to spend their time in the services together. The army seemed dull, colourless, and unromantic; the RAF sounded exciting, but only if you could get selected as aircrew—and neither of them had the educational qualifications necessary for that. Then there was the Navy, which seemed to put more value on individuality than the army: perhaps the Royal Navy or even the Merchant Navy might provide the opportunities that they needed.

It was the sort of discussion that they had had before—the sort, indeed, that was going on in pubs all over Britain. Perhaps the impending reality of a move away had made them excited, or perhaps they had drunk too many bottles of Younger's Scotch Ale. Probably it was no more than showing off—but as they made their slightly unsteady way past the nearby Bull's Head on their way home, Vernon swung himself up onto the fire escape that led to the roof of the Market House, and began to climb.

Kenneth followed him, Vernon drunkenly reciting poetry into the night, and his older brother urging him to be quiet. From the roof, they could look across to the Bull's Head that was part of the same building. For some reason, Vernon broke a pane of glass, and then the two brothers jumped down onto the flat roof of the hotel. There, Vernon tried half-heartedly to open a window. Inside the room, a woman screamed, and he backed off, mumbling nervously that there was nothing to be frightened of, and looking round anxiously for Kenneth, who had disappeared. It was shortly afterwards that the porter of the Bull's Head arrived, alerted by the noise. He told his story in court later:

> I saw the defendant turn towards the left, and I got out myself. I found him in an alcove on the left side of the window and caught hold of him, saying 'Are you coming up quietly?' The defendant replied, 'Oh, all right, I won't shoot.'[5]

When the police appeared a few minutes later, Vernon was still sounding cocky and derisive. Why was he on the roof, asked the inspector; 'Just looking for the moon', he replied. Back at the police station, though, it became clear that the police didn't share the joke, and believed that he and Kenneth might have been trying to break into the Market House or the hotel. Perhaps, they hinted heavily, he had been 'up to something else' when he briefly opened the window into the woman's room. Vernon, thoroughly scared and sober by now, began to sound more contrite. 'I was on the roof. I broke the pane of glass in the door. It was only mischief', he pleaded. After a brief and unconvincing effort to persuade them that he had been alone, he admitted that Kenneth had been part of the escapade: surely now that he was cooperating fully, he reasoned, the police would accept that it was no more than a stupid prank by a couple of boys who had had too much to drink?

But the law took its solemn course, and a few days later, the brothers were standing shamefacedly before the magistrates, facing charges of breaking and entering. Their solicitor was persuasive, if ponderous—'They were indulging in what I will call "this drunken escapade" on the roof and in the building known as the Market House. You have to be satisfied that these men went there with the criminal intention of stealing', he told the Bench. There was no evidence of that, he submitted. Luckily for the Bain brothers, the magistrates agreed, and dismissed the more serious charges, fining them £1 each for wilful damage.

But more worrying than the fine was the front-page headline in the following week's newspaper: 'Aylesbury Brothers in Court—Easter Saturday night incidents on Bull's Head Hotel Roof and in Market House'. For

Vernon, it was a threefold disaster. The Old Man had always been fond of saying that one day he would swing for one or other of his two sons, or maybe both together; a respectable organization like the British Equitable and General Assurance Company Limited would not be likely to approve of one of its employees appearing so publicly in the dock; and perhaps worst of all, Barbara would have read the whole story. Now she would know that he was only eighteen years old.

To James Bain, the *Bucks Herald* story was an embarrassment rather than a shock, since he had gone with Kenneth and Vernon to the police station on the night of the offence and stood glowering at the side of the room while they were fingerprinted and charged. Perhaps he was so outraged that even violence seemed inadequate to express his anger; perhaps there was a degree of smug satisfaction to be had in the thought that his two ne'er-do-well sons had finally proved him right and demonstrated the depths of their depravity—either way, his only response to the incident was a disgusted snarl of 'Get out of my sight!' when they arrived home.[6] It was such an anticlimax that it was almost disappointing.

At the office where Vernon worked, there was a predictably humiliating interview in front of one of the partners, who had travelled over from Oxford. It might almost have been another court appearance, with the young offender summoned brusquely to the partner's office and standing like a naughty schoolboy in front of him, trying not to look at the newspaper spread on the desk with its headline shouting his shame out loud. But instead of being sacked, Vernon surprised both himself and his employer by pre-empting the decision and declaring that he was planning to leave anyway, to join the Forces. 'RAF Aircrew', he said, decisively, forgetting his earlier preference for the Royal Navy and blurting out the first thought that came into his head. Maybe, too, he remembered the RAF advertisements seeking volunteers who were 'fit, intelligent, and possess dash and initiative'. The partner, clearly relieved, made comforting noises about how he didn't need to leave, and how nobody would remember the newspaper report in a week or so, but the die was cast.[7]

And as for Barbara, her response was, as far as Vernon was concerned, the most surprising of all. As he'd suspected, she was more interested in his age than in what he had got up to on the roof of the Bull's Head, but once she had made a couple of perfunctory protests about his deceit, it seemed to make him more attractive rather than less. The 'drunken escapade' with Kenneth proved to be the curtain-raiser to what he later recalled as a 'long, heartless and beautiful summer…of Elysian delight, of rapture both physical and metaphysical'[8]. But first, there was the little matter of the RAF to be settled.

(iii)

The Old Man's response to Vernon's announcement that he was going to join the RAF was predictably encouraging: 'You couldn't fly a paper kite, never mind an aeroplane', he scoffed. Unfortunately, this time he was proved right.

RAF Cardington, near Bedford, was famous as the birthplace of the ill-fated R-101 airship, which crashed in France on its maiden international flight in 1930, killing forty-eight people. In April 1940, with the airship-building business confined to history, it had a more mundane role as the RAF's No. 2 Recruitment Centre, an unattractive jumble of good intentions, office buildings, and concrete and red-brick barrack blocks. The young Vernon Bain arrived with his treasured Methuen *Anthology of Modern Verse* in his overnight bag, ready to breeze through the medical examination. After all, he was young and strong, and six years of boxing and regular training had left him leaner and fitter than most of the other aircrew candidates.

But once the tests started, it took the Medical Officer only a few minutes to find that he was both colour-blind and astigmatic—either one a good enough reason for him to be rejected for aircrew. Instead of a glamorous role as an air gunner, the flight sergeant who was acting as recruiting officer decided that his defective eyesight, combined with three years' experience in an office, reasonable spelling, and the ability to type with two fingers on each hand added up to the ideal qualification for an RAF clerk, grade three. Instead of Vernon swaggering home a hero, His Majesty proposed to invite him to swap one boring office job for another.

An hour or so later, he was lined up with about fifty other recruits, each of them issued with a bible on which to be sworn in. It was only when the warrant officer standing in front of them began to bark out the oath for them to repeat that Vernon realized that there was still a way out. 'I've changed my mind', he said, like Oliver Twist asking for more. The warrant officer was only a little less outraged at his ingratitude than Mr Bumble the Beadle, and in a few moments Vernon found himself, still a civilian, standing outside the gate of the depot. Anyone with the insolence to turn down the opportunity to serve the King in the capacity of clerk grade three was clearly not entitled to one of His Majesty's travel warrants and, in the middle of the morning of one of the hottest days of the year, he set out on the 35-mile journey home to Aylesbury.[9]

With a lot of walking and the help of a passing lorry driver, he was home by nightfall. Before he had even joined the services, Vernon Bain had started a running battle with authority that would last on and off for the next seven years.

(iv)

But the most memorable and most exciting of Vernon's Elysian delights was his eager and enthusiastic exploration of the intriguing territory of sex that he had started to investigate with Barbara. She, it sometimes occurred to him, seemed to know the landscape slightly better than he did, but he pushed the knowledge away. Over the next few months, he recalled fondly later, 'We both seemed to be possessed by a kind of erotomania.'[10]

The warmth of the spring and summer nights meant they could avoid the quizzical glances of the hotel staff by making love out of doors, and they did so at every opportunity. They would go for drinks in the local pubs—including the Bull's Head, which seemed to have taken a fairly relaxed view of the Bain brothers' embarrassing indiscretion on the roof. Despite the warm and settled weather, Vernon would be incongruously dressed in a long, shabby old raincoat as they sat and impatiently sipped at their drinks and then, walking home on a long, circuitous route to Barbara's lodgings, they would find a secluded spot in the trees and the raincoat would be spread on the ground as a makeshift groundsheet for a few minutes' snatched and urgent, frantic passion. Sometimes they would go together to see films in the local cinema; there were weekend trips to London, where they splashed out on an occasional night in the Strand Palace Hotel near Covent Garden, or on tickets at the Old Vic to see *King Lear* directed by Harley Granville-Barker and *The Tempest*, with John Gielgud as Prospero. Closer to home, they would go walking in the Chilterns, or bathing in the reservoir at Weston Turville, 3 or 4 miles away down the Wendover road, and later in the summer there were even clandestine assignations on the couch in the old flat in Kingsbury Square—but most of their meetings ended in the same constantly exciting way:

The evacuation of allied forces from Dunkirk had begun and, in a few weeks' time, the Battle of Britain would be waged against a backcloth of ironically tranquil blue skies and lavish sunshine, but I was happily preoccupied by images of [Barbara's] naked welcomings which were intermingled with the music, and ripple and rush, the flash and thunder, lilt and flow of Shakespeare's verse.[11]

Several months earlier, Vernon had fended off questions about this new girlfriend he was seeing by telling his father that Barbara had left Aylesbury and gone to London, but eventually—inevitably—the truth came out. There was a confrontation in the street near the Manor Road house, with the Old Man accusing Vernon of lying to him, and punching him in the head when he did not like his reply. This time, though, it was different: Vernon hit him back with a slightly half-hearted right-hander that left James Bain nursing a black eye and a rather more severe bruise to his pride. It was not a big punch compared with the ones that Vernon was used to exchanging with his opponents in the boxing ring, not even compared with the ones his father had dished out to both his sons through their childhood, but it was a momentous one. It marked the end of eighteen years of bullying. James Bain never hit either of his sons again.

But there was another violent incident connected with Barbara—one that seems even more significant in the light of Vernon's later experiences. Barbara's parents lived some 20 miles away in Buckingham, and she would go back there on the weekends when she and Vernon did not have some excursion planned. One Sunday night, as he was waiting to meet her bus in Kingsbury Square, he was sitting in the Bull's Head when he overheard a young man boasting about having met a girl at a dance in Buckingham, taken her outside to the car park, and had sex with her in the back of his car. It was the typically graphic description of a drunken adolescent show-off, but it was not the back-seat sexual antics that excited Vernon. What struck him was the name of the girl that was being shouted around the bar. It was Barbara Phillips.[12]

He knew the young man slightly, and when he met Barbara off the bus, he quizzed her about the dance. Yes, she'd been at a dance a couple of weeks before. She'd gone with her sister. No, she hadn't thought to mention it to Vernon. Yes, she thought the man he mentioned had been there, she said, bemused at the insistent questioning. Vernon didn't hit her, but he grabbed her by the arms and shook her violently, telling her what had been said in the pub. It wasn't true, she replied calmly. That, she added perceptively, is the way boys talk.

If Vernon had stayed with her another moment, he admitted later in *Drums of Morning*, he might have turned his mounting rage on her. 'Vengeful anger dominated completely and I was shaken and sickened by the urge to smash, to hurt, to destroy',[13] he says. Later in his life, similar emotions would overwhelm him, and he would do serious damage—but this time, his response was to run frantically back to the pub, which was about to close, and without a word punch the young man in the face, knocking him off his stool and onto the floor. Then he went home alone.

Barbara was lucky. He had no reason to believe that she was lying, but that night, remembering his earlier suspicions that she might have enjoyed rather more sexual adventures than he had, he was beyond reason. He described in his memoirs, written more than fifty years later, the graphic image that flooded his mind—'hideously but powerfully exciting'[14]—of his girlfriend with her skirt pushed up and her legs spread in the back of the man's car. It was the sort of uncontrollable, unreasoning, all-consuming sexual jealousy that would spark rages in him throughout his life, and the same sort of violent response. This time, though he worried for several days about what had happened, there had been a straightforward, well-defined ending to the incident: he had vented his anger on a loud-mouthed drunken show-off with a single punch, in much the way that the Old Man had often boasted about. In the future, the endings would be much messier, much less clear.

(v)

That incident seems to have marked the beginning of the end of the long, hot summer of love. Vernon and Barbara still met when they could, still had sex on the couch in the Old Man's studio, but the innocent urgency, the all-consuming passion that had marked their relationship through the summer was gone. And anyway, the war had forced itself into their lives.

Earlier in the summer, when they had been walking home through the darkened streets from the pub, or even when they had been writhing under the trees on the treasured overcoat, they had sometimes heard the distant drone of enemy bombers heading for Luton, Coventry, or Birmingham—an unobtrusive but unsettling grumble, the 'low and unrelenting threat' of 'Black-Out', that would remain a powerful image of unappreciated danger. In London, the Blitz started in earnest in early September—like many young men, Vernon and Kenneth travelled up to the capital one Saturday night to see the excitement almost as if it had been a firework display. In Aylesbury, the glow of the fires away to the south-east could sometimes be seen in the night sky. Aunt Clarice, 'a sour and unattractive elderly woman'[15] according to Vernon, duly arrived in Manor Road to take shelter from the bombers. They had always passed Aylesbury by—but on Wednesday, 25 September, the war finally arrived.

Details of bombing raids were never published at the time, and newspaper reports of the first bomb to strike the town seem coyly anonymous today. 'A S.E. town had its first taste of the indiscriminate bombing of the Nazi raiders last week', says the *Bucks Herald* report. The bomb had fallen in the centre of Aylesbury, and although casualties were light—'one death and a number injured' according to the newspaper—the effect on the town was salutary. Many of the injured had to be dug out of their homes, and the house where the bomb landed was destroyed:

> The rear of the house and all the other property around lies a shattered ruin bordering a blackened area of kitchen gardens…Windows in shops in the town's main shopping centre were smashed.[16]

Compared with the destruction being visited upon London, it was a minor incident—but it shocked the people of Aylesbury out of any complacency they might have felt about their own vulnerability. Certainly it had that effect on the Bain family: Elsie, Clarice, and thirteen-year-old Sylvia packed their bags and left for the Cotswolds, while James Bain hurriedly sublet the Manor Road house and moved back into Kingsbury Square with his two sons. The family, such as it was, would never be together again.

(vi)

Soon after the return to Kingsbury Square, Vernon started to work for a local garage, the Aylesbury Motor Company, selling spare parts and accessories. It was better paid than his old office role in the firm of accountants—£1 15s. a week[17] rather than the £1 5s.[18] he had been receiving before—but it was boring, repetitive work with little hope of promotion and no prospects. He was marking time, waiting for—something. He didn't know what.

But he needed the job. Although he had told Kenneth the full story of what happened, he had never confessed the debacle at RAF Cardington to his father—indeed, he had told him that the RAF had accepted him as an air gunner. It was only a matter of time, he had said, before the papers came through for him to go and join his station, but now, seven months on, the story was beginning to wear thin.

In any case, Vernon was facing another crisis—one that he never mentioned in his memoirs or in articles or interviews about his life. Whether because of his explosion of jealous rage or just because the two of them were growing weary of each other, the passion and excitement had seeped away from his affair with Barbara. In the normal course of events, as with many highly charged relationships, they might just have drifted apart, in the way that his memoirs suggest that they did. In fact, in a letter in 1967, he referred with nostalgic sentimentality to his 'first proper love affair—very romantic and doomed'.[19] But it wasn't quite like that. Sometime in August or September, Barbara came to tell him that she was pregnant. Exactly how she broke the news, or how it was received by the Old Man, isn't known—but at some stage Vernon presumably plucked up the courage to tell him. By the end of November he was married—a step which, at the age of eighteen, he would only have been able to take with his parents' permission.

In fact, the two never even lived together: Barbara went back to her parents' house in Buckingham to prepare for the baby, and Vernon continued with his desultory work at the motor company. But everything had changed. With a dead-end job, no money, and no prospects, and just six months after larking about like a drunken teenager on the roof of the Market House, he was a married man, expected to take on the responsibilities of a husband and father and settle into some simple role of staid domesticity. No matter that he no longer felt any particular affection for the girl who was to be his life's partner, or that she felt much the same about him: no less was demanded of a young man with a pregnant girlfriend.

In fact, the Old Man may have been too distracted with the complications of his own life to rage at Vernon's immorality. Perhaps there were other reasons than fear of the bombers for Elsie's sudden departure, because about this time Vernon found out that his father was having an affair with a mysterious woman who called him on the phone and was occasionally seen around Aylesbury in his car. The old photographic studio in Market Square would have been a useful place for his assignations as well as his son's. He and Elsie never lived together again.

There were no angry confrontations as far as we know, no late-night discussions between James Bain and either of his two sons, but there is no

(a)

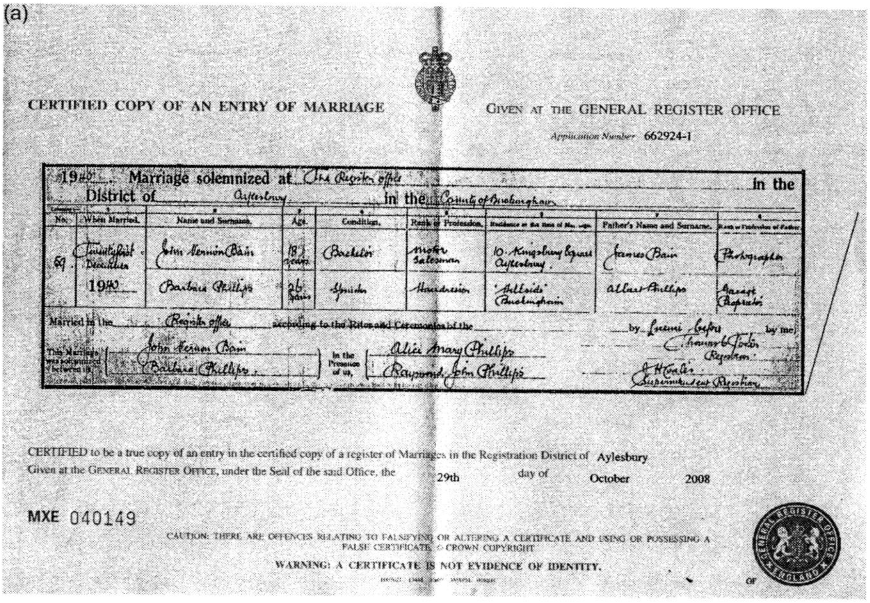

CERTIFIED COPY OF AN ENTRY OF MARRIAGE

GIVEN AT THE GENERAL REGISTER OFFICE

Application Number 662924-1

1940 Marriage solemnized at The Register office in the District of Aylesbury in the County of Buckingham

No.	When Married	Name and Surname	Age	Condition	Rank or Profession	Residence at the time of Marriage	Father's Name and Surname	Rank or Profession of Father
69	Twentyfirst December 1940	John Vernon Bain	18 years	Bachelor	motor salesman	10 Kingsbury Square Aylesbury	James Bain	Photographer
		Barbara Phillips	26 years	Spinster	Hairdresser	'Hillside' Buckingham	Albert Phillips	Garage Proprietor

Married in the Register office according to the Rites and Ceremonies of the ... by ... by me

This Marriage was solemnized between us, John Vernon Bain, Barbara Phillips, in the Presence of us, Alice Mary Phillips, Raymond John Phillips

CERTIFIED to be a true copy of an entry in the certified copy of a register of Marriages in the Registration District of Aylesbury

Given at the GENERAL REGISTER OFFICE, under the Seal of the said Office, the 29th day of October 2008

MXE 040149

CAUTION: THERE ARE OFFENCES RELATING TO FALSIFYING OR ALTERING A CERTIFICATE AND USING OR POSSESSING A FALSE CERTIFICATE. ©CROWN COPYRIGHT

WARNING: A CERTIFICATE IS NOT EVIDENCE OF IDENTITY.

(b)

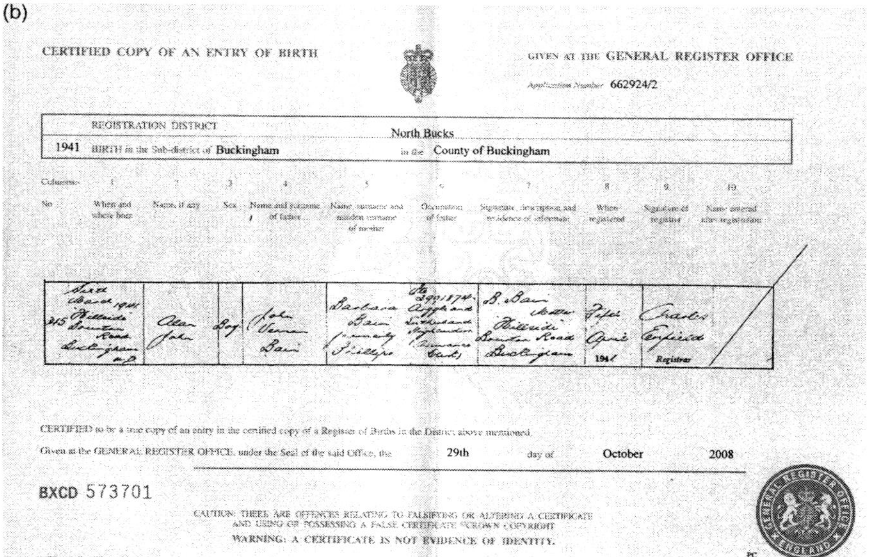

CERTIFIED COPY OF AN ENTRY OF BIRTH

GIVEN AT THE GENERAL REGISTER OFFICE

Application Number 662924/2

REGISTRATION DISTRICT North Bucks

1941 BIRTH in the Sub-district of Buckingham in the County of Buckingham

No.	When and where born	Name, if any	Sex	Name and surname of father	Name, surname and maiden surname of mother	Occupation of father	Signature, description and residence of informant	When registered	Signature of registrar	Name entered after registration
215	Sixth March 1941 Hillside Gawcott Road Buckingham	Alan John	Boy	John Vernon Bain	Barbara Bain formerly Phillips		B. Bain Mother Hillside Gawcott Road Buckingham	Fifth April 1941	Charles Enfield Registrar	

CERTIFIED to be a true copy of an entry in the certified copy of a Register of Births in the District above mentioned.

Given at the GENERAL REGISTER OFFICE, under the Seal of the said Office, the 29th day of October 2008

BXCD 573701

CAUTION: THERE ARE OFFENCES RELATING TO FALSIFYING OR ALTERING A CERTIFICATE AND USING OR POSSESSING A FALSE CERTIFICATE ©CROWN COPYRIGHT

WARNING: A CERTIFICATE IS NOT EVIDENCE OF IDENTITY.

Figure 6a and b. Marriage certificate and birth certificate. The day after Vernon's first, forgotten, wedding, Barbara went back to live with her parents in Buckingham. That is where the couple's son was born just over three months later. (Photocopies of originals). Also see plate section.

doubting Vernon's lasting anger at what he saw as his father's betrayal. Some thirty-five years later, in a poem called 'Our Father', he referred to his father as 'a sadist, liar and a fornicator'—that last word, surely, in the light of Scannell's own life, a classic case of a rather grubby pot throwing insults at a battered old kettle. But by now the Old Man and his sons were living separate lives anyway, eating their lunch in separate cafés around Aylesbury, and snatching a slice of bread and cheese in the evening. Not even an unwanted pregnancy or an illicit affair provided common ground on which they could meet.

In any case, the final and irrevocable break was about to come, and in a most unexpected way. Scannell's version of the story[20] was that he was snooping around his father's bedroom one night while he was out when—almost accidentally—he came upon a leather wallet stuffed with pound notes hidden away in a wardrobe. The Old Man had boasted several times that he did not need to worry about the tax man, and here was the reason why: the wallet contained something like £400,[21] presumably in undeclared earnings from his business. It was more money than Vernon had ever seen in his life. He talked over with Kenneth what they should do about it, but there was never any doubt. A couple of days later, he took a handful of the cash while his father was out of the house, and the two boys set off for London, secure in the knowledge that their father could not report the theft to the police without answering some awkward questions about where he had got the money in the first place.

(vii)

The whole episode seems to mark one of the less creditable moments of Vernon's early life. It was not only the Old Man that he was escaping from, of course. Back at her parents' home in Buckingham, he was leaving behind his pregnant wife of a few weeks to have her baby and bring it up on her own. He seems conveniently to have forgotten about her, the marriage, and about his still-unborn son—when, just three months later, he signed up for the army, it would be as an avowedly single man with neither wife nor dependants. He must have believed that he was walking out of Barbara's life forever; it would be another eight years before she walked back into his, in the most embarrassing circumstances.

Apart from a few brief and unsatisfactory meetings later in his life, he was leaving behind his father too. The theft of his money was a shabby and underhand way to end even such a cruel and dysfunctional relationship as they had experienced, and Vernon seems to have realized it. In his memoirs, he describes how he and Kenneth agreed, rather unconvincingly, that their father 'owed' them the money, and explains why he had taken only some of the banknotes rather than stealing the lot:

> I had felt, as I reached for the wallet, something like the same inhibition that had prevented me from hitting the Old Man with my full strength when we had fought on that summer night near Manor Road. Taking only a portion of the money was something like pulling my punch at the last moment had been.[22]

It sounds rather like someone who knows he is behaving badly, and is trying to salve his conscience. Vernon could often find excuses for the things he did wrong, but one of the redeeming features of his character was that he generally did not quite believe them.

But for the moment, he and Kenneth were conscious only of their new-found freedom. As they sat on the train and counted the money they had stolen, they realized that they had £37 each,[23] more than enough to fund them for a few days in wartime London. Apart from a vague and half-formed awareness that the war had finally caught up with them and that they would have to end up joining one of the services, they weren't thinking much further ahead than that.

London—at least the west of it—was abuzz with wartime excitement and possibility. They stayed in a twin-bedded room at the Regent Palace Hotel in Piccadilly—not as exciting, perhaps, as the double bed he had shared with Barbara at the Strand Palace, but a much more luxurious place than he was used to. And outside, the streets were filled with uniforms—the bright kilts of Highland soldiers, the occasional glamour of foreign service-men, and the ribbons and gold braid of senior naval and Air Force officers, as well as the usual drab khaki. There was Donald Wolfit to be seen in *King Lear*, and the pianist Myra Hess giving her famous morale-boosting lunch-time recitals at the National Gallery, its paintings now being hurriedly shipped out to the safety of Gloucestershire and Wales. There were the bookshops of Charing Cross Road—*Palgrave's Golden Treasury of Verse* and W. B. Yeats's *Oxford Book of Modern Verse* were among the volumes Vernon later remembered they had bought there. And of course there were the bars and pubs of Soho: for two young men with more money in their pockets than they had ever had before, there was more than enough distraction.

It was a week before they began to realize how quickly they were getting through the cash. With the glamour of life as RAF fliers now apparently unattainable, they had decided that volunteering for the Merchant Navy might offer the combination of élan and individuality they craved, and they set off east for the Shipping Federation Offices in Aldgate. The journey itself was a reminder of the reality of war; in this part of London, houses, shops, factories, and warehouses lay in crumbled ruins, marked off by sagging lengths of tape; the people in the streets had a hang-dog, almost furtive look that was foreign to the bustling excitement of the West End. This was where the bombs had fallen.

There comes a time for most young men when they realize that they are not quite as special as they thought, and that dreams are cheap, and jobs hard to find. For Kenneth and Vernon, that time came in the unlikely setting of the offices of the Shipping Federation, the merchant ship-owners' organization. They wanted to go to sea, they said brightly.

So what could they do, came the slightly bored reply from the former sailor behind the desk, who had probably already seen quite enough of the sea and enough of the young men in front of him to know that the answer was 'Not very much.' The sea, he told them bluntly, was no place for unskilled dreamers who wanted to strut about in smart uniforms, and in a couple of minutes they were back on the pavement outside, chastened but defiant.

But the officer in the Shipping Federation was doing them less than justice if he thought that they would just give up. From London they caught the train to Cardiff, hoping that they might be able to find a job on a ship in the docks at Tiger Bay. And when that didn't work, they travelled up to Glasgow, their dreams of a seafaring life gradually crumbling around them. There, too, the answer was the same.

By now they were staying not in smart hotels like the Regent Palace, but in seedy rooms that demanded payment upfront, and after a few days of half-heartedly scanning the Situations Vacant columns of the local papers in the public library, they discovered that their limitless fund of cash had dwindled away to almost nothing. That was when they noticed the army recruitment poster asking for volunteers between eighteen and twenty to serve in a Young Soldiers Battalion. If they lied about Kenneth's age, they reasoned, they could be enlisted as twins and hope to spend the war together. And anyway, they wanted to eat and have a roof over their heads.

The army was third choice, after the RAF and the Merchant Navy. But that was where the Bain brothers were going to spend the war.

4

Gone for a Soldier

They reach the starting line in night's disguise.
It isn't fear exactly that he feels:
excitement, certainly, and something else,
a small black living thing inside his gut
that grows and squirms as sudden livid weals
are slashed across the dark face of the skies.

'Baptism of Fire', from *Of Love and War* (2002)

I

More than twenty years later, early in 1962, Vernon Scannell was standing at
the bar of The George in Great Portland Street, in London's West End—the
BBC's local. He was forty years old, and an established writer, with five
novels and three books of poetry to his name, and a fourth collection of
poems due out later that year.[1] The name Vernon Bain and the war seemed
far behind him. Scannell was talking to the poet George MacBeth, who was
an influential poetry producer at the BBC. MacBeth, who was born ten
years after Vernon, in 1932, was suggesting that poets like himself, too young
to have seen action, lacked the capacity to write about battle with conviction.
By contrast, he said, warming to his theme, Scannell could speak about these
things with authority. After all, he had fought in North Africa and on the
beaches at D-Day. Perhaps younger poets like himself should confine themselves to other themes, and write about subjects on which they could bring
personal experience to bear?

Scannell was always a perceptive and honest, if sometimes acerbic, critic
of his contemporaries' work. Although he had published very few poems
by 1962 which dealt specifically with battle—his first volume, *Graves and*

Resurrections, published in 1948, included a single sonnet entitled 'El Alamein' and a twelve-line poem called 'After Conflict'—the lingering effects of the war on those who had taken part in it had been an occasional theme of both his poetry and his novels.

The clash that MacBeth described between imagination and experience interested Scannell all his life, and that night in the pub, he sought to set his friend's mind at rest. A poet, he argued, could create scenes and events from his imagination as effectively as he could from his memory. It was the emotion, not the facts, of a poem that had to be truthful. A little later, in a letter that he wrote after reading a book of MacBeth's poetry, he was more specific:

> Reading your 'Paras' poem reminded me of you saying one night in The George that you felt the lack of having seen action or experienced extremes of danger, violence, and so on. Your poem splendidly proves my point that one can write about it without having done it. I'm certain no paratrooper could create such an authentic and convincing thing.[2]

MacBeth's poem, 'The Drop', in which a French soldier graphically describes the gut-wrenching combination of terror and excitement of a parachute assault during the French-Algerian war, certainly does support that argument. And, as will become clear, the letter makes a highly significant point in the context of Scannell's own life too.

II

Private 2991874 John Bain—on the rare occasions that anyone in authority used a Christian name, the army dropped the Vernon that his parents had always used and settled for plain John—was not a good soldier. That much was established very early in his military career: in the very act of signing up as a member of the Argyll and Sutherland Highlanders, he demonstrated the blithe disregard for officialdom and military discipline that would characterize his service career.

The document to which he puts his name is clear: 'You are hereby warned that if after enlistment it is found that you have given a wilfully false answer to any of the following four questions you will be liable to punishment.' One of the questions and answers that follow—'How many children are dependent upon you?' 'None'—is at least technically true, although

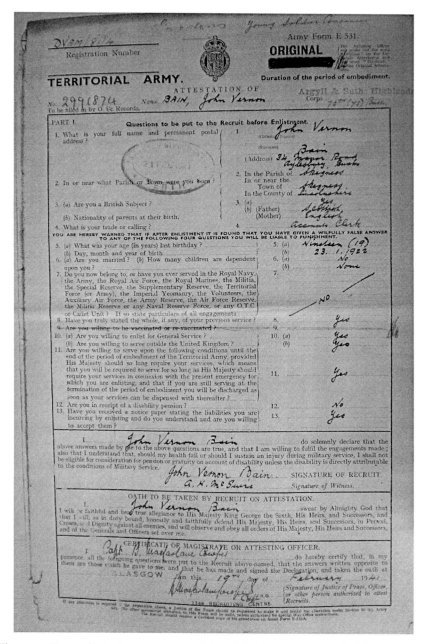

Figure 7. Vernon's signing-up papers claimed that he was unmarried, but no one cared that he was lying. Barely two months later, his wife and son were listed as his dependants. (Photo: Andrew Taylor). See also plate section.

Vernon knew by then that within a month he was likely to become a father. But another is clearly a deliberate lie:

'Are you married?'
'No.'

Bain's name, in his rounded, schoolboy writing, is signed below, formally confirming that what he says is true. His next of kin is listed as his father, James Bain, with the Manor Road address. He had rubbed his new wife out of his life like writing off a blackboard. Not for the last time, he was simply shaking off unwelcome memories of the past: he did not want it to have happened, so it hadn't.

It's not an attitude to the truth that would have been likely to find favour with the military authorities in peacetime—but in 1941, with a war to fight and an army to recruit, nobody much cared. By 1 April, John Bain's military record noted the existence of his wife, Barbara Phillips of Buckingham, and the birth of his son, Alan John, on 6 March. Apart from a couple of brief meetings when the child had grown up, he would never see the son he had left behind.

The inaccuracy on his recruitment form seems to have been ignored, but with his posting to the regiment's 70th (Young Soldiers) Battalion for basic training, he quickly won himself a reputation as the recruit who was never on time, whose kit was never polished or tidy, and who was always the one to be late back from a weekend's leave. In his diaries, he wrote later:

> I found the only way I could deal with the boredom, loneliness, and discomforts of service life was to allow myself to become brutalised. I drank and cursed and fought on pay-nights, I became known to my superiors as Bolshie and a trouble-maker, and I spent spells in the guard room as well as the glasshouse.[3]

To make matters worse, the army seemed to have a trick of seeming to promise comfort, even a degree of luxury, and then snatching it away at the last minute in favour of a regime of hard floors, harder work, and even harder discipline. On the way with his brother to join their regiment for the first time, he had glanced down at the travel warrant in his hand. It said they were to report to The Bay Hotel, Stonehaven in Aberdeenshire:

> I remember saying to Kenneth as we were travelling on the train, 'That sounds jolly good—it's going to be comfortable. Nice, being in a hotel.' I really

thought we'd be in beds; probably have room service and things. It was rather surprising when I discovered that there were no beds at all. We slept on the floor, with a couple of blankets. So that shows how naïve I was. Yet I don't remember being either particularly perturbed or surprised—I just thought, 'Hello, no beds—OK, we'll sleep on the floor.'[4]

If the lack of beds didn't dispel any illusions, then the kit with which he was issued should have done. The recruits were given rough blankets, kit-bag, soap, toothbrush, uniform, fatigues, boots, socks, underwear, cap, overcoat, and—because armies always prepare to fight the last war rather than the next—gas mask. Some of it was new, but most was second-hand: this was still an army being equipped on the cheap and in a hurry.

And there were more nasty surprises in store, with his first glimpse of his unit's new billet. Duff House, in Banffshire, had once been the luxurious country seat of the Earls of Fife, and its magnificent eighteenth-century Baroque architecture still retained, from a distance, an aura of luxury. That initial impression was as illusory as the beds of The Bay Hotel.

The house had been commandeered by the War Office in 1939, first for use as a military hospital, then as a transit centre for Italian civilians who were to be interned, and then as a prisoner-of-war camp—during which time, a stray Heinkel bomber had scored a spectacular own goal by unloading its bombs and killing not only two of the guards, but also six of the German prisoners. Now, as the Argylls' training base, it still had the eight-foot barbed wire fence, the machine-gun emplacements, and the watchtower of its previous incarnation. Behind the grand façade, Duff House was a grim, cold place.[5]

Just a short distance away, the beaches that had been so popular before the war were banned to civilians, and protected by more coils of barbed wire, mines, and concrete blocks. Bain's task during long hours on sentry duty was to protect Duff House from the mythical German paratroopers dressed as nuns who haunted the popular imagination in 1941; more realistically, it was to turn back any locals who might still insist on dodging past the elaborate defences to use the grounds as a short-cut from the town to the nearby bridge over the River Deveron.

The coast of Banff is further north than Moscow, and winter was bitterly cold, with the icy wind howling in off the North Sea:

> ...stropped to such
> Fine and steely sharpness that
> It might slice off a shrivelled lobe or finger[6]

Figure 8. Gone for a soldier—a photograph taken soon after Vernon joined the Argyll and Sutherland Highlanders in 1940. Within two years he was transferred to the Gordon Highlanders for the journey to North Africa. (Photo: Not known. Scannell family collection)

Huddled in his army greatcoat, Bain felt that he had reached 'the *Ultima Thule* of human misery'.[7]

In fact, the occasional respite that he found from the rigours of the camp came from the very locals he was supposed to be guarding against. Off-duty, he and his friend Tommy McGuire would occasionally stroll across the bridge for a couple of pints in the Fife Arms in Macduff—or even better, down into Banff for a traditional high tea with Gavin Alexander and his wife, who kept the chemist's shop.[8] The Alexanders had a son of their own in the forces and, like many of the locals, were happy to show their hospitality to the young soldiers. They offered them fried local fish or sometimes chicken with chips, followed by generous plates of scones, jam, and Mrs Alexander's homemade chocolate cake. Then Gavin would get out a bottle, and the young men would sit drinking his malt whisky and smoking his cigarettes with him until it was time for them to weave their unsteady way back to the barracks. Vernon would later remember that part of his time in Scotland as 'an idyll of peace, safety and human kindness'[9]—a break from the harshness of life at Duff House just as his grandparents' house had been a break from the harshness of life at home when he was a child.

Back at the camp, they lived a different life. Again and again, the new soldiers dismantled and reassembled the standard British army Bren gun—named from Brno in Czechoslovakia, where it was designed—until it was almost second nature. Firing 500 rounds a minute of .303 ammunition, the same as they carried for their Lee-Enfield rifles, the Bren would become their best friend, often their lifesaver. Training was disrupted by heavy snow during the bitter winter, but the constant aim from reveille to lights-out was to turn ordinary young men into battle-ready fighting soldiers who would be capable not just of handling machine guns and all the complex technology of twentieth-century warfare, but also of ripping an enemy's guts out in hand-to-hand combat. It was all about choking any feelings of empathy, humanity, or pity in these young men, still in their late teens and early twenties. There was bayonet practice with a screaming and almost comically aggressive sergeant:

> 'Right lads,' he barked, 'you see them sacks?
> I want you to forget
> That sacks is all they are and act
> As if they was all Jerries – wait!
> . . . You've got to understand, you must
> Be brutal, ruthless, tough
> I want to hear you scream for blood
> As you rip out his guts and see
> The stuff he had for duff.'[10]

Bain was no gentle flower—his boxing experiences had left him tough, hardened, and ready enough with his fists—but neither did he have any desire to fire a shot in anger if he could possibly help it, still less disembowel an enemy with his bayonet. He was, simply, not cut out for a military life.

By four in the afternoon, the men were usually dismissed to their barracks. Some—Bain not among them—would spend their time shining their boots, blanco-ing their webbing, and polishing their brass buttons; others would lounge about reading, playing cards, or maybe writing letters. He had few, if any books: looking back later, as Vernon Scannell, he would claim that he read virtually nothing during his four years at war, apart from a dog-eared copy of George Moore's *Esther Waters*, tossed to him by a guard in the military prison in Alexandria. However, he did manage during that first year in the army to squirrel away at least one poetry book, the *Pelican Anthology of Religious Verse*, in which he found a short poem called 'Carol', by the little-known Westmoreland writer John Short. Its eight lines, depicting the infant Christ in 1930s poverty, 'poor as a Salford child', stayed with him, 'part of my mental furniture',[11] and nurtured a love for Short's work that would run like a thread through his life.

Moments like that, though, were kept secret. To survive in the rough, macho, blustering world of the barrack-room, he had to bury any sensitivity or intellectual interest so they could not be seen:

> My comrades were mostly sub-literate, embittered children of the General Strike, from the slums of Glasgow and Edinburgh. The only way I could form any kind of working relationship with them was to suppress the side of my nature that they would have found not only incomprehensible but even sinister, and let the Caliban in me grow big, flex his muscles, and out-roar the roaring boys.[12]

He could do it—he was a strong man, well able to handle himself in a fight and ready to roar with the best of them—but there was a heavy price to pay. There were times in Scotland, and later, of utter dejection and a feeling that any hope of a fulfilled, rewarding life was over:

> He had known, suddenly and with utter certainty, that the war would not end during his lifetime, that he was condemned to remain in this drab khaki world, becoming steadily more and more dehumanised, until all memory of a previous existence was extinguished by death or indifference.[13]

On 8 August, less than six months after he had joined up and signed his name to an oath to 'be faithful and bear true allegiance to His Majesty King George the Sixth, His Heirs and Successors', he decided he had had enough, and slipped out of the barracks early in the morning. For the first time, but definitely not the last, Private Bain was on the run.

He was absent without leave (AWOL) for nearly three weeks, but the army seems to have taken a fairly relaxed view of this first offence: he was fined twenty days' pay, just about covering the period he had been away from the barracks, and a few months later was promoted to corporal—the only military promotion he ever received, and, as it turned out, a short-lived one at that.

So why had he joined up in the first place? He was, after all, a volunteer, not a conscripted man. Was it, as no doubt it was for many young men in the dark days of 1940, a fervent patriotic response to the danger of invasion, an idealistic wish to see the scourge of Nazism swept from the world? Not exactly, he confessed later. 'I had no understanding whatsoever of the political realities', he said. 'None whatsoever. It was a kind of silly, half-baked notion of adventure.'[14]

It is a dismissive and self-deprecating explanation that would have appealed to the older Vernon Scannell. As an old man musing over the published diaries of a pacifist who had campaigned against the war, he looked back in bemusement on the boy he had been when he marched off to war. 'The contrast between her adult, intelligent, fairly well-informed responses to the war and my own ignorant, silly reaction as an eighteen-year-old amuses and fascinates. Those civvy grown ups *were* so *frightened*. I wasn't. Not because I was brave, but because I was crassly stupid and childishly ignorant.'[15]

But that confession also ignored another reason why he had volunteered for his khaki battledress: joining up meant leaving Barbara and escaping not only the responsibilities of marriage and fatherhood, but also the miserable memories of his childhood and his dysfunctional relationship with the Old Man. Running away from them, like running away from the army, had not solved any of his problems, but it had certainly put them behind him for a while. 'Taking a powder' was a tactic that he would turn to again and again.[16]

III

But however unhappy he was, the young Private Bain had signed up, and in the summer of 1942, he was transferred to the Gordon Highlanders. They had already started training at Aldershot in England, but although it was clear that a move abroad was in prospect, nobody had told them where they would be sent. All the Gordons knew was that they were heading for combat, and that their training was reaching its peak: they dug slit trenches, and then squatted there while Churchill tanks were driven over the top of them, inches from their heads; they practised advancing in open order towards machine gun posts, ducking instinctively as the bullets whistled above them.

It was only after they had left British waters that they were told they were heading for Egypt. German and Italian naval patrols and air power barred the short route through the Mediterranean, and the 10,000-mile journey to

war took them around the southern tip of Africa, and then north, hugging
the east coast as far as the British base at Aden to refuel, and on up the Red
Sea. By the time they disembarked at Port Tewfiq, at the southern end of the
Suez Canal, they had been at sea for nearly eight weeks.

There followed several weeks of further training in the heat and dust of
the desert, before they finally moved quietly into their battle positions. This
was the place, between the Mediterranean Sea to the north and the soft,
impassable salt marsh of the Qattara Depression about 30 miles to the south,
where in July the British forces had made their final stand against the
German and Italian advance.

The Arabs called it the Place of Two Flags—El Alamein.

The new commander of the Eighth Army, General Bernard Law
Montgomery—brilliantly summed up as 'an abrasive, opinionated little
cock sparrow of a man' in one authoritative history of the North Africa
campaign[17]—had a simple view of warfare: for him, it was simply about killing the enemy. One of his early messages to the men under his command
read, 'Everyone must be imbued with the desire to kill Germans, even the
padres—one for weekdays, and two on Sundays.' Winston Churchill, slightly
more poetically but just as bloodily, told the soldiers during the build-up to
Alamein, 'Gentlemen, you will strike an unforgettable blow against the
enemy. The corn will be ripe for the sickle and you will be the reapers.'
Bearing in mind the slaughter that was to follow, the response might have
been an adaptation of another of his famous remarks: 'Some corn, some
sickle.'[18]

Such bellicose posturing would have revolted Bain both as a young soldier, and as an old man. He was never opposed to war on principle—years
later, writing in opposition to what he called the 'imprudent and aggressive
jingoism' of the Falklands campaign, he stressed, 'I am not and never have
been a total pacifist ... I believe that in certain circumstances the use of military force can be justified, and that the war against the Axis powers was one
such instance.'[19]

But the war left him, like many other combatants, with memories that he
could never shake out of his mind. Much later in his life, his partner Jo
Peters would wake him from nightmares when he would be sweating and
shouting that he was too old for the army:

> He had one memory that was particularly vivid. I don't know exactly where
> this was, but he remembered the first dead body he had ever seen. It was

covered with a blanket, and all he could see was the hand. Later on, of course, he saw hundreds of things that were worse, like people being blown up, but that first image stayed with him.[20]

Looking back on the war as an old man, he would tell her that his aim from the start had been to get through it without being killed and without killing anyone else. An entry in his diary in 1951 recorded bluntly: 'I detest Field Marshall Montgomery.'[21]

IV

But this was Montgomery's moment. It was time for killing.

The battle that started with the crash of a single heavy gun at exactly 9.40 p.m. on 23 October was like a ghostly scene from one of the First World War stories that had so fascinated Bain as a child—the concerted, earth-shattering roar of almost 1,000 pieces of artillery pounding the German and Italian defences, followed by the eerie sight of long snaking lines of officers and men making their way west towards the noise of the explosions. Painstaking and dangerous work by the sappers had cleared narrow corridors for the advancing troops through the thickly strewn minefield: now the job of the advancing soldiers was to push forward through the constant rattle of machine-gun fire and the shivering explosions of mortar shells beyond the enemy's main defences.

Sergeant Felix Barker of the 5th/7th Gordons recalled the advance later:

> It was a moonlight walk to places called First and Second Objective with death in every form lying between the walkers and their destination ... it was an endless journey—five miles or ten? You couldn't tell how far you had walked—and all the way the steady, remorseless taking of position after position, stumbling into enemy machine gun and mortar pits, passing over the bodies of Germans and Italians lying in their holes.[22]

The sun rose on a scene of widespread confusion, but it gradually became clear that the Allied forces had succeeded in forcing a huge bulge in the enemy lines. Now they faced ten days of waiting and watching while the tanks battled it out in front of them. Stories filtered back of friends killed, wounded, or missing, but there was nothing they could do but smoke and wonder how the battle was going.

The next infantry assault was mounted under a savage aerial bombardment from dive-bombing Stukas and Messerschmitts, but after a day's fierce
fighting, the Germans began to retreat. The wall had crumbled, and the
Eighth Army poured through the gap. A week later, the enemy had been
driven out of Egypt, and Allied troops were streaming into Libya, which had
been an Italian colony. Tobruk, which the Germans had seized five months
earlier, was retaken; and then Benghazi. With US and Allied troops already
established in French North Africa, to the west of the retreating Germans
and Italians, the hope in the 51st Highland Division was that the Axis forces
might surrender once the Libyan port of Tripoli fell, ending a desert campaign that had brought them nearly 1,000 miles from El Alamein. Rumours
were rife that they might even go back to Britain, and the Gordon
Highlanders marched into the town on 23 January 1943—the day after John
Bain's twenty-first birthday—amid the swirling and skirling of kilts and
bagpipes, so smartly turned out that soldiers from other units wondered
where they had managed to keep their kilts through the long campaign.
Most had had no sleep for forty-eight hours; they had been working like
navvies to repair the craters in the road left behind by the retreating Germans;
and now they were ready for a few days' rest.

Shortly afterwards, Winston Churchill himself, reportedly with tears running unashamedly down his cheeks, took the salute in the town's main
square. Along with his commanders, he had paid a surprise visit to the
Eighth Army back in Egypt, a few weeks before the Battle of El Alamein:
the army that marched past now was very different from the one they had
inspected then. 'The last time we had seen them was when they arrived in
the Middle East—then they were still pink and white; now they are bronzed
warriors of many battles and a victorious advance. I have seldom seen a finer
body of men, or one that looked prouder of being soldiers', said Field
Marshal Alan Brooke, Chief of the Imperial General Staff,[23] who watched
the march-past with him.

V

The Gordons' regimental history is justifiably proud of its part in what had
been achieved:

> Wherever the enemy had stood he had been attacked and forced to continue
> his retreat. Despite minefields and demolitions, sandstorms and rainstorms,

shortage of water, petrol, ammunition and all supplies, the pursuit, though sometimes slackening, had never ceased. Untried in battle before they attacked at El Alamein, the Highland Division were now war-hardened and desert-hardened.[24]

But what of John Bain's part in the campaign? Nearly thirty years later, writing by now as Vernon Scannell, he says in his memoirs that he remembers little about the fighting:

> I have since wondered if I was not indeed in some kind of self-induced hypnotic state which preserved me from panic and disintegration. On the other hand, it might be that my memory is refusing to recall much of what happened because it knows that such recollection would not be good for me. Of something like eighteen months of action in the Western Desert, Tripolitania and Tunisia I remember, in precise detail, not more than a few hours, though the experience has left in the memory a shifting impressionistic canvas of enormous size but seen in bad light and from too far away.[25]

Later in his life, though, some of the memories seemed to return. He produced several moving poems about El Alamein; in one, he wrote about the terror of soldiers as they struggled in 'a storm / Of killing thunder they must battle through',[26] and in another, he described the heroism of a Scottish piper at the height of the battle, standing at the entrance to the narrow corridor that had been cleared though the mines:

> And at the gap one piper
> Played *Highland Laddie* for
> Our comfort and encouragement,
> Like a ghost from another war.
> Of course that brave young piper
> Did not stand there long;
> Shrapnel or a Spandau-burst
> Ended that brief song...[27]

Nearly sixty years after the battle, again as Vernon Scannell, he spoke movingly to the writers John Bierman and Colin Smith, who were preparing their history of the North Africa campaign, about his personal experiences in the bullets and shrapnel:

> There was a sergeant who was quite close to me who always seemed to me almost a kind of father figure – rather a tough, leathery kind of man. And he was badly wounded and hearing his voice sort of sobbing and in fact calling for his mother, his mum, you know, seemed to be so, I don't know, demeaning and humiliating and dreadful.[28]

It is a vivid image of personal breakdown under fire. Like the description of the piper's death, it takes the blood, noise, and confusion of battle and focuses them on the single, suffering individual. The sobbing of the dying sergeant and the ghostly figure of the tragic piper, George MacBeth might have said, could only have been described by someone who had seen and heard them.

And yet, in the three volumes of memoirs in which Scannell quarries his experiences from the war years, there is no significant mention of the fighting at El Alamein, which was thought of as the turning point of the war and which must have been a defining experience for anyone who took part in it. Keith Douglas's classic *From Alamein to Zem Zem* describes his own part in the battle and in the advance which followed, until he was seriously wounded by a mine at Zem Zem just east of Tripoli in north-west Libya.[29] Scannell's memoirs, by contrast, contain virtually nothing in detail about the North Africa campaign until the Battles of Mareth and Wadi Akarit in mid-March, nearly five months after the start of El Alamein, and two months after Douglas's injury. An incident in *The Tiger and the Rose*, in which he accidentally drops a pile of landmines, 'might have been at Zem Zem, or it might have been later, when we had passed Tripoli and were facing the Germans in the Mareth Line'.[30] This is one of a very few passing references to the pursuit of Rommel's retreating forces across North Africa.

Bierman and Smith, reading *Argument of Kings*, certainly noticed the oddity. 'I notice that your story begins at Wadi Akarit but does not mention Alamein—which is the focus of our book—and the events in your life leading up to it',[31] Bierman wrote to him in 1999. Scannell's reply refers to his accounts of the later battles at Mareth and Wadi Akarit. At Alamein, he says, there was nothing for him to write about:

> I haven't written about it in prose because, I suppose, nothing specifically 'personal' happened. I mean, there are already hundreds of accounts of first experience of battle, including El Alamein. I wrote about Mareth and the 'Mock Attack' in *The Tiger and the Rose* because my Company Commander deserted 'in the face of the enemy' when I was his Company Runner.[32]

Perhaps that is true, although it seems bizarre that he should have found nothing to interest him in his participation in one of the biggest set-piece battles of the Western Front—that nothing of note happened to him as he advanced under fire, as the night sky was lit up by the exploding shells, as he heard wounded and dying men crying out in pain. Or perhaps, as he said in

The Tiger and the Rose, there was not enough clarity in his 'shifting impressionistic canvas of enormous size' for him to attempt to write about Alamein and the succeeding weeks—but there is another, simpler reason than either a lack of interesting material or self-induced hypnosis.

Nothing of interest happened to him because he wasn't there. According to his army records he was still in England when the Battle of El Alamein was fought. The official record shows that all the exploits of the Gordons in the 51st Highland Division, from the initial training in England to the carnage of Alamein, took place without John Bain. He wasn't at Tobruk, or Benghazi, or Tripoli either, whatever he told Bierman and Smith, and whatever most of his friends in later life believed. In the memoirs, too, he was happy for the reader to have that impression. But the army records say that he wasn't even a member of the Gordon Highlanders regiment until after they had left for North Africa—their ship left British waters on 21 June, and John Bain's record shows his transfer to join the regiment on 2 August.

Although there is no specific claim in *Argument of Kings* or elsewhere in his memoirs that he was at Alamein, there is the 'something like eighteen months of action in the Western Desert' in *The Tiger and the Rose*, and the passing reference to Zem Zem and the accident with the landmines. There is an old-soldierish nonchalance in his observation that he 'knew about the trip wires, the booby-traps, the malevolence of the stray shell, the sniper's bullet, the dive-bomber screaming down at you from what had, moments before, been a clear sky'.[33] No doubt you learn about these things very quickly in battle, but the implication of those words, describing his approach to the Battle of Wadi Akarit in early April 1943, is clearly that he had been part of the long trek westwards from Egypt that preceded it. Years later, when asked, he would tell his friends that he had fought at El Alamein.[34]

He hadn't, because by the time of Wadi Akarit, if the records are to be believed, he can have been in Africa for no more than six or seven weeks. The entry is clear. The Battle of El Alamein was fought between 23 October and 5 November 1942, and the military history sheet in John Bain's official army record shows him as serving at home—in Britain—from his enlistment on 19 February 1941 until 20 December 1942. It then shows his service in Egypt as starting the next day, 21 December—but since this service is counted from the date of his embarkation, he still had to make the eight-week journey to the Red Sea by ship. He cannot have been in North Africa before mid-February at the very earliest.

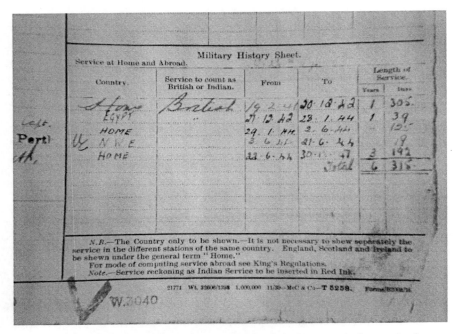

Figure 9. The Military History Sheet on Vernon's Army records shows clearly that he left for Egypt on 21 December 1942—nearly seven weeks after the Battle of El Alamein. Photo: Andrew Taylor. See also plate section.

Records, of course, can be mistaken—but apart from that entry, there is a separate note of an appearance for a disciplinary hearing before his commanding officer in the UK on 23 September—about a month after he would have had to set sail to reach North Africa in time for the Battle of El Alamein. It is inconceivable that two army clerks should have made mistaken entries—so if we are to believe the army record, John Bain cannot possibly have been in Africa until some four months after El Alamein, after the retaking of Tobruk, after Benghazi and after Tripoli. He arrived in Africa not as part of the first force of the Gordon Highlanders who were to turn back the German and Italian forces west of Alexandria, but with the reinforcements who joined them later.

There is no shame in that—since he was only transferred to the Gordons in August 1942, he could hardly have been ready to leave for Africa any earlier. 'I came as quickly as I could', he might have said to those who had fought through El Alamein and after. And the army record does not suggest that Scannell was telling direct untruths in his memoirs. In 1968, as he was mulling over whether to write *The Tiger and the Rose*, his first autobiographical memoir, he worries about whether he will be able to write an honest book about his life:

> The more I think of doing an autobiography up to the time of going to North Africa, the more I like it. I think I could be honest over that period. Then, perhaps, a subsequent volume taking up the story in 1945.[35]

There were, as we shall see, other aspects of his military service that he was not prepared to talk about at that stage—but it still seems odd to seek to erase the entire war years from his life story.

He decided eventually, of course, to go ahead and write about his military service—and it's important to note that where they *do* describe specific engagements, the details he sets out tally with those of the history books. He doesn't specifically claim in either *The Tiger and the Rose* or *Argument of Kings* that he was at El Alamein, and as for the poems, he was justifiably insistent that readers should not look for literal, factual truth, and still less for autobiography, in poetry. The death of the young piper who was playing 'Highland Laddie' in the poem that Scannell wrote in the 1980s is in fact described in the regimental history of the Black Watch[36] published in 1950, in which the piper is named as Piper Duncan McIntyre. There is no reason why moving, sincere poetry should not be written about experiences in battle in which the poet did not share, and that is exactly what Scannell has done in the Alamein poems. As he said to MacBeth all those years later, 'One can write about it without having done it.'

It is not to say, either, that he had no battle experience in North Africa. It is almost certain that he was at the Battle of Mareth Line in March 1943, and quite certain that he took part in the assault on Wadi Akarit twelve days later—described by General Douglas Wimberley, commander of the 51st Division, as the finest battle his men fought in either North Africa or Sicily.[37] There is no doubt either that he was on the beaches at D-Day in June 1944. However dismissive he may be about his military record, that last experience alone is surely enough to establish his credentials as a soldier. Throughout his life, Scannell was the last man either in public or private to brag about his prowess as a fighting man—'I see myself as the archetypal "bad soldier" ', he noted in his diary,[38] and in *The Tiger and the Rose* he mocked his unsoldierly bearing, with his battledress trousers 'far too slack at the waist and the seat [hanging] low and baggy like a Muslim's pantaloons'.[39] But on the other hand, he must have seen the brief biographical note in *The Terrible Rain*, Brian Gardner's influential anthology of Second World War poetry published in 1966, which says that he 'served in the 51st Highland Division, from Alamein to Tunis'.[40] He never corrected it, just as he never did anything to correct the impression that his service in North Africa was longer and more impressive than it was.

VI

In 1998, more than fifty years after Alamein, there were allegations that another English poet, in another war, had been less than scrupulous in his account of his experiences. An article in the *Spectator* by the writer Simon Courtauld claimed that Laurie Lee, author of *Cider with Rosie* and *As I Walked Out One Midsummer Morning*, had exaggerated his exploits during the Spanish Civil War. Lee had been dead for some seven months and Scannell, who was a personal friend, wrote sadly and with great humanity in response:

> Simon Courtauld . . . claims, with some justification, that Lee in his third autobiographical prose book, *A Moment of War* (1991), describes adventures during the Spanish Civil War that he could not have experienced and events at which he could not have been present. It is perhaps a pity that the lie has been uncovered, but in the end the best of the poems in *The Bloom of Candles* (1947) and *My Many Coated Man* (1955) and the rhapsodic account of a prelapsarian rural existence in *Cider With Rosie* will survive unblemished.[41]

As I Walked Out One Midsummer Morning ended with Lee's walk over the Pyrenees into Spain in 1937. It was another twenty-two years before he published *A Moment of War*, which described how he went on to military training with the Republican fighters, and killed a man in hand-to-hand fighting at the Battle of Teruel. 'Did it take him that long to decide to tell such a whopper, or perhaps for his imagination to fertilise?' Courtauld sneered. Scannell published *The Tiger and the Rose* in 1970, twenty-eight years after Alamein, and *Argument of Kings* another ten years later. In neither book does he explicitly describe experiences or events 'at which he could not have been present', but to a cynic today, his defence of Lee may seem double-edged, even self-serving. It was undoubtedly sincere—but, even if the word 'lie' is a harsh and unfair term for anything that Scannell may have been guilty of, his words about Laurie Lee provide a fitting postscript to his own North African war service.

VII

In fact, two days after the Gordon Highlanders joined their ship in Liverpool, John Bain was doing what he did best as a soldier. Once again, he was on the run. He had still not been transferred to the Gordons, of course, but the records show that he was officially declared a deserter from the 2nd Highland Regiment on 23 June, having gone missing at 6 a.m. At 11 a.m. on 16 July he rejoined his unit, and nine days later he was standing trial before his commanding officer, and forfeiting twenty-four days' pay. At the same time, he reverted at his own request from the rank of corporal to that of private.

Maybe that was a mark of contrition, or maybe, despite a note on the record saying that he was demoted 'at own request . . . and not with a view to avoiding trial by Court Martial', it was a way of avoiding more serious punishment—but either way, less than two months later, he went AWOL yet again. He had been transferred to the Gordons on 2 August, and this time, the record shows him losing another ten days' pay after going missing from 4 September to 13 September—the absence that resulted in his appearance before his Commanding Officer (CO) on 23 September. Before he finally embarked for Egypt, there was yet another absence without leave of nine hours forty-eight minutes on 17 November, followed by an attempted escape from custody the next day. This time, he was given a week's detention, and the loss of a day's pay. By the time he got on the ship that was to take him to war, John Bain was already a serial absconder.[42]

But when he did arrive at the front—still pink and white from England, in contrast to Field Marshall Brooke's 'bronzed warriors'—there was still fighting to be done. The Gordons' hopes of home were quickly dashed: there would be no convoy back to England. They had marched out of Tripoli in the first few days of February,[43] resuming their pursuit of the remnants of the Afrika Korps and the Italian army, which had set up a final defensive position along the Mareth Line, some 200 miles to the west, in a narrow pass between the coast and the Matmata Hills. It was a tough march from Tripoli, with the Gordons, along with an armoured brigade and the 131st Infantry Brigade, out ahead of the main body of Montgomery's forces.[44] There was frequent shelling and sniper fire from the retreating Germans and Italians, the road was often impassable through craters, and booby traps were scattered across the route. Landmines of a new and frightening design, made mainly of wood, and thus largely undetectable by the sappers' equipment, were hidden beneath the surface—the Gordons' War Diaries refer laconically to 'odd mines here and there to catch the unwary foot soldier'.[45] Scores of officers and men were killed or injured by them.

If the official record is correct, it seems likely Bain was among a group of reinforcements who joined the advance during this march. In *Argument of Kings* he refers to his 'fear, privation and pain during the advance from Wadi Zessar towards the Mareth Line'[46] and the Gordons' War Diaries record the battalion arriving at Wadi Zessar on 23 February, about eight weeks after the date of his departure from England.

Before them, beyond a broad and deceptively inviting grassy plain strewn with the wrecked remains of Rommel's defeated tanks, stood the Matmata Hills and the defensive fortifications of what had become known as the Maginot Line of North Africa.

The Axis forces were in full retreat, and Rommel had lost the charisma and dash that his earlier victories had brought him—back in Berlin, senior officers sneered openly that he always seemed to have enough petrol to retreat, but never enough to attack.[47] To the west, American and British troops and armour were massing on the borders of Tunisia, having landed in Morocco and Algeria the previous November at the start of Operation Torch. The aim was to clear the Axis powers out of North Africa by trapping Rommel's retreating soldiers between the chasing Eighth Army·and these new forces in their rear. The immediate challenge, however, was to clear them out of the heavily defended Mareth Line.

It was late on 16 March, more than a month after they left Tripoli, that the Gordon Highlanders were among the units tasked to cross the steep-sided Wadi Zigzaou that lay before the Mareth Line, and clear out the defenders from their well-dug-in positions. It was a daunting obstacle:

> Bank to bank, it stretches for 300 yards, and the whole had been strewn with mines. Beyond it was the anti-tank ditch, and when the position was examined after the action, it afforded matter for marvel that it was ever carried.[48]

The Mareth Line itself, originally erected by the French in the 1930s as protection against possible Italian attack from Libya, ran some 22 miles from the sea to the supposedly impassable Matmata Hills. Now the Germans and Italians had taken it over to mount a defence of their base in the port city of Sfax, which was Montgomery's next objective. Again, there were mine-fields, tripwires, and machine-gun posts high in the rocks to be negotiated, often under heavy artillery bombardment. It was a daunting place for a young soldier to get his first experience of battle.

The plan was to mount an outflanking movement around the Matmata Hills—Montgomery's 'left hook'—and the Gordons were to create a diversion further north with a mock attack. Scannell remembered that phrase ironically later:

> It sounded quite comforting; not a real attack, but an exercise like one of those schemes we used to do back in Blighty, using blank ammunition and getting back to barracks or camp for sausage and chips in the NAAFI.[49]

But there would be no sausage and chips: they advanced like First World War Tommies behind a creeping artillery barrage, Scorpion tanks flailing the ground in an attempt to clear it of mines, machine guns chattering in the dark, and white-hot shrapnel ripping through the air. At one point, the advancing soldiers overran their own barrage, so that the 25-pound shells from the British guns were falling amongst them; at another, there was a brief panic as the men mistook the swirling clouds of a smoke-screen for an enemy gas attack. In 1970, he remembered it all vividly in a poem:

> We moved, ton-booted, in.
> Then everything went wrong: we advanced too fast,
> Were pulverized by our own artillery.
> A Spandau got a fixed line on the gap.
> We heard its black jabber; tracers like burning embers
> Slid through the slick dark, chirred past our ears,
> Our skulls bulged with the din; it was time to dig in.
> We dug.[50]

That night, Vernon heard for the first time, a sound that he and thousands of other soldiers would remember for the rest of their lives—the hopeless dying screams for help of a wounded man. Years later, that noise would waken him from repeated nightmares.[51]

It was here that the incident to which he referred in his letter to John Bierman happened. He had been designated runner, ordered to stay close to the company commander to carry messages to the troops on the front line of the attack. It was a high-risk job, and they found themselves pinned down, lying side by side with their faces pressed into the ground while bullets whined above their heads and the soft dust and pebbles rained down on them. Scannell claimed later that he looked up after a few minutes, hoping that he wouldn't be needed to run any message—to find that the company commander was missing. 'He had taken a powder, got off his mark, vamoosed, or in the more formal language of military jurisprudence, he had deserted

in the face of the enemy',[52] he said later. The officer was, he claimed, later
hospitalized as shell-shocked, given an administrative job, and promoted to
major. That, of course, was nothing more than a rumour, and the account
of the desertion itself sounds a slightly self-serving story, bearing in mind
Vernon's own future experiences—but the battle was the first military
action of which he offers any direct personal account.

After the first attack, there followed three days of sustained artillery bombardment, Bain and his companions crouching in slit trenches while shells
and mortars exploded around them—'the next worse thing to Alamein', as
veterans said later.[53] But the outflanking movement that Montgomery had
planned had been successful, and during the night of 20 March, the German
forces pulled back. As the weary soldiers made their way into the deserted
positions, relieved that the fighting was over, they were able to see the magnitude of their achievement:

> The Mareth Line was an imposing sight, its block towers well sited and cam-
> ouflaged, its communication trenches six feet deep, and an anti-tank ditch
> supplementing the formidable obstacle of the Wadi Zigzaou. Needless to say,
> the mine and wire defences were elaborate in the extreme.[54]

The next day, pressing forward, they marched through a small village lying
to the east of Mareth itself. Its name—fittingly, many of the soldiers thought,
was Piste Djorf.[55]

VIII

Later in his life, Scannell said that he kept jottings of odd words, phrases, and
ideas for poems during his time in North Africa[56]—but apart from that,
he was writing nothing. Another soldier-poet in the Eighth Army, the
22-year-old Captain Keith Castellain Douglas, recovering from his wounds
in Port Said, was by contrast putting the finishing touches to the journal
that he would eventually turn into his famous memoir, *Alamein to Zem
Zem,* and even sending new poems back to London.

There was a good reason, of course, why Bain should not have been
inspired to write poetry about the experience of fighting: his experience at
that stage was more of the guard-room and the glass-house than the battlefield. But even after Mareth and Wadi Akarit, which was to come, even
after the landings on D-Day and the advance through Normandy, he wrote

nothing about the horrors of the battlefield. His experiences certainly burned themselves into his consciousness—the last verse of the last poem in his last collection, published shortly before his death in 2007, is a memory of Mareth—but for years after the war, he remained silent.

That he did not write during the war may be in part a reflection of the difference between the life of an officer like Douglas and that of an ordinary soldier, but it also highlights an important difference between them as poets. No one questions Douglas's bravery, even heroism, still less his sharp-eyed observation as a poet, but he had a confidence, a brash patriotism that was completely absent from John Bain and, one suspects, the great mass of the soldiers fighting on either side. Douglas was frantically getting everything he could down on paper—fortunately, since within eighteen months he would be dead. He describes his enthusiasm for combat in *Alamein to Zem Zem*:

> I enlisted in September 1939, and during two years or so of hanging about, I never lost the certainty that the experience of battle was something I must have...It is exciting and amazing to see thousands of men, very few of whom have much idea why they are fighting, all enduring hardships, living in an unnatural, dangerous, but not wholly terrible world, having to kill and be killed, and yet at intervals being moved by a feeling of comradeship with the men who kill them and whom they kill, because they are enduring and experiencing the same things.[57]

Bain—or Scannell—was by contrast one of those 'thousands of men' who had little idea what they were fighting about, and it is impossible to imagine him expressing such a self-indulgent thrill of anticipation. The words 'exciting' and 'amazing' are notable by their omission from his accounts of the war. When his experiences did begin to flood into his poetry, they had been filtered through the suffering of an older man: where Douglas's work, like that of Wilfred Owen, is the poetry of the young fighting man in battle, Scannell's is that of the veteran brooding on the experiences and suffering of a generation. The wounds are older, and they ache with a different pain.

Scannell sincerely admired Douglas as a poet. He praised the toughness of his poetry, its 'total lack of self-pity and the absolute refusal to indulge in nostalgic evocations of the joys of civilian life, of peace, security, love and home'.[58] He noted the greater introspection of his writing compared to that of Wilfred Owen, but added:

> The best of his war poetry, with its hardness of edge, wit, vision, compassion and disciplined intelligence will prove to possess at least the lasting qualities of the best of Wilfred Owen.[59]

The point of Owen's poetry, of Douglas's war poetry, is generally the brutal pathos of what happens in combat—the poetry, as Owen memorably said, is in the pity. But where they write about the victims—the dead German soldier in 'Vergissmeinicht', or the choking infantryman in Owen's 'Dulce et Decorum Est'—Scannell deals instead with the survivors. What happens to them afterwards is a quieter, darker, and generally untold story. Some fall apart, like the veteran in Scannell's memorable villanelle, 'Casualty—Mental Ward', who is chillingly aware that:

> Something has gone wrong inside my head.
> The sappers have left mines and wire behind;
> I hold long conversations with the dead.[60]

Many more, on the other hand, lead lives of studied ordinariness, with hell bubbling beneath the surface. Scannell's subjects weep silently in bars, as in 'Incident in a Saloon Bar'; they are terrified by fireworks, as in 'Gunpowder Plot'; they forget names and faces in their old age, but find that:

> certain memories will never die:
> Tom Fenton's smile, part naughty urchin's grin
> yet just a little sad,
> before the bomb blew it and him star-high
> near Mareth as our Company moved in
> and the universe went mad.[61]

It is about these silent, suffering survivors and their memories of incidents like this that Scannell writes. If Douglas had survived the war, of course, he might eventually have written the same sort of poetry as Scannell; the point is that Scannell was never interested in writing poetry like Douglas's. Perhaps his responses, like his life, are closer to those of the ordinary soldier who survives the battle, but has to deal with its consequences for years to come.

IX

The taking of the Mareth Line was a qualified victory—although the Allied forces had achieved their objective, the Germans had avoided being trapped and had been able to retreat to set up another defensive line a few miles back towards Tunis. Battered and bloodied from the conflict, the Gordons moved on over open country and on rough tracks towards the port city of Gabès, where, Scannell said later, the soldiers enjoyed a brief pause:

They had changed out of winter battledress after the forced march from
Mareth when they had bivouacked near Gabès. Mobile showers had been
brought up and they had got rid of their lice-infested, filthy uniforms and for
the first time in many weeks they had been able to soak their grimed and
verminous bodies and put on clean shirts and shorts.[62]

This volume of Scannell's memoirs, *Argument of Kings*, was written throughout in the third person. 'In the forty or so years that have elapsed since the
actions I deal with, I have become someone quite other than the twenty-
one-year old who was the protagonist', he explained. 'I naturally think of
that young man as "him", not as "I".'[63] But even so, the clear implication of
the description of the lice, vermin, and filth, is that he, too, had endured the
same privations as the rest of the men. Perhaps so, but not for nearly as long
as they had.

In front of them now lay yet another obstruction, the Wadi Akarit, bris-
tling with desperate defenders. This time, there was no possibility of an
outflanking movement: the only way to pass the defensive lines was with an
all-out full-frontal assault. The Gordons were to provide support, moving
forward after the Seaforth Highlanders had mounted the initial attack, and
Bain spent the night before taking turn-about with his mate, a tough and
fiery-tempered Glaswegian machine-gunner named Hughie Black, sleeping and keeping watch as they squatted in a hastily dug trench with their
knees up to their chests. It was just before dawn when the first of the
Seaforths moved silently past them towards the hills. A few minutes later
came the rattle of machine guns and the flash and crump of exploding mortars. The noise of battle intensified, and in the dim half-light it was possible
to see tiny figures on the hillside, some of them moving in little clusters, but
others lying still and alone. After a while, the shooting stopped, and soon the
Gordons were on the move again, in single file, climbing steadily, unwillingly, up the rocky path.

The fighting was over. Dead bodies littered the track, and when they
reached the enemy slit trenches, now empty and silent, there was the sickly,
cloying smell of death. The dead, German and British, lay waxy skinned and
twisted, like that first body he remembered seeing. A light coating of dust
was already beginning to settle on their weapons, their clothes, and their
features. Bain watched in silence.

It seemed that there must have been an order to fall out, because men
from his section and from the other platoons were wandering among
the dead, both Seaforths and Germans, gazing down at them with a fixed

intensity which seemed at first to be an expression of grief. First one man and then another fell to his knees beside a corpse; others bent low over the bodies, delicately rearranging their clothing. Then, to Bain's horror and disbelief, he saw one turn a body over with a casual, uninterested nudge from his boot, and he realized that they were not grieving but looting the corpses. Watches and rings were stripped from dead wrists and fingers; pockets were ripped brutally open, and papers and personal possessions riffled through greedily.[64] Soon the vultures would be circling in the sky, but the bodies they were watching and waiting for were already being picked clean.

After a few moments, he turned away and started to walk, quite slowly and deliberately, back down the way that he had come, his rifle still slung over his right shoulder, and his head sweating under his heavy steel helmet in the blazing heat. He wrote later:

> I just remember all those dead Seaforths lying there and our blokes going round, settling on them like fucking flies, taking their watches and wallets and Christ-knows-what, and I just got up and walked. It was like a dream.[65]

No one shouted or tried to stop him, and he did not look back.

X

It was one of the defining moments of his life, but for nearly forty-five years he never mentioned it even to his family and close friends. His public acknowledgement of what happened came in his memoir, *Argument of Kings*, written shortly after he had taken part in a BBC Television programme [66] about soldiers in combat and his own experiences. In the programme, he said, his interviews had been factually honest as far as they went, but he had never mentioned his desertion or the three-year sentence that followed it:

> My concealment of this fact was caused, at least in part, by shame. The curious thing to me is that I did not experience this sense of shame at the time of my flight, court martial and sentence ... This feeling of shame seems to have been born some years later and it has steadily grown as the years have passed.[67]

He needed, he said, to set down what happened 'as honestly as I can'—a need, as we have seen, that seems not to have extended to a straightforward description of his time before Wadi Akarit. But the shame was genuine—even after the publication of *Argument of Kings*, he would frequently break into uncontrollable fits of sobbing when he mentioned his desertion in late-night conversations. He would wake sweating from nightmares in which his guilt was paraded before a contemptuous world, and he would torture himself by going over and over the incident, the events that led up to it, and his motives in walking away.

Was the reason he had given—an instinctive revulsion at the callous pickpocketing of the corpses—the true one? Certainly the image of theft from the helpless victims of war stayed with him—in 'The Bombing of the Café de Paris, 1941', written nearly forty years later, he describes a survivor lying semi-conscious in the rubble of the nightclub, and seeing someone making his way towards her:

> 'Rescue!' she thought
> As by her side he knelt upon the floor,
> Reached out to finger at her neck and take
> Her string of pearls in one triumphant paw.[68]

Shortly after featuring an interview with Scannell about the publication of *Argument of Kings*, the Bradford *Telegraph and Argus* received a letter giving more details about the death of Eric Anderson, a stretcher-bearer who won a posthumous VC at the Battle of Wadi Akarit:

> Apparently his mother was told that no possessions were returnable because whatever he had in his pockets etc. were destroyed when he was killed. A comrade, however—and this is documented—saw his body was not badly damaged, and it seems he was killed by a single bullet. In other words, it's obvious that he was a victim of the 'vultures' of his own unit. At least this suggests my account of the looting at Akarit is accurate and not a self-justifying false memory.[69]

The sense of relief in that diary entry is unmistakable. The story about Private Anderson may not be conclusive proof, but it is certainly corroborating circumstantial evidence to back up Scannell's account of what happened.

On the other hand, he was well aware that it certainly did not prove that he did not run away because he was scared. That possibility tormented him, and the theme of courage in battle, or the lack of it, appears repeatedly in novels, poems, and in his private moments. David Marshall, a character in his novel, *The Face of the Enemy*, for instance, is clearly drawn from the officer he claimed had run away at Mareth, but the story of Marshall's

cowardice under fire has a distinctly personal edge to it. Scannell's memories of the battle are there—the soldiers pounded by their own guns, the
screaming of the injured man, the smoke bombs and the Scorpions—but
rather than the hospitalization and promotion he says his company commander received, the character is court-martialled like John Bain.

> 'I got back to Battalion Headquarters and went to the M.O. and tried to get
> him to say I was bomb-happy. What he did say was, "The only thing wrong
> with you, Marshall, is you're a bloody coward." And of course he was quite
> right'...He said softly, 'And that's what Daddy did in the Great War, my
> boy.'[70]

In the book, Marshall redeems himself by going back to face the members
of the ex-servicemen's club who he expects will reject him after he has been
exposed—and finds that they are understanding and compassionate.

Marshall was guilty of desertion in the face of the enemy—a significantly
greater crime than John Bain had committed. In *Argument of Kings*, Scannell
explains the difference to a fellow prisoner as they sit in a cell, beneath the
warders' spy-hole.

> 'You was done for scarpering in a forward area, wasn't you? That's not as bad
> as in the face of the enemy. That's right, ennit? You wasn't done for the face of
> the enemy job, was you?'
>   John looked up at the judas-hole. Then he said, 'No, I fucked off in the arse
> of the enemy.'
>   Chalky was quiet. Then he said, 'What you mean?'
>   'Jerry was on the run. Got his back to us when I took a powder.'[71]

Alone though, sitting in lonely judgement on his own case, he was less for-
giving: 'I am a physical coward: the war proved that to me if prove [*sic*] were
necessary' ,[72] he wrote in his diary. Another entry deals with his lack of
candour in his earlier autobiographical memoir, *The Tiger and the Rose*, published in 1971:

> The omission of my walk-away at Wadi Akarit and my time in the nick was
> caused by shame.
>   The more I think about physical courage, the more important as a human
> attribute it seems. And I sometimes feel that cowardice is one of the worst of
> human weaknesses; it might even be a crime. The idea, put about, I suspect, by
> cowards, that there are many kinds of courage, that the physical coward may
> show great moral courage, is baloney. Moral courage and physical courage are
> I think inseparable.[73]

It was hardly the swashbuckling, romantic role he and Kenneth had imag-
ined for themselves in the pubs of Aylesbury, and not quite a match for the
North Africa experiences of Keith Douglas. It is impossible to miss the par-
allels between the two men when Scannell writes about the famous poem,
'Simplify Me When I'm Dead', which Douglas wrote just before he left
England,

> That a young man of twenty-one, about to sail to Egypt to fight in a war
> which at that time looked as if it would go on for many years and would
> probably end in an enemy victory, that he could contemplate his own death
> so calmly seems quite extraordinary, and the lack of orchestration in the poem,
> the total absence of heroics, seem to me guarantees of its honesty and
> seriousness.[74]

Scannell, of course, was even younger than Douglas when he left for North
Africa—but in the same book, still without mentioning himself, he puts his
finger on a more telling comparison. Soon after the start of the Battle of El
Alamein, Douglas abandoned his post as camouflage officer 20 miles in the
rear and fibbed his way into a front-line role.

> Technically he was absent without leave, if not a deserter, and he must be the
> only soldier in the British Army, or any other Army for that matter, who
> deserted in order to get into battle rather than escape from it.[75]

It would be more than ten years before *Argument of Kings* at least attempted
to tell the truth about his own record, but Scannell's words reverberate with
memories of his desertion. There is no mention of his own time in North
Africa, no comparison of their experiences or reactions, no sense of fellow-
feeling with Douglas as poets or soldiers. No doubt this reticence is partly
proper critical objectivity—but it is hard not to see it too as a sort of wistful
diffidence, an awareness that Douglas, unlike him, had no burden of guilt to
carry.

Today, John Bain would almost certainly be diagnosed with post-traumatic
stress disorder—a condition that would have a horrible relevance for him
and for those close to him for the rest of his life. In those less enlightened
days, however, and in the context of an army fighting a war for survival, he
could expect a much more rigorous response.

5

Military Prison

Although I miss you, dearest heart
I would not have you with me here
To see me play this clownish part
Clad in penitential gear.
More than pain or loss I fear
Humiliation's sickly taste:
The sky seems one enormous sneer
As I crouch here, ashamed, debased.

'The Defaulter's Song', from *Soldiering On* (1989)

I

It is hard to know whether Bain realized as he walked away from Wadi Akarit how serious an offence he was committing. He had already acquired an unenviable reputation as a truculent, scruffy, and generally uncooperative soldier who was more at home on a charge in the guard-room than he was in the barracks—a man who occasionally ignored or disobeyed orders, was late back from leave, or vanished for days at a time into the pubs and bars of the nearest town whenever he got the chance. Before he had even left Britain, he had forfeited a total of nearly two months' pay and served a week's detention as various senior officers tried to find a way of forcing him to observe some semblance of military discipline.

But this was different. In the First World War, men were shot by firing squad for leaving their units—it was only in 1930 that the death penalty for desertion had been abolished, and shortly before the Battle of El Alamein Montgomery's predecessor, General Sir Claude Auchinleck, had to resist heavy pressure to reintroduce it. The fighting at Wadi Akarit might have been over when Bain left, but in leaving his unit in a front-line position, with the enemy in the immediate vicinity, he was still committing one of the cardinal sins of military service.

His own account, written from memory years afterwards, sounds as though he walked away almost in a trance:

> He walked unhurriedly but quite steadily, not looking back, his rifle slung on his right shoulder. And still no one shouted. It was as if he had become invisible. He plodded onwards and downwards. The sun was strong now, and he felt the heat biting through his KD [khaki drill] shirt. Sweat was soaking his hair under the steel helmet. He did not look back but kept his eyes down, seeing no more than a few yards in front of him. If there were any sounds he did not register them. He moved without any sense of physical exertion as if he had been relieved of a great burden and could enjoy an easy, almost floating sense of effortlessness as he walked onwards, down to the level ground and onto a rough track.[1]

He sounds like a man walking away without a plan, with no firm intention of actually escaping, and indeed the various stories he told to people he met along the way—a young lieutenant who gave him a lift in a staff car, a small detachment of Ghurkas, and an RAF driver in a lorry who drove him most of the 100 miles or so to Tripoli—were so varied and so unconvincing as to sound as though he almost wanted to be challenged. The most believable—that he was carrying a dispatch for Brigade Intelligence—was actually suggested by the officer as he chatted in the car, but the others—that he had been cut off from his regiment and was wandering back to Divisional HQ, or that he had escaped from the Germans and was heading on foot for a transit camp some 250 miles away in Tripoli—seem not to have fooled anyone. The Ghurkas laughed at him, and the RAF driver, giving him tea, a razor, and cigarettes, told him not to talk bullshit. When Bain admitted that he was on the run, the driver did all he could to help him, although he warned him that he had no chance of avoiding capture.

In fact, the so-called 'other ranks' seemed to be extremely sympathetic. Rather than any resentment of him as a deserter, a man who was leaving his colleagues in the lurch, there was the instinctive fellow-feeling of men who had experienced combat for themselves and who could understand why he wanted to get away. Certainly, none of them seem even to have considered handing him over to the military police. Even more remarkably, he claims to have found a similar response among the other soldiers of his unit, the men he was supposed to have betrayed, when he finally rejoined them many months later. The only complaint they had about his conduct was that he hadn't stopped to take them with him.

Bain spent two days and nights on his journey, partly on the road and partly stumbling over the sand and scrubland, and sleeping by the side of the track. He headed first towards the port of Gabès, and then gratefully accepted the offer of a lift in the RAF lorry towards Tripoli, some 250 miles in the opposite direction. He had, clearly, no firm idea of where to go—and if he *was* walking in a dream, it was a dream that was very like a nightmare. Images of the dead soldiers from Wadi Akarit, picked over by the living, were repeatedly before him, along with memories of other bodies he had seen. He ate tinned meat from abandoned Italian rations, and froze as he kicked a discarded jerry-can in the dark, his experiences of the past few days having left him terrified of mines.[2]

At the same time, though, he retained enough presence of mind to leave the road, where he might be spotted by passing army traffic, and walk for some of the time in the shelter of a wadi running alongside it. When the lorry driver warns him in *Argument of Kings* that the military police are certain to catch him, and that the imprisonment in the glass-house that he can expect will be 'bloody terrible. Worse than in Blighty. And that's saying something', his reply is telling: 'I never thought about it...Nothing could be worse than action.'[3] It's not just the revulsion at the casual plundering of the dead soldiers that has led him to desert, in other words, but the whole experience of battle and being under fire.

Probably like most deserters in the field, he realized that he had little prospect of avoiding arrest. The lorry driver was right:

> Sooner or later, he would be picked up. Attempts to delay the event were a waste of effort. It did not matter to him whether they got him now or the next day or in a week's time. The consequences would be the same, though the exact nature of the consequences was something that his mind was unable to contemplate, partly because he had only a vague idea of the procedures that would follow his arrest, but also because the future had become unthinkable. It seemed almost as though he had been left with the dead soldiers on the stony hillside at Wadi Akarit.[4]

But as he reached Tripoli there came thoughts, however unrealistic, of possible escape—the lorry driver, anxious not to be accused of aiding a deserter, had dropped him off a few miles short of the town, and as he approached the coast, he got an unexpected whiff of the sea:

The sea meant ships and ships were more than mere symbols of escape and freedom: they were practical agents of these things. If he could get to the docks where no doubt troops were employed unloading the ships it might be possible to sneak aboard a merchant vessel and hide. Fantasy began to project its unlikely, sanguine images on the walls of his mind: he saw himself hiding in a cargo hold and being discovered by a sympathetic sailor who would keep his presence a secret and bring him food and drink and civvy clothes.[5]

It was, of course, no more than a dream, but it was still in his mind as a 15 cwt truck screeched to a halt behind him and a corporal in the military police leapt out. Alone in the street, unshaven, unwashed, and half asleep, Bain was an obvious target for an alert policeman on the look-out for deserters.

He made a half-hearted and desultory attempt at one final lie to explain his presence, but he knew the game was up. He handed his rifle over to the corporal, and clambered wearily into the back of the lorry for the short trip to the military police barracks and into another world.

II

This was not like the times he had been confined in the guard-room before. Then, he had treated military discipline almost like a game, but now he was under close arrest, locked in a cell in the Tripoli barracks until transport could be arranged for the journey back to his unit at Wadi Akarit. He could expect, the sergeant at the military police barracks told him with relish, something between five and ten years in a military prison that would make hell seem like a rest camp.

The day Bain left, Montgomery recorded later in his campaign diary, had seen 'the heaviest and most savage fighting we have had since I have commanded the Eighth Army'.[6] Dealing with a deserter was not the highest priority in the aftermath of such a battle, and it was several days before he appeared before senior officers of his regiment for the formality of a remand for trial by court martial, accused of desertion in a forward position. It was not as serious a charge as desertion in the face of the enemy, but still one that could bring heavy punishment. When he finally stood before the court, presumably still affected by the fatalism that he had felt for much of his time on the run, he said nothing beyond confirming his name, rank, and number. The young lieutenant tasked to defend him, 'embarrassed and almost apologetic', suggested several possible vague excuses that could be made to the court, such as 'troubles at home', or 'things on his mind'. All Bain could find to say to him was that he hated the whole business of war.

Their interview is reflected in a meeting between Jeff, the central character in Scannell's novel *The Wound and the Scar*, published in 1953, and the defending officer in his court martial:

> The officer was obviously bored at being detailed for the job… He produced a small notebook and pencil and said, 'What did you desert for?'
> Jeff, who had been overcome by a sense of unreality and an odd drowsiness, replied without thinking, 'I hate the army.'
> The officer said irritably, 'Thousands of us hate it, but we have to stick it. That won't go down very well at the court.'[7]

In court, Bain would not even accept the suggestion that his desertion had been a spur-of-the-moment act that he now regretted. 'It just happened. It seemed inevitable. I didn't seem to have any choice', was his only response.

Not having any choice but to desert, like hating the army, seemed like an unprofitable argument to put to a military court, and in the end the defending officer made the point that when Bain had left the scene of the battle, the fighting was over and the enemy was on the run. But Bain himself could see no reasoned or coherent explanation he could give for having deserted when the immediate danger seemed to be over; and anyway, his disciplinary record was so bad that there was nothing for him to say.

Some recent academic studies suggest that officers during the North Africa campaign handed out disproportionately stiff sentences because they believed that there was a crisis of morale in the British army. One suggests that average prison sentences of around 2.7 years more than doubled after October 1942.[8]

> The details of individual cases were often overridden in the name of discipline and military efficiency… Many men found guilty and punished by Courts Martial in North Africa in the crucial period 1942–1943 may well have been treated differently in other circumstances.[9]

Had Bain been charged with the more serious offence of desertion in the face of the enemy, he could have gone to prison for more than ten years— so in the circumstances, he may have been lucky with the sentence of four years' penal servitude that the court imposed. Then, nineteen days after the court appearance, came word that Montgomery, as commander of the Eighth Army—or his staff officers—had remitted one year of it. It is unlikely

that Bain realized it, but bearing in mind his record, he had got off remarkably lightly.

It had taken the Eighth Army nearly six months to fight their way west-
wards from the scruffy little railhead that bore the now-famous name of El
Alamein—through Tobruk, the crucial port that had finally been relieved
by Montgomery's forces after a German siege lasting 240 days; through
Benghazi, which they had lost and won and lost and won again; past
Mussolini's grandiose Arco dei Fileni, referred to dismissively as 'Marble
Arch' by the Allied soldiers, which marked the border between the Libyan
provinces of Cyrenaica and Tripolitania in what had once been the Italian
empire; and on to the bloodletting and slaughter of Mareth and Wadi Akarit.
These were names that would echo in military history. If a soldier was asked
what he had done in the war, Churchill had said in Tripoli, 'It will be quite
sufficient for him to say, "I marched and fought with the Eighth Army." '[10]

But once he had been through the brief formalities of his court martial,
Bain's journey back was swift and ignominious, handcuffed to another prisoner in a small cargo boat that made the short voyage down the coast from
Tripoli to Alexandria. There were six convicted men on board, all in full
marching order with ground sheet, rolled blanket, water-bottle, belt and—
making the point that they were no longer fighting men, but prisoners—
empty ammunition pouches. With them, embarrassed by their task and
clearly with some sympathy for the men they had to guard, were a sergeant
and three privates. On arrival at the port in Alexandria, the bedraggled and
dispirited little group was bundled into a military truck that bumped
through the streets of the city until it reached a massive white building that
dazzled in the sun so it was impossible to look directly at it. This was their
destination—the Mustapha Military Prison and Detention Centre. With the
prisoners and escorts standing stiffly to attention, the sergeant pressed a
small bell at the side of the heavy iron-studded door.

There was a grating noise, and a small barred opening appeared in the
door, with a shadowy face peering through it. This feeling of being inspected
by an anonymous face on the other side of a door was one to which the
prisoners would become accustomed. A few curt words were exchanged
between the face and the sergeant, who held up a sheaf of official papers—
the army documents that would define the prisoners and circumscribe their
lives for the full term of their sentence. Then there came more grating and
rattling sounds as iron bolts were pulled back, and the door opened slowly

and unwillingly. The sergeant removed the men's handcuffs, handing them
to the escorts to hold, and marched the prisoners inside.

The man who had opened the door was in immaculate khaki uniform
with razor-sharp creases and a cap whose shiny peak came down almost
vertically over his forehead, hiding his eyes and practically touching the
bridge of his nose. Once they were across the threshold, it was clear that the
prisoners belonged, body and soul, to him. His orders were curt, dismissive,
threatening:

> From now on, you are S.U.S.'s—Soldiers Under Sentence. You will do every-
> thing at the double. You understand? Everything. You do not move unless it's
> at the double. I'm Staff Hardy. I'm going to hand you over to Staff Henderson.
> He'll look after you. Right. Double...march! *Left*-right, *left*...Mark time!
> Get them knees up! *Left*-right *left*-right *left*-right *left*...[11]

III

The experiences of the following months seared themselves into Bain's soul.
If he was paying for his desertion, then he and the people closest to him
would continue to pay for the rest of his life. Long after the war, in his diary
for Tuesday 17 April 1951, he would note:

> Eight years ago today I began my sentence of six months detention in the
> Military Detention Barracks at Alexandria... For years afterwards, I had irra-
> tional sadistic & homicidal impulses, particularly if I'd been drinking...I'm
> sure that the 6 months detention made me into a much nastier person than I
> had been before.

In *Argument of Kings*, Scannell describes the NCOs and the relish with
which they run the prison: they squeal their orders like the pigs in *Animal
Farm*; they fly into sudden and irrational rages; they are aggressive, bullying,
and sadistic. The commandant, Captain Babbage, is pudgy, balding, and
overweight, and his sweaty, ill-fitting uniform is in stark contrast to the military smartness of the NCOs—but he, too, treats the prisoners with dismissive contempt. 'You're here to be punished', he tells them. 'You're here
because you've committed crimes. In your case—all of you—it's the crime
of desertion. You're all cowards. You're all yellow. You think you're tough
guys but you're not. You're soft and you're yellow.'[12]

The descriptions are almost certainly more vivid than fair—the sort of bitter, vengeful images that would naturally be brooded over by any one of the prisoners in their charge. The prison staff themselves might justifiably say that they had been given a job to do, and that they were doing it to the best of their ability. But Scannell's account of his first day at the prison, and indeed of the three months that followed it, depicts a system that was designed not simply to punish the men in prison but to humiliate them. The long, narrow cell that the six new prisoners had to share with three men already serving sentences was a gloomy, airless corridor fifty feet long and eight feet wide, with only one door and three small windows. A spy hole in the door meant the guards could secretly check on them whenever they pleased. The cell stank of sweat and of the contents of the slopping out buckets, which the men were permitted to empty each morning. They were there to be punished, but they were also there to be broken.

They were given pointless, repetitive tasks to carry out—scrubbing the stone floor of the parade ground, cleaning rusty old cooking pots with sand and rags, carrying buckets of sand from a pile in one corner of the parade ground to make a pile in the other, and then returning the sand, bucket by bucket, to the pile it first came from. There were apparently random, capricious punishments—Bain, screwing up his eyes in the glare of the midday sun, was sent for three days solitary confinement on a charge of 'smiling on parade'. There, his 'flowery'—flowery dell, rhyming slang for cell—was around eight feet by six feet, with a single small window set high in the wall. It was empty, except for a slopping out pot and a bucket of water—he slept on the bare concrete, with two threadbare blankets which were taken out of his cell in the morning and returned at night. His punishment diet, known as jockeys' diet or bread and desert soup, allowed him one piece of bread in the morning and another at four in the afternoon—and when he decided to keep part of his morning bread to eat later in the day, it was taken from him. 'You are not allowed to hoard food. You eat your ration at the proper time or not at all. You understand?'[13]

Everything, as the NCO had warned at the prison gates, was done at the double—and all the time, everywhere the prisoners turned, there was the constant, aggressive, challenging contempt. 'You're a horrible, dirty, stupid little man. What are you?'; 'Get those greasy bellies off my nice clean parade ground!'; 'We've seen your kind before. Thousands of you. And you're all the same. Shit!' Step out of line, and the punishments were severe, and not always official: there was the body-belt, a wide leather strap that went around a man's waist, with steel cuffs to fasten his hands by his sides. Once that was on, he could not move his arms, and there were plenty of stories whispered around the cell to suggest that the guards would not be above taking advantage of his defencelessness to administer savage beatings.

Bain's response to this sustained psychological and physical attack reflected different aspects of his character. First and simplest was the reaction of the boxer, the strong, fit, trained fighter who imagined meeting one or other of the guards sometime in the future, far away from the prison, when the war and Mustapha Barracks would be no more than a memory. One day, he told himself, knowing that it was no more than a fantasy, he would smash the bastards.

Alone in his punishment cell, there was the reaction of the poetry lover, remembering and reciting some of the verse that had been so important to him—Thomas Hardy's 'Afterwards', for instance, or Sir Henry Newbolt's 'He Fell Among Thieves', which he remembered from the age of nine. Different snatches of poetry recalled different moments in his childhood and adolescence. Keats gave way to A. E. Housman, who gave way to D. H. Lawrence and T. S. Eliot, each one with a particular memory attached. John Bain must have been the only man in history to recite Eliot's 'Love Song of J. Alfred Prufrock' to himself and find that it brought back to him the smell of mingled sweat and embrocation from the dressing room before a boxing bout.

He also pondered, as he sat on his own with the minutes and hours dragging past, on the reasons for his desertion. Were the sneers and taunts of the guards justified? He had told his defending officer, and himself too, about his unbearable disgust at the whole idea of war, of revulsion at the sight of his fellow-soldiers going through the pockets of the dead and stealing their possessions—were these ideas just self-serving excuses to cover his cowardice? Was he simply yellow, a coward who had let his mates down and left them to fight while he ran away? Sometimes, he felt that the case was proven; at others, looking back at his stumbling, dream-like walk down the hill away from the battlefield, he could find no trace of fear or cowardice in the thoughts that had gone through his mind. Back in his childhood and adolescence—a lifetime ago, it seemed, and a different world—he had been a brave enough boxer in the ring, but he was too intelligent to believe that this offered any evidence about his character one way or another. It takes one sort of courage to face someone who wants to punch you on the nose, another to stand fast when someone is trying to blow you to pieces. So was his desertion some sort of protest against the lunacy of war, or was it just that he had run away because he was scared, as everyone seemed to believe? Or was the truth a mixture of the two? This uncertainty about his motives, about what his desertion said about him as a man, would stay with him for the rest of his life.

In his mid-sixties, for instance, he was still pondering the question of courage. In one diary entry, convinced of his own cowardice, he half-heartedly mulls over the possibility that the lack of courage may not always be a bad thing:

> I have thought occasionally that cowardice must be one of the very few human failings that might have beneficial consequences. If everyone were as craven as I there would be no more wars. But I really know that courage is not only admirable but also valuable. The courage of the mountain rescue crew, the lifeboat men, firemen etc is essentially the same courage that is required of the combatant in war. Is this true? I think so. I fear so.[14]

Another entry ponders whether courage may be a natural gift, like the ability to do woodwork—Scannell was hopelessly impractical—or solve mathematical problems:

> Why should I be more ashamed of my lack of courage than of my lack of practicality, *if* these things are simply gifts of God or Providence over which we have no control and for which we should not claim or accept credit? There is, of course, a moral dimension to courage and its lack which is absent from the business of practicality, mathematical ability etc. It involves life and death. An inability to mend a puncture, read music, construct a bookcase, does not hurt other people. Cowardice can end the lives of other people.[15]

Each time, he rejects the proffered consolation. Cowardice, he seems to be saying, is his own not-very-secret failing. In his seventies, his poem 'Family Secret' tells the story of an old man looking far, far back on a day when he was a small boy, scalded by boiling water. He knew his father had been killed in the First World War, and when one of the uncles with whom he lived had urged him to 'Be a brave soldier', he had replied, 'I will. Just like my dad.' There had been an awkward, brittle silence in the kitchen, and it had been years before he found out why:

> His Dad had been no hero but a child,
> A frightened boy who'd sprawled face-down in mud
> With no salutes, no wild
> Or mournful bugle calls, no flags,
> But dawn's death-rattle of the firing-squad.[16]

Another deserter, in fact. Another coward. The guilt, the uncertainty, the self-doubt that grew out of John Bain's desertion in 1943 were instrumental in shaping Vernon Scannell as a man and as a poet. They reinforced his distrust of military virtues and politicians who prattle about them, and they brought to his poetry a sympathy for the weak, the morally compromised, and for those 'frightened boys' who had failed to meet the challenges that life had set them. But his image of himself remained tainted by doubt about his physical courage—with typical black humour, in 1988, he celebrated a medical all-clear (premature, as it turned out) from the hospital:

> I should rejoice because there's nothing wrong with me except for haemor-rhoids, failing eyesight, enlarged prostate, emphysema, impotence, vanity, cow-ardice, mendacity and infantilism.[17]

There it is again, that word 'cowardice', hiding away in a list of the common complaints of old men, disguised perhaps by a wry smile, but still revealing a wound that had never healed.

IV

That same ironic, self-deprecating sense of humour also came to his rescue in prison. He noted wryly that one of his fellow-prisoners, serving ten years for desertion in the face of the enemy, boasted a tattooed dagger in the middle of his chest, with the words 'Death Before Dishonour'. The same tattoo, with the same ironic inscription, would reappear on another prisoner in his novel *The Wound and the Scar* in 1951, where the Mustapha Barracks was presented as an example of the worst and most brutal military prison in the British army. At the time, Bain's only thought was the self-mocking one that in the unlikely event that he might have a similar tattoo, the inscription would have to be reversed to read 'Dishonour Before Death'.

With care—very great care, because the penalty for being detected would have been dire—he found it was also possible to mock the prison guards. He was forced to write a letter home each fortnight and, since he had no desire to write to his mother or his father, since he had long forgotten his wife Barbara, and since he had no idea where Kenneth had been posted, he began composing letters to an entirely fictitious family at an imaginary address of Radcliffe Hall, Hampshire. The letters had to be read over by Captain Babbage, acting as censor, before they were sent out. He presumably missed the ironic exaggeration of their messages of shame and regret but there was delight to be found in the outrage that the echo of the name of the lesbian novelist Radclyffe Hall would have caused, if the Captain had ever heard of her. In addition Bain filled the letters with as many long words as he could think of in the certain knowledge that the Captain would have to turn again and again to a dictionary to help him get through it. Childish pleasures, perhaps, but there was very little other light relief in the Mustapha Barracks.

The guards in the prison were all-powerful—any complaint about the prisoners' treatment, about unfairness or illegality, had to be made to the commandant, and received short shrift. 'I'll tell you where it'll get you', he is told, when he protests at the confiscation of his meagre bread ration. 'Right back in here, sonny, where you belong. Right back in a single flowery for another wee dose of desert soup. Now do you understand?'

There was one occasion, like the Oliver Twist moment in front of the RAF recruiting officer three years before, when Bain challenged authority directly and, astonishingly, won. It was one evening when Staff Sergeant Brown, one of the prison guards, had come into the men's cell to lock it up for the night. As he turned to leave, Bain spoke up.

'Excuse me, Staff.' It was shocking enough that an S.U.S. should speak to a guard without being spoken to, but the guard stopped in amazement when he heard what Bain wanted to say. He asked for a book. He had been told that Prison Regulations said that any prisoner who had served fifty-six days or more was entitled to a book or a magazine to read, and if he was entitled to one, then he would like one. Please.

The other prisoners were as stunned by his temerity as the staff sergeant. Would anyone else like to claim their rights, Brown asked, looking round challengingly. No one spoke. He stalked out, slamming and bolting the door behind him, but returned a few minutes later to toss a magazine onto the floor where Bain was squatting, rubbing at his rusty cooking pot with a sand-covered rag. For a moment—just a moment—Bain was astonished and delighted. Not only had he fronted up to Brown and not been slapped down like a dog, he had actually got something to read. And then he looked at the magazine: it was in Arabic.

For a second, he finally lost control and hurled himself at the smirking Brown with a roar of anger. If he had reached him, weeks of pain, humiliation, and frustration would have been packed behind every punch—but the consequences would have been much worse for him than for the man he was hitting. For that brief moment, he forgot the body-belt, the kickings, the beatings, the bread-and-water diet, and the extra time he would have to serve for assaulting an officer. All he wanted was to smash that self-satisfied, contemptuous, hateful face to a pulp. He was only prevented by his friends, who seized his legs to drag him back, and by the nimble footwork of Staff Sergeant Brown, who stepped smartly outside the door and slammed it shut behind him, his little joke over.

The other prisoners had no doubt about what would happen next—up in front of the commandant, another term in solitary, and then a brutal late-night kicking by the guards. 'They did it to a mate of mine in the Black Watch … half killed the poor fucker',[18] said one, comfortingly. As the adrenalin drained from his system, John felt a crushing despair. It was not just the punishment and the beatings that would surely follow soon—he had also lost the only protection he had against the harsh prison environment. Until that moment, he had refused to react to the pain, the insults, and the taunts, nursing a belligerent resignation that meant a little bit of him remained unbowed and undefeated. Now, paradoxically, in fighting back he had shown his weakness. Now he had no defence.

Through the next day, he waited for the inevitable summons to the commandant's office. And the next. Brown, it seemed, was taunting him, probably revelling in the knowledge that John would be on tenterhooks, waiting for the axe to fall. But it was several more days before it was Brown's turn to lock up the cell again. Bain sat on the concrete by his blankets with his eyes on the rusty tin dixie he was polishing, determined not to look up, not to react to anything that was said or done.

'Here you are, Bain.' And something was tossed onto the floor next to John. It landed with a slap, a flutter of paper, and a slight skid across the concrete as Brown shut the door and the metal bolts ground home.

It was a book, a battered and stained Penguin paperback. When John picked it up, he turned it over for a moment, expecting another trick. But it was a copy of George Moore's *Esther Waters*: the first book Bain had held in his hands for several months. The deeply sentimental late Victorian tale of the seduction and abandonment of a religious young girl, her struggles and dilemmas, and her final happiness, seems an odd one to find in an Alexandria military prison, and an even odder one to interest a 21-year-old squaddie, but to Bain it was a lifeline. He would read ten pages a day, and make it last well over a month, he decided. And when he had finished it, he would start again at the beginning.

V

However much the prospect of reading *Esther Waters* excited John, he never finished the book. Some three weeks later, he was summoned to the commandant's office after the morning parade in the barrack-square, and told that he should report later that day for an interview with the Sentence Review Board. It was a complete shock—there had been rumours for months that the eventual opening of a Second Front in Europe might mean an early release on suspended sentence for prisoners who would return to action, but he had long since abandoned any hope that he might be one of them. Hope, he had learned, was corrosive.

That afternoon, he was marched back into the office to find a lieutenant-colonel sitting in Captain Babbage's chair, with a major either side of him. This was the panel that had the power to take John out of the Mustapha Barracks, or to leave him there to fester for another two and a half years.

The army was looking for troops with battle experience to join the invasion that would be mounted sometime in the near future at an unspecified place on the coast of Europe. John's case, said the lieutenant-colonel, was 'one of the less disgraceful kind'—and now they wanted to know whether if he were back in battle again, he would desert again. 'Can you promise that you would not do the same thing again, the thing you were sent here for?'

John had no illusions about what he was being offered: it was the chance to take part in an operation that would very likely see him killed. 'Nothing could be worse than action', he had told the RAF driver who had given him a lift on the road away from Wadi Akarit; but now he knew better. 'Yessir', he said. Then, once again, he faced the question he had been asking himself, the one he didn't know how to answer. Why had he deserted in the first place, when the battle was over and the danger past, one of the majors demanded.

But six months' military detention had taught John how to play the system. He'd had a letter just before the battle, he lied, saying his girlfriend was pregnant—clearly by somebody else, since he had been away from England for almost nine months. He was confused, upset, he told the panel, sounding as confused and upset as he knew how, while all the while thinking of nothing but the tantalizing prospect of freedom. Outside, he knew that his fellow prisoners were jogging from corner to corner of the square with full buckets of sand as the guards shouted at them. That night, he would be shivering on the concrete floor in the sweaty, stinking cell with all the rest—but tomorrow, if he could only convince these three officers, he could be a free man again.

Even if that meant he would be dead in a few short weeks or months, he wanted it. Why hadn't he mentioned his girlfriend's pregnancy at his court martial, the major asked. He hadn't thought it was any excuse, he replied, sounding suitably sincere and manly. Then why had he mentioned it now?

> I've had a lot of time to think about it, Sir. I came to feel that it had upset me more than I realised at the time. I think I felt that we were supposed to be fighting to protect our loved ones at home and that was the kind of thanks we were getting. I know it's no excuse, but I think that's what I felt subconsciously.[19]

It was a bravura performance of wounded innocence and regret for the shameful crime his predicament had led him into, and the sort of story that was calculated to resonate with any soldier who had been fighting away from home for months on end—but although the officers made vaguely sympathetic noises, it was probably wasted anyway: nobody by now was really interested in why he had run away. He was a Soldier Under Sentence, but he was still a serving soldier, and if they had wanted to, they could simply have ordered him to pack his bags and report for duty. All they wanted was some assurance that he would not desert again.

The staff sergeant who gave John the news that he was to be released tomorrow was incredulous, but determined to squash any feeling that he might be getting away with something. They were letting him out to get himself killed, he said.

But John knew that. And he didn't care.

6

Back in Action

So when this civvy poet says they 'fell
With faces to the foe', it don't sound right.
My pal, he never fell. A Jerry shell
Smashed him up to smithereens that night.

'A Binyon Opinion', from *Views and Distances* (2000)

I

Bain had been in North Africa for a total of one year and thirty-nine days—long enough, despite his unimpressive record as a soldier, to entitle him to the Africa Star when the medals were handed out later, even though more than six months of that time had been spent marching around the parade ground at the detention centre rather than fighting Germans. His stay in the Mustapha Barracks had left him angry, bitter, and resentful, and with unspoken but deep-seated doubts and fears about his own character: the word 'coward', snarled, shouted, sneered, and snapped at him so often over the past six months, would not go away. The long-term psychological effects of his stay in Alexandria would begin to become clear over the next few years, but within days of walking through the prison gate, he had a sudden physical reaction.

> When I was released I returned to my battalion, where the Medical Officer had me put in hospital immediately. I was ill in a queer, undiagnosable way for a month: sick, unable to sleep or eat or find succour in anything.[1]

Queer, undiagnosable illnesses, of course, are relatively common, particularly among soldiers who have disciplinary records as bad as Bain's, although the fact that the medical officer at the military base in Egypt saw fit to send him to hospital for a month suggests that there was more wrong with him than an acute case of malingering. But there was neither the time for a detailed diagnosis, nor the official interest in it: the army needed its soldiers for the Second Front, and Bain was put on a transport back to England. Then, after a few days in a transit camp near Southampton, he was sent away on a week's leave before rejoining his unit.

He had no intention of going to see Barbara, who had left Buckingham and was now living with their son, Alan, in Preston Street, Brighton. They had been excised from his life from the moment that he got on the train to London with Kenneth all that time ago. He had no way of contacting Kenneth, no idea where he was serving, and no intention of telling even him where he had spent the last few months. That would remain a secret from his family for years to come. There was only one place for him to go to spend his leave.

Years later, in his poem 'On Leave: May 1916', he thinks of a soldier returning home on leave from the front—the 'Fluting and flutters of welcome, kisses and tears', the 'khaki itch, stiff wool' stripped off, the luxury of the steaming bath, and the sensuous welcome to the 'unsurprisable bed'.[2] In the poem, he is remembering a different war, but the parallel with his own journey home in uniform on the train, is close enough for the contrast in the reception that awaited him to be powerfully affecting.

Aylesbury cannot have been a very welcoming place, although at least he must have been sure of being free from too many probing questions from his parents about what he had been doing. They had never taken much interest before, and were unlikely to start now. With the threat of bombing much reduced, Elsie and Sylvia had returned from the Chilterns, but the Old Man was now deeply involved in an affair with the mystery woman from his photographic studio, who had gone to work as his assistant shortly after Elsie left. The return of their younger son—physically and psychologically battered and bruised—was more of an inconvenience than a delight. 'My mother was frightened I'd eat her butter ration and the old man tried to avoid being on his own with me in case I tried to tap him for a couple of quid', he says in *Argument of Kings*.[3] There may also, of course, have been more than a little tension over the money that the two boys had stolen from their father—not something Bain would be likely to talk about.

That was his responsibility, of course—he was the one who had stolen the money in the first place. And it's possible, too, that he might have had a loving, sensuous welcome of his own on his return, like the soldier in his poem, had he behaved differently—he had, after all, walked out on his wife and new-born son when he left Aylesbury three years earlier. In the poem, the soldier's return is ultimately blighted by his horrific dreams and memories of the thunder of artillery and the landscape of combat:

> The crazy scribblings of barbed wire, the fat
> Bulges of stacked sand-bags, shattered trees,
> The livid stripped forked branches…[4]

Bain had all those images of warfare in his head and, with his months in the Mustapha Barracks behind him, more beside. Within two days, he had left for the less complicated pleasures of London.[5] The place had changed radically from the way he remembered it when he had arrived with Kenneth fresh from Aylesbury, his pockets stuffed with the Old Man's money. There had been a buzz and excitement in the streets then, but now, to a casual observer, many parts of the city seemed to have been occupied, swamped with the American servicemen who had been flooding into the country in preparation for the invasion that must be imminent. They were young men, far from home, with money in their pockets, and they knew that they might die soon. General 'Pete' Quesada of IX Tactical Air Command was a good example: at forty, he was old enough to be almost a father-figure to many of his men, but still felt the need for proper supplies during his time off in London. He wrote home to his mother asking for regular parcels of Montecristo cigars, stockings, and lipsticks.[6] There were thousands more like him, in the pubs, bars, and nightclubs, spending their money and chatting up the women, and Bain, like most of the British soldiers wandering the streets of London looking for fun, felt very much the poor relation. He stayed at the Union Jack Club, a downmarket haunt of servicemen in Waterloo, and drank through what was left of his pay as hard and as fast as he could. By the time he boarded the train for Chalfont in Buckinghamshire, where he was to rejoin his unit, he had spent his last pound and smoked his last cigarette.

II

If London had changed while Bain had been away, so had the war. While he had been in prison and then recovering from it in hospital, the Germans had finally been driven out of North Africa; allied troops had battled their way up the Italian peninsula, forcing an Italian surrender and gradually pushing back a determined and bloody fighting retreat by the Wehrmacht; Soviet forces, having stopped the German army at the Battle of Stalingrad, had been pushing westwards, and by the end of September 1943, the Germans had retreated nearly 700 miles to the River Dnieper in Ukraine. Stalin's demands for a second front in Western Europe to enable his forces to drive forward even more strongly had become more insistent, and Montgomery's old adversary, Erwin Rommel, one-time hero of the Afrika Korps advance into Egypt, was now preparing defences along the French coast to fend off the expected Allied invasion. The tide had turned, and where people in England had been waiting in fear for a German invasion, now they were expecting news of Allied troops storming ashore into northern France.

But the question troubling Bain as his train chugged sedately through the Buckinghamshire dark was the reception that he could expect from his former comrades. He was wearing his greatcoat, collar turned up against the January cold; his kitbag was beside him, and his rifle propped up in one corner of the compartment. All over the south of England, there were stores of ammunition, mines, building materials, and engineering equipment in corrugated iron dumps by the roadside; row upon row of tanks, jeeps, and other military vehicles stood in farmers' fields; tents and Nissen huts had sprung up in rural villages and out in the countryside. The whole of the south of England had been turned into one sprawling military encampment as preparations went ahead for the great invasion of Europe that was to bring the war to its final stages: Bain looked like any one of thousands of other soldiers on their way to rejoin their units for more training after a few days of leave. Only he knew what was different.

Senior officers had gone out of their way to reassure him that his desertion would not be held against him. They had thrown around well-meaning clichés like 'learned your lesson', 'fresh start', and 'wipe the slate clean' in an effort to set his mind at ease. But it would not be senior officers with whom he would be training, eating, drinking, and sleeping—it would be men who would know that only a few months ago, he had turned his back on them and walked away. Since the last time he had seen them, they had fought on into Algeria and then, the Afrika Korps finally defeated, sailed not for home, as they had hoped, but on to Sicily. Instead of the hard-fought and bloody landing they expected there, they had left their landing craft virtually unopposed, and there had been relatively little resistance for the rest of their twenty-five days on the island—but even so, he could hardly expect an enthusiastic welcome from the men he had left to fight on their own.

Vache Camp, where the Gordons were based, was one of four army camps near the village of Chalfont St Giles, some 25 miles north-west of London. Sixty or so concrete and iron prefabricated huts were huddled together in little clusters on either side of a rough track. A large square of concrete was used to park trucks and heavy vehicles, and also to provide a parade ground for the troops. Everywhere else was mud and gravel, leading the soldiers to suppose that the camp—actually named after the Norman family who used to own the land—was called Vache (the French for cow) because only cows should be living there.

In the event, John's fears about his reception were groundless. He recognized only a few of the men with whom he was to share one of the huts—some of his former colleagues had been transferred to other units, others were recovering in hospital, some had died. There were many new recruits—young, eager, fresh-faced boys of eighteen or nineteen, without the haunted look of the veterans like John who, at twenty-two, had grown up and grown old as they huddled in holes in the ground, teeth clenched and eyes shut, with artillery shells exploding around them. Montgomery's plan, and the reason for Bain's release from the Mustapha Barracks, was to stiffen the untried, unblooded youngsters by mixing them with the supposedly hardened veterans of his North Africa campaign—so it was ironic that, at least according to Bain's own memoirs, the only word of criticism that he heard from them came from Hughie Black, the man who had been his Brengunner in North Africa. Why, Black wanted to know, had John deserted alone, and not taken him with him?

No doubt there would have been many who shared his feelings, particularly among the North Africa veterans, many of whom felt considerable resentment about the fact that they were once more being thrown into the front line. Some army divisions had not yet fought in any theatre, but there were regiments of the Eighth Army which had been away from home for six years and more. It seemed to be time for somebody else to bear the brunt of the combat.

Everyone, on both sides of the Channel, knew that an invasion was in prospect. In the United States, President Roosevelt had warned the American people that grim times were coming. 'The war is now reaching the stage when we shall have to look forward to large casualty lists—dead, wounded, and missing', he had said in a Christmas Day broadcast in 1943. In France,

Rommel was busily commissioning a series of underwater obstacles and anti-personnel mines to kill Allied soldiers as they tried to wade ashore, part of a wall of fortresses and gun emplacements that stretched from Holland to the Atlantic. Churchill, Roosevelt, and their chosen supreme commander, General Dwight D. Eisenhower, had fixed on May for the date of their invasion, and the beaches of Normandy for its location—two of the most closely guarded secrets of the war.

On 12 February, Eisenhower received his formal orders from General George C. Marshall, Chief of Staff of the United States army: 'You will enter the continent of Europe and, in conjunction with the other United Nations, undertake operations aimed at the heart of Germany and the destruction of her armed forces.'

All over the south of England, hundreds of thousands of soldiers from Britain, the United States, and Canada, along with others from Australia, Belgium, Czechoslovakia, France, Greece, the Netherlands, New Zealand, Norway, and Poland, were practising endless mock attacks and deployments. The black comedy of the swinging bags of straw ripped apart in bayonet practice was ancient history now: this was hard, professional soldiering, rehearsal for the biggest seaborne invasion the world had ever seen. There were new weapons to be mastered—the terrifying Wasp flamethrower, for instance, which would hurl its jet of fire over 100 yards—and new techniques to be mastered, such as crossing rivers and finding ways through mines laid, not in the desert sand, but in the deceptively gentle-looking farmland of northern France. [7] Again and again they went through the procedures for charging out of a landing craft and deploying onto the beach—something that was not new to those of the Gordons and the rest of the 51st Highland Division who had seen action in Sicily. Platoons of soldiers rehearsed the advance to contact, while others mounted mock assaults on hastily constructed enemy pillboxes and gun emplacements; snipers honed their deadly skills and practised camouflage and concealment. There was practice in street fighting in the bombed ruins of east London. And when the exercises were finished, there were always assault courses of water jumps, barricades, and hanging ropes to be negotiated. [8]

The 1st and 5th/7th Gordons were part of 153 Brigade of the 51st Highland Division, alongside the 5th Black Watch, under the command of Brigadier Horatius 'Nap' Murray. Early in March, the division moved camp to Halstead in Kent, and then on 16 May to a massive encampment near Grays in Essex, on the road between Tilbury and Southend. Now, as they settled into the tiered bunks packed into the bell tents that dotted the fields like grotesque swollen mushrooms, even the Spartan conditions of the Nissen huts they had left behind seemed comfortable by comparison. Scores of similar gated camps, surrounded by coils of barbed wire, were dotted along the road towards London, erected specifically to marshal the invading army. Those few civilians who were allowed in the area—several hundred square miles in total—had their papers repeatedly checked by suspicious military policemen, and were quizzed in detail about where they were going and why.

Still no one had any idea of the date of the invasion, but they knew it had to come during the summer, so it could not be far away. Training and practice assaults were abandoned, and an uneasy lassitude settled over the men. There were lectures about the kind of country they would be fighting in, the weapons that the Germans would be likely to use against them, and the tactics they might expect to encounter, interspersed with football and other games, either official or unofficial. For two or three weeks, there were even one-day leave passes for soldiers to make trips to London.

There was a lot of rowdy drinking, occasional flying fists, and outbreaks of violence thinly disguised as laddish boisterousness and high spirits. One young officer who had acquired a reputation for pomposity and humourlessness—his nickname, 'Adolf', says all that is necessary about the way he was regarded by the soldiers—was tossed up and down in a blanket in a grim parody of some long-forgotten public school story, eventually being allowed to hit the earth from a height of twelve feet or so. These were men who knew they were likely to be dying soon.[9]

> Discipline was not easy to enforce because what, under other circumstances, might have been a potent threat of detention was now regarded by many of us as a desirable reprieve from very probable execution on the beaches of Normandy. Some of the young recruits who had joined the Battalion on its return from the Middle East were excited by the prospect of action, but we old hands, with our Africa Stars and wound stripes, listened to their prattle with sour amusement. They would learn.[10]

During the tense, weary times between lectures, games, and other organized activities, Bain continued to mull over the question of his recent desertion and his supposed cowardice. In *Argument of Kings*, he describes a conversation with Hughie, who wants him to desert again before the invasion starts, and take him with him. What follows may well be a literal account of what happened, but perhaps it is more likely to be a dramatization of Bain's own

inner dilemma and the way he resolved it. 'It's to do with my own feelings
about myself', he explains to Hughie in the book:

> 'Self respect, I suppose you've got to call it. When I fucked off at Akarit it
> wasn't planned. I told you, didn't I? It was like being hypnotised, as if I'd got
> no choice...I never thought about being a coward. Not until I was in the
> nick. Then that's about all I heard. I'd been yellow. I'd run away and left my
> mates to face it.
>
>   'I'm not going to take a powder. I've got to have another go. And I don't
> mind telling you, I'm shit scared. But if I fucked off now, I'd never know,
> would I? And I don't know why, but somehow I've got to know. I've got to
> find out if those bastards in the nick were right or wrong.'[11]

But the process of reaching that decision seems to have been harder than
Scannell ever admitted. He had been warned that if he deserted again, he
would be sent back to serve the rest of the three-year sentence that he had
already incurred, as well as any new sentence that the court might impose—
but on 5 March, as his unit was preparing to move from Vache Camp to
Halstead, he had gone missing again. His army record, with military preci-
sion, notes that he was 'Absent from 2359 Hrs. 5/3/44 to 0815 Hrs 20/3/44
(14 Days 8 Hrs 16 Mins)'.

Since there is no mention in the record of his having been under close
arrest at any time, he almost certainly returned to the camp voluntarily—
but if he wasn't intending to try to escape back into civilian life and desert
permanently, going AWOL was an act of breathtaking stupidity. It could
have seen him back in some military prison like the Mustapha Barracks for
several years—but then, John Bain's desertions were seldom considered and
thought through. Rather, hating army life and military discipline as he did,
he periodically walked out practically on a whim. It seems likely this time
that he just slipped quietly away from the camp—as many soldiers did—to
go on an illicit bender in London, without thinking of the possible consequences. If so, he was lucky: he was never officially declared a deserter on
this occasion, and was simply docked a total of twenty-two days' pay as
punishment. With D-Day looming, the army had no interest in putting its
soldiers behind bars—after all, there was every chance that they would be
dead in a few weeks anyway.

No doubt the guards on the camp were getting stricter as the invasion
drew nearer; after the move first to Halstead and then to Grays, it would
have been harder to get away anyway. But the eventual decision to face
down the temptation to desert and to stay with his unit was a significant

one; it may have called for a different kind of courage from the cheery, square-jawed derring-do of the comic books and propaganda, but it took courage all the same. He had no idea where the Gordons would be in the line of battle—no idea, either, where or when the invasion would come— but like everyone else waiting on tenterhooks in the camp, he knew that the chances of being killed were very great indeed. 'Cannon-fodder' was the word that the soldiers used about themselves—and many of them reached a different decision from John Bain's. Between D-Day and the end of the war, some 36,000 soldiers who had gone missing just before and shortly after the invasion were tracked down and arrested by the military police, and more than 10,000 of them charged with desertion.[12]

At the end of his life, Bain looked back on his emotions as the moment to go onto the Normandy beaches approached. In his poem 'War Words' (2007), as soldiers returned from the Iraq war, he mused on D-Day, and on the modern soldiers diagnosed with post-traumatic stress disorder. What he had shared with the other soldiers more than sixty years before, he said:

> Was *pre*-traumatic stress disorder, or
> As specialists might say, we were 'shit-scared'.[13]

It is a typically self-deprecating line, with its confession of fear and its old man's wry dismissive side-swipe at 'specialists', and yet it sums up the dogged courage shown by Scannell and hundreds of thousands of other soldiers on D-Day and the days that followed.

The original target date for the invasion had been May, but by the spring it had been put back to June. First leave was stopped, and then mail. On 8 May, General Eisenhower and his senior advisers studied the weather forecasts, the moon, and the tides, and settled on 5 June. Fifteen days later, on 25 May, the gaps in the wire around the tented camps in Essex were suddenly closed without notice. Armed military police patrolled the perimeter, and every entrance was strictly guarded round the clock. No one left except under escort, and then only to another sealed military camp. Even the sick were sent to special secure hospitals, behind more coils of barbed wire. Now, any lingering thoughts about possible desertion were no more than idle daydreams. The guards and the wire were there not to prevent intruders getting in, but to stop the soldiers inside from getting out: the camps had become prisons. The hot, sunny weather that might have been summery and relaxed under other circumstances now seemed sultry, sweaty, even threatening.

Alastair Borthwick, then serving in another regiment of the 51st Highland Division, told later how he and the other officers were briefed on the day that the camps were sealed:

> We climbed into trucks and drove in convoy to another camp, passed a red-cap at the gate who checked our identity cards and admitted us through the wire, and left our trucks in a park inside. Ahead of us was a second belt of wire manned by sentries. Again we produced our cards, and again passed through. There was a third wire barrier, this time set in a circle one hundred yards in diameter. In the centre of it, fifty yards from the nearest sentries, was a big black hut. We went in.[14]

Still they heard no details about where the attack was to be, and the map that plotted the initial invasion plans was on too big a scale to give them any clues. On 3 June, as the first ships that would be involved in the operation—the warships that would stand offshore and pound the German positions with artillery shells—were steaming south from the Clyde, the Gordons' commanding officer addressed the soldiers on parade. They would be embarking in landing craft the next morning, he told them; they would have the honour of being among the first seaborne troops to go ashore. Even then, neither the men nor their officers had any idea of exactly where they would be going.

They were issued with their ammunition and emergency rations—'a peculiarly unpleasant chocolate bar, bitter, brick-hard and gritty in texture, a cube of dehydrated porridge, a self-heating tin of soup, biscuits, barley-sugar sweets and cigarettes'.[15] Then there was a parade for inspection in full battle-order—not one of the pernickety occasions from the past, where NCOs sneered and barked at soldiers like Bain with unpolished buttons, scruffy webbing, or boots without the regulation shine, but a deadly serious check to see that every man had the equipment he would need for fighting. Their lives might depend on it.

They wore steel helmets and battledress, their webbing festooned with ammunition pouches, water-bottle, entrenching tool, and respirator. Bain carried a Bren gun, while others clutched either their rifles or a two-inch mortar. In a pocket was an emergency field dressing, and on their backs they carried a pack containing their rations, an anti-louse shirt and underwear, a small camp cooker and water sterilizer, a lifebelt, anti-seasick chewing gum and a vomit bag, waders, and a small supply of French currency. Altogether, the kit weighed about 70 lbs.

A message was read out from Field Marshal Montgomery, the commander whom Bain had loathed in North Africa and whom he loathed now. 'To us is given the honour of striking a blow for freedom which will live in history; and in the better days that lie ahead men will speak with pride of our doings. We have a great and a righteous cause', he said. It is easy to imagine John Bain's response.

III

It was a bad start. Reveille had been at 5.30, and at 6.45 the men had been on parade ready to board the trucks that would take them to Tilbury and the landing crafts in which they were to cross the Channel. It was a wet and windy morning and, during the short drive to Tilbury docks, each man was handed half a dozen extra sick bags. Clearly nobody believed that the single one they carried in their backpacks would be enough for the crossing ahead.

The men huddled awkwardly on the narrow seats that lined the steel sides of the cramped landing craft, smoking and talking in low voices, as the flotilla made its way downstream. At Southend, they joined a huge assembly of similar boats, all rocking uneasily at anchor just off the coast. And there they waited, in the shelter of the Thames estuary, as rough seas in the Channel made it impossible to start the crossing. Extra seasickness tablets were handed out, two to each man, their recipients noting with grim humour that they contained 'a strong drug as used on drunks'.[16] They had been due to leave at 8 a.m. on 4 June, but it was more than twenty-four hours after that before the anchors were hauled on board and the little boats nosed nervously out of the estuary and into the open sea. By the afternoon, they were off Dover, and maps and final instructions that finally divulged the secret of their destination were unsealed. The soldiers of 153 Brigade were to take the lead as first support division behind the initial assault on the Normandy beaches near the town of Courseulles. Few if any of the 200 or so men on board had heard of the place—but they knew only too well what the order meant. Even if the first assault troops succeeded in blunting the edge of the initial German defence, there would be savage fighting over the next days and weeks as they struggled to break out of the beachhead. But by now, many of the soldiers were no longer interested in what was waiting for them: as the sweet smell of diesel combined with the effects of the heavy swell, nerves, excitement, and raw fear, most of them were preoccupied with retching into their sick bags, and the stench of vomit filled the boat. As they reached the Isle of Wight, they changed course to head south, still pitching and rolling in the waves.

This was the scene that Vernon Scannell remembered when, more than sixty years later, he wrote with calm restraint in one of his last poems about 'troops who sail away to where great danger waits'.[17] The poem, 'Missing Things', is on the surface a wistful meditation on his approaching death: he imagines the books on his shelves looking down at him with the same valedictory goodwill as crowds on shore might show towards the departing soldiers. The words on the page are simple, straightforward, and universal in their meaning: the soldiers could be Greek hoplites setting out on an Athenian trireme, or red-coated marines sailing away to some corner of Queen Victoria's empire. All we know about them is that they are already on board the ship, so there is no going back; perhaps there is a suggestion of calm acceptance in 'sail away', which suggests that they are travelling voluntarily, or at least with resignation. The danger they face, too, is unspecified: all we know is that it is waiting for them, ominously and unavoidably, at the end of their journey.

This deliberate lack of detail, as though the scene is in soft focus, contributes to the poem's lyrical, elegiac quality, but it is impossible to believe that Scannell could have written those words without remembering the much more brutal and physically realized voyage that he made as John Bain all those years before, with the smell of fear and vomit in the boat, and shrapnel, bullets, and a probably bloody death waiting for the men when they landed in France. Perhaps, too, there is a parallel between the boat that the soldiers can't get out of and the deathbed that Scannell can't get out of, and from which he is writing the poem. Boat and bed, after all, are very likely heading for much the same destination. It is an image, like many in his poetry, with a starkly personal, autobiographical resonance, much more intense than it appears on the page. But when he asks, at the end of the poem, 'Then why so sad? And just a bit afraid?' the gentle querying of the general atmosphere of calm acceptance is more forceful and more poignant because we know something of the young man's pain and fear that still torment the old man on the point of death.

IV

In fact, the 5/7th Gordons were scheduled to arrive by the village of Courseulles-sur-Mer on Juno Beach just a few hours after the initial assault by some 14,000 troops of the 3rd Canadian Division. At 7.49 a.m., following a two-hour bombardment from the Royal Navy cruiser HMS Belfast and a naval task force which included one other cruiser and eleven British, Canadian, French, and Norwegian destroyers, the first Canadian landing craft had approached the shoreline. The waiting German artillerymen and machine-gunners held their fire until the ramps were down and the soldiers had begun to disembark, and then unleashed a hail of machine gun bullets and artillery rounds that scythed through the advancing soldiers.

Backed by amphibious tanks, they struggled forward, encountering fierce resistance every step of the way. Many never made it off the beaches. It was well into the afternoon before they had control of the town, and even then detachments of follow-up troops had to deal with snipers hiding around the beach. On that first day alone, more than 350 Canadians were killed either on the beach on in the countryside around it.

The Gordons, by contrast, picking their way cautiously through a mass of anti-aircraft ships, landing vessels, floating piers, and wrecked tanks and boats, were astonished at how little initial resistance they met. Scattered across the sand and shingle, they could see the small dark humps which they knew were the bodies of Canadian soldiers who had died on the beach. Some still lay in the shallow water, among wrecked boats and abandoned vehicles that had been inadequately waterproofed; others seemed tantalizingly close to the shallow trench at the top of the beach where they would have found a moment's relative safety. They had almost made it.

But Bain and the rest of the Gordons had no time to sympathize. From beyond the dunes where the first assault forces were fighting their way forward, they could hear the sound of gunfire.[18] On the beach itself, there was sporadic shellfire and a few half-hearted bombing runs by enemy aircraft. Later, in *Argument of Kings*, Scannell described the occasional 'iron chatter of machine gun fire',[19] although the Gordons' regimental history says there was no sound of small-arms fire.

Even so, any mistaken impression that the Germans might collapse under the weight of this massive invasion was soon dispelled. The men struggled ashore with their heavy kit through four or five feet of water, hanging onto a rope held on shore by a platoon commander who had waded ahead to the beach. It was a precarious lifeline: as Bain waited for his turn to jump into the water, he saw one short, stocky Glaswegian, waves slapping into his face, stumble and let go. Weighed down by his kit and by the extra weight of the heavy mortar bombs he carried slung around his neck, he was dragged by the strong undertow under a neighbouring vessel. There was no time to stop and rescue him: his, Bain knew, was the first life to be lost by their company.

At the water's edge, a sergeant was frantically waving his Sten gun in the direction the platoon had to go up the beach:

> John, soaked and squelching in his water-logged boots, felt the pack and blanket on his back dragging at his shoulders with the huge weight of sea water but he managed to move forward in a stumbling canter across the strand where he now saw that the dead lay quite thickly. From over on his left he heard an explosion followed by hoarse shouts and one high scream and he tried to move faster, but the weight he was carrying proved too great and he could only manage to sustain his clumsy lope.[20]

In the ditch, they paused and caught their breath for a moment. The mines that scattered the dunes and the marshland beyond had yet to be cleared, so there was only one exit from the beach, and that was clogged by the Canadians' vehicles, still struggling to get inland and snarled up in a massive and incongruous traffic jam—but even so, all the Gordons were off the beach by 8 p.m. and making their way inland to a little village called Banville, where they were to make their base for the night.

V

Banville was about 4 miles inland, well behind the front line that the Canadians had pushed forward some 7 miles from the coast, but there were still isolated pockets of German resistance and hidden snipers dotted throughout the countryside. Bain's platoon found themselves in a farmhouse on the edge of the village, where a half-eaten Camembert, several open bottles of wine and an unfinished letter lying on a table showed that the German occupants had left in a hurry. They dug their slit trenches in a nearby field, close to the road, and settled down for a cold, miserable, and sleepless night.

At about the same time, infantryman James Cramer, a sergeant in the 6th Airborne Division, was touching down in a glider near the village of Ranville, about 15 miles away—another soldier, but one who had flown, rather than sailed, to the great danger that was waiting. Cramer's memoirs later described the sort of trench where Bain was taking shelter:

> Our slit trenches were, as far as I can remember, four feet by three feet across, four feet deep to start with, then deepened so that you could stand with your

elbows on the front of the trench facing the enemy with a berm of soil behind the trench. As time went on you lengthened the longer side so that you could sleep comfortably.[21]

But there was little comfort for Bain or Hughie that night. They were together as a Bren-gun team, and they squatted awkwardly facing one another with their bent and helmeted heads just below the parapet. Their experience in North Africa had left them in no doubt that a slit trench provided the safest shelter under fire. Only a direct hit from an artillery shell could penetrate its reassuringly solid earth walls. They had done their best to wring the seawater out of their clothes and the contents of their backpacks, but they were still soaked through, and they sat and shivered through the night, flinching at the occasional nearby bursts of machine-gun fire.

Further inland they could hear the deep rumble of artillery, and back over the coastline orange tracer rounds from Bofors anti-aircraft guns were jabbing into the sky, seeking out marauding Luftwaffe planes. It was the sort of night that cements friendships, and Bain and Hughie—their old closeness from North Africa already reinforced by Hughie's acceptance of Bain's return to the unit—became virtually inseparable over the next few days.

The next morning, they were ordered to move west to the little village of Ste Croix sur Mer, where they were greeted with relief by the residents, who had been warned by the Germans to expect savage Russian invaders and where, since their motorized transport had still not arrived, they commandeered a donkey and cart to fetch blankets from the beach. Then it was further inland to Le Fresne Camilly, and on to a new position south of Hermanville. For three days they were constantly on the move, digging in and taking shelter in their slit trenches and then being roused and moved on through the churned and blasted Normandy farmland. The fields were scattered with dead cows, some grotesquely broken and bloated, and others stretched on the ground as if asleep—a bizarre mingling of blood and bucolic. The memory of two cows in particular stayed with Bain:

> An older memory of a field
> Which I would rather far forget…
> Both were still; the toffee one
> Lay on its back, its stiff legs stuck
> Up from the swollen belly like
> A huge discarded set of bagpipes.[22]

Elsewhere, the grassland had been planted with rows of jagged and broken stakes in an attempt to stop the gliders carrying Cramer and his companions from landing; occasional crashed planes, 'like the broken bodies of great prehistoric birds',[23] showed where they had either succeeded or failed. The war here was being fought out in a deceptively familiar environment, unlike the ominous, drab desert landscape of North Africa—'cider country, rather like Dorset'.[24] Only the smell—the mixture of cordite, sweat, and decomposing bodies—was the same. For Bain, though:

> The essential experience was just as it had been before and would always be: the sense of being dehumanised, reduced to being little more than an extension of your equipment and weaponry, the constant feeling of being used as an object, manipulated by blind, invisible hands, controlled by a force that was either malignant or stupid, the sense of being quite lost, of staggering about with no conscious direction in a metaphorical and quite often literal darkness, of being exhausted, frightened, sick, sometimes so weary that you slept on your feet like a horse. And ignorance, stupefying, brutalizing ignorance.[25]

By now their transport had arrived, and during the evening of 10 June they were carried east across the River Orne ready for an attack on the village of Touffréville, from which a detachment of British paratroops had just been forced to withdraw. As night fell the Gordons were lying in a field with the artillery shells of their barrage whining over their heads as they clenched their teeth in fear and buried their faces in the ground. Returning salvos of mortars crashed around them, showering them in clods of earth.

The advance, when it came, took them through thick woods on the approach to the town, bullets ripping through the branches around them from German patrols and snipers who seemed to be scattered through the woodland. Until they arrived in France, the soldiers had never fought among trees, and they quickly learned that the sense of safety that came with concealment was a mirage. The trees offered no shelter, and the covering of branches was perfectly placed to burst incoming shells at the very height where they would do most damage. Bain's company took up positions around a farmhouse on the outskirts of the village and sat there for the next two days, under a constant barrage of mortar and machine-gun fire.

Bain was not the only one on whom the stress of constant tension and fear was beginning to tell. In *Argument of Kings*, he describes one of the eager young recruits who, back in England, had been among the most gung-ho and enthusiastic about the prospect of battle:

The neatly shaped, alert features had melted and blurred, the mouth was sagging, and the whole face, dirty and stubbled, seemed swollen and was smeared with tears and snot. He was making wordless, bleating sounds from which every now and then an identifiable phrase would surface and when this happened the words were recognised as a frightened infant's cry for its mother.[26]

There is a striking honesty about the response in himself that he goes on to describe—contempt, even a degree of sadistic hatred, but at the same time 'a kind of envy of the boy's shameless surrender to his terror, and an intolerable suspicion that he was witnessing something of himself'. Perhaps this sense of being complicit in the young soldier's breakdown, of privately sharing his humiliation, was another effect of the self-doubt that he had felt ever since he had walked away from Wadi Akarit—certainly, years later, he seemed relieved to hear more evidence that, as he had once told Hughie Black, 'not everyone can be a hero'.

On 5 June 1994—now Vernon Scannell, not John Bain—he appeared briefly in a television programme marking the fiftieth anniversary of the D-Day landings. Some of the other veterans spoke of their feelings of excitement in battle, leaving Vernon, he noted afterwards in his diary, to wonder whether distance had not lent enchantment to their memories. But what really interested him was the contribution of a medical officer who had worked in a casualty clearing centre on the beaches, and who 'spoke of those casualties whose wounds in hand or foot were indicative of self-infliction. They were treated, but placed under arrest for later court martial. It seems that these cases were quite numerous, so it seems that my reaction to battle was not after all so uncommon.'[27]

In fact, the idea of using the veterans from North Africa to stiffen the resolve of the new recruits in the landings was leading to unforeseen problems in the 51st Highland Division. Rather than 'battle-hardened', the soldiers seemed to be battle-weary. In the days following the attack on Touffréville, the division was supposed to advance some 4 miles south towards Cagny, east of Caen, as part of a pincer movement that aimed to force the German defenders out of the city of Caen. The attempt, the divisional history later recalled, was an embarrassing failure:

The fact must be faced that at this period the normally very high morale of the Division fell temporarily to a very low ebb...A kind of claustrophobia affected the troops, and the continual shelling and mortaring from an unseen enemy in relatively great strength were certainly very trying.[28]

If that word 'trying' has all the studied nonchalance of a military historian writing after the event, a more graphic version comes from a Canadian paratroop major who was involved in the same action. 'The thing that shocked me was 51st Highland Division', he said. 'Three different times our division restored a situation for them. If you could have seen our lads come up to help them out on one occasion and call them yellow bastards when the Scotties threw their weapons and equipment away and fled!'[29] A couple of weeks later, Montgomery was considering sending the whole division back to Britain for retraining—an astonishing prospect in the middle of a hard-fought invasion campaign. 'The 51st [Highland] Division is at present not—NOT—battleworthy. It does not fight with determination and has failed in every operation it has been given to do', he wrote.[30]

In the event, Montgomery contented himself with replacing the divisional commander, and left the 51st in the field[31]—but by that time, Bain's direct involvement with the 51st Highland Division and with the war itself was at an end.

Bain's unit was not directly involved in the attempted advance to Cagny, having been ordered back to the town of Escoville to defend it against an expected German attack. He himself had suffered a series of the random, second-hand experiences that were demoralizing so many of his comrades. He describes them in *The Tiger and the Rose*: one of his company, a boy of about eighteen from Aberdeen, had killed himself by blowing his head off with his own rifle under a mortar barrage;[32] in a deserted farm, Bain walked in upon the dead body of an old woman, lying peacefully in her bed; in the centre of Touffréville, he had turned a corner into a small public park to see a number of dead British paratroopers hanging from trees by their parachute shrouds, like horrific dangling fruit. Other bodies were lying on the grass and the cobbled road:

> We went into one of the deserted cafes and helped ourselves to bottles of Calvados before we headed out of the town, back to our positions. We felt no shame at leaving those airborne soldiers behind, only a nervous gratitude for our own survival. It was only later that guilt began, that those hanging paratroopers and their sprawled comrades on the ground began their ceaseless whispers of accusation.[33]

But there was still a worse experience to come.

He was dug in close to a ruined farmhouse alongside Hughie Black, experiencing once again the inexpressible terror of bombardment, his hands clutched instinctively but pointlessly over his testicles for protection—'Montgomery may not take care of his privates, but by Christ, I take care of mine', he had told Hughie grimly, during one bombing attack.[34] They were being pounded by the Nebelwerfer multi-launchers, Moaning Minnies, as the soldiers called them, and the mortar bombs screamed and howled in the air like banshees, thirty of them in a single salvo, before the two cowering soldiers were showered with the soil and stones of each deafening explosion. From the woodland beyond the farmer's field, bursts of machine-gun fire swept across the landscape like deadly showers of rain; the occasional crack and whine of a sniper's bullet was a powerful reminder to keep their heads down. The onslaught lasted for nearly two days, with occasional very brief and unpredictable pauses during which they could make the hazardous run to the farmhouse for water or to relieve their bladders.

It was on one such run that Hughie was killed. Bain, left alone in the trench, had his head down after the mortar barrage had suddenly restarted, and when he peered nervously over the edge, it was to see his mate stretched out on the ground about twenty yards away. Bain ran to him; so did their corporal, Gordon Rennie, but there was nothing they could do. A piece of shrapnel had ripped away the front of his friend's body, killing him instantly.

There was little time for grieving. Within an hour or so, Hughie's body was in the ground, and that night the unit pulled back from Touffréville to be redeployed a short distance away at Escoville, a village known among the troops for its mines and its mosquitoes.

VI

Hughie was one of three men killed, twenty-one wounded, and four missing during the exchanges,[35] and now, added to the feelings of shame and self-doubt that followed his desertion at Wadi Akarit, Bain carried an additional burden of guilt for his friend's death—survivor's guilt, not rational or reasonable, but still a painful and powerful feeling. He had survived, and Hughie had not. Perhaps that emotion made him particularly sensitive to his surroundings—but somewhere on the journey from Touffréville to Escoville, at a time when Bain was so tired that he said he had literally fallen asleep on the march, came an experience that would be imprinted on his memory and would eventually form the centrepiece of one of the Second World War's finest poems.

It was a brief and simple incident, but almost religious in its intensity—
the appearance just as dawn was breaking of a convoy of ambulances carrying wounded soldiers back to a casualty clearing station for treatment. His
mind still clouded by the death of Hughie Black, Bain and his new partner
had dug themselves into a position close to the Caen Canal when the
ambulances jolted past through the mist. The image stayed with him, and he
wrote about it on several occasions, although the first time was not until
eighteen years later. His poem 'Walking Wounded', written in 1962, describes
first the ambulances, 'stumbling and churning past the broken farm', and
then, a moment or two later:

> ... the walking wounded,
> Straggling the road like convicts loosely chained,
> Dragging at ankles exhaustion and despair.
> Their heads were weighted down by last night's lead,
> And eyes still drank the dark. They trailed the night
> Along the morning road. Some limped on sticks;
> Others wore rough dressings, splints and slings;
> A few had turbaned heads, the dirty cloth
> Brown-badged with blood. A humble brotherhood...[36]

By the time he wrote these lines, of course, he was Vernon Scannell, not
John Bain. 'Walking Wounded'—not only one of his most moving and
evocative war poems, but among the best poems of the Second World War
by any poet—goes on to present a vision of wounded men like these in
their thousands, struggling onwards eternally:

> And when heroic corpses
> Turn slowly in their decorated sleep
> And every ambulance has disappeared,
> The walking wounded still trudge down that lane,
> And when recalled they must bear arms again.

It is easy to see why the subject—the endless unregarded suffering of the
common man, no hero or martyr, but a walking embodiment of the unknown
soldier—would resonate with a man who was so tortured about his own
military record. But the poem, and the genesis of the central images within
it, offer a fascinating insight into the way Scannell thought and felt, and how
he approached writing and the craft of poetry.

In an interview in 1963, a year after writing the poem, he said it was
based on his specific wartime memory. 'It had been lying there for nearly

twenty years before I found my way to writing it', he said.[37] But according to his diaries, the immediate impetus to turn the memory into a poem came from a sudden fascination for the phrase 'walking wounded'. On 20 November 1962, without having mentioned the ambulances, the Caen Canal, or the war, he suddenly notes, 'I would like to write a poem called *Walking Wounded*…It seems to me a packed phrase, very evocative.'[38]

But evocative of *what*? A day later, he is still not sure:

> Scratched away for an hour or so at a very rough prose draft of *Walking Wounded*. I'm not at all sure that poems are made like this, but I'm going to try it. First, a rough prose piece, written quickly; then see if any natural cadences occur upon or around which a rhythmic basis could be constructed. Then versify it and see what happens. The trouble is, I don't think I have anything to say about the subject. I remember the wounded on Jeeps and in ambulances in Normandy and then the phrase 'Walking Wounded' conjures up a vision, an image, a picture of men, tired, dejected, unheroically, undramatically injured, limping and stumbling back to a dressing-station where they will be patched up and returned to the fighting. There is some wider reference, I'm sure, but I'm damned if I can quite focus it. I suppose the big traumas dignify their victims, but the little, nagging hurts, which we have to face again and again are more to be feared. Or is this the glib casuistry of one who has never been really walloped?

The starting point, then, is the phrase itself, with its implications of continued suffering, relatively minor compared with that of the killed or maimed victims of battle. The words bring to mind the scene from eighteen years earlier, and the main body of the poem is a series of graphic and specific images culled from that memory—a dead German motorcyclist, still holding the handlebars of his machine; the ambulances themselves, and the 'amputated signpost and smashed trees' of the shattered landscape. Scannell was always for the concrete image—'Let the image do the work. Let the emotion come from the reader', was the advice he sometimes offered.[39]

In 1971, nine years after 'Walking Wounded', he returned to the ambulances in prose, in his memoir *The Tiger and the Rose*; and sixteen years after that, he told the story for a third time in his account of his military service, *Argument of Kings*. It was clearly an important and evocative memory for him. There are some differences in detail between the two prose accounts—in *The Tiger and the Rose*, for instance, he names the soldier who was accompanying him at the time as Bill Grey, and in *Argument of Kings* as Alec Stevenson; in the first account, the arrival of the ambulances is preceded by 'a couple of jeeps carrying stretchers fixed above the heads of the drivers, and flying Red Cross pennants', while the second has a dozen or so. These, perhaps, are mistakes of detail that could be accounted for by a fading memory over several decades—and in any case, as we have already seen, Scannell often changed the names of people he mentioned in his memoirs.

A more significant discrepancy, though, concerns the 'walking wounded' themselves. In *The Tiger and the Rose*, as in the poem, they appear shortly after the ambulances have disappeared—a moving and memorable sight:

> There was something haunting about the sight of those men...They moved like sleep-walkers; they were shocked and exhausted and their eyes had about them a remote, stunned look, as if they were still gazing on the scenes of carnage that had raged about them on the previous night.[40]

Clearly, too, from the detail of the description, they have passed very close to the watching Scannell. The scene, he says, 'has been fixed in my memory ever since'. But in *Argument of Kings*, they have vanished. The ambulances pass, and Scannell goes back to sleep. Had he simply forgotten about them in 1987? Decided that they were no longer relevant? Or when he was writing in 1971, was his memory coloured by the poem he had written and the scene he had imagined for it?

Perhaps he saw the men and the ambulances on the same morning, perhaps not—there must, after all, have been plenty of groups of wounded soldiers making their way painfully towards treatment centres. In his diary, he says that the picture of the men is 'conjured up' by the phrase 'walking wounded', so it seems that they have been added in some way to his original memory of the scene, either drawn from his imagination or remembered from a different occasion. In writing the poem, then, building on a single phrase which he found evocative and tightly packed, he has taken a specific incident from his past, described the sight and the sound of it with striking detail—

> Crunch of mortar, tantrum of a Bren
> Answering a Spandau's manic jabber

—and then enlarged upon it with new images, either imagined or drawn from other incidents, but still sharply drawn, precise, and concrete.

And then for the final seven lines, the men return in a silent, ghostly dream sequence drawn entirely from his imagination, presenting the 'wider reference' about which he had been so unsure as he began the poem. It has developed its own momentum, growing organically out of Scannell's images and taking its meaning further than the original thought in his diary that 'the little, nagging hurts…are more to be feared' than the 'big, dramatic traumas'. Its conclusion is bigger, more serious, more profound, and its reference both universal and personal. The soldiers must march again when 'recalled' to service, but also when 'recalled'—remembered—by Scannell. These eternal victims of war are the masses of unsung soldiers who have to fight, who suffer wounds that don't heal and aren't remembered, and who are subject to an undefined but irresistible compulsion. From an instinctive sense of the potential of a single phrase, coupled with the vivid recapturing and reworking of his personal memories, he has created a dream-poem of universal relevance that bears comparison with Wilfred Owen's 'Strange Meeting'.

VII

Shortly after the ambulances had passed, Bain's unit was on the move again—a three hour single-file trudge on towards Escoville, past wrecked and abandoned vehicles and grim skull-and-crossbones warnings of landmines, and accompanied by the sound of nearby explosions and the occasional welcome roar of a passing RAF fighter-bomber. He had long abandoned the thought that had come to him shortly before he had left Alexandria, that nothing, not even sheltering from the bombs and shrapnel, or advancing towards the bullets, could be worse than life in the military prison—and now he was also coping with an all-enveloping, irresistible tiredness. Each foot was planted in front of the other through instinct rather than will, and each time he paused, standing or sitting, he would fall asleep, a cigarette smouldering unheeded between his lips.

The company reached Escoville and dug in once more, in a field close to a church, overlooked again by an area of woodland. The inhabitants of the village were long gone, and almost every building was pockmarked with the scars of bullets and shrapnel. For a couple of days the war seemed to be going on around them, but on the third day, another bombardment opened up, sending them scurrying to their holes again. Again, there was the overwhelming, almost suffocating terror as the mortars rained down, and the panic-stricken conviction that each shell was aimed personally, individually, at him:

The fury of artillery is a cold, mechanical fury, but its intent is personal. When you are under its fire, you are the sole target. All that shrieking, whining venom is directed at you and at no-one else. You hunch in your hole in the ground, reduce yourself to as small a thing as you can become, and you harden your muscles in a pitiful attempt at defying the jagged, burning teeth of the shrapnel. Involuntarily you curl up into the foetal position except that your hands go down to protect your genitalia.[41]

The next morning, with the barrage apparently over, news came that Bain and his section—about a dozen men—were to mount a reconnaissance patrol to see whether the Germans had pulled back. Their orders were to move out in the cover of the hedgerows and make their way down the road and across the fields towards the woodland. If they came under fire, they were to withdraw at once.

Bain was carrying one of the Bren guns when there was a sudden burst of fire from the sergeant leading the patrol, followed at once by an answering burst from the other side of the bushes. A German patrol had been creeping along the same hedgerow on the other side, and they had practically walked into each other. Bain froze:

Then he saw the German helmet rise, quite slowly it seemed, above the hedge leading to the next field and he looked straight into the eyes of its wearer. He heard Alec's voice behind him screaming 'For fuck's sake, Johnny, shoot! Shoot the fucker!' as the German raised his Schmeisser machine pistol—again it seemed that the movement was accomplished with hypnotic slowness—and aimed it at John's stomach.[42]

From the moment he had first gone into uniform, he had prayed that he would never have to kill anyone, but he raised his own gun to fire—only to find that nothing happened when he pressed the trigger. There was a shot from behind him, a burst of fire from the Schmeisser, a sudden blow as though someone had kicked his leg from under him, and a brief cacophony of firing from every direction at once. Then the shooting stopped, and he felt two of his mates lift him with his arms around their shoulders, and half-drag, half carry him back towards the shelter of another hedgerow and a low bank of earth.

Back at Battalion Headquarters, a medical orderly cut away Bain's left trouser leg, dressed the wound where he had been shot, and gave him an injection of morphine to deaden the pain. One of the soldiers who had gone back with him told him what had happened: the rest of the patrol had opened fire on the German who had the Schmeisser and killed him—but not before he had fired off a burst that had hit Bain in the right leg. A second bullet had hit him in the left ankle. And as for the Bren gun with which he might have protected himself and the rest of the patrol—he had forgotten to take the safety catch off. It was not only because he was generally scruffy on parade and late back from leave that Bain had a reputation as a bad soldier.

He had the wound that all the soldiers used to talk about—a clean hit from a bullet which would heal in time, but which was enough to guarantee him a return to England and a break from active service. It felt as if he was leaving his mates in the lurch for a second time, and there was yet another burden of guilt to bear. Years later, he would return to Ranville cemetery:

> What little could I remember of the dead? Not much. My friend Gordon's manic, broken-toothed laugh; Peter Ross's choirboy face that didn't seem to own more than half its nineteen years, and Sergeant Jameson, leathery and profane, a rough but humane father-figure to these very young ones experiencing their first taste of action. And there, incredibly, was his age, carved in the white stone: 27.[43]

But back then in 1944, all he knew was that Hughie had died, and he had survived, and that the men who had carried him back to safety were going back into the bombs, bullets, and shrapnel that might well kill them too. But he was going home.

The army might argue about it—and would—but Bain's undistinguished military career was effectively over.

VIII

The Emergency Military Hospital at Winwick, near Warrington in Cheshire, was a grim and forbidding place. It had been a Victorian lunatic asylum—more of a prison than a hospital in those days—and had only recently been converted to provide treatment for wounded soldiers. The beds were crowded close together, with forty-two patients in a ward intended for twenty-eight, but the sheets were clean, the mattresses were comfortable, there was no one shouting orders, and there were no sudden artillery barrages or sniper's bullets.

Bain's right leg was plastered up to the thigh, and his left to just below the knee—'both legs encased in plaster like the icing on a rather old birthday cake'.[44] For the first three or four weeks he was confined to his bed, but he rapidly discovered a member of the Women's Voluntary Service who brought him books from the public library. There was *The Oxford Book of English Verse*, William Faulkner's *The Sound and the Fury*, and T. S. Eliot's *Collected Poems*—for practically the first time since he had picked *Esther Waters* off the floor of the Mustapha Barracks, Bain could sit with a book in his hand. For a while, it was like heaven, but with the smell of hospital.

And for all its forbidding appearance, the hospital welcomed relatives of the patients. Bain, of course, had no inclination at all to invite either of his parents—but he realized within a few days of his arrival that Winwick was less than 15 miles away from Eccles, where he had lived with his father's parents when he was eight years old. As he remembered again some forty-five years later in a poem written for children, his relationship with his grandmother there had been one of the few bright spots in his own bleak and miserable childhood:

> For ages I remembered her faint scent
> Of lavender, the way she'd never scold
> No matter what I'd done, and most of all
> The way her smile seemed, somehow, to enfold
> My whole world like a warm, protective shawl.[45]

He wrote to her at the old house in Bardsley Street, and her visit brought him—possibly for the first time in his adult life—a brief taste of simple, uncomplicated love and affection:

> A tiny frail old lady. It was weird.
> She hobbled through the ward to where I lay
> And drew quite close and, hesitating, peered.
> And then she smiled: and love lit up the day.[46]

But her visit was only a brief hour or so in a long and tedious stay. He was tired, battered, and emotionally drained by his experiences under fire, and he had no wish to join in the constant banter and laughter among the other patients. The noise they made, either snoring and occasionally crying out with pain, or talking and joking with each other, stopped him sleeping at night and from reading during the day. Even if the ward had been silent, he found that he had lost the ability to concentrate. By the time the cast was removed from his left leg after four weeks, he had had more than enough.[47]

It was with a shock of something approaching delight that he realized that removing the cast meant not only that he could move around, slowly and painfully, on his crutches, but that he could apply for a pass to leave the hospital on a day's exeat. In his hospital blues—shapeless blue woollen jacket and trousers, worn with a white shirt and red tie—he looked and felt more like an inmate of the Victorian asylum than a recovering patient from the modern hospital, but the addition of his Glengarry cap and Gordons regi-mental badge, and a slit in his right trouser leg to accommodate his remain-ing cast, gave him a slightly more soldierly appearance. During the weeks in action in France, and subsequently in hospital, he had had little or nothing to spend his pay on, and he now had more than £3 in his pocket—the equivalent of around £110 in today's money.

He knew exactly what he wanted to do with it: his plan was simply to make his way into Warrington, just a couple of miles away, and enjoy a pint in a pub. It was a deceptively simple idea—perhaps its first weakness was that, for Bain, pints of beer never came in the singular—and it began to unravel even before he had left the ward. The pubs in Warrington, the other patients told him, had all been told not to serve soldiers in Winwick blues. He would have to travel to either Liverpool or Manchester.

The fact that his pass entitled him to go no further than Warrington hardly crossed his mind. By midday, after a bus ride into Warrington and a brief train journey, with his crutches propped up beside him and his plas-tered right leg stretched out on the seat opposite him, he was standing outside Manchester London Road station,[48] with a cigarette in his mouth and the warm August sun on his back. Bare-legged girls in summer dresses strolled down the street without a care in the world; the doors of the pubs were wide and welcoming; on the street, the traffic moved freely. Even the scratchy material of his hospital suit was reassuring: it had no badges, no webbing—it could, at first glance, be taken for civilian clothing. The drab, khaki existence of army life, and the war itself, seemed to belong on another planet:

> His sense of freedom was intoxicating…He thought: 'I'm on my way out. They'll never get me again. I'll never be shot at, or shouted at or fucked around by brainless, big-mouthed NCOs or pissed on by public school pre-fects with one pip. I've got the army by the short hairs. I can do what I like. They can't send a one-legged man to the glasshouse.'[49]

Even by then, it must have been clear that the 8.30 p.m. deadline on his hospital pass might as well never have been written. Bain would not be reporting back at Winwick that evening: he was primed and ready for a bender.

The account of the next two days that he gives in his memoirs—grateful civilians noticing his military cap and plying him with drinks in various bars; meat pies in down-at-heel cafes; waking in a park; bloodshot eyes, dry and rancid mouth; his surroundings slipping in and out of focus; his voice, slurred and unfamiliar, sounding to him as if he was hearing it from a great distance away; and finally vomiting painfully, humiliatingly, messily in the street—could probably have been a description of many of his illicit away days from the army. What he describes sounds almost like a vivid enactment of a Hogarthian series of Rake's Progress illustrations, but it was probably very similar to the kind of night out that many soldiers felt entitled to after they came back from the war.

Women, brassy, flirtatious, and tantalizingly available to different degrees, float vaguely through the story; spivs and chancers tap him up for drinks and fleece him of his money, while good-natured strangers fill his glass; a friendly couple help him out of the street, give him a cup of tea and a night on their sofa. And typically, when he wakes before dawn, he decides that the next day is going to be different:

> He would not make the mistake of drinking too fast and too much. He would take it easy. Box clever. Not go crazy. And not be taken for a ride by con men and old whores. It was going to be a glorious day.[50]

Predictably, glorious though it was in many ways, the next day doesn't turn out like that. After leaving the house where he had spent the night, Bain finds his way to a YMCA café, where he settles down for breakfast. There he meets a young Scottish girl—named Maxie in *Argument of Kings*—who is serving as an anti-aircraft gunner with the Auxiliary Territorial Service. She seems to be as keen on finding a drink as he is, and by 11 a.m. they are in the first pub of the day. From there—Bain still swinging gamely along on his crutches—they move from pub to pub until mid-afternoon, when he lies down to rest on the grass in a cemetery near Maxie's billet, while she goes back to fetch a bottle of Scotch that she has stored there.

After finishing the bottle, they agree to go back to the ATS encampment, where Bain, who is by this time decidedly unsteady on his crutches, will crawl under the wire so that they can spend the night together. He is half-way through when the guards catch him, and while Maxie is marched off by an ATS sergeant, he is taken to the guard-room before being driven back to Winwick in an army truck by two military policemen in the middle of the night. The next morning, Bain is up before the hospital commandant—'a pouchily dyspeptic major'[51]—to be sentenced to fourteen days confined to barracks and fined a week's pay, and the story ends with him glumly attending physiotherapy sessions and peeling potatoes.

It is a good tale, with John Bain in the central role as a hapless and semi-comic Just William figure, buffeted and tossed around by circumstance in a cruel and implacable world, at the mercy of officers as William was at the mercy of uncomprehending grown-ups—but it is almost certainly more a carefully stitched together patchwork of escapades from his various times on the run than an accurate account of a single incident in 1945. Once again, the official army record tells a different, more complicated, and ultimately more sombre story.

His first absence from hospital—presumably the one featured in *Argument of Kings*—began on 16 July, but rather than the two-day jolly he describes, in which he goes absent almost by accident, simply 'forgetting' to return to Winwick, it lasted for a full week. He reported back at the hospital at 5.15 p.m. on 23 July, and was sentenced not to fourteen days confined to barracks, but to a week in the guard-room. *Argument of Kings* goes on to describe him receiving a letter from Maxie, and slipping quietly out of the barracks a few days later, while still serving his sentence, to meet her again at the YMCA in Manchester. Again, perhaps the meeting happened—perhaps, as he says in the book, they spent another evening drinking beer and whisky, were turned away from the Piccadilly Hotel, and finally spent the night together in a house owned by a crippled pervert who kept trying to spy on them. Again, it's a good story, but it certainly didn't happen the way it is described.

It would have been much harder for him to escape from detention in the guard-room rather than from a sentence confined to barracks—but his record demonstrates that he never escaped at all. His second absence began on 3 August, two days after his release. This time, instead of the brief two-day fling which *Argument of Kings* describes, ended by smirking military policemen who bundle him into an army truck and back to the hospital, he was on the run for ten days, returning to Winwick at 11.30 in the morning on 13 August.

According to his account, the commandant took a stricter line—particularly in view of the fact that he had now had his second plaster cast removed, and might therefore think it would be even easier to escape.

'This hospital, as I expect you know, used to be a loony bin. That means there are padded cells available. And that's where you are going…Right Sar'nt. Take him over to the cells and lock him up. You let him out only once a day for physiotherapy and then under escort. Otherwise he's to be kept locked up at all times.'[52]

The sentence noted on his army record of thirty-six days' pay docked and ten days' detention presumably relates to this time in a padded cell, of which Winwick did indeed retain several from its days as a mental hospital. From there, rather than spending several weeks having further physiotherapy at the hospital as he might have expected, he was to be sent back to his regimental depot—out of the hospital blues and back into standard army regulation khaki—before another move to a convalescent depot in Hamilton, Scotland.

The official record lists another five spells of absence over the next eight months, ranging from two days at the beginning of September to ten days in April 1945. In that period, he served a total of forty-three days either confined to barracks or in detention, with another ten days for a separate charge of neglecting to obey the order of a superior officer. During his time in hospital and convalescence, he was docked a total of eighty-six days' pay.

Life in Hamilton, he said later, was 'exclusively masculine, drab, sweaty, obscene and monotonous'[53]—a collection of adjectives that could just as well describe his experience of army life in general. But, even though he was back in the hated khaki battledress, this apparently obsessive record of absconding and absenteeism came at a time when the regime was as relaxed as any time he had known in the army. There were exercises to be done to ease the stiffness in his legs, but it was not the gruelling and demeaning labour that he had known in the Alexandria Barracks; there were opportunities to visit the bars and fish and chip shops in Hamilton, and frequent drunken nights in the barracks. There were too, as there had been in Banff, back in that distant, relatively innocent world when he had been a young recruit, occasional invitations to join local families for cups of tea, sandwiches, and hospitality. They didn't always go well.

In *The Tiger and the Rose*, he tells of one occasion when he arrived with a friend—'a large Aberdonian…a good drinker and useful ally in a brawl'[54]—on the doorstep of a middle-aged woman who had invited a couple of soldiers round for tea and scones. She had 'that look of firmly set solidity that the young associate with older aunts', while her friend, another middle-aged woman with a husband away in the military police, 'looked as though she would make a pretty formidable red-cap herself'. However, when the two young men caught sight of the bottles of beer ranged on the sideboard, it seemed as if an enjoyable evening might be in prospect—but they had not allowed for the entertainment that the two women had in mind. Switching off the lights, they climbed heavily onto the young soldiers' laps:

> I felt her hospitality deserved some kind of repayment so I tried, without enthusiasm, to respond, but my hand encountered what felt like corrugated iron corsets and capacious, slippery bloomers and these, with the hot smell of tobacco smoke and beer that she was breathing into my face, were too much for me.[55]

Horrified, Bain and his friend heaved the amorous women onto the floor and blundered clumsily out of the darkened house, grabbing their glengarries and greatcoats as they went. It was one of the few occasions in a long life when Vernon Bain, John Bain, or Vernon Scannell turned down the offer of a sexual adventure.

The way he tells it, the tea-and-scones adventure sounds like another of the 'Just William' scrapes that peppered his army career. But Bain's record of absences doesn't sound like that of a man sneaking the occasional night off for a few illicit drinks and a night on the town—he could, after all, have got those at the barracks or on his frequent forays into Hamilton without running the risk of another spell in the guard-house and a large sum docked from his pay packet. Rather, it speaks of a man with a deep-seated and passionate loathing of army discipline and army life, coupled perhaps with the beginnings of alcoholism—not Just William, in fact, but a man with a serious problem. Physically, he was slowly recovering from his wounds—his broken right leg had healed completely, but he was still unable to flex his left ankle or walk properly. Developments in Germany, with American and British forces now east of the Rhine and the Russians knocking on the door of Berlin, meant that there was very little possibility of his being called back for active service, and the institutions where Bain found himself must have been some of the safest and easiest places in which to sit out the rest of the war. There was no question of cowardice, of running away from danger.

But he must have known that he was playing with fire. Any one of Bain's absences would have been enough for him to be dragged before a court martial and have the balance of his Mustapha Barracks sentence reimposed, as he had been warned when he was released. Perhaps he had been right when he told himself that the army could no longer touch him, as they could hardly send a wounded soldier to the glass-house; perhaps, though this seems unlikely, the engaging personal charm that always got him both into and out of trouble worked its magic on the senior officers who sentenced him. Or maybe, with the war dragging towards its end, there simply seemed no sense in wasting rations on a man who was clearly never going to be any use to the army.

At the beginning of May, however, it seems that they ran out of patience. Bain had pushed his luck too far, and a terse entry notes that he was 'in close arrest awaiting trial'. Perhaps, finally, the authorities had decided to crack down on this serial deserter, and maybe even impose that outstanding two-and-a-half-year sentence. If so, they never got the chance: on 8 May, before a court martial could be set up, came news of the German surrender, and on that very day, late in the afternoon, Bain packed his haversack with his shaving kit, a towel, and a toothbrush and—close arrest or not—walked out of the barracks for the last time.

The army, meanwhile, was responding in the way that large bureaucracies do—slowly, clumsily, and inconsistently. On 15 May, a week after he had gone on the run, the West Scotland District Command portentously announced: 'Sentence of 4 years P.S.[56] awarded on 22.4.43 and Suspended on 25.10.43 is Remitted.' He probably never knew it, but he was now officially free from the threat of prison.

Or he would have been if he hadn't gone on the run already. Nine days later, he was officially declared a deserter again. But by that time, he was far away.

IX

Bain's days as a soldier were over, but he was not escaping unscathed.

As he limped away from the convalescent depot in Hamilton looking for a friendly truck driver to take him south, he knew that the war—*his war*—was over. It would be another three months before the Japanese forces surrendered in the East, and there were still British and Allied troops fighting there, but like most people at home, he felt that the German surrender marked the end of a conflict that had convulsed a continent and cost millions of lives all over the world. He had been lucky: his left ankle was still giving him pain, but he knew that it would eventually heal. Other men he had lived and fought with, such as his fellow machine-gunner Hughie Black, or his friend the corporal, Gordon Rennie, would never be going home. Neither would some 380,000 other British servicemen.[57]

Hundreds of thousands more had been wounded—some suffering relatively minor wounds like his own, from which they would recover, and others losing arms or legs and crippled for life, or suffering hideously disfiguring burns.

But many, maybe most, of the five million or so Britons who were under arms in 1945 had other prices to pay. For all of them, the war had disrupted their lives—some would find it hard to return to the drab drudgery of civilian life after the excitement of war, while others, like Bain, had spent years confined in an institution that they found crushingly brutal, unsympathetic, and inhuman. Many had seen death at close quarters in ways that would haunt them for the rest of their lives; many, again like Bain, had crouched in terror under artillery bombardments or heard bullets whine past their heads, expecting with a horrible certainty that the next one, the one that they did not hear, would kill them. Their bodies might be scarred and battered, or they might have escaped without visible wounds, but their minds, their personalities, their souls, were damaged in ways the doctors could not see.

The figures for deaths and physical injuries in a war that lasted six years and engulfed the whole world are necessarily approximations and best guesses, but there can be no figures at all for the secret, invisible mental scars that these former combatants bore. The war cast a long, black shadow: the various traumas suffered by those who fought would break out in the years to come in drunkenness, depression, loneliness, and violence. Wives would find their husbands changed—silent, brooding, bitter, and moody, sometimes forever. Young men would find that the world they remembered from the innocent years before the war had become a greyer, grimmer, more sombre place. They were the walking wounded who would straggle through Vernon Scannell's dreams.

For many, it would be several years before these insidious effects of their time under arms would begin to become apparent. John Bain was among them: his stiff and painful ankle would prove to be the least of his problems.

7

On the Run

'I drink to forget.'
But he remembers everything, the lot:
What hell war was,
Betrayal, lost
Causes best forgot.

'Six Reasons for Drinking', from *The Winter Man* (1973)

I

Mid-May 1945, and in a capital city that still could not quite believe that the war with Germany was over, two men faced each other warily, suspiciously, at the door of a flat in an impressive Victorian block called Sinclair Mansions in Shepherd's Bush, West London. Each of them had his own long-running battle with authority that was still going on, surrender or no surrender, and each wanted to be sure that the other was not one of the enemy.

The man who had just opened the door to the flat was short and stocky, with pale and unwelcoming eyes. He wore a loose-fitting checked woollen shirt and old corduroy trousers, and he looked narrowly at the tall, hungry-looking figure in front of him in his all-enveloping army greatcoat. The new arrival was thin and drawn, but he had the air of a man who was used to getting his own way, and even under the greatcoat it was clear that he had big, muscular shoulders. Not a man to tangle with. There was a long silence; the stranger had just asked who lived there, and the man at the door seemed to be deciding whether to reply.

There was a sudden movement behind him and a young, pretty, fair-haired girl aged about eighteen appeared at his shoulder, peering curiously out at the stranger. 'Vernon!' she exclaimed.[1]

II

John Bain—still Vernon to his family—had made his way to Shepherd's Bush after being dropped off in Cricklewood, North London, by a lorry driver who had given him a lift. He had persuaded his mother to give him the address of the flat in London where his sister Sylvia was staying, but she had said nothing about anyone else living there. He had learned to trust no one when he was on the run. Sylvia's boyfriend Cliff Holden, for his part, had spent the last six years dodging the police as a conscientious objector who had refused meekly to follow the orders of the magistrate and find himself a job in food production on a farm. He was always waiting for the knock on the door or the tap on his shoulder that might announce his arrest.

But once Sylvia had explained who he was and John had told the story of his latest desertion, all the tension between the two men drained away, and he was invited in to join them in a meal. There were two others in the flat—a slight, bearded young man called Peter Ball who was, like Holden, an avowed anarchist, conscientious objector, and fugitive, and a dark-haired young French girl called Yvonne who was, unknown to Vernon, the daughter of one of General de Gaulle's senior aides. It was the sort of raffish, Bohemian environment that Bain loved—the two men were supporting themselves in a succession of doubtfully legal odd jobs and occasional stints as artists' models, while keeping half a step ahead of the police.

This latest escape from the army could have been just another one in Bain's long series of desertions, to end with an ignominious return to the convalescent depot, another brief appearance in front of an increasingly exasperated commanding officer, and another spell in the guard-house—but in Cliff and Peter he had found two people who were more than willing to keep him out of the hands of the police, and who had the skills and contacts to do so.

Holden was a talented artist—he went on to be a founder member of the Borough Group, and exhibit at the Tate, the Whitworth Gallery, and various other galleries and museums in England, Scotland, and Sweden—but, more importantly for Bain at the time, he was well practised as a fugitive. Throughout the war he had produced an underground newspaper, *War Commentary*, and occasionally been the subject of articles in the press about a mystery man who led a shady secret organization. 'That was quite silly because it wasn't any secret at all. We published pamphlets against the war with names and addresses and telephone numbers', he says now:

> It was rather easy on the run because we had a number of safe houses all over the country that the police didn't know about, and you just moved from one safe house to another and managed to avoid them. I was on the run all through the war, and only landed in jail for two or three days. And even then I was bailed out by the Independent Labour party.[2]

When Bain had deserted before, he had generally stayed in uniform, doing his best to avoid the police but simply relying on being taken for a soldier on leave. This time, Holden told him, it was going to be different. 'I helped him desert. Of course, the war was over, so he wasn't running away from anything except the dehumanising effect the army was having on him', he says. 'He was very depressed at the time, but Sylvia brought him in and we made a meal, and then I took his uniform off and we sat in the sitting room and burned it in the grate. We got him some civilian clothes.'

Holden gave him an old dark-blue shirt, while Ball dug out a down-at-heel pair of sandals. Since Bain was so much taller than either of them, he had to give some cash to Sylvia to go out and buy him a pair of heavy, workmanlike corduroy trousers. Not dapper or fashionable, perhaps, but few people on the streets of London in the months after the end of the war looked dapper or fashionable. Now he looked less like a wandering soldier, and more like one of thousands of battered civilians trying to make ends meet. And Holden had an even more important gift for him—one, as it turned out, that would last him for the rest of his life.

> I had a friend—well, not exactly a friend, but I knew him quite well—who ran a brothel. He was able to get a lot of identity papers, which was very useful during the war. So we got Vernon a new name—I don't know whether the papers came from a dead man or whether they'd been stolen from a client at the brothel, but they were in the name of Vernon Scannell.

So John Bain and Vernon Bain were both consigned to history. John, or Johnny, would emerge a few times over the next few years as the name of a professional boxer, as a shamefaced prisoner in the dock, and once, bizarrely, as the winner of a BBC poetry competition—but from this moment on the tall, thin, oddly-dressed figure standing by the cold ashes of his army uniform in the grate would be known as Vernon Scannell. That would be the name he would give to his children, the name that would appear on his books, the name that would finally appear in his obituaries, and the name that is carved today on his memorial in a little Dorset churchyard. By taking it, he was not only seeking to avoid capture—he was cutting himself off from his past, from the bullying father who bore his old name, from the marriage on which he had turned his back, and from all the miseries that John Bain had suffered as a soldier.

He was starting a new life.

III

Holden—'a nice little chap but tends to be over-earnest about things in general and himself in particular', according to Scannell some years later[3]—was a widely read and dedicated anarchist. He could, and would, quote constantly from leading Russian figures in the anarchist pantheon such as Peter Kropotkin and Mikhail Bakunin, or present the modernist, Marxist, and anarchist views of the English critic and theorist Herbert Read. Peter Ball was less committed politically—'an odd character, very negative in many ways, very critical about everything', Holden says—but was an avid and discriminating reader.[4]

During his five years in the army, Vernon Scannell, as he now was, had barely read a book. In hospital, he had found it impossible; his mind, he was beginning to feel, was closing down almost before it had fully opened up. But as he wandered around the flat, he found novels, volumes of poetry, and plays in abundance, and he had the time, the inclination, and the ability to immerse himself in them. His new life was beginning in more ways than one:

> Those earlier weeks are still bright in the memory with unfailing sunlight, the sense of liberation that was spiced by danger, the comfort of companionships that were not imposed by necessity...I listened to music and nosed among the books that were scattered around the Shepherd's Bush flat. My reading was desultory but luxurious: a sip of Rilke, a large bite of Kafka, a bender on Baudelaire, a jig with MacNeice and banquets with Yeats and Auden. I was not getting down to the systematic reading I knew I needed but I was, as it were, limbering up and getting a lot of pleasure from it. They were good days, or they seem to have been.[5]

And he was not only reading—for the first time since his childhood, apart from the few rough notes and ideas he used to scribble down on scraps of paper as he marched through the North African desert, he was writing too. As far as we know, none of these early efforts has survived, although one or two might have formed the basis of poems which later appeared in *Graves and Resurrections*, the collection that he published in 1948, and which he later disowned as 'woolly and wordy' and a 'grave embarrassment' whenever poems from it turned up in anthologies.[6] Holden remembers that he would write these early poems secretly and then leave them to be found:

> While he was with us, Vernon started writing poems on slips of paper, and just leaving them around the kitchen. It was as if he didn't dare show them to us, so he just left them around. Neither of us took them very seriously—we read them, but we didn't talk about them, because he was obviously nervous about criticism.[7]

After a couple of weeks, Holden found Vernon a job with a friend of his who manufactured dolls' heads in a shed in Leake Street, Soho. Their memories differ over the details—Holden recalls him as 'a Hungarian, with pretensions to being an artist', Scannell in *The Tiger and the Rose* as 'Pat, an ex merchant seaman'—but whatever his name, he was clearly part of the fly-by-night, underground economy that thrived in wartime London. The two men were paid half a crown an hour[8] to boil up a foul-smelling rubber mix on a small stove, pour it into moulds, and then dust down and smooth off the finished heads. They were paid, of course, in cash, with no questions, no tax, and no papers: it was not much, but it was enough for Vernon to move out of the Shepherd's Bush flat and find himself a room of his own in Chalk Farm until the dolls' head business went bust. Then, with no money to pay the rent, Vernon did a moonlight flit. The owner of the business, who had become a friend of Vernon's as people tended to, gave him and Cliff a couple of hundred dolls' heads each in lieu of the money they were owed, and put him up rent-free in his own house in Hampstead for a few weeks.

The job in the dolls' head factory had been not just a welcome source of income, not just a reintroduction to the shady world of under-the-counter work outside the army—it was also a reminder of the joys of Soho, which Vernon had first sampled with Kenneth when the two brothers had run off to London with the Old Man's money, all those years ago. There were slightly more elevated pastimes—he remembered fondly, years later, trips to the Promenade concerts at the Royal Albert Hall to hear Vaughan Williams's 5th Symphony and Grieg's Piano Concerto[9]—but it was the pubs of Soho and Fitzrovia that defined his life. He became a regular—or as much of a regular as his limited funds would allow—at The Wheatsheaf, the Fitzroy Tavern, and others he would remember as 'the pubs in Soho where the poets met'.[10]

They were slightly seedy, beery haunts—Holden took him to the Fitzroy Tavern, for instance, at the corner of Charlotte Street and Windmill Street, where the flags of the allies hung from the ceiling, and the sawdust-strewn floorboards were sticky with spilt beer, and thick with yellowed and discarded Woodbine fag-ends. On the walls were old cap badges and flags from the First World War, but the bar was usually too gloomy for anyone to look at them. The elderly painter Augustus John, grey-haired by now, but still leering lasciviously at young women at the bar from under saggy eyelids, used to claim that, like Clapham Junction or Piccadilly, The Fitz was a place that everyone passed through sometime in their lives. Or, in contrast, there were the two small bars of The Wheatsheaf, brightly lit but thick with the cloying smell of stale sweat hanging in the air. There was an odd reddish tinge to the light because of the heavy stained glass windows; incongruously, squares of tartan decorated the walls, to mark the Scottish background of the pub's owners, the brewers William Younger. The Wheatsheaf was a particular favourite of Vernon's, because it sold the same strong Younger's Scotch Ale that he had drunk in Aylesbury—one of the few happy memories he had from his time there.

Then there were the others—The George near the BBC's Broadcasting House, or the nearby Stag's Head, another Younger's pub, where Louis Macneice had his regular chair in the corner, and where frequent visitors included the writers Laurie Lee, Henry Reed, the argumentative and quarrelsome Roy Campbell, and, either roaring or sitting morosely alone, Dylan Thomas. There was the Yorkshire Grey, better known for reasons no one could remember as the Whore's Lament, or the busy, chattering Marquis of Granby, famed for its clientele of guardsmen, men in anonymous raincoats, and flamboyant homosexuals, and for the sudden punch-ups that would flare up if one of them made a play for the wrong person. Huddled in among them was the 91 in Charlotte Street, a sleazy dive referred to as Tony's Café but run by a Maltese immigrant called George, whose face was disfigured by razor scars but who had the reassuring reputation of a kindly family man. He served tea, coffee, and food to a clientele that included at various times Macneice, Dylan Thomas, Lucian Freud, and the composer Elisabeth Lutyens, alongside Soho's usual shifting cast of villains, spivs, and prostitutes. It was in the 91 that, twenty years or so later, the writer Jeffrey Bernard would unwisely challenge Scannell to put up his fists, only to end up sprawled unconscious on the floor amid a tangle of upset chairs and tables. And then in Dean Street was the York Minster, which everyone called the French pub because of its landlord, the elegant and extravagantly mous-tachioed Victor Berlemont, where only five years earlier Charles de Gaulle had prepared his famous BBC address calling on his countrymen to join the Resistance, and where drunks would be thrown out with such disarming Gallic charm that they never realized they had left until they were outside on the street.[11]

These, rather than the down-at-heel bedsits where he laid his head, were the places Scannell called home. Pubs, he said later, were useful for poets. 'I've always found them fascinating places. You meet a lot of interesting people, and you overhear things that do seem to be useful to a writer.'[12]

A chance meeting in one of these Soho bars led to a brief, undistin-guished, and entirely unqualified stint as a grandly titled Assistant Electrician at the London Coliseum, where he was paid £4 a week[13] to manage a spot-light, until a combination of inattention and incompetence resulted in a series of disasters as the star of the show reached the climax of his act. Vernon fled, without waiting to be sacked.

For a while, he moved back in with Cliff Holden, who had split up from Sylvia and moved into another flat in a cul-de-sac in Notting Hill Gate. The two men had become firm friends—a friendship, says Holden, that survived even the travails of poverty:

> I remember we had a barrel of fish that we got somehow at Petticoat Lane street market one Sunday morning. It was raw fish, a very Swedish idea. We would eat some of that, and then go out for a pint, and maybe fool around with some boxing when we got back. Once I slipped, and hit him harder than I meant to, and broke a couple of his ribs, which gave him a bit of pain for a fortnight.[14]

It was a scrappy, hand-to-mouth existence, but the possibility of arrest never stopped the two friends from going drinking together or searching for women. Cliff would often leave the flat by climbing out of an upstairs win-dow and making his way over the rooftops into the next block, avoiding a policeman who was watching for him outside. Even though the police seemed to take little interest in Vernon, it was courting disaster for a man on the run to live with someone who was being so actively sought, so it was a considerable relief when he eventually moved in with a young blue-eyed blonde woman called Jackie, whom he met in The Wheatsheaf.

Jackie lived, Scannell says[15], in a flat in Monmouth Street which had no bathroom, but was conveniently close to the Holborn Public Baths. She

shared it with a Singhalese short-story writer and a frustrated Welsh intellectual with a stammer, two characters who sound like classic figures from
the Soho *demimonde*. Jackie—according to Holden—is merely a single representative of a number of women on whom Scannell relied as he struggled
to get through these difficult months on the run. Holden says:

> There were various girls. Vernon was tall and handsome, and he was very suc-
> cessful at living with women. He would find one who had a good job, and
> then he would make her happy for a while. When there were troubles with
> his girlfriends, he would change them.[16]

It was Jackie's idea, as summer slowly turned to autumn, to collect the dolls'
heads which the owner of the bankrupt business was still looking after for
Vernon. She made bodies and dresses for a couple of dozen of them, and
together they hawked them around the pubs of Soho at 12s. 6d. a time.[17]
With a chronic lack of toys in the shops, they were quickly snapped up.

Then there was another venture with Cliff Holden, who had an Indian
friend who had been manufacturing perfume at home. He supplied several
gallons of it, along with a large number of tiny scent bottles, and Scannell
joined him one Saturday afternoon decanting it into the bottles and selling
it at Walthamstow Market. Again, they were helped by the post-war short-
ages. Vernon describes it as 'terrible stuff',[18] but Holden is more upbeat. 'It
was genuine perfume. There was nothing artificial about it', he remembers,
'but the only trouble was that we couldn't get the smell off us. It was very
embarrassing if you got on a bus.'

But occasional money-making ventures like that were not enough, even
though Jackie was happily paying the rent, and supplementing their meagre
income with an occasional few pounds that she would filch from the hand-
bag of an elderly relative whom she sometimes went to visit in St John's
Wood.[19] It was a daily struggle to make ends meet. Vernon was wearing old
clothes that had been given to him by his former employer in the dolls' head
business; often, long evening hours were spent sitting outside the Fitzroy
Tavern, The Wheatsheaf, or the other pubs in Soho, without the money to
venture inside but smelling the familiar, fuggy, and enticing mixture of beer
fumes and tobacco smoke, and listening longingly to the music of the piano
drifting out through the open door.

One night, having scraped together enough for a couple of half-pints of
beer, they were sitting inside one of the pubs when Scannell idly picked up
a copy of *Boxing News* magazine that was lying on the bar. It was more than

seven years since he had put the gloves on for a properly set up boxing bout—the few contests he had fought while in the army had been little more than organized punch-ups, against opponents who had much more heart than artistry. However, the paper brought the old excitement he had felt in the ring so long ago flooding back. In it, he found a classified advertisement from a retired heavyweight called Wally Dakin inviting boxers and managers to contact him about a series of professional boxing matches he was planning.

The next morning, he walked to Bill Klein's gym in Fitzroy Square looking for Dakin. As soon as he walked in, the smell of massage oil, the patter and squeak of boxing boots on the wooden floor, the slap of a skipping rope and the rapid staccato of blows hitting the punch bag took him straight back to the nights in Aylesbury's Castle Street Hall. Once more he felt the thrill of anticipation, the tension in his stomach, and the tiny worm of fear. Bill Klein had seen a lot of ambitious amateurs, and wasn't particularly impressed—but he told him how to find Wally Dakin's house nearby.

The ex-boxer, too, was sceptical at first. He quizzed Scannell about his record—'Finalist in the British Schoolboys' Championships, North West Divisional Junior Champion. The war stopped me going in for the Senior ABA's'[20]—and asked a few questions about individual fighters he had faced. The answers seemed to satisfy him, and they arranged that Scannell would come back to the gym that evening for a trial session. If Dakin thought he had the makings of a professional boxer, he would sign him up.

As he set off home back to Jackie's flat to borrow the money to buy his kit—the Singhalese short-story writer had just sold a story to the BBC, so could be touched for a couple of pounds—there was a new, confident spring in Scannell's step that had been missing for months. If the dozen or so bouts in the army had been less than testing for him as a boxer, the hard physical lifestyle had turned him from an ambitious young boy into a hardened fighter. He had, he noted later, 'developed a right hand punch that would knock a man cold'.[21] The rough, boorish, macho aspects of army life that he hated were the very things that had toughened him, given him a streak of recklessness, and made him a ruthless opponent in the ring:

It was not until I joined the army that I became a really formidable boxer. The rigorous discipline, unaccustomed exercise, route marches, PT, solid food and general animalism of the life strengthened and brutalised me. Exiled from the life of the mind and spirit, dressed in the anonymous and ugly uniform, surrounded by the instruments of pain and death, and forced into close and inescapable intimacy with the stupid, the vicious and profane, I made myself, or allowed myself to become, also, stupid, vicious and profane.[22]

But this, he told himself, was no time for the life of the mind and spirit. That could come later: right now, he needed money, and this was a way that he could get it. Stupid, vicious, and profane would do very well for a while.

But as he walked back, rather more slowly, towards Bill Klein's gym that night, carrying his bag with the cheapest boxing boots he could find, the embarrassingly crisp, new shorts, and the home made gutta-percha mouth guard, the bravado was steadily leaking away. He could feel his lack of boxing experience over the past few years in every step he took; his timing would be off, and his stamina would let him down. Lack of food had stopped him putting on weight, but there was still a pudgy slackness around his waist that would tell any half-fit opponent that here was a boxer ready for the taking.

Even so, once he was stripped ready for the ring, Dakin looked him up and down like a horse dealer and seemed satisfied. After Scannell had gone a couple of trial rounds with a wild-eyed, flailing, hard-hitting Irish opponent, he agreed to put him up for his first professional bout. Inexplicably, he was boxing under his real name of Johnny Bain—the name the army knew him by, the name that would be on the military police list of absconders. As it turned out, he was right in his assumption that there were unlikely to be any inquisitive redcaps watching the undercard at Ipswich for his first bout, or at Lime Grove Baths in London or Watford Town Hall where he also fought during the next few weeks—but it was an odd decision for a man on the run. He had three six-round fights and won them all—the first one by a knock-out—and he found that his fitness and timing improved with each training session and each bout. More importantly, perhaps, he made himself £5 a time,[23] less 10 per cent for his Boxing Board of Control licence.

Dakin was ready to take the next step up and put him in for an eight-round contest in Ipswich. It seemed, briefly, as though he might have found at least a temporary answer to his money problems—but then came a meeting that would end both his professional boxing career and his relationship with Jackie, take him out of London, bring him as close as he ever got to a university education, and, eventually, get him into a great deal of trouble.

IV

In his memoirs, Scannell describes how he met a male medical student from Leeds by chance one night in the Fitzroy Tavern in Soho. Unusually, he does not give him a name, but this obliging new friend, in London to take his exams, was horrified to hear from a drunk and garrulous Scannell that he was on the run from the military police. He warned him anxiously that London was a dangerous place for deserters. Occasional raids on bars and cafés led to anyone of military age having their papers checked; it was only a matter of time before he would be picked up and marched back to the glass-house—this time, for an even longer stretch. Why did he not come north to Leeds, where he would be safer, the cost of living would be lower, and he would not only be able to find some kind of a job, but would also have the chance to concentrate on the writing career he was still talking about?

That's Scannell's version, and it all has the ring of truth—except that the 'male medical student' who is described as taking such an active interest in his welfare was actually a slim, petite, and strikingly attractive young *female* medical student with flashing dark brown eyes, a strangely intense manner, and a thick tumble of coppery auburn curls that fell in luxuriously thick waves around her face. Her name was Estella, or Ella, Cope. It was entirely in character that she should want to help Scannell avoid the police: when she was still at school, she had got into trouble for raising money for the International Brigade in the Spanish Civil War, and she had no doubt about whose side she was on in any confrontation between an individual and the military.[24] And of course, Scannell was tall, good-looking, and irresistibly romantic: as Cliff Holden says, he was good with women, and he had just found another.[25] In *The Tiger and the Rose*, Scannell says that he discussed with Jackie the possibility that she might come to Leeds with him, which seems unlikely—but in any case, he says, that relationship had run its course:

> I knew that I was living with Jackie under false pretences. I liked her well enough but I certainly did not love her, nor did I even find her physically attractive, so our relationship was a demoralizing one. She cried for a while when I said I was definitely going, but then she cheered up and said, 'You'll be back inside three weeks. But don't be surprised if I've got another boy-friend by then.'[26]

True or not, it's an account of Scannell's ideal for ending a relationship—with him in control, no guilt, and no final goodbye. But if Jackie really thought he would be coming back, she was mistaken. He never saw her again and when, many years later, a friend told him casually in a Soho pub that she had died, he could barely remember what she looked like.[27]

The Tiger and the Rose describes Scannell's arrival in Leeds on a damp wintry day. He ate a traditional Yorkshire fish and chip supper, and settled down in his new friend's room, 'shivering on his floor under a thin blanket and a couple of coats'. In view of later developments, it seems highly unlikely that his first night in Leeds with Ella was spent quite so chastely. In the book, he says that 'the medical student, on his own ground and busy with his work and friends with their specialised interests, quickly lost interest in me and my circumstances', but in fact, shortly after he arrived in Leeds, Ella told him that she was pregnant.

Far from losing interest, she was madly in love with Scannell—but now she was in tears, distraught; pregnancy would mean the end of her studies, she said, and her parents would be furious. Scannell's response was immediate, generous, unrealistic, and completely thoughtless. They would have to get married, he told her, and on Saturday, 12 January 1946, at Leeds Register Office, that is what they did. Ella's parents, a successful Leeds timber merchant and his wife, were aghast at the idea that she should marry such an obviously unsuitable person—some of Vernon's friends said later they had even offered him money to stay away from her—but Vernon had made up his mind, and Ella was eager to become Mrs Scannell. Vernon had done much the same six years earlier, of course, when he married the pregnant Barbara in Aylesbury—but the difference this time around was that, standing in front of the Registrar in Leeds, he was committing a serious offence. In marrying Ella, he was committing bigamy.

There were other differences too: just one day after the ceremony in Aylesbury, Barbara had gone back to her parents' house with her baby son, her marriage no sooner started than it was over, but Ella and Vernon's wedding was the start of a brief but intense and passionate relationship. In one of his last poems, 'Missing Things', one of the memories the dying Scannell calls to mind is 'Black Leeds, where I was taught love's alphabet', and although he had already enjoyed several preliminary lessons under the canal bridge in Aylesbury and slightly more advanced tuition in various London bedrooms, it was Ella in Leeds who did most of the teaching. The two became known as a couple around the university and in the pubs and bars where the students met. Years later, contemporaries asked Scannell's friends what had happened to 'that pretty student that Vernon was always with'.[28]

Even before her sudden and scandalous marriage, Ella had fallen out with her well-off parents who, she felt, had pushed her against her will into the medical studies that she loathed—indeed, one of Vernon's attractions might have been that he seemed to offer her a way out of their influence. The two newly-weds lived a hand-to-mouth bohemian existence in a little flat in the Leeds suburb of Oakwood, Ella slipping back to her parents' home occasionally to steal food from their pantry—Vernon's lack of a ration book with which to buy food was an inconvenience, but not a serious problem. None of this, of course, features in any of Scannell's memoirs or personal writings about Leeds: whether he found it hard to come to terms with when he came to look back on his life, or was ashamed of the way he had behaved, or worried about upsetting Ella by publishing the story, he later wrote her ruthlessly out of his life—but at the time, he took full advantage of the connections she had to offer.

With a few vague assurances about an entirely imaginary London University degree, he found himself one or two pupils for coaching in English, history and—desperately keeping one lesson ahead in Teach Yourself primers—French, Latin, and even mathematics. He was, he said later, preparing them 'for examinations I had never even heard of'.[29] The ten shillings[30] an hour he was paid was not much, but it might almost have begun to seem like the start of a new, settled phase of his life. With luck—particularly if he could manoeuvre Ella and her parents into some sort of reconciliation—he might even have been able to provide a home for the new baby.[31]

Except that there was no baby. Two or three months after their marriage, Ella came home one day with the news that she had been running for a bus, and the strain had been too much for her. She had lost the baby. It was a sketchy, unconvincing story, but Vernon—as naïve and ignorant as most men in those days about pregnancy and 'women's issues'—believed it implicitly, at least at first. It was only later as he began to feel trapped in the marriage, that he started to wonder whether he had been tricked into it all along.

It is impossible to say exactly when or how the relationship began to unravel. Undoubtedly Vernon's doubts about how Ella had behaved played a part in it, but probably the initial testosterone-fuelled rush of excitement was fading anyway. At that time of his life, certainly, he was not a man for long relationships: by the end of the year, he was living on his own in a flat in the seedy Chapeltown district of the city:

> An attic in a tower above a street
> Where shifty mongrels cock suspicious eyes
> And nonchalant legs, and prowling cats investigate
> The trash in gutters and front garden bins.[32]

It was a grim little garret in the same building as the headquarters of the North Leeds Communist Party, high under a steepled roof through which the rain dripped down the walls. It cost him 7s. 6d. a week;[33] there was no bathroom, and the only toilet and wash basin were down a flight of stairs. Thirty-five years later, still living in a rented flat in Leeds, he would look back on it all—'that little attic in Francis Street, the rudimentary furniture, a table, a couple of chairs, the tiny electric fire which had to be turned on its back to be used as a cooker, the ramshackle bed'.[34] The winter was cold, damp, and hungry, and whatever hopes he might once have had for the relationship with Ella were dead.

Certainly the couple kept in touch—Scannell had an amazing capacity for 'leaving without leaving', for retaining a claim on the affections of the women from whom he walked away. The loyalty, affection, even love that his friends, family, and former lovers continued to feel for him bear witness to the strength of the emotions he inspired—but there could also be something slightly threatening about this emotional possessiveness. For Ella's twenty-fifth birthday in late December, he wrote her a strange, cold-eyed poem[35]—addressed to her, significantly, in the initials of her unmarried name—imagining her life as a book whose twenty-fifth page was just turning:

> Stained with dim ghosts of fallen tears
> Shed for your Autumn whose death was a symbol
> Of something
> Elusive, something suffering…

So far, perhaps, so conventional and sentimental. But the poem asks who will write upon that page, and then gives the answer:

> I bring you a birthday gift of knowledge:
> No anonymous author will fill this page.
> Take courage my darling, accept me ever,
> Your permanent collaborator.

There is something impenetrable and sinister in that final word, 'collaborator', particularly when written so soon after the end of the war—a sense of

shared guilt, as well as the more obvious literary collaboration. But the overall meaning of the lines is clear enough: no one else is going to take my
place. Ever. Many of the various women who shared Vernon Scannell's life
would recognize that sentiment.

V

However, Vernon was involved in a new love affair, which was growing into
one of the most permanent attachments of his life. He was gradually falling
in love with Leeds and the north of England. He would betray that passion,
too, several times in his life, and flirt with Surrey, Dorset, South Wales, and
London, but Yorkshire was the love to which he would always return.

It had not started well. When he first arrived among the soot-blackened
Victorian buildings, he had hated the place:

> The air was polluted not simply by industrial dirt but by a drab melancholy
> that the town seemed to breathe out. I felt that I had made a journey not in
> space but back through time to the period of the General Strike. I had not
> known that such slums existed any more. It seemed that all human aspirations
> must wither in this dark air and in this cold earth. The voices seemed harshly
> alien, not hostile perhaps but excluding.[36]

But gradually, encouraged by his reading of W. H. Auden's poetry of unlikely
urban beauty, he began to develop an affection for Leeds, its spark-spitting
trams, its ubiquitous fish and chip shops, and the solid confidence of its civic
buildings. Even the down-at-heel slums of the inappropriately named Belle
Isle district of the inner city would later inspire a poetic tribute to their

> small, warm, certain
> Houses huddling, cuddling
> Together defying
> The too real terrors of the night.[37]

For the rest of his life, he looked back on Leeds as the place where his creative life began. Some eighteen years after his first arrival, when he had lived
in Leeds, left, and then returned again to stay, he wrote:

> I think of Leeds with affection because, in a sense, I was born there, or I
> should say, re-born there, for I never saw the place until 1945 when I was
> twenty-three years old.[38]

In particular, Scannell loved the shadowy, comforting warmth of the Leeds pubs: even though he was short of money, he always managed to afford a drink. Gregarious and sociable as he was, he had rapidly made friends of his own in city-centre bars such as *The Pack Horse*, *Whitelocks*, or *The Victoria*, first with Ella's fellow students and then with the other university figures, journalists, and artists who drank there. There was Jacob Kramer for instance, a leading expressionist artist in his day, but now a pale shadow of his former self, drinking heavily and telling stories of his friendships with Augustus John, Wyndham Lewis, and David Bomberg. By the time Scannell knew him, he was dreaming beerily of the past and sketching out on the bar plans for ambitious new paintings that would never see the light of day.

> He would take a drop of beer and slop it on the bar and say 'I've got this marvellous idea for a painting—a wonderful landscape. You can see this great range of hills here, and the way the river moves and shapes here, and echoes and rhymes with these shapes.' He'd go on like this, and you knew this marvelous vision, this painting, would never go further than that bar and would be mopped up in seconds.[39]

In *The Pack Horse*, close by the offices of the *Yorkshire Post* newspaper and its sister title, the *Evening Post*, he would drink with the poet and journalist R. C. Scriven, universally known as Ratz, who would peer short-sightedly around the bar, bringing his glass up to an inch or two from his nose to see if it was empty. Within a few years, Ratz would be carrying a white stick, both deaf and blind. 'He was a very strange little man—a gifted poet', Scannell recalled later:

> When I knew him, he was art critic for the Yorkshire Observer. Even then, he couldn't see very well. He must have been the only blind art critic in the business.[40]

There was Kenneth Severs, then a PhD student, and in time a leading figure in the BBC, who was his real entrée to the English Department at the University. Through him, Scannell met the poet and critic Wilfred Childe, who lectured at Leeds; the Shakespearean scholar George Wilson Knight; and the University Professor of English, Bonamy Dobrée—'almost a parody of the dandy and the scholar, in whose company I always felt uncouth and clumsy, but a fine teacher who cared deeply both for his subject and for those of his students in whom he might glimpse a reflection of his passion for the literature of the eighteenth century'.[41] With Childe, he talked about John Short's poem, 'Carol', which he had read during his early army days, and he was delighted when Childe responded a few days later by giving him a copy of the poet's recently published collection, *The Oak and the Ash*. It was a gift that he treasured:[42] he still knew nothing about Short himself, but the new poems fed his love for the poetry and his curiosity about the poet.

However, not all the people he met through his university friends were agreeable. In Whitelock's, for example, there was the soon-to-be-angry young man John Braine, whom he got to know through Wilfred Childe, and whose successful novel *Room at the Top* was still ten years away. Scannell remembered him later as 'a desperately insecure, pushy mixture of aggression and sycophancy'.[43] Another was Robin Skelton, who later became the well-known author or editor of over a hundred novels, anthologies, and books of poetry, criticism, and witchcraft. He, Scannell said dismissively, was 'a rather dirty and very opinionated and thick-skinned youth' who 'used to follow me around like a terrier'.[44]

VI

Bonamy Dobrée's dapper vanity, incongruous in post-war Leeds, is witnessed by the Indian writer Mulk Raj Anand, who described him as 'obviously of independent means. He dressed in suits made in Savile Row, and had a finely trimmed brown beard, which made him look like the younger brother of George V.'[45] His kindness, generosity, and open-heartedness were not in doubt, particularly towards people who wanted to learn, and he could see that Vernon was one of those. Through Ella, though never officially a member of the university, he had begun to meet people who would change his life.

The first time he met Dobrée, he hid his feelings of inadequacy behind a veneer of brash self-confidence, listing the novels and poetry he had devoured during his first months in Leeds. 'Have you read a lot?' Dobrée asked him.

'Yes', replied Vernon, desperate to impress his new friend.

'You know, it's a rather frustrating thing,' said Dobrée gently, 'but I find that the more you read, the more you realize how little you've read.'[46] It was the mildest of rebukes from a university professor of English to a blustering and slightly nervous young man. Dobrée could see that, despite his lack of formal education, here was someone with a genuine passion for literature that should be encouraged.

Through his influence, Vernon became first a frequent visitor and then an unofficial student at Leeds University, with no formal standing but with an open invitation to attend lectures in the English Department. Within weeks, he was accepted as a guest in Wilson Knight's tutorial groups. It was the company and conversation that he relished as much as the lectures and tutorials: Severs, he said was 'incomparably better read than I was, and his tastes were more sophisticated',[47] and in Childe, Dobrée, and Wilson Knight he had found three academics who were more than ready to give their time to support his studies.

From a severely practical point of view, bearing in mind that the Francis Street attic had no bathroom, he was able to take baths and showers in the university gym. He also began to box again, representing the university and winning the Northern Universities Championships at welter, middle, and cruiserweight—conveniently forgetting that his flirtation with a professional career had rendered him ineligible to box as an amateur. Boxing in other amateur competitions in Huddersfield, Bradford, and other towns around the north of England brought him silver cups and canteens of cutlery as prizes which he was able to sell to make a few extra pounds.

Scannell had also discovered the Leeds City Library, and he was spending increasing amounts of time there, either taking advantage of the free warmth and shelter in the reading room, or carrying home armfuls of books to Chapeltown. Money was still tight, and he was eating cheap toad-in-the-hole or shepherd's pie in the British Restaurant at the Town Hall, where no one asked for ration coupons—but he still found enough from his earnings as a tutor and his occasional boxing prizes for frequent visits to second-hand bookshops. This was when his reading became serious, purposeful, and directed:

> There are still books on my shelves that I acquired in Leeds: the Home University Library anthology of sixteenth and seventeenth century poetry in which I first enjoyed Henry King, Marvell, Herbert and Donne; a 1943 edition of Matthew Arnold's Poems of Wordsworth, picked up secondhand for two shillings; the Faber Selected Poems of Auden and the Collected Poems of Edward Thomas. And it was then, in early 1946, that I first read the novels of Dostoievsky, Hardy and Melville. Somehow I stumbled across Djuna Barnes's *Nightwood* and William Faulkner's *The Sound and the Fury,* heady stuff on an empty stomach. By the same blind luck I found in the public library I.A. Richards's *Principles of Literary Criticism* and was led on to Coleridge, Hopkins, Eliot and Yeats. Again by chance, I found Hart Crane's poems and was dazzled, bewildered and excited by them ... Life was charged with wonder and danger and promise.[48]

But the most important development of this time in Leeds was that Scannell started to write seriously, and to send his work off to magazines such as the left-leaning *Tribune*, where probably the first of his published poems appeared. 'One Who Died', in the magazine for 25 October 1946, is a strangely angry and over-excited poem for a 24-year-old poet to have written, about the indignity of ageing:

> the flesh decaying;
> The bones grown brittle in anticipation
> Of the ultimate disintegration.[49]

Other poems appeared in the Chicago-based *Poetry* ('Love Among the Tumblers', July 1947) and *Adelphi* ('Belle Isle', January–March 1948). At last, he was a published poet. Working through the bitter winter of 1946 in the cold and damp of the attic flat, he produced thirty-six poems that would eventually be published two years later, along with these three, as his first book of poetry, *Graves and Resurrections*. He said later that all the poems in this volume were written in the Francis Street flat, although it is possible that some—particularly most of those written for Ella—date from his earlier time at Oakwood. He had written a few bits of poetry as a child, of course, and there had been the odd scraps that Cliff Holden remembered finding around the kitchen of the Shepherds Bush flat, but this was the first time he had written with the intention of seeing his work in print.

Vernon's life was starting again: there was a slightly unreal feeling about everything he did, with the shadow of possible arrest hanging over him, but at times it seemed as if the five years of misery he had endured in the army might now be firmly behind him. In January of 1947, the government announced a 'period of leniency' for the thousands of deserters like him who had refused to wait to be demobbed by the army. Perhaps, he must have wondered, there really might be a future for him.

And then, one Sunday afternoon, he was sitting alone in the flat reading *Crime and Punishment* when there was a clattering rush of heavy footsteps on the stairs outside and the door crashed open. Two men charged in and dragged him to his feet.

'All right', one of them said. 'We're police officers. We know all about you.' Scannell's two years on the run had come to a sudden and brutal end.

8

Court Martial Again

I pray
Into the unresponsive dark that they,
My better, braver, comrades will forgive
Not just this unheroic urge to live
(Small doubt of that) but chiefly this regret
That I must bear the burden and the boon
Of living on beyond their brief forenoon.
I think that they would wish me to rejoice
Without regret and would approve my choice
Of opting for old age in civvy street.
I hope that's so.

'Compulsory Mourning', from *Of Love and War* (2002)

I

There was no point in lying. Back at the Central Police Station, Vernon admitted that his name was John Bain, and that he was a deserter from the Gordon Highlanders. They knew that already, but the questioning continued: deserters, having no identity papers that would enable them to get legal jobs, were often forced into the world of crime, and the police wanted to know what he had been up to. Sometimes they were chatty, even friendly, sometimes they were cold and formal, and sometimes they were brusque and bullying, but he had nothing to tell them. Through his boxing activities, he had come into contact with various more or less shady characters around the city—when he was not drinking with the blameless scholars and intellectuals of the university, he could occasionally be found sharing a pint with large, flashily dressed men with flattened noses, cauliflower ears, and oddly unexplained sources of income.

That, though, had been the limit of his involvement with the under-world. Apart from the occasional fib about his teaching qualifications—and the little matter of a bigamous marriage, which did not figure in their inquiries—he was in the clear as far as the civilian police were concerned.

The Redcaps, however, were a different matter. After a brief, formal appearance before the magistrate the next day, he would have to wait for the Gordon Highlanders to send an NCO and two guards to escort him back to the depot in Aberdeen. He was going back to the army, back to the guard-room, back before the commanding officer, up before a court martial, and then, no doubt, back to some military prison for a long time. He sat glumly in his police cell—'lavatorial tiled walls and a wooden bunk and three grimy looking blankets'[1]—and thought about his prospects.

Writing in *The Tiger and the Rose* some twenty-four years later, he claimed to have no idea how the police had tracked him down. 'I never did discover who, if anyone, put the police on my track, and I have never felt much interest in the matter',[2] he said. At other times, he suggested unconvincingly and disin-genuously that someone might have recognized him by chance in a recent boxing match and told the police. But he did have his suspicions, and he cer-tainly felt considerable interest in the matter: several of his acquaintances might have guessed his secret, but only one knew person for sure—Ella. What had been a close, affectionate, passionate relationship had been going wrong: he had started to wonder about her story of the lost baby, and even to talk about pos-sibly leaving Leeds. Perhaps she might have told her parents, who had never liked or trusted him, that he was on the run, and they might have contacted the police. Perhaps she had told them herself. For the rest of his life, even though there was no evidence to support his belief, he was convinced that, either directly or indirectly, Ella was responsible for his arrest.

II

It was five long, cold days before the military escort arrived and Vernon, in handcuffs, was marched onto the train for the miserable journey to Scotland. He had known from the moment that his flat door burst open that his new life had been irrevocably shattered, but the fact was really brought home to him when his civilian clothes were confiscated at the Brig o'Don barracks, and he was issued once more with the hated khaki uniform. The army was claiming him as its own: after two and a half years as Vernon Scannell, he was John Bain again.

The court martial was brisk, and, in its way, efficient. Vernon had already admitted who he was and what he had done, so he had little option but to plead guilty. George Wilson Knight and Bonamy Dobrée had both volunteered to speak or write on his behalf, but no one seemed particularly interested in what they might have had to say. The defending officer briefly and nervously made the point that the prisoner's desertion, coming at the end of hostilities, had not been the action of a coward, that he had been wounded in Normandy, and that he was probably at the end of his tether when he left. Then Vernon was allowed to address the court in person:

> I said that I had spent almost five years in the army and had found the life, both in and out of action, totally destructive of the human qualities I most valued, the qualities of imagination, originality, sensitivity and intelligence. I had felt whatever traces of these qualities I might possess being steadily destroyed and I knew, in May 1945, that I would either have to surrender to the extinction of my humanity or escape from the military life.[3]

It was an honest account of his feelings, but it's hard to think of a case that would be less attractive to the three career officers sitting in front of him. The president of the court martial was bemused: why would a soldier decide to desert when his wounds meant he would sit out what little remained of his service in an easygoing office job at home? It made no sense. He quizzed the prisoner about his plans for life after the war, in an exchange that provided Vernon with one of his favourite stories:

> I explained, as I thought reasonably, that I wanted to write, that I had to get away, otherwise I'd be finished. He said, 'What do you want to write?'
> I said, 'Poetry.'
> He said, 'Send him to a psychiatrist.'[4]

It's a good story, and it tells what happened but, unsurprisingly, it is less than fair on the army, or on the president of the court martial. In 1947, there were still nearly 20,000 deserters like Scannell at large in the country;[5] but the war was over, there would have been nothing useful for them to do even if they were still in uniform, and there was a rapidly diminishing official appetite for tracking them down. The army was no good for people like Vernon Scannell, and they were most certainly no good for the army. Keeping them in prison would be a waste of everyone's time and money, so, in this case, giving a psychiatrist the opportunity to rate him medically unfit must have seemed an ingenious way of getting everyone off the hook and solving an intractable problem.

Vernon, of course, knew nothing of that at the time. When, after several more days in the cells, he finally reported to the army psychiatrist at Glasgow's Maryhill Barracks, he still had no idea what would happen to him, and after a brief and unsympathetic interview, he was firmly convinced that he would soon be on his way back to prison. The only question in his mind was whether he would be back under the hated military regime that he remembered from Alexandria, or sent to a civilian prison. The general feeling among the other prisoners was that he could expect a two-year sentence.

But three days later, with just a few minutes warning, he was under escort again and on the way to Northfield Military Hospital in Birmingham, the army's centre for its psychiatric services. Its main purpose during the war had been to get patients back to the front line, and in fact the so-called 'Northfield experiments' in the use of community therapeutic care instead of the authoritarian regime of a traditional military hospital had a lasting influence on psychiatric thinking. Scannell arrived at the gates after a 5-mile train journey from Birmingham followed by an hour's walk uphill with his kit, to be faced by a dark, grim set of buildings with the unmistakeable look of an institution. Inside, his footsteps echoed in long, stone corridors as he passed sparsely furnished wards and ominous locked doors. His fellow patients included failed suicides, manic depressives, epileptics, and others who prowled the wards with anxious, hunted faces, neither speaking to anyone nor responding if they were spoken to.[6]

Perhaps word had been passed to the hospital authorities about Vernon's record of absconding, because he began his time there in a locked ward, under constant supervision. He stayed there for about two weeks, wondering whether he might not just be left in the hospital for months or even years, forgotten about. Perhaps a military or civilian prison might have been a better option. But then, without warning, he was taken in to see the psychiatrist again, to be told that he was to appear before a Medical Board. The hospital would do him no good, the doctor admitted: both the army and the medical authorities wanted him out. Within a few weeks he would be a free man again.

The general atmosphere of the hospital, the claustrophobia, and the occasional outbursts of violence among the other patients all made it impossible for him to concentrate on reading or writing—in his weeks in Northfield, he said later, he 'read Walton's lives of Donne and Herbert and...got about half-way through The Prelude, but otherwise I read nothing but thrillers and

I wrote nothing at all'.[7] On the other hand, the doctor had assured him that the Medical Board would be a pure formality, leading to a certain discharge, so there was little reason for him to do anything but sit and wait.

But then, back in Scotland two years earlier, he would have been pretty confident that he would have been demobilized within a few months. The sensible thing to do then too would have been to sit tight—but he hadn't done the sensible thing that time, and he didn't do it now. On 10 October, instead, he slipped out of the hospital and went off on another of his illicit benders, for fifteen days this time. When he finally returned, it was to be marched before the hospital's commanding officer for yet another deduction of pay and another seven days' detention. It was a final gesture of defiance: shortly afterwards he appeared before the Medical Board, to be formally declared to be suffering from 'anxiety neurosis' and thus unfit for the army on grounds of ill-health.

The final printed note on his army record reads 'Discharged 30-12-47. Rank: Pte. Permanently unfit for any form of Military Service.' Underneath, in longhand, the Record Officer at the Perth Infantry Records Centre has added, as if the army were determined to have the last word: 'Military Conduct—Bad'. He could boast a military record under fire in the service of his country; he held the Africa Star, and had the scars to prove that he had been no D-Day dodger, but a real front-line soldier—but when Vernon Scannell finally walked out of the Northfield Hospital, the army was seeing the back of one of the most determinedly uncooperative soldiers it had ever had. It's hard to know whether Scannell or the army would have been the more relieved.

III

There was never any doubt about where he would go. His relationship with Ella had petered out, but he still had friends in Leeds. The city he had originally found so grubby and unfriendly had now become his home. Since he had officially left the army, he had a grey chalk-stripe demob suit to wear and some £60[8] from his gratuity left in his bank account. Instead of the chilly garret in Francis Street, he found himself a room in a large house in Cromer Terrace, near the university, and began to look around for a job.

But if the Redcaps had finished with John Bain, the civilian police still had an interest in Vernon Scannell. His arrest for desertion had established the link between the two names, and quite probably it was that, rather than anyone actually informing on him to the police, that led to another knock on his door soon after he got back to Leeds. His marriage to Ella might be history as far as he was concerned, but to the police, it was a clear case of bigamy, and on 19 February 1948 he was back in court—a civilian court this time—with Ella standing beside him. He was facing a possible seven-year sentence on a charge of bigamy and a further charge of making a false statement, and she was charged with aiding and abetting his crime.

He had little choice but to plead guilty: in the Register of Marriages, produced in court, he had declared that his name was Vernon Scannell—wrong, it was John Vernon Bain. He had given his age as twenty-six—wrong, he had been twenty-four in January 1946. He had claimed he was a bachelor—wrong. He had said he was a journalist—wrong. He had given his father's name as Patrick Scannell, and his father's profession as commercial artist. In fact, the only true statements in the register were his address and the date of the marriage.

But the law had to take its solemn and ponderous course. The sad, lonely figure of Barbara appeared in the witness box, like a pale ghost from the

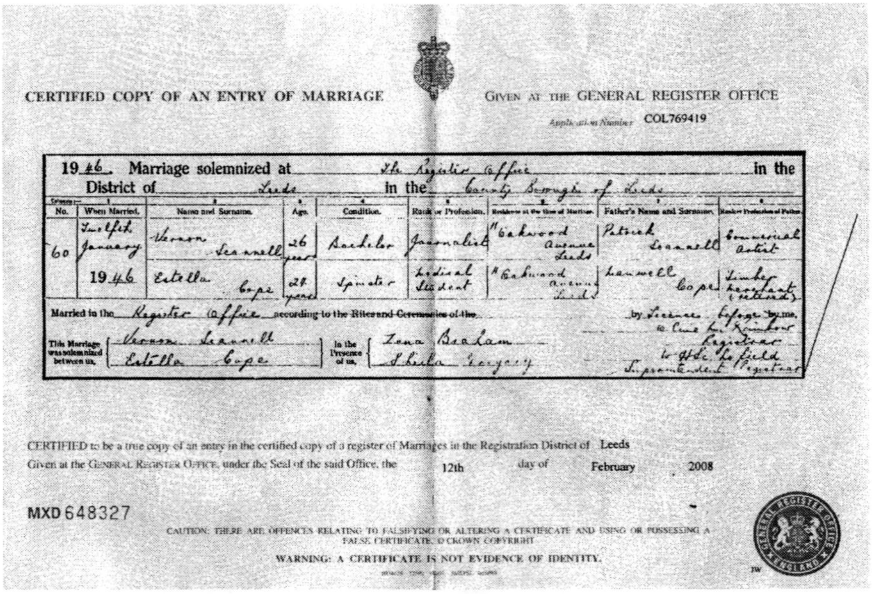

CERTIFIED COPY OF AN ENTRY OF MARRIAGE

GIVEN AT THE GENERAL REGISTER OFFICE

Application Number COL769419

1946. Marriage solemnized at The Register Office in the District of Leeds in the County Borough of Leeds

No.	When Married.	Name and Surname.	Age.	Condition.	Rank or Profession.	Residence at the time of Marriage.	Father's Name and Surname.	Rank or Profession of Father.
60	Twelfth January 1946	Vernon Scannell	26 years	Bachelor	Journalist	11 Oakwood Avenue Leeds	Patrick Scannell	Commercial Artist
		Estella Cope	27 years	Spinster	Medical Student	11 Oakwood Avenue Leeds	Hanwell Cope	Timber Merchant (retired)

Married in the Register Office according to the Rites and Ceremonies of the by Licence before by me,

This Marriage was solemnized between us, Vernon Scannell, Estella Cope

in the Presence of us, Zena Beeham, Sheila Gregory

[illegible] Registrar

[illegible] Superintendent Registrar

CERTIFIED to be a true copy of an entry in the certified copy of a register of Marriages in the Registration District of Leeds

Given at the GENERAL REGISTER OFFICE, under the Seal of the said Office, the 12th day of February 2008

MXD 648327

CAUTION: THERE ARE OFFENCES RELATING TO FALSIFYING OR ALTERING A CERTIFICATE AND USING OR POSSESSING A FALSE CERTIFICATE. ©CROWN COPYRIGHT

WARNING: A CERTIFICATE IS NOT EVIDENCE OF IDENTITY.

Figure 10. A bigamous marriage certificate. Practically every detail about Vernon is false. (Photocopy of original). See also plate section.

past. She seemed to have no bitterness, but she did not want to be there, reliving an unhappy part of her life that she had been trying to forget, and her evidence was brief and factual. Yes, she had married the accused on 21 December 1940. After one day, she had gone back to live with her parents. Her husband had joined the army in February 1941. There was one child.

And then it was Ella's turn. Scannell's friends always stood by him, but never more bravely than this. In the past, as he tried to wile away the hours in military custody, he might have had his doubts about Ella's loyalty; he might still believe that she had informed on him to the military police. But now, at considerable risk to herself, she spoke up for him bravely. Rather than claiming that she had been deceived by a cynical trickster—a tactic which would have increased the pressure on Scannell, but which might well have led to her acquittal—she declared that she had known from the moment she met him that her marriage was a sham, and that he already had a wife and child:

> We became very much in love. At that time I was having domestic difficulties with my parents and left home. I naturally went to Vernon. He later suggested marriage. In my belief it was a purely quixotic gesture, knowing the middle class background and circle in which I mixed, and not wishing to attach any scandal to me.
>
> I wish to say I knew of his previous marriage and there was never any attempted deception on his part. The tragic circumstances of his earlier life and the fact that we were very much in love somewhat blinded us to the seriousness of what we were doing.[9]

She must have been aware by now that their relationship was over, and yet a police witness told the court that she had told her interviewer that she would stand by Vernon 'no matter what happened'. There is a directness, a dignity, about her court statement which is curiously lacking from Vernon's. He sounds plaintive, almost whiney: he had married Barbara at eighteen, but because she was so much older than he was, there had never seemed to be any hope that the relationship would be successful, he said. His assertion that the 'neurotic condition' resulting from his army service was 'largely responsible' for his bigamous marriage sounds forced and decidedly ungallant; and when he went on to claim that he had married Ella to 'avoid placing her in an embarrassing position', an onlooker might have been excused for asking him exactly what sort of position he thought Ella, and Barbara too, was in at that moment.

He was more convincing when he explained that he had used the name Scannell for the marriage not so much for any purpose of concealment as because it was the name by which he was known in Leeds and in the magazines to which he contributed, but all in all, it was far from his finest hour. It is hardly surprising that he expunged all mention of it from his memory, never mentioning it in his memoirs or in interviews. Even his children were astonished to hear about the bigamy case after his death.

The court, however, seems to have been impressed by Ella's loyalty and honesty if not by Vernon's excuses. Although they were both sent for trial, they were given bail, and when the case was finally heard, they were released without any punishment.

IV

More than sixty years later, the 89-year-old woman sitting in the wheel-chair in a care home in southern England still has the same striking dark brown eyes that caught Vernon Scannell's attention. The red curls have gone, replaced by straight white hair, and the gentle face is wrinkled, with a slightly vague, puzzled look.

At first, Ella remembers nothing of Vernon. The name brings no spark of recognition. She remembers Leeds, and Oakwood Avenue where she lived, her father's business as a timber merchant, even the Fitzroy Tavern in Soho, but she takes only the mildest interest when told that Vernon was the man she had believed she had married in 1946. 'He says that, does he?' she asks. A few minutes later, told that her evidence helped him in court, she says softly, 'Good.' Reminded that he had deserted from the army, she shakes her head and whispers, 'That's no great sin.' But to every other question, she replies only with an apologetic smile. Her hand moves against her cheek, as if brushing aside those coppery red curls that used to tumble around her face, and she murmurs, 'Memory.'

But then, after a few moments silence, she suddenly says, unprompted, 'Vernon let me down.' And that is all she remembers, or all she wants to remember.

Among her personal possessions, her relatives found a single piece of paper that seemed to be a brief summary of her life. It included the brief note, '2 + Vernon', which seems to refer to the years they spent together, and then the single line '1945–47 Marriage?!' No more. That chapter of her past has been closed for many years.

V

For a few months Vernon worked as a proofreader and editor for the educational publishers E. J. Arnold and then, worried that the boring work and long hours were leaving him no time or energy for his own writing, found himself a job as a teacher in a small preparatory school. It was a step up from the hand-to-mouth casual coaching that he had turned to before, and it provided him with an introduction to a career that would serve him well for nearly twenty years. Although he always saw working in schools simply as a way to make money to support his writing, many of his former pupils still bear witness to his flair as a natural teacher, a man with the gift for passing on his passion for literature. In a letter years later to the poet and novelist Peter Redgrove, he summed up his own view of his qualities as a teacher with typical self-deprecation:

> I had little formal education, so when I found myself called on to teach old-fashioned English grammar—clause analysis, parsing and so on—I had to swot it all up and, in the face of much contradiction from people in education, I am convinced that exercises of this kind have some value ...
>
> I had quite a lot to give as a teacher simply in terms of my enthusiasm for my subject and sympathy for the less gifted child—as an old dunce, that was quite easy to hand out.[10]

He had moved on from the room in Cromer Terrace—and also found himself a replacement for Ella. He had first met Jean Stead soon after he came to Leeds—a young *Yorkshire Post* reporter, drinking in the Pack Horse pub with the rest of the journalists—and they had quickly become friends. Barely twenty, she was fascinated by his poetry and his literary and artistic knowledge, impressed by the obvious regard that university figures like Dobrée, Wilson Knight, and Childe had for his intelligence, and bowled over by his wit, his charm, and his conversation.

> Some people tended to look askance at him a bit because of what had happened, with his arrest and the bigamy case and so on. Then he started chasing me and before I knew where I was he'd actually moved into my flat. That was always the way with Vernon—he needed somewhere to live, and he saw women as people who could get him a flat and money to write his poetry.[11]

The couple lived together in the flat above a bicycle shop in the cosmopolitan district of Hyde Park, Scannell continuing with his teaching and also

Figure 11. Scannell in 1949. With his Army service, his two years on the run, and his time in Northfield Military Hospital behind him, Vernon embarked on a career as a poet with the publication of Graves and Resurrections in 1948. (Photo: Not known. Scannell family collection)

pressing on with his writing. Childe, Wilson Knight, and Dobrée were now firm friends with whom he would remain in contact for years to come, and to whom he would turn for advice about publishing or testimonials when he sought new jobs.

Graves and Resurrections appeared later in 1948, published by R. A. Caton's Fortune Press. With it came a glowing recommendation from Wilson Knight, who declared on the book's jacket that the poems showed 'a quite remarkable memory—a contact with childhood days of a particularly pure sort—a recapturing as it were of childhood's innocence; though this is balanced by an acute awareness of those harsher realities normal in modern poetry and the expression throughout is that of a gifted, controlled and mature mind'. The reviewers, too, were generally positive: 'A new and authentic voice has arisen among the English poets', said the *Northern Review*, while the *Yorkshire Post*, although grumbling that 'many of the lines seem to be exercises in the manner of Eliot or Auden than the fruit of deep personal feeling', admitted grudgingly that the book showed 'undeniable promise'.

The Fortune Press had begun on the fringes of the law, its specialization in gay pornography leading to a court appearance for Caton on a charge of obscene libel. It remained a one-man operation working from a dingy basement flat in London's Belgravia, but since its seedy beginnings Caton had

changed its focus from pornography to poetry. Over the years it had published the first books of Larkin, Kingsley Amis, Graham Greene, William
Golding, and Cecil Day Lewis, among others. Scannell had every reason to
be delighted.

But he wasn't—or at least, not for long. He agreed with the *Yorkshire Post*
reviewer that the poems, a mixture of pointed childhood recollections, bitter
memories of combat, and the love poetry addressed to Ella, were derivative
and immature, and felt them to be an embarrassment.[12] Some twenty years
later, he refused permission for the inclusion in an anthology of 'The Return',
a poem from *Graves and Resurrections* about the 'embered ruins and one dark
waiting tomb' that remain after combat. He replied to the anthologist: 'The
poem is from a book of juvenilia which I regret having published and I
would rather not have it reprinted.'[13] Although he relented towards the end
of his life, and said that there were poems in the book that he would include
in a planned but never completed new collected edition of his work, it is
hard to find in *Graves and Resurrections* many examples of the terse, mordant
language or the subtle imagery that would come to characterize his poetry.

But he continued with his writing—throughout his life, despite occasional pauses when he looked on his efforts with dejection, disappointment,
and disgust, he would continue to write poetry. It would be some time
before he had the confidence to abandon teaching and became a full-time
writer, and he would break off several times to work on novels or radio
plays to make money, but he was never in any doubt about his priorities.
Above everything else, he was determined to be a poet.

After *Graves and Resurrections*, Leeds seemed a smaller and less exciting
place, soured by the bigamy trial. He still loved the urban landscapes and the
nights in the pubs, but it felt limiting and provincial—and if he wanted to
build a poetic reputation for himself, he knew that this was not the place to
do it. Even though he was less than enthusiastic about the poems he had
published, he felt that his first book should mark the start of a career as a
poet. And for that, it seemed at the time, he would have to go back to
London—particularly since he no longer had reason to fear the military
police. For all her steadfastness and loyalty in court, he seems to have parted
from Ella without a backward glance. He was unwilling to leave Jean, whose
flat he had been sharing, and to whom he had been growing increasingly
close over the past few months, but there was a chance that she might take
up a role as her paper's London correspondent. Everything seemed to be
pointing him south again.

VI

For a few weeks, Scannell worked for £9 a week[14] in the London offices of an American trade magazine, handling the layout of the advertisements—a job for which he had about as much experience as he had brought to his earlier role as a theatre electrician. The result was much the same—incompetence, chaos, and a brisk and sudden exit. From there he went to wash dishes in a West End hotel, until he sold a children's story to a magazine for £50[15] and abandoned that job too. His plan now was to write a novel—10,000 words a week for six or seven weeks should do the trick, he reckoned, and his £50 would keep him going at about £6 a week. It was a fairly unrealistic plan, the more so as he had no idea what he would write about.

Jean Stead had come to London, as he had hoped, and was working in the *Yorkshire Post*'s Fleet Street office. For a few weeks, they lived in separate flats, but then moved in together again in a basement flat in Campden Hill Road, just off Kensington Church Street. It was a lively time: there were the Soho pubs to get acquainted with again and, at home, Vernon decided to teach Jean the rudiments of self defence:

> He was worried about me walking across Hyde Park safely—it was a danger-
> ous time in London just after the war. So he taught me how I could throw a
> very heavy bloke over my head, by letting him come at me, going all slack,
> and then putting both feet into their middle.[16]

And, for a bright, inquisitive young girl, there was also the infinitely greater excitement of watching and occasionally sharing in Vernon's work. Just as he had done in Cliff and Sylvia's flat, he would leave pieces of paper around the flat covered in notes and odd lines of poetry. 'It was very important if you saw a scrap of paper lying around not to throw it away, because it might be about his poetry', she remembers now:

> I was very young, and for me, it was like living in another world, a world of
> higher intelligence. His friends would come round and they would sit talking
> late into the night, and I would just sit on the floor and listen. Looking back
> on it, I think I owe all that I know now about literature, the arts, and painting
> and music to Vernon.

And then Kenneth arrived. The two brothers had not seen each other throughout the war: Kenneth had been married and divorced, like Vernon, and had just left a job as an agricultural labourer on a farm in Hertfordshire after being demobbed. Like Vernon, he was broke—but as soon as he heard about the £50 windfall, he came up with an alternative to the idea of eking it out over six weeks of hard writing. The three of them, Vernon, Kenneth, and Jean, would set off together on a visit to France.

It was one vague and unrealistic plan replacing another—little more, in fact, than buying rail and boat tickets to Paris and then hoping to hitchhike south and get some sort of job for a few weeks, or maybe even months. It would mean not only abandoning the novel before it was even started, not only using up the precious £50, but also selling Vernon's books to raise more money. At that point, Vernon jibbed: he was not going to sell his books. For the rest, though, he was prepared to follow the lead of the older brother he idolized, and a few days later, having bought a couple of the ex-army packs that he had thought he was done with forever, and having arranged with a friend to look after his precious books, the two brothers and Jean boarded a train for Newhaven on the first stage of their expedition.

It was an adventure in the same mould as most of Scannell's escapes from military service—an extended bender, fuelled this time not by beer and whisky but by litre bottles of cheap red wine and glasses of Pernod as their limited funds dribbled away. In Paris, they swam in the Seine, their skins chill, white, and English compared with the tanned bodies around them; in Tours they had a drunken late-night fist-fight that left them both even more sick and sore than usual; and by that time, Jean had had enough:

> It was a mistake for me to go. The first night in Paris, they'd gone out and got drunk together, and that's how it went on. In Tours, I'd booked into a separate hotel, and there was this huge noise outside in the square. I had no idea what it was, and then I saw it was Vernon and Kenneth punching each other, with what seemed like the whole town cheering them on. Eventually Vernon knocked Kenneth out, and dragged him away into a hotel. So the next morning, I went home.

Nothing and nobody could come between the two brothers, even when they were trying to punch each other's lights out. Jean got back to London just in time to keep her job with the *Yorkshire Post*, and moved her belongings out of the Campden Hill Road flat. The affair was over, even though she and Vernon remained friends for the rest of his life.[17]

Vernon and Kenneth, though, staggered on to Poitiers, where they passed a couple of weeks lying by the river drinking red wine by day, splashing in the water when the sun got too hot, and reeling from bar to bar drinking more red wine during the evening. The whole journey was punctuated by crippling hangovers and blanks in their memories of what had happened the day before.

Both men had been heavy drinkers since their first teenage escapades with bottles of Younger's Scotch Ale in Aylesbury all those years before, but now Vernon was settling into a pattern of drinking that would stay with him almost all his life. During his first spell in London, according to Cliff Holden, he would take a drink early in the morning to recover from a hangover and immediately be drunk again. Holden says bluntly, 'He was an alcoholic.' But it was never as simple as that: he would go for long periods without having a drink, and would then suddenly find himself embarked on massive benders, often lasting several days, that would leave him drained, his head pounding, and his mind filled with guilt, regret, and a sense of hopelessness. It was the hangover, not the drunkenness, that fascinated him when he was sober:

> It is the hangover that seems to induce a state that is related, however obliquely and distantly, to mystical experience, not the mystical ecstatic but its dark reverse, a condition not so very different in kind, I imagine, from what St. John of the Cross meant by the 'dark night of the soul'...I have known hangovers in which I have been filled with a sense of self-disgust, feelings of unfocused anxiety and terrible loneliness which cannot be so very different from the anguished Christian's feeling of separation from God.[18]

His diaries are peppered with references to hangovers and lost days, weekends, and occasionally even weeks. Sometimes he affected a grim pride in his own stamina:

> Today I have walked in the Valley of the Shadow of Hangover. I suppose I could write an authoritative treatise on the Geography of the Hangover. It is a territory which I have explored with great thoroughness at one time or another.[19]

More often, though, he is consumed with guilt at the way his 'great, mauling, life-sucking hangovers'[20] keep him from writing and cripple his personal relationships. He might enjoy drinking 'with my lewd well-natured friends, drinking to engender wit', as he wrote in his diary,[21] but he was all too well aware that it would be followed by 'agenbite of inwit, misery, sterility, hangover, angst, spleen, the shakes, the horrors, and no sign of light on the horizon'.[22] Again and again in his diaries, a passionate determination to stay sober is mixed uneasily with a fatalistic realization that he won't: he spent much of the rest of his life climbing determinedly on the wagon and falling joyously off it again.

At his best, according to his friends, he could be a witty, engaging, and amusing drunk—but he could turn suddenly and unpredictably into a violent and aggressive one, as Kenneth presumably found out in their late-night brawl in Tours. Kenneth could look after himself, but the intimate link between drink and violence would blight Vernon's life and the lives of those closest to him.

In France, predictably, they found no work, and when their money ran out in Poitiers they bluffed their way by train to Paris, persuading a ticket inspector who was more generous than they deserved that they had lost their tickets. Then they argued a slightly less congenial British Embassy official into lending them the money to get home and so, tired, hungry, dishevelled and penniless, they limped back to Victoria Station.

VII

Vernon knew the only place he could go was his mother's home in Aylesbury, even though he also knew that he wouldn't be particularly welcome there. She was now divorced from his father, and living on her own. There is something deeply sad about his description of her, still as cold, undemonstrative, and unemotional as he remembered her from his childhood:

> She disapproved of alcohol, tobacco and sexual pleasure, and held strongly to the belief that a man should work hard at a respectable occupation, behave always in a way that would frustrate scandal mongers and arouse the envy of neighbours. Her two sons were a disappointment to her, except that the word 'disappointment' seems too strong a word for the way that she nodded and sighed in an almost self-congratulatory style as if she could have long ago predicted our various failures in love, work and social advancement.[23]

He told her about the trip to France—leaving out the details of the drinking and the hangovers—and explained that the jobs they had been promised had fallen through. He would need to stay with her while he looked for work, he said and, despite her sceptical response, that is what he did. He studied the 'Situations Vacant' columns of the newspapers in the local library each morning, applying for jobs as kitchen porter, newspaper library assistant, encyclopaedia salesman, and—with slightly more optimism—teacher in a London school.

Nothing seemed likely to provide him with the chance to earn a living, until one day in the street he bumped into Eddie MacSweeney, an old friend from his days at Queen's Park Council School. They went for a drink together—Eddie paying for the beer, since Vernon had no money—and then, again at Eddie's insistence, went off to visit a fair that had come to the town. Quite unexpectedly, he was about to find another way in which his boxing prowess might help him earn a living.

Eddie's idea was for Vernon to win some money in the fairground boxing booth and, emboldened by the beer, by his native optimism, and by his belief in his own strength and skill, Vernon agreed. The stage from which the barker was appealing noisily for challengers to take on one of his four boxers was framed with flashing coloured lights, and Vernon knew as he climbed the rickety steps that the fight would be fixed. He just had no idea how fixed.

He was standing in the ring, being introduced to the crowd, when the barker put a hand over his microphone and whispered to him that he should take a dive in the sixth round. But the deal that had been announced was a £5 prize for lasting eight rounds, and £10[24] for knocking the other boxer out, and Vernon, even with three pints inside him, had his mind set on winning the £10. It was clear within a couple of minutes that he would have no trouble doing so, but for the referee. In the first round, he knocked his opponent down, but the bell went for the end of the round; in the second, he knocked him down again, but the barker—who was refereeing the bout—warned him for punching low. In the third, he hit the other boxer with another blow to the chin that should have ended the fight, only for the referee to stop the fight again and warn Vernon's second for giving advice while the round was in progress. Then in the fourth round, when Vernon had decided that he would have to end the contest once and for all, the fight was suddenly stopped again. The referee rubbed a towel over Vernon's forehead, surreptitiously nicking the skin of his eyebrow with his thumbnail, and then declared that the fight would have to be stopped. It would not be safe to let Vernon carry on with blood coming from his face.

Instead of his £10 prize, he was given £2 in appreciation of his game performance, and then invited to take round a hat to the spectators for their tips—'nobbins'. He was literally begging, cap in hand.

He needed money, though, and he was in no position to be too choosy about where it came from. A shamefaced shuffle around the crowd with the boxer he had just fought at his side yielded the grand total of £4 18s. 7d.,[25] which they shared, half for Vernon and half for the fairground team. Even with the £2 he had been given in the ring, it was still far short of the £10 he had been hoping for, and practically nothing compared with the money that the barker had collected earlier for himself. It was not just the crowd who had been cheated. On the other hand, Vernon was walking away with more than £4 for less than ten minutes' work, and before the pubs closed too. He was able to buy Eddie MacSweeney a drink back.

What was more, he had been invited to go back to the boxing booth as one of the team when the fair moved on from Aylesbury to High Wycombe a week later. His job would be to stand in the crowd and seem to respond to the barker's challenge, and then get into the ring for the 'fight'. If he was told to fall down, he would fall down—then they could set up a return 'match' for him to get his revenge, and even more spectators would flock to the booth. It was a sad and undignified end to a sporting career that had begun with a small boy dreaming of being one of the boxing greats, and taken him into the fringes of professional sport—but on the other hand, it was a fairly pain free source of money at a time when he was flat broke. With magazines appearing to be as uninterested in his poems as various employers were in his job applications, he seemed to have few other options.

And anyway, there were things to learn even in the tawdry setting of the boxing booth. Once he had been proud of the power of his right hand: now he learned how to deliver a right cross with his fist slack so that he could pull the punch at the last minute, making an impressive noise but causing no more damage than a gentle flick. Once he had delighted in his ability to read an opponent's intentions and slip his body inside a punch so it sliced harmlessly through the air: now he was adept at opening his guard to a painless open-gloved slap on the jaw. Once, he had been proud to keep standing: now he learned how to make a spectacular crashing fall to the canvas. It was, he said later, not boxing but acting; he was not a fighter, but a boxing illusionist.[26]

His career at High Wycombe, however, was a brief one. He had only fought three bouts—or put on three carefully rehearsed performances, as he put it—when he received a letter from the Director of Education of Clark's College, a group of independent schools in London. Wilson Knight, at Leeds University, had encouraged him to apply for teaching jobs. 'Teaching is the soundest basis for anyone wanting to write', he wrote:

> Nothing else gives both (1) stability and (2) leisure. You may be a slave in term, but you become a real gentleman in the holidays...The relation between teacher and pupil is the quintessence of all poetry, properly understood.[27]

And he offered not just realistic careers advice, but also a glowing testimonial, which impressed the college so much that they were ready to offer Vernon a job teaching English and history at their school in Ealing, West London. The salary of £6 a week[28] was not much, but it was enough to enable him to walk away from the humiliation of the boxing booth and move out of his mother's home. It was time for another new start.

VIII

Rather than the dull suburbs of Ealing, close by the school, Scannell chose to return to the basement room in Campden Hill, near Notting Hill Gate, where friends of his had moved in after he had left for France. Even though it was some 5 or 6 miles away, there was more buzz and excitement than Ealing could offer—and more pubs. It was a room that must have reminded him of the chilly Francis Street garret in Leeds:

> [It] smelled of dead cats and its furnishings were simple: a table, two upright chairs, an armchair and a divan bed. There was a gas fire and a ring, like an old rusted doughnut, for cooking on. I shared a bathroom with the occupants of the flat on the first floor.[29]

It is indicative of Scannell's priorities that, after a mention of the public library in Kensington High Street and the second-hand bookshops of Notting Hill, his most vivid memories were of the pubs in the area. There was the Windsor Castle on Campden Hill Road where he and the poet Roy Campbell ('soft and mild, though of substantial size', he said[30]) were thrown out for not being posh enough; another in Kensington Church Street where painters and artists met; The Prince Albert where he played bar billiards; the big glitzy pub near the underground station where a fleshy and gone-to-seed ex-boxer would while away the evenings; the Catherine Wheel where Vernon and Kenneth drank late into the night with a stranger who kept on quoting A. E. Housman at them; the big anonymous bar next door to an undertaker's, where he was fed double scotches by a drunken Glaswegian tart who thought he was Polish; or the one on Holland Park Road where he played darts and drank with an Irishman from Shepherd's Bush, funded by the money his wife made as a prostitute. And many more besides.

The school where he was starting teaching was a mixture of boys and girls aged from about twelve to seventeen, who were studying either academic subjects to General Certificate of Education Ordinary Level or typing and secretarial training to fit them for office work. Former pupils remember a strange assortment of teachers. 'They were definitely an odd lot', recalls Natalie Bartington, whom he taught there. 'There was one who had shell shock, and another very young man who was supposed to teach us electronics, but who was so nervous that he could hardly speak.'[31] And then, of course, there was Scannell himself, whom she remembers as something of a disciplinarian, and always dressed in corduroy trousers with heavy brown shoes. Occasionally, she says, he would come into lessons looking pale and hung over—a memory that ties in with Scannell's own account of one of the other teachers, a tough but bibulous ex-para called James Corris who taught mathematics. He was, Scannell says, by far the best teacher in the place:

> He loved his subject and he could communicate that love, originally and unpedantically...James's flaw was his habit of going off on periodical alcoholic jags of epic scale, on many of which I was a pie-eyed partner. I have never, before or since, known such a drinker.[32]

Their 'jags' must indeed have been monumental for Scannell, who had some experience of similar adventures, to remember them in such terms. More than once they were arrested together for being drunk and disorderly; on another occasion, alone this time, Scannell was fined £7 for attempting to drive away a car without the owner's consent. 'I was quite drunk, of course. Three days' drinking at a total cost of over £18—and now I can't afford to get my shoes repaired', he noted ruefully in his diary. 'If I don't stop drinking soon, it will stop me.' [33] But, other than leave them looking pale and fragile, their late-night drinking sessions, brushes with the law, and occasional nights in the cells seem not to have interrupted their work at the school unduly. Natalie Bartington remembers Scannell as an inspiring teacher:

> He was very good with poetry, and his lessons were always interesting. But he seemed to be very left wing, and you knew he had no time for the Conservative Party or people who supported it. The Headmaster used to come in sometimes and talk to us about political issues, putting a right wing slant on them when Vernon had been giving us all the left-wing ideas.[34]

Scannell's political views surprised people all his life. By the time he left the army, he had already acquired the slightly throaty voiced, officer-class Received Pronunciation that would characterize his poetry readings—one of his favourite stories of his army days was about asking another soldier on a station platform which train they were to board. A nearby NCO wheeled round to answer, stiffening to attention as he did so—only to find himself facing, not the senior officer he expected, but a grinning Private. Scannell in his ill-fitting and unpressed uniform. The voice, the upright, military bearing, and the sternly traditionalist ideas he sometimes expressed about literature, prepared people for an unbending conservative view of the world.

Nothing could have been further from the truth. Listing 'Hating Tories' as one of his hobbies in *Who's Who* might have been slightly ironic—certainly he didn't hate them enough to turn down the offer of a £300 grant from Edward Heath or a £700-a-year Civil List pension from Margaret Thatcher[35]—but he had a lifelong, deep-seated and almost instinctive sympathy for society's underdogs. In his diary, for instance, he notes his reaction to the proposals of the new Conservative government in 1970:

> A disgraceful Tory budget plan: increased health charges, school meals, no free milk for the over-sevens, everything designed to soak the poor and make the rich still richer.[36]

It was not a carefully thought-out political philosophy, but a visceral dislike of Conservative policies and politicians. Of one member of Margaret Thatcher's Cabinet, he noted:

> He is a repulsive specimen. He wears always an expression that is both commonplace smirk and a wince of fastidious distaste for the murkier reaches of existence. His hair is always carefully brushed, combed, lacquered. He is the worst kind of Tory—utterly egotistical, heartless, snobbish, hypercritical and mendacious. Loathsome.[37]

And later, watching the Party Conference in 1990, he confided in his diary:

> My God, they're a smug, lying, hypocritical, mean, greedy, materialistic bunch of shitbags![38]

What his views lacked in subtlety, they more than made up for in passion: perhaps it is hardly surprising that a little of that bile should have seeped out into his lessons at Clark's College and elsewhere.

IX

In the evenings, and sometimes while he was at the college as well, Scannell was writing—usually in exercise books 'borrowed' from the school store cupboard. *Graves and Resurrections* may have been a false start, but now he was serving his apprenticeship as a poet and a writer. That meant sending his work off to weekly and monthly magazines, hearing nothing for weeks on end, and then getting a curt refusal. In his diary, on 5 April 1951, he notes anxiously:

> Went by bus to Notting Hill Gate to buy typing paper and to see if my poem had appeared in *The Month*. The current *Month* was out, but *Jairus's Daughter* was not in it. I suppose it will appear in the May issue.

In fact, 'Jairus's Daughter', a dramatic monologue reminiscent of Robert Browning, was printed four months later, in August. And there were other successes too over the next few months, with his name beginning to appear in magazines such as *The Listener*, *The Spectator*, and *Time and Tide*. In poems such as 'Early Summer in the City', published in *Time and Tide* in May 1952, a description of new cricket bats lined up in a shop window shows how early he acquired his gift for the needle-sharp evocation of the beauty and possibility of ordinary things:

> Clean as bone
> Or almonds newly peeled, the brave display
> Of cricket bats brings promise of bright
> Noons of sun and green and graceful white.

In 'The Visitation', a poem that would eventually appear in his next collection, still seven years in the future, it is possible to see him feeling towards the subtle menace that would be characteristic of much of his mature work:

> Bird calls from night's dark hill
> Imperious; the candles weep, the fire burns low,
> The clock is ticking but the hands are still.[39]

Over the next few months he began also to establish himself as a contributor of poems, talks, and short stories for the BBC, where his friendship with Kenneth Severs in Leeds had brought him introductions to some influential young producers. He would privately fret over the way that writing for the BBC was distracting him from the real business of his life. 'There is no defence for having spent the entire evening writing a rather silly short story of over 2,000 words for the BBC', he noted in his diary[40]—although, in a different mood, he admitted that there was indeed a very obvious defence. ''Tis pity I'm a whore—but I have to live.'[41]

It provided some distraction from the College, where work was frustrating him so much that not even the occasional benders with Corris could disguise his boredom and disillusionment. 'Why should I now, a dissolute and lazy man, compel these children to read about things that don't interest them, things which, because of the limitation of their actual experience, can have little or no meaning in their eyes?' he asked himself.[42]

And even though his poetry was being published, and he was gradually beginning to make a name for himself as a writer, the work that he was producing failed to enthuse him. His poems appeared with gratifying regularity in the magazines, but he was desperate now to find a publisher who would bring out another collection. A letter from Bonamy Dobrée, sent from his home in Blackheath, South London, cannot have been much encouragement:

> I think I ought to say quite frankly that I think the chances of publication at the moment are extremely dim. Most publishers won't even look at poetry now, as far as I can hear.[43]

He was frustrated and deeply dissatisfied with what he was achieving, as he would be all his life, but at the same time he was thinking seriously about his craft, looking for his own distinctive voice:

> I don't think I've ever been less confident about the value of my poetry than now; and yet more of it is being published than hitherto. The best of it is fairly good by contemporary standards, but I can't rid myself of the feeling that I am merely nibbling at the raw material, not immersing myself...
>
> I think the only way to acquire an effective personal style—and this is the mark of the poet of stature—is to be completely honest. The experience from which the poem is to be distilled must be felt with all the faculties working at their highest pressure; the objects and symbols which emerge must be examined steadily, then recreated as faithfully as possible. Literature, other people's verse, should be forgotten. No falsification for the sake of effect, no dragging in of the flashy image which has no place there, no distortion to arrive at a preconceived assessment or concept. The poet's only allegiance is to the truth, not to a formal dogma, but the truth as he sees and feels it. To speak the truth is style.[44]

Scannell's perennial guilt about his supposed idleness was matched only by his astonishing capacity for sudden bursts of relentless hard work; and now, teaching at Clark's College, agonizing over his poetry, and turning out scripts for the BBC, he was also working on the novel that his French adventure with Jean and Kenneth had postponed. Once again, he had little confidence in his ability—but at least this time he had a clear idea of what he was trying to do.

He began writing—still in the 'borrowed' school exercise books— what he planned as the first English novel to be set in the world of professional boxing. The big title fight, he thought, might work as an allegory for the pressures and conflicts that beset human relationships, and his personal experience of the boxing world, in and out of the ring, would help him to create an environment that was convincing, vibrant, and alive. Like most first novels, *The Fight*, as it would be called, contained several half-digested gobbets of autobiography—one of the main characters was a heavy-drinking journalist, Philip Dobson, who remembered his love of poetry as a child, and also how his father had encouraged him to box. Like Scannell, he had been fascinated by the sport, and had found it hard to decide whether his ambition should be to win a Nobel Prize for literature or to become lightweight champion of the world. There is, too, a sickening moment in the book where another character, a trained boxer, punches his girlfriend full in the face: Scannell knew about violence both in and out of the ring, and he poured his knowledge into the book.

But though his initial surge of enthusiasm carried him through 50,000 words of the novel, after a few weeks he was starting to lose heart in that as well. 'I can't tell whether there is any hope for it, but I suspect not', he wrote in his diary. 'It has less form than a dumpling, and will probably prove as indigestible.'[45]

The novel was abandoned. Scannell's diaries at this time depict a young man who was uncertain of his own ability, resentful of the years he had lost in the army, and aware that time was slipping away. Other people of his age had started to build productive, comfortable lives, and he was still flitting from one down-at-heel bedsit to another, constantly counting the pennies, and struggling to make ends meet. More importantly, he was twenty-nine, an age by which, he realized, many poets had already produced their finest work, and he had hardly begun.

Perhaps it was depression, as well as drink and simple shortage of cash, that led him into another foolish escapade reminiscent of his blundering around on the roof of the Bull's Head in Aylesbury. Late one Saturday night in April, drunk and penniless after a night in the pub, he found himself in Ealing, outside Clark's College. The building was dark and empty; the street, too, was deserted. This, he told himself, was his chance:

I broke into C[lark]'s. I broke in for the excitement of it, but once inside the building, I began to look around for something to steal—money, I mean. It began as an adventure, an antidote to boredom, and suddenly changed into a job. Working in the darkness, my hands encountered a tin box, fairly heavy, which rattled reassuringly. I left with this hidden under my coat, and when I got home I opened it. It was full of rusty keys, screws and nails! I took it back and replaced it, and left for the second time, undetected.[46]

Unlike the drunken night in Aylesbury, his luck held—he escaped without getting caught, and his break-in was not even noticed—but the incident was a symptom of his dissatisfaction with his life as a teacher and a struggling poet. He had no idea what he would have to do, but he knew he would have to do something.

Once again, it was a woman who saved him. Elspeth Fairbrass[47] was in her mid-thirties, five years or so older than Vernon, slim and curly haired, and she taught shorthand and typing at Clark's College. They had caused quite a stir among the pupils by being seen around together in Ealing, and moving in with her seems to have helped to drag him out of the Slough of Despond into which he was sinking. She began by encouraging him to start work on his novel again. She washed for him, cooked for him, and brought him coffee as he worked away at the manuscript after school, at weekends, and through the Easter holiday. Then, when he had completed piles of scribbled pages in his scrawled, barely decipherable handwriting, she volunteered to type it out for him, taking it down in shorthand at his dictation, and then typing up her notes. And finally, when the excitement of seeing his work neatly typed and properly presented had begun to wear off, and he was once more beset by doubts about whether it was any good, she encouraged him to press ahead and send it off to a publisher. A few weeks earlier, he had met the poet and translator Margaret Crosland, and her husband agreed to act as his agent. Together, they agreed to give it to a publisher called Peter Nevill, who had a small business producing biographies, classic poetry, and books of psychology and was trying to build a list of contemporary novels.

Vernon's advance was £50,[48] half to be paid at once and half on publication. It was not a huge amount, but that was not the point: it was a professional expression of confidence in his novel, and it was enough to encourage him to start work at once on another one. Taken with the money he was earning from the BBC and from the poems that had been appearing in weekly magazines—and added, optimistically, to the royalties that he hoped to be paid—it was also enough to tempt him to hand in his notice at Clark's College.

9
Marriage

They ignored all warnings
and advice; they settled down together
to discover, after ten years,
the sweet and heady spice
of carnal love no less delicious, even
tastier than it had been in the past...

'The Long Honeymoon', from *Views and Distances* (2000)

I

Early in the New Year, Scannell made an entry in his diary that reads very much like a reminder to himself about the simplicity and directness he wanted to achieve with his writing.

In the greatest works of art there is a quality of innocence. It is to be found in the works of Melville, Conrad, Blake, the Elizabethans, Thomas Hardy, and Edward Thomas. It is the child vision: the clear, astonished and awed gaze of the child seeing its first miracle. Such writers as these have not consciously woven the mantle of greatness; they have put absolute trust in their genius and have often followed blindly. This innocence is conspicuously absent from the work of Eliot, Graham Greene, and indeed from most contemporary writers, Dylan excepted.[1]

II

For all her enthusiasm, the move away from Clark's was the death knell for Scannell's relationship with Elspeth. Washing and cooking for him, typing out his manuscripts, and generally cheering him up had been one thing while they were both paying the bills, but now that he was relying on occasional small cheques and they were having to live almost entirely off her income, it was a much less attractive proposition. There was, Scannell said later, growing tension between them,[2] and when she had the opportunity to improve her qualifications by going off to a Teachers' Training College, there was little to hold her back.

Looking back, Scannell implies that, on her side if not on his, there had been the hope that this might prove to be more than just another brief flirtation, but he is quite matter-of-fact about the parting:

> I had never been able to give her the totally committed love she hungered for and deserved... I do not think I was especially sentimental in my view of romantic love, believing in the existence of an ideal, predestined Miss Right, yet I was sure it would be a mistake to marry unless the decision involved the consent of the whole being, allowing for not the least thread of doubt or reservation.[3]

Elspeth, simply, had not been Miss Right. All that remained of their relationship was the almost anonymous dedication on the title page of *The Fight*: 'For E.F.'

Earlier in his time in London, Scannell had mused lugubriously about his semi-itinerant lifestyle:

> Always I seem to return to the same place, whether it be W5, W8 or NW makes no difference—the obscene jug, basin and slops bucket are the same, the ageing curtains and cheap frayed rugs, gas ring and hungry meter, and of course insufficient covering on the bed.[4]

It was not just that he was irked by the shabby, inconvenient, and uncomfortable lifestyle, not just that he wanted someone to cook and clean for him, do his typing, and handle all the day-to-day jobs that got in the way of his writing, not even just that he wanted regular, uncomplicated sex—although all those things were true. Another part of him wanted a settled, lasting, committed relationship. The trouble was that each time he came close to one, he threw it away. He had been in love with Jean, for instance, and had almost deliberately sabotaged the relationship with his heavy drinking. Then, when he heard that he had definitely lost her, he noted in his diary:

> J[ean] S[tead] gets married this weekend. I hope and pray that she is going to be content. My own feelings are a slight sadness mixed with a definite sense of reprieve.[5]

Now, with Elspeth gone, there were practical considerations: he could no longer afford the flat, so he was back among the jugs and slops buckets. For several months he stayed in various scruffy rooms and bedsits—including, according to *The Tiger and the Rose*, a spell with a drunk and lecherous old couple who made money by hawking pies filled with stale bread around some pubs and placing bogus charity collection boxes in others; who had sex in the kitchen and also pilfered his possessions on the sly. Even when *The Fight* appeared early in 1953, and the second half of his £50 advance was paid, he had no money to move, since he had already borrowed most of the advance from his agent.

This time, it was the BBC who came to his rescue. He submitted a number of poems to the poet and critic John Wain, who was presenting a new radio programme called *First Reading*, and had a positive response. 'I greatly admire your poems...had it not been for the pressure of space, I should have liked to keep all of them', Wain wrote back.[6] He chose two poems for broadcast immediately, and *First Reading* became an important outlet for Scannell's poetry over the next few months—even though there was a tart rebuke from a senior producer a little later in the year when it emerged that two more poems used on the programme had already been published in a magazine. 'Scannell ought to be rebuked for playing this trick on us...Would you like to tell him off, or shall I?' the producer, Howard Newby, wrote brusquely to Wain in an internal memo.[7] Whoever finally did it, the telling off does not seem to have been too rigorous, since Scannell's work continued to feature on *First Reading* and other programmes.

Around the same time, he found another job as a teacher of English and history at another west London tutorial college which paid him £12 10s. 0d. a week[8]—enough and to spare, with the more regular money he was now getting from the BBC, for him to afford a more comfortable room close to Ealing Common. In October, too, came the first royalties from *The Fight*, which had sold a respectable 3,000 copies—easily enough to persuade Peter Nevill to take another novel. Like the advance, much of the royalties had already been borrowed from his agent and spent long ago—but there was certainly enough to finance another massive alcoholic bender lasting several days.

> It seems that I have no control over this insane compulsion to spend my money on booze...I'm sure it is a childish thing. Give a poor child a sum of money which seems to him princely, and he will gorge himself with chocolates, sweets, ice creams and so on. I have exchanged the lollipop for

the point of beer, the ice cream for the double scotch, but the greed is the same as the child's.[9]

His second novel, *The Wound and the Scar*, was due out in a few weeks' time, and he had been working for several months on a third, *Dark Sacrament* or *A Taste for Violence*. It sounds as if he might have felt he was on the verge of a career as a novelist—but his diary tells a different story. 'Not bad for a first novel',[10] he says grudgingly about sales of *The Fight*, and then adds about *The Wound and the Scar*: 'It might not be the worst novel ever published, but it must be the worst published by someone who has some talent.' About his third novel, he is uncharacteristically optimistic—but only briefly. 'I think it's the best thing I've done in prose', he writes cheerfully, but then adds, 'It could be that and still no great shakes. Now I can write the things I want to—poetry and criticism.'[11]

The Wound and the Scar, in particular, was probably a book that Scannell had to write in an attempt to deal with the past. Nightmare scenes from his past occur throughout the book, whose central character is Jeff, a young soldier on the run after deserting from the army. 'I'm a coward. I've always been a coward', he says. He recalls dead, bloated cattle scattered in the green fields of Normandy, the sickly smell, waxen skin, and sightless eyes of soldiers sprawled in an orchard in Touffréville, and the bodies at Wadi Akarit, 'lying like wax dolls on the rocks, like dolls somebody had got tired of playing with'. Jeff is court-martialled and sent, like Scannell, to a mental hospital, where a psychiatrist arranges his discharge and tells him, 'You're no damn good to the army, and the army's no damn good to you.'

But the diary entries, terse as they are, sum up Scannell's attitude to novel writing. He is cheerful enough, for all his grudging tone, about the sales of *The Fight*—the money that it makes—but he dismisses the others as mere potboilers, and welcomes the fact that they are now out of the way. There was no doubting his priorities: even though he had been disappointed by the one book of poetry that he had published, it was as a poet that he wanted to be judged. He might pour his deepest fear and pain out onto the pages of his novels, but they were written to finance his poetry; rewriting or editing them was a chore, and one that he often skimped. Rewriting his poems, by contrast, was a passion. Another diary entry sums up his feelings:

The poet's first concern is with language, with the look of language, the sound of language and the feeling of it. He uses it as a sculptor uses clay or stone—he manhandles it and loves it. His audience may be more interested in reading his pseudo novels, but he is more concerned with his undisguised poems.[12]

III

There was—it is tempting to add, 'of course'—another woman in Scannell's life by now, unmentioned in his memoirs and known in his diaries only as Dorothy. He had moved with her into a flat in Craven Terrace 'in that strange, haunted territory between Bayswater Terrace and Paddington',[13] which was sublet from a friend-of-a-friend in Leeds. Once again the relationship seems to have caused at least as much pain as pleasure: when she left after a few months, his diary noted dispassionately, 'Dorothy has left me, sensible girl, and I'm all alone and at the moment, rather happy.'[14]

For several weeks, by then, they had effectively been living separate lives in the flat, Vernon's latest novel abandoned, and the poems he had started left untouched for days at a time. He was drinking late into the night, and then spending the mornings in bed, rising around lunchtime:

> Apathy is the disease from which I suffer most acutely . . . I cook myself a meal, and then sit and smoke or read until about three o'clock. Mind you, I don't read anything worthwhile—usually a newspaper or a novel. The prospect of performing the slightest task becomes unbearable. I don't work or shave for 48 hours. Then I am tortured by guilt and the sense of loss.[15]

He had kept in touch with many of his friends from Leeds—Kenneth Severs, in particular, was occasionally in London, and they would meet for pub crawls around Soho. In the summer of 1953, Severs announced that he was coming down for a party with some BBC colleagues, and suggested that they should meet outside Broadcasting House. When Kenneth arrived, he was in an open-topped Austin being driven by an artist friend from Leeds, a dark-haired and strikingly attractive girl named Jo Higson, who taught painting in the Fine Arts Department of Leeds University's Art School. He had been trying unsuccessfully to persuade her to marry him—but as soon as she met Vernon, Severs must have known it was a lost cause.

'I can picture it to this day. Vernon walked across in a green shirt and green corduroys that I ironed for many a year after that', she remembers now. 'Kenneth had told me about this poet friend of his—said he was a bigamist and a drunk, and a pretty tough guy—and then I met this rather mild-speaking chap...'[16]

Scannell was struck with her too:

> She seemed rather shy, but not gauche, happier to listen to us talking about our concerns than to discuss her own, and willing to go along with whatever we wanted to do. Not that she was negative or over-anxious to please. You sensed her intelligence and humour and she impressed by not making the least attempt to impress. I liked her very much, and thought she had unusually beautiful eyes.[17]

The three spent the rest of the day drinking before Scannell staggered back to his flat, and Jo—long before the days of breathalyzers—drove off to her parents' home in Kent, safe in the knowledge that he had written down her name and phone number and promised to call her. He didn't— he said later that he had lost the number—and it was almost a year before they met again.

Figure 12. Jo Higson, the talented art student who was soon to become Jo Scannell. (Photo: Not known. Jo Scannell collection)

During that time, Scannell was beginning to get better known in literary circles. The publication of *The Wound and the Scar* had brought him another £25 advance[18] (most of which vanished over the bar of one of the Soho pubs within a few hours), and his poems continued to be read on the radio and published in well-known and prestigious magazines such as *The London Magazine* and *Encounter*. Stephen Spender, then co-editor of *Encounter*, was so impressed by his poetry that he invited him to the magazine's Haymarket offices, and asked him to write about Dylan Thomas's new radio play, *Under Milk Wood*. The article was never published, but Spender's rejection note contained a sentence that was more valuable to Scannell than the few pounds' fee that he might have received. 'You write good poetry, and that's what matters', he said. Perhaps it was a condescending comment for an older, established poet to make to a struggling young man, but Scannell did not see it that way.[19]

There were other disappointments—his third novel, now renamed *Plague of Violence*, came back from the publishers with a demand for a complete rewrite, eliminating 'morally bad' characters and 'obscene' passages; an application for a job with the BBC as a programme assistant in Leeds was turned down, and a test as a possible boxing commentator on the radio also failed. Since the job at the West London tutorial college had lasted only a few months, 'the bad demon alcohol being responsible, as usual',[20] these failures hurt. He was back to scrabbling for occasional cheques wherever he could earn them. His failure to get the boxing commentator's job, in particular, brought on another fit of self-doubt. After all, he knew a lot about the sport, and he was beginning to be convinced that he had a good broadcasting manner.

> But I don't really fit in with the BBC wideboys, and I can't imagine myself as a future Raymond Glendenning or Eamonn Andrews. On the other hand, I am equally out of my depth with the intellectuals, the booksie boys. They make me feel clumsy and earnest, and I usually get drunk if there's liquor at hand. I suppose my lack of education and breeding hampers me more than I realise.[21]

But there were successes too—more talks on the radio, even a prize on the BBC's Third Programme (the precursor of Radio Three) for a parody of Graham Greene, submitted, oddly, in the name of John Bain. Best of all, two of his poems were selected for the prestigious 1953 PEN Anthology of new poetry.

At the Chelsea party to celebrate the new anthology, Scannell mingled with some of the leading figures of the world of poetry whom he would later come to know well. There was Roy Fuller, later to become Oxford University's Professor of Poetry; Laurie Lee; Robert Conquest, with whom Scannell would later enjoy a lengthy, witty, and occasionally scurrilous trans-Atlantic correspondence; Stevie Smith, 'black-haired then, just as elfin, with eyes like amused and very clever currants';[22] the Welsh doctor-poet Dannie Abse, who would become one of his closest friends; Thomas Blackburn; and Michael Hamburger. Some of them, like Fuller and Abse, he had already met less formally in Soho or Fitzrovia—but now he seemed to be accepted as part of literary London. Scannell must have felt, for a night at least, as if he had truly arrived as a poet, and he celebrated in the way he knew best.

The next morning, a night of 'staggering drunkenness'[23] behind him, he awoke to find the poet John Heath-Stubbs sprawled across his couch, fast asleep, having seen Scannell safely home. A few years later, Heath-Stubbs would be completely blind; even then, his eyesight was failing. The fact that he had felt so anxious about Scannell's well-being as he staggered out of the party says a lot about him, and also about the condition that Scannell must have been in.

A few weeks later came a suggestion from Vernon's brother Kenneth, who was working in a bookshop in Dundee. Would Vernon like to join him for a few weeks while the proprietor was away? It meant selling books in the shop and coffee in the coffee bar beneath—hardly demanding work, and a welcome opportunity to get away from London, and the constant reproach of novels abandoned and poems not written. Best of all, it would mean three weeks with Kenneth, surrounded by books.

But the trip to Dundee and the PEN party were two bright spots in a bleak time. Discontented and unsure of himself, Scannell was disenchanted with novel writing, and although his poetry was being published, he could still see no prospect of its ever providing him with a living. He had moved back into Craven Terrace and Dorothy had wandered back into his life, but both the flat and the relationship were still as draughty, chill and uncomfortable as they had been before.

IV

That was Scannell's mood in June 1954, when he found himself in Notting Hill Gate with an hour or so to kill before he went to the pub. He took a newspaper into a nearby coffee bar and sat down to read, vaguely aware of a girl sitting at the counter. It was only when he looked up after a few minutes and their eyes met that he realized that it was Jo Higson. She was as surprised and excited to see him as he was to see her. She had left Leeds and was living in a flat around the corner in Kensington Park Gardens—and within a couple of days, so was Scannell. He described the meeting affectionately in *The Tiger and the Rose*—a passionate, romantic, life-changing encounter:

> I had met no other woman quite like her. She was herself, unique, inimitable, and already so precious to me that I was in a fever of apprehension in case I should lose her.[24]

And yet, Scannell being Scannell, it was all slightly more complicated than he suggested. He didn't mention in the book, for instance, that he was sitting with Dorothy at the time, which must have made the encounter slightly more awkward than he describes. Jo Higson—now Jo Scannell—remembers:

> I hadn't realised it was him, but I was looking at this couple, and just thinking 'Lucky her'. And then he looked up and I recognised him, and when he spoke I was highly embarrassed because I thought he must have thought I was staring at him . . . In a way, it wasn't like moving in together when he came to my flat. We just got drunk one evening and went home, and there we stayed. Together. I suppose it was a bit daring—I had a boyfriend at the time, but he wasn't important to me . . . It was an emotional thing right away. I recognised that there was something there that appealed to me—I know now it was his intellectual honesty. What Vernon said, he meant. And he would never compromise about that.[25]

Intellectual honesty or not, he would still slip away every now and then for the next week or so, saying that he was going for a drink—and going round to see Dorothy again. Once again, Vernon was finding it very hard to close the book and say goodbye.

But for the next few happy, hectic months he and Jo were lost in each other like two teenagers, though Vernon was thirty-two and Jo twenty-nine. Life with Vernon was like his driving—never dull, but occasionally frightening. The first night they went out together should have told Jo what she could expect; Kenneth came as well, and the two brothers got roaring drunk, as they usually did:

> Vernon picked me up and put me over his shoulder, and then fell down and grazed my arm badly. My father was taking me to Glyndebourne that night, and I had agonising pains, but I was pleased to have them because they reminded me of Vernon . . . I woke up the next morning clutching his first

book of poems, and I thought, 'How marvellous! Now he can't get away!'
Right from the beginning I knew it was very special.

Vernon went to meet Jo's parents at Edenbridge in Surrey, and formed a
lasting friendship with her father, a First World War veteran. By the end of
June, he was writing to a BBC producer who had commissioned a script
from him:

> I think I'm going to be married fairly soon. She is a painter, very intelligent
> and modest and not a bit phoney. An additional attraction for me is that she
> turned Kenneth Severs down.[26]

It was, he told another BBC correspondent 'an unnerving but oddly exhilarating prospect'[27] And then, in October—Vernon having this time dutifully
seen to the formalities of his divorce—they were finally married at
Kensington Register Office.

After their wedding, they left Jo's tiny studio flat in Kensington
Gardens—and presumably, at last, Dorothy as well—and went for six
months to take care of a Scottish farmhouse called Pennymore on the
shores of Loch Fyne owned by Dick Broomin-White, a friend of Jo's parents, an MP, and a one-time senior intelligence officer in MI5 and MI6.[28]
It sounds like a rural idyll:

> The nearest pub is eight miles away so I'm becoming clear-eyed and rather fat
> since I've suddenly taken to eating huge quantities of chocolate...I go out
> occasionally with a gun and a spaniel, but so far no rabbit has called my bluff,
> thank God. We have a three mile walk every day to fetch milk; no electricity,
> but manage to live pretty comfortably.[29]

The idea was that they should live rent-free as caretakers, so that Jo could
paint and Vernon could revive his faltering ambitions as a novelist. In five
months, in and among chopping wood for the fire that was their only
source of heat and breaking the ice on the stream from which their water
came, he had finished another novel, called *Confessions of a Mystified Sinner*,
taking his title from James Hogg's nineteenth-century classic, *The Private
Memoirs and Confessions of a Justified Sinner*. Flushed with optimism, the disappointment of *A Taste for Violence* now forgotten, he packed it up and sent
it off to a publisher.

This attempt at a novel was no more successful than the last, but just
before they were due to return from Scotland, Vernon received a letter from
the liberal journalist George Scott, editor of the weekly political review

Truth. Scott was trying to build a new reputation for the magazine, which had been badly damaged by wartime allegations of fascism and anti-Semitism, and he had already recruited future journalistic stars such as Bernard Levin, Philip Oakes, and Alan Brien to his team of writers. He was looking for someone to write a regular sports column and thought that Scannell, whom he had heard talking about boxing in one of his broadcasts, might be the ideal candidate.

Scannell was in no position to turn down the offer of regular employment: within weeks of the wedding, they had discovered that Jo was pregnant. Their rent-free tenure of Pennymore was coming to an end, the hope of money from the novel was fading, and he needed an income to support his wife and child. The problem was that he had no particular knowledge of, nor interest in, any sport other than boxing—but he was not about to tell Scott that. He would cross that bridge when he came to it.

His first column, of course, was on boxing, but then he wrote on point-to-point with Jo's help, on international rugby with the advice of her father, a dedicated former player, and over the next few weeks on cricket, hockey, and tennis, always relying on the knowledge of different friends and acquaintances. Then, as he grew more confident, he began to write on other sports without any knowledge at all, relying on his writing skill to give his columns the appearance of authority. 'If I learned anything from my stint as a sports journalist,' he said later, 'it was to view all experts with suspicion.'[30]

He was enjoying this light-hearted, easygoing writing—but now that they were back in London, living again in the little studio room in Kensington Park Gardens, he needed more money than *Truth* was paying him. Answering an advertisement in the *New Statesman*, he was offered an even more unlikely job, writing promotional literature for the National Anti-Vivisection Society. Vivisection was not a subject he had ever thought much about, but for £500 a year,[31] which was the pay the Society was offering, he was more than happy to have strong enough feelings to produce a monthly newsletter on how evil it was, and drive off to different places a couple of times a month to give lectures to 'bored schoolchildren, mad vegetarian societies and sceptical audiences from youth clubs'.[32]

Together with the income from his column in *Truth*, it was just about enough to support them, even though money from writing seemed to have dried up. In any case, the work that he was doing allowed no spare time for poetry or novels. *Confessions of a Mystified Sinner*, which carried so many of their hopes, came back from a third publisher, then a fourth, and finally a fifth, each time with a kind and more-or-less encouraging note explaining why they were not interested in publishing it. Eventually, almost terminally disheartened, he threw the manuscript in the bin.

This time, it was the birth of their first child that lifted him out of his depression. He had never expected to feel more than 'mild curiosity' about the baby girl, whom they named Jane—the only other time he had become a father, after all, he had walked away before the child was born and never looked back—but her arrival fascinated and enthralled him—even though, in a note to a friend at the BBC, he joked that she 'looks like Sydney Greenstreet in one of his more sinister roles'.[33] Perhaps it was Jane's birth that started him writing poetry again: his former lover Jean Stead, now Jean Bourne, had a child around the same time, and the poems he wrote for the two babies spelled out the hopes and fears he felt for their futures. In 'First Child—for John and Jean Bourne' he remembers the common apprehensions of all first-time parents about broken nights and lost liberty, but then focuses on the real, unforeseen terrors for the vulnerable newborn baby, the illnesses and accidents that threaten 'That innocent and O, so fragile head'.[34]

'Poem for Jane', like Philip Larkin's 'Born Yesterday', which was written a couple of years earlier, considers the wishes that poets often express for beauty, happiness, love, and other gifts for new born babies, only to reject them as inadequate. Larkin opts for ordinariness, Scannell not for love but for 'a deep capacity / For loving'. He wants that, he says, not for the lucky person whom she might grow up to love:

> But because, without it, you
> Would never know completely joy,
> As I know joy through loving you.[35]

In *The Tiger and the Rose*, he describes the sudden realization that, with children, love could go further than the fleeting romantic passion he had felt for some of the women in his life, further even than the feeling he had for Jo, who still seemed to him to be the Miss Right he had been searching for. Jane's birth brought a new tenderness into Scannell's poetry:

> I suddenly realized that this tiny person had altered me, fundamentally and irrevocably, that her advent had created inside me areas of feeling that had not previously existed, that for the first time in my life I was capable of experiencing something approaching selfless love. I was deeply and humbly grateful for the change.[36]

Whatever other shortcomings he might prove to be guilty of in his relationships and in his family life, there was never any doubting his love and affection for the children which Jo bore him. 'I remember when we were little,
he was fun more than anything else. For his time, he was a pretty hands-on
father', Jane recalls now. 'He was around more than other people's fathers,
and he was very funny—right to the end of his life. I remember things like
him asking us questions and having quizzes—we enjoyed that at the dinner
table. He wasn't testing us, just having fun.'[37]

  With other children, too, whether his grandchildren, the young relatives
of people he was close to, or pupils in the many schools where he taught or
gave readings, he could be kindly, avuncular, and understanding. All these
qualities might often be hidden behind an assumed grumpiness when talking to other people, or behind a stern and demanding classroom persona,
but Scannell was a man who could love, understand, and empathize with
children and young people. Perhaps because of his own harsh and loveless
upbringing, he had an instinctive sympathy for the child struggling to com-
prehend the unfriendly complexities of the adult world, whether in the
classroom or outside. That is not to say that he was openly emotional, as Jane
herself pointed out wryly some forty years later:

> When my father felt anything, he wouldn't tell you, he'd go away and write a
> poem about it. Work was the centre of his life, at least until the later years,
> when we were grown up. *To Jane* is a good example of that: it is focused on
> me, his daughter, but it is above all a piece of work.[38]

It was not until the late sixties that he began writing poetry and novels
specifically for children, but Scannell always believed passionately in
W. H. Auden's much-quoted and incisive observation that 'While there are
some good poems which are only for adults, because they presuppose adult
experience in their readers, there are no good poems which are only for
children.'[39] Like all good children's poets, he treats his young audience seriously and without condescension, offering them complex and difficult ideas
expressed directly and honestly: his books for children contain many poems,
such as 'Growing Pain', 'Elaine's Story', or 'Nettles' that also fit well into his
adult collections. 'Apple Poem', on the other hand, published in 1987, is a
complex and serious meditation on existence, on the echoes of myth,
memory, and potential that resonate around a physical object. It is hardly a
poem for children—but there, nestling amongst the philosophical specula-
tions, is a description of the apple in which any child could take delight:

> domestic, familiar as a pet,
> Plump as your granny's cheek ... [40]

It was with the birth first of Jane, and then of Jo's other five sons and daughters that this sympathy with childhood began, and with the various joys and tragedies that they brought him that it deepened into the mature understanding of both a father and a poet.

More practically and more immediately, the arrival of Jane meant it was important to find somewhere to live that would give the family more room than the little flat in Kensington Park Gardens. Life as an ambassador for the National Anti-Vivisection Society was dull, repetitive, and uninspiring, and when Jo suggested that a friend of her father's might be able to find Vernon a job as an English teacher at a prep school near the family home in Kent, there seemed to be little to keep them in London. In September 1955, the little family of three moved to the village of Limpsfield, where Vernon would resurrect his teaching career at Hazelwood School.

1. Vernon at Otley in 1998. (Photo: Alan Benson)

2. James and Elsie Bain, with (left to right) Kenneth, Sylvie and Vernon. Vernon never forgave his father for his brutality or his mother for her lack of affection. He was, he said, 'fairly unhappy'. (Photo: Not known. Scannell family collection)

3. Vernon described days like this with his older brother: 'Both my brother and I were literary children in a way, We both were able to read fairly unusually young…it was he who taught me to read.' (Photo: Not known. Scannell family collection)

High Street, Limpsfield

4. Redfern, the Scannell's final Limpsfield home. The poet Richard Church lived here for ten years shortly after the First World War. (Reproduced by permission of Patricia Hall)

5. Jo Scannell with Jane and Nancy at their home in Limpsfield. (Photo: Not known. Jo Scannell collection)

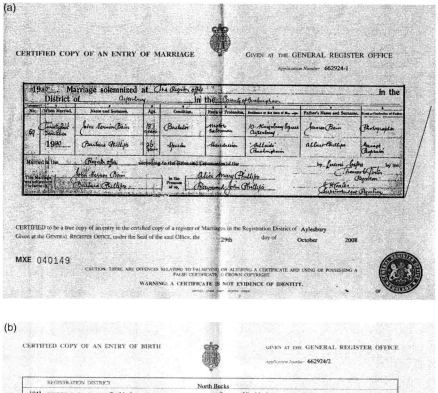

(a)

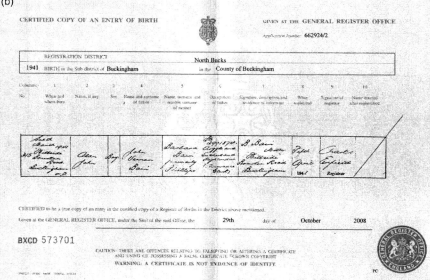

(b)

6. (a) and (b). Marriage certificate and birth certificate. The day after Vernon's first, forgotten, wedding, Barbara went back to live with her parents in Buckingham. That is where the couple's son was born just over three months later. (Photocopies of originals)

7. Vernon's signing-up papers claimed that he was unmarried, but no one cared that he was lying. Barely two months later, his wife and son were listed as his dependants. (Photo: Andrew Taylor)

8. Folly Cottage, the Dorset home to which Vernon and Jo moved in 1967, was originally three cottages for agricultural labourers. (Photo: Andrew Taylor)

Military History Sheet.

Service at Home and Abroad.

Country.	Service to count as British or Indian.	From	To	Length of Service.	
				Years	Days
~~Home~~	British	19·2·41	20·12·42	1	305
Egypt	"	21·12·42	28·1·44	1	39
HOME		29·1·44	2·6·44	—	125
NWE		3·6·44	21·6·44	—	19
HOME		22·6·44	30·1·47	3	192
			Total	6	315

Left.
Part I.
At.

N.B.—The Country only to be shewn.—It is not necessary to shew separately the service in the different stations of the same country. England, Scotland and Ireland to be shewn under the general term "Home."
For mode of computing service abroad see King's Regulations.
Note.—Service reckoning as Indian Service to be inserted in Red Ink.

21771 Wt. 3366/138 1,000,000 11/39 McC & Co T 5258. Forms/Books/24.

W.3040

9. The Military History Sheet on Vernon's Army records shows clearly that he left for Egypt on 21 December 1942—nearly seven weeks after the Battle of El Alamein. (Photo: Andrew Taylor)

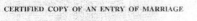

CERTIFIED COPY OF AN ENTRY OF MARRIAGE   GIVEN AT THE GENERAL REGISTER OFFICE

Application Number   COL.769419

19 46   Marriage solemnized at _____ the Register Office _____ in the

District of _____ Leeds _____ in the _____ County Borough of Leeds

No.	When Married.	Name and Surname.	Age.	Condition.	Rank or Profession.	Residence at the Time of Marriage.	Father's Name and Surname.	Rank or Profession of Father.
60	Twelfth January 1946	Vernon Scannell	26 years	Bachelor	Journalist	"Oakwood Avenue Leeds	Patrick Scannell	Commercial artist
		Estella Cope	28 years	Spinster	Medical Student	"Oakwood Avenue Leeds	Lionwell Cope	Timber merchant (retired)

Married in the _____ Register Office _____ according to the Rites and Ceremonies of the _____ by Licence, before me,

This Marriage was solemnized between us, { Vernon Scannell / Estella Cope } in the Presence of us, { Zena Beaham / Sheila Gregory } _____ Superintendent Registrar

CERTIFIED to be a true copy of an entry in the certified copy of a register of Marriages in the Registration District of **Leeds**

Given at the GENERAL REGISTER OFFICE, under the Seal of the said Office, the   **12th**   day of   **February**   **2008**

MXD 648327

CAUTION: THERE ARE OFFENCES RELATING TO FALSIFYING OR ALTERING A CERTIFICATE AND USING OR POSSESSING A FALSE CERTIFICATE. © CROWN COPYRIGHT

WARNING: A CERTIFICATE IS NOT EVIDENCE OF IDENTITY.

10. A bigamous marriage certificate. Practically every detail about Vernon is false. (Photocopy of original).

11. Family man. Vernon and Jo in 1967 with (left to right) Nancy, John, Jake, Toby and Jane. 'He was always fun, never cross with us, never laid a finger on us. In fact we rang rings round him', says Nancy. (Photo: Not known. Scannell family collection)

12. Angela Beese. 'She was delightfully and piercingly, almost unendurably beautiful. I love her', Vernon wrote in his diary. (Photo: VS)

13. Vernon with Jo Peters at Otley. 'I love her so much. I'm sure that this is really my first experience of wholly committed love for a woman,' he said. (Photo: Not known. Jo Peters collection)

14. The boxer Freddie Mills, former World Light-Heavyweight champion, lends a hand at the launch of Vernon's first novel in 1953. (Photo: Not known. Scannell family collection)

15. Four poets: Laurie Lee, Jeremy Robson, Vernon Scannell and Dannie Abse at a Poetry and Jazz Special broadcast by Harlech Television. (Photo: Not known. Jeremy Robson collection)

16. The launch of *Soldiering* On at the Imperial War Museum in 1989. With Scannell, from left, are Anthony Thwaite; Roy Fuller; Bruce Kent, then Chair of the Campaign for Nuclear Disarmament; Ruth Fainlight; Norman WIllis, then General Secretary of the TUC; Scannell; Alan Sillitoe; Jeremy Robson; Kit Wright; Peter Porter; Gavin Ewart. (Photo: Not known. Jeremy Robson collection)

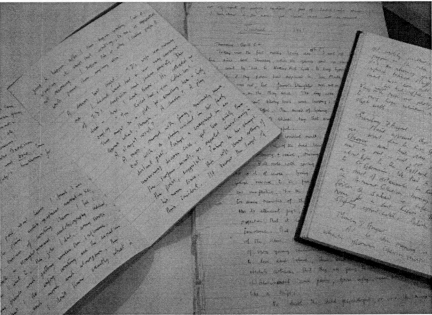

17. (a) and (b) Twelve volumes survive of the thirteen in which Scannell kept his diaries from the early 1950s until the end of his life. (Photo: Andrew Taylor, Leeds University Library)

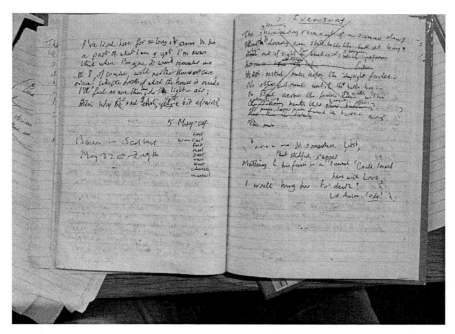

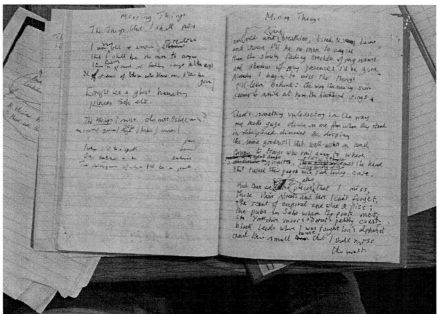

18. (a) and (b) Scannell's notebook jottings for *Missing Things*. (Photo: Andrew Taylor, Leeds University Library)

19. The portrait of Vernon painted by Charlotte Harris in 2003. Harris said she tried to catch his half smile, and the sadness and humour in his eyes. (Reproduced by permission of Charlotte Harris)

10

Schoolmaster

And now another autumn morning finds me
With chalk dust on my sleeve and in my breath...

'Ageing Schoolmaster', from *A Sense of Danger* (1962)

I

In Limpsfield, the family lived in a little cottage on Detillens Lane that had been the home of Vernon's predecessor at the school. It was 'a tiny, crumbling place that was supposed to date back to the fourteenth century'[1] by Vernon's account—'a nasty little place, damp and unfurnished and uncomfortable',[2] according to Jo. Limpsfield was a well-to-do village surrounded by National Trust countryside and boasting a greengrocer, a butcher, and a bakery. Frederick Delius, one of Scannell's favourite composers, lay buried in the churchyard. Stockbrokers and city workers mixed with local farm workers in The Bull, just around the corner, which, with other nearby pubs such as The Wheatsheaf, the Haycutter Inn, and the Grasshopper Inn would become a much-loved haunt over the next ten years.

A mile or so away, in a large, opulent Victorian mansion set in 25 acres of woodland with cricket and rugby pitches, tennis court, and croquet lawn, stood Hazelwood School. It was a very traditional institution, which aimed to prepare the young sons of prosperous parents to go on to public school at thirteen. The curriculum was necessarily geared towards the Public Schools Common Entrance exam—therefore, in Scannell's view, 'discouraging originality from either teacher or pupil'. It seems an odd place to find a man with his instinctive left-wing views, and his memories of the school are dismissive:

Figure 13. The first house in Limpsfield at Detillens Lane—'damp and unfurnished and uncomfortable', Jo called it. (Photo: Not known. Scannell family collection)

> There was something dreamlike about much of school life, moments of Alice-in-Wonderland craziness, an unnerving sense of lunacy in command, together with a vague sense of déjà-vu which I think must have come from vague memories of my reading the *Magnet* and *the Gem* when I was about the same age as the boys I was teaching.[3]

But in fact, Hazelwood suited Scannell, and not only because, since the headmaster was a friend of his father-in-law, no one was going to be too pernickety about his complete lack of qualifications. The traditional English prep school's concentration on sports—the whole school had compulsory games for two hours each afternoon—meant that his interest in boxing could be given full rein, and one of the first things he did when he arrived was to ask the headmaster if he could erect a temporary ring in the gymnasium. And, of course, however dull and unimaginative he affected to find the curriculum, his own essentially conservative view of English literature would have been broadly welcomed.

He had high standards and high expectations of the boys he taught. One of them, Dudley Treffry, still has a reading list that Scannell handed out to a class of twelve-year-olds for the summer holiday:

Conrad—The Secret Agent
Milton—Paradise Lost
Hemingway—A Farewell to Arms, For Whom the Bell Tolls
Gorky—My Childhood
Galsworthy—Strife (about struggle between capital and labour)
Orton—Loot
Henry James—What Maisie Knew
Lawrence—Sons and Lovers
Garrett Mattingly—The Defeat of the Spanish Armada
Shakespeare—Antony and Cleopatra ('Hamlet will come later', Scannell
    commented)
Gibbon—Decline and Fall (Not all of its seventy-one chapters, Scannell reas-
    sured his pupils, 'but a taste')
Tolstoy—The Government Inspector[4]
Dostoyevsky—The Gambler
John Gunther—Inside South America
Osbert Lancaster—With an Eye to the Future (autobiography)
Orwell—Homage to Catalonia
Osborne—Look Back in Anger
John Arden—Left Handed Liberty
Somerset Maugham—Collected Short Stories ('Just one or two to get a feel')
Bullock—Hitler, a Study in Tyranny
Shirer—Rise and Fall of the Third Reich
Mark Twain—Life on the Mississippi or any other of his works
Giuseppe (di Lampedusa)—The Leopard
Samuel Butler—The Way of All Flesh
Pasternak—Collected Poems

It is a demanding list, and it is not recorded how many boys actually read
how many books—but that was not the point. 'He was not saying, "You've
got to read this", but encouraging us to try to read widely before we went
off to secondary education', says Treffry. 'There was nothing patronizing
about his lessons—for instance, he would start talking about his admiration
for John Milton's attitude towards censorship, expecting us to be aware of
the whole historical context—but because his language was so crystal clear,
the class very quickly got hold of what he was getting at.'[5] He remembers
Scannell with affection—a towering figure in a green corduroy jacket, yellow v-necked sweater and checked shirt, who could be impatient with
those who did not respond to his passion for poetry, but who was colossally
enthusiastic with those who did. He had a burly, boxer's build, and his temper was occasionally volcanic, leading him to shout, roar, and bang the

blackboard with his fist or even hurl the wooden blackboard cleaner theatrically around the room—but his enthusiasm was infectious. Treffry recalls:

> He was inspirational without a question, and very passionate indeed about language—almost a force of nature, with the sort of charisma that silenced a room when he walked into it.

Another former pupil is the journalist Simon Jenkins, who wrote about Scannell in *The Guardian* newspaper shortly after his death:

> He did not teach English, which presumably was his job. He simply read poetry from start to finish. He read the entire canon and made us read it back. We had to learn nothing by heart, but he did insist that we 'recognise by heart' what he was reading. This rough diamond of a man would recite Marvell's To His Coy Mistress when close to tears (from his memoirs I can perhaps tell why)...
> ...Keats, Wordsworth, Tennyson, Hardy, cascaded from the walls. In particular Scannell read the war poets, Owen, Brooke and Sassoon, with a feeling and a savagery that must have tested the headmaster's patriotism (if he ever knew). Poetry must always tell a story, he said, but do so by employing meter, scansion and song.[6]

Jenkins was also enthusiastic about his weekly boxing classes in the winter, although Treffry remembers boys desperately trying to avoid catching Scannell's eye when he came into lunch, searching for contestants for one of the inter-house matches that he used to arrange. However, a third pupil, Mike Jordan, recalls an incident that might show not just Scannell's enthusiasm for the sport, but also his understanding of what it could achieve, and his empathy with small boys:

> I was bullied a lot as a little boy—I suffered from undiagnosed deafness, and I'd lived in Italy, both things that maybe made me different. Whatever the reason, I used to hide away at break to avoid the bullies.
> Vernon Scannell used to teach all the boys boxing, and one day, it was my turn. I've never known whether this was deliberate, but he matched me for a bout with the leader of the bullies. I remember thinking that I could either get beaten up in the ring, or I could just do my best, and I ended up hammering the bully and winning the bout.
> I was never bullied after that. It was a turning point at school for me.[7]

And there was another reason why the boys treated Scannell with awe and fascination. Thrilling rumours filtering back into the school from Limpsfield suggested that he was not at all the type of English teacher that their parents might have expected for their young sons. In a letter sent to Scannell in 1987, Dudley Treffry told him about the excitement that swept through the dormitory as the stories were told breathlessly of Mr Scannell 'blind drunk in the pub and battling with the bobbies'.[8] Treffry recalled later that there was sometimes visible evidence of these nocturnal adventures.

'Sometimes he would come in after a night at the pub with black eyes and wounds all over his face. It gave him a sort of heroic stature in our eyes as word got round about his pub fights. On one occasion, someone said that it had taken four bobbies to hold him down.'[9]

In his reply to Treffry's letter, which also recalled the strict discipline in English lessons, Scannell, maybe tactfully, made no mention of fighting in the pub, but did give an insight into his own attitude towards teaching:

It was rather a shock to learn I was a figure of terror: I've always thought I was a benign, avuncular creature—not quite Mr Chips, perhaps, but not Mr Squeers either... I was never really a professional teacher—I was doing it only until I could refloat myself as a freelance writer after getting married and having children. All the same, I did care very much about what I was trying to do—instil a love of language and literature, and a regard for the efficiency of the left jab.[10]

II

At the beginning of his career at Hazelwood, the boys knew nothing of Scannell's 'real job' as a poet, a man who, in a literary sense, practised at home what he preached in the classroom.[11] And in fact, he had all too little time for writing poems. His teaching duties kept him busy during term time, and despite Wilson Knight's earlier promise that as a teacher and 'a real gentleman in the holidays',[12] he would find time for poetry, he had so little money that he found himself taking on private coaching jobs to make up the shortfall. When he *was* writing, he was often diverted by work on short stories for the BBC which he hoped—wrongly—might also bring in a significant income. With a wife and child to support—and, by now, another baby on the way—he was even more tightly enmeshed in the trap of having to spend time on earning a living that he would have preferred to use in creating more poems. He was also, incidentally, adding to his own problems with a string of late, drunken nights and self-induced, massive hangovers.

And, however tight money was, he was not a man who could be easily patronized. Staying at The Wheatsheaf at Limpsfield was a man who had recently won nearly £260,000[13] on the football pools, and had started investing in West End theatrical productions. Robert Crick, the son of the landlord of The Wheatsheaf, remembers that he considered backing Vernon financially:

> He was very rich and condescending, and invited Vernon for lunch at the Ivy. He offered to put up some money to sponsor him but said that he should start writing more commercial poetry—and that's when the lunch ended. Vernon stood up in a temper, knocking the table over and scattering the glasses everywhere, and told him just what he thought of him. And that was that.[14]

During his first months at Hazelwood, he heard from the poet Dannie Abse, who was co-editing *Mavericks*, a new anthology of modern English poetry, and wanted to include some of Scannell's poems. The collection was planned as a riposte to the emergence of The Movement, a group of young poets who had just been featured in an anthology called *New Lines*, collected by Robert Conquest. The Movement poets—Conquest himself, Philip Larkin, Dennis Enright, John Wain, and Donald Davie among them—focused on discipline, form, and style in their writing and saw themselves as producing poetry of 'order, severity, and correctness'[15] that was 'not precisely satirical but of a dry anti-romantic flavour'.[16] In fact, they were united by little more than a dislike of Dylan Thomas's work and the fact that they generally had a university background. Abse said they had little in common with each other, 'except perhaps their antagonism towards sensibility and sentiment and their corresponding emphasis on being "tough"'.[17] In *Mavericks*, he and his co-editor, Howard Sergeant, sought to give a voice to other young contemporary poets who were 'making a valid attempt to grapple with problems beyond those of technique (important though these may be) and to communicate, lucidly and honestly, what they feel to be significant experience'.[18]

Where Scannell stood in a literary spat of half a century ago hardly seems important—fitting poets into groups or movements is generally a fairly futile exercise, and in any case, several of those listed as part of The Movement later denied that it ever existed as a coherent alliance with its own programme and philosophy. But what is significant is that this was another appearance in an important and influential anthology to follow his inclusion in the PEN collection. With only a single unsatisfactory collection of poetry behind him, he was acknowledged as, in Abse's words, one of the contemporary poets 'unafraid of sensibility and sentiment, who are neither arid nor lush... working from the heat of personal predicament and common experience.' He was worth listening to.

Some of the leading figures in The Movement, such as Conquest and Enright, would later become Scannell's good friends; John Wain had given him his first big break on the BBC; and Philip Larkin he would later name as among 'the poets I most enjoy and admire'.[19] But at this stage of his career he had little patience with what he called 'the University half-wits' composing their 'metrical crossword puzzles'.[20] In another diary entry a few days later, he sneered at 'Aimless Amis, Vain Wain, Davie, Larkin and others' as 'beginning to imitate themselves... not poets, but together they make up a composite and anonymous versifier, a glib oracle speaking mechanical triolets. Automation threatens to put even poets out of business.'[21] And even though, the next day, he confessed that he was being too hard on the poets themselves, his considered verdict on The Movement remained damning:

> It is altogether too conservative, unadventurous, decorous, and even if the ideal were to be attained, the result would scarcely be electrifying. It is sad to see the young people at the universities treading this neat and cosy path. If they don't aim at 'the roll, the rise, the carol, the creation' now, they never will.[22]

On the face of it, there might seem to be a degree of perversity in that judgement: Scannell, after all, shared the concern of The Movement poets for form, rhyme, and structure, although the romantic, lyric quality of much of his poetry meant that he would never be considered one of them. He did aim at Hopkins's roll, rise, carol, and creation. But the vituperation comes from a different source: as a poet, Scannnell had all the experience, self-reliance, originality of thought, and mental toughness of a genuinely self-educated intellectual, but he still felt at a disadvantage all his life when dealing with the 'booksie boys', the confident, sometimes supercilious representatives of the exclusive Oxbridge élite like the leading Movement poets.

A few years later, there is a clear note of whistling in the dark as he writes in his diary about watching himself on a television discussion programme:

> I saw nothing to feel narcissistic about, but I am forced to admit that I did feel just a little flicker of self-congratulation as I said to myself, 'Well, boy, you've fooled them all right. Nobody would know you weren't a real educated gent up there with a Cambridge don and the Professor of English Literature.[23]

The amiable, sociable Scannell didn't quite belong. And he never would.

III

At the same time as Abse and his co-anthologist, Howard Sergeant, were compiling their book, Scannell had also been putting together a collection of the poems he had written over the past eight years, and had interested a publisher called John Sankey, who ran a small company in North London called Villiers Publications. The collection, to be called *A Mortal Pitch*, would be the first since the disappointment of *Graves and Resurrections*, and for Scannell it was an opportunity to break away from the daily trials of domestic life and relaunch himself as a poet. He noted in his diary:

> I long for the kind of small success that would act as an incentive to further work. Life is difficult at the moment—Jane is teething and not sleeping at night, and Jo is being horribly sick and also suffering from toothache. I am suffering from fatty degeneration of the sensibility and chronic hangover.[24]

Among the thirty-four poems in *A Mortal Pitch* were the five already selected for the *Mavericks* anthology, including the wry and rather wistful 'Unsuccessful Poet':

> At the age of thirty or thereabouts when he says
> That he is a victim of an evil age where all
> Standards are debased, remember not to raise
> Sceptical brows or blunt instruments; and above all
> Do not judge when he goes quietly to his hovel
> To put his head in the oven, or write a novel.[25]

It is a sardonic dig at The Movement, with its agonizing over 'debased' standards, and also a grim reflection of the 35-year-old Scannell's view of his own novel-writing activities.

In fact, he was beginning to break into a new and optimistic period of his life as far as his writing was concerned. His second collection was in the shops, and a third, to be called *The Masks of Love*, was well under way. He had a job, and plans for another novel, a thriller, which he hoped would bring in some more money. The poetry, too, was at last beginning to flow. He was starting to work at it more regularly than he had done for months, and to sense the development of an individual and consistent tone of voice emerging in his work. But there were also more immediate and pressing priorities for him and Jo: on 4 December, with Jane just eighteen months old, their second daughter, Nancy, was born.

The first thing was to find a bigger place for the four of them to live, and Jo's mother, who had been worried from the moment they moved in about the damp in their original home, suggested a deal that would enable them to start again in a house that was for sale in Limpsfield's High Street. She would buy the house, and they would repay her the interest on the money that she spent in the form of rent. It was a generous gesture, and it meant that in the spring of 1958 the family was able to move into a bigger house, called Redfern, a double-fronted Queen Anne cottage with three bedrooms, a garden for the children, and built-in bookshelves in the front rooms for Vernon. Since the new 'rent' was less than they had been spending on the old place, they saved money as well. It had also been, Vernon discovered later, the home during the 1920s of the poet Richard Church, who praised both the house and the village in his memoir *The Voyage Home*: [26] if he had believed in such things, that might have seemed a good omen.

Jo Scannell remembers now how romantic and sentimental Vernon could be—but ever since they had moved in together, she and Vernon too had been struggling with a terrible and secret problem that would turn into something of a pattern throughout his life. Most nights he would go to The Wheatsheaf, The Bull, or one of the other pubs in the neighbourhood, and settle down with the other locals in the bar, witty, jovial, and popular. Five or six pints were usual, nine or ten not uncommon.

And often, this literate, friendly, and sensitive man would stagger home drunk and beat his wife until she bled. Looking back on it now, Jo can hardly believe that it happened, or that she tolerated it:

> Most of the time, he was the gentlest person with me. But right from the beginning, when we were living in Kensington Park Gardens, he could be very violent when he was drunk. When he was in that state, it became part of his persona—he would fight people in pubs, and then he would come home and attack me.
>
> The whole basis of it was jealousy—he was immensely, pathologically sexually jealous. I remember when I was pregnant with Jane we went to a party and I was wearing a very pretty dress—a Dior copy that I was very proud of. We came home early because I wasn't feeling well, and he was really violent, pushing me around, hitting me, and shouting. I fled out of the house and he chased me around the streets for a while.
>
> Then he cut up this dress with my nail scissors and put the pieces in a brown paper bag. He couldn't bear me talking to anyone else, or even looking as if I might talk to another man, and he was convinced I'd dressed up for somebody else. [27]

By the next day, it would all be forgotten—literally, in Vernon's case:

> After we got to Limpsfield, I would hear him coming up the stairs in our little
> house, and at first I would think, 'Oh lovely, he's back.' But he would come
> straight in and grab me by the hair, pull me out of bed and push me down-
> stairs. He wasn't vicious—I would never call Vernon vicious—but he was very,
> very rough. Perhaps I should have done something about it—but in the morn-
> ing, there he'd be, complaining about his hangover, and I'd bring him a cup of
> tea, and we'd giggle about something.
>
> Remember, I was just a young middle-class girl who had never experi-
> enced anything like that. There was no such thing as domestic violence in
> those days. I just used to think it would be all right tomorrow as long as I shut
> up: the thought of being without him was terrifying to me.

This was the hidden violence that blighted her life and his, and would also
cripple virtually every long-term relationship he had. One of his most
famous poems, produced a few years later, gives a stark insight into his state
of mind at the time. 'A Case of Murder',[28] one of many poems written by
Scannell that can be read either by adults or by children, has been popular
in school English classes for years, although its ostensible subject—the killing of a cat by a nine-year-old boy—has occasionally made it controversial.
The poem was turned down for the BBC's *Woman's Hour* because the editor was worried about her 'more squeamish listeners'. Scannell was asked to
supply another, with the suggestions that 'if you could avoid actually *squash-
ing* an animal, we should feel much happier'.[29]

More than forty years after its first publication, the *Scotsman* newspaper[30]
ran a story about parents complaining that such 'violent literature' could
damage their children. The chairman of the Campaign for Real Education
declared that it might 'upset or desensitise' pupils and 'put ideas into their
heads'.

The row, such as it was, was a good example of Scannell's own frequently
repeated lament that the general public does not read poetry. Even a cursory
look at 'A Case of Murder' shows it to be a poem about guilt and regret.
After teasing, prodding, and finally killing the cat, which is caught—possibly
accidentally—in a slammed door, the boy cries in terror at what he has
done, and hides the body in a cupboard under the stairs. In a macabre conclusion, moving from horrifying realism into the realm of nightmares,
Scannell describes how, although dead, the cat grows over the years until:

> the cupboard swells and all sides split
> And the huge black cat pads out of it.

It is frightening, in the gruesome way that many children enjoy being frightened, although it is hard to see how such a poem might give its readers the idea of slamming cats in doors.

But Scannell was fond of quoting T. S. Eliot's observation in *The Use of Poetry and the Use of Criticism* that a poet uses 'meaning' in a poem much as a burglar uses a piece of meat with a guard dog, to keep the reader quiet while the poem does its work upon him. We should, in other words, look sceptically at what a poem appears to be 'about'—a very useful caution in reading this poem.

Eighteen years after writing 'A Case of Murder', in his book *How to Enjoy Poetry*, Scannell describes how the idea of the poem came to him. An acquaintance had told him how he and his wife had returned from a shopping trip to find their nine-year-old son in tears because he had somehow 'accidentally killed the cat'. That was it. There was no suggestion that, like the boy in the poem, he had hated the animal, or poked it with a stick, or that there was any real doubt—as there is in the poem—over whether the 'accident' was actually deliberate. At the time, however, Scannell had been reading a study of the brutality and sadism of SS guards in the Nazi concentration camps, written by a former prisoner, and began to think about the infliction of suffering, of remorse, and of guilt. He had, he says, no *conscious* intention when he began the poem of focusing on these emotions: 'I surprised myself by the ending and, having written it, had to ask myself what I meant by it. I believe that it proceeded from my own preoccupations with "man's inhumanity to man", and that the poem explores to some extent the nature of sadism, violence, repression and guilt.'[31]

Other people have read the poem in different ways: the cat is black, and Scannell was congratulated at one poetry reading on having written a poem about Black Power, which he agreed was a perfectly reasonable interpretation. 'Provided that the reader does not actually misread the poem, that is, misconstrue the literal meaning—and it would surely be very difficult to do so—then he is free to attribute whatever significance he wishes to the symbolic or allegorical elements in the writing.'[32]

So, although it remains a challenging poem, it is still surely one that would be suitable for use in school. Young children may find the ideas of sadism and repression difficult to deal with, but they have plenty to say about violence and guilt. It is a gripping story, brilliantly told, which can start all kinds of interpretative discussions, and from which they can learn a huge amount about the craft of poetry.

However, Scannell often notes that writers may reveal much more about themselves in their poetry and imaginative work than in their avowedly autobiographical books, and there is another underlying meaning to 'A Case of Murder' which reflects that. Within the poem, there is a description of brutal sexual violence, the excitement that it engenders, and the suffering, guilt, and shame that follow from it. Scannell is dealing in his poem with a subject that he could not face in his life.

The cat the boy hates is warm, inviting, and 'plump as a cushion'. The way that he plagues and abuses it is significant: he takes 'Daddy's stick' and prods at the cat under the couch with it:

> He followed the grin on his new-made face,
> A wide-eyed, frightened snarl of a grin,
> And he took the stick and he thrust it in,
> Hard and quick in the furry dark,
> The black fur squealed, and he felt his skin
> Prickle with sparks of dry delight.

It seems fairly clear that those excited thrusts of 'Daddy's stick' can be seen as a description of delight in violent and abusive sex. The cat for which he feels such irrational loathing—warm, enticing, and feminine—has already been described as a 'muff', which is not only a hand-warmer but also a slang term for a woman's pubic hair. The 'wide-eyed, frightened snarl of a grin' of the boy as he closes on the animal is unsettlingly reminiscent of the 'peculiar half-grin, half snarl' that Scannell remembered on his father's face at the start of one of the bullying, sadistic outbursts that scarred his childhood.[33] He is writing a poem which on one level at least revisits his father's violence and confronts his private guilt and shame about his own violent behaviour. There is no doubting the literary quality of 'A Case of Murder': it takes a simple story of a child left alone in a flat, and draws the reader into a compelling and troubling world of Hitchcock-like psychological horror—but it is, on this reading, a disturbing poem which deals with violent misogyny, and with the anguish Scannell feels over his drunken, brutal attacks on his wife, and over the pleasure that he takes in them. Scannell himself said, in an introduction to the poem printed in a poetry book for schoolchildren, that it was 'about aggression and violence and the necessity to face the fact that these things exist. There are no abstractions in the poem. It attempts—with some success I think and hope—to *embody* its theme.'[34]

The violence in his life could be hidden most of the time. Bob Ball, a journalist with *Time Magazine* who lived in Limpsfield, used to drink with Vernon in The Bull, which was run by a 'formidable' landlady called Maisie. He says he never saw Vernon fighting drunk, either struggling with police-men, as the boys at Hazelwood claimed, or staggering home in a condition to beat up his wife, as Jo describes. 'I guess our drinking was substantial but decorous. We'd drink for an hour or two, and he would become either jolly or melancholy as the evening went on, but I never saw him even stumbling drunk', he says. But even so, both he and his wife had some idea of what went on behind locked doors and closed curtains.

> There was some domestic violence there. Once or twice you could see that Jo had been hit—she would have a black eye, bruises or something. But she would always have a story about it. We sort of looked the other way, I guess.[35]

IV

The probable roots of Scannell's violence stretch right back through the war and into his early childhood. Dr Felicity de Zulueta, a consultant psychia-trist and head of the Traumatic Stress Service at London's Maudsley Hospital, says that his story, and specifically 'A Case of Murder', represent a classic account of post-traumatic stress disorder (PTSD) triggered by his wartime experiences:

> It is almost a perfect textbook example. The poem tells the story of how the little boy is playing with the cat, and how the play gets more violent and more exciting, until he is acting out the violence that Scannell remembers from his own father. In the poem, though, he can go further, and the cat actually dies—at which point the other part of his brain, the victim side, becomes aware and is horrified and terribly upset. The guilt and pain just grow and grow—any psychiatrist would recognize this story from among their patients. I certainly wouldn't have been surprised by Scannell's story if he had walked into my clinic.[36]

This, of course, is an attempt at an explanation, not an excuse for the vio-lence, and it is based on Scannell's story as it emerges from his diaries, his writings, and the accounts of other people. It is impossible to make a detailed diagnosis of a patient who is not there in the consulting-room—but violence, fear, and raging jealousy are all common effects of PTSD, a chronic, longer-lasting, and intractable version of the 'shell-shock' with which soldiers in the First World War were diagnosed. Sufferers may experience severe depression, difficulties in forming lasting relationships, feelings of total ineffectiveness, and an overwhelming sense of shame. It all goes back to the experience of conflict and the childhood abuse before. De Zulueta goes on to say:

> Not everyone who goes to war suffers from PTSD, of course, but someone like Scannell, who had a cold mother in his childhood who failed to protect him from his violent father, would be very susceptible to it. In his childhood, it seems that he experienced the classic triangle of abuse, with himself as the victim, his father as the perpetrator of the violence, and his mother as the accomplice who allowed it to happen. As a result, he may well have been unable to cope emotionally with his wartime experiences.
>
> He hated his father, yet in many ways he emulated him. Under stress, he almost *became* his father. At one minute, he was the loving husband, and then suddenly he became the perpetrator of the violence. He would have been in a state of sheer terror. He did to Jo what was done to him by his father.

Scannell seems to have been uneasily aware of how he was copying his father's violence. In a poem published in 1962, he said that he saw his father's face in his shaving mirror each morning, 'Or something like a sketch of it gone wrong'.[37] The poem says he still cannot love the Old Man, although he can forgive 'the blows, the meanness and the lust'—but it ends, looking at his own face, on a clear note of self-disgust:

> ... These eyes in the glass regard the living
> Features with distaste, quite unforgiving.

Apart from the disturbing phenomenon of identification with the abuser, says de Zulueta, it's also common for children in a cold, abusive and violent relationship to latch onto another individual who they may feel understands them, and with whom they then develop an unusually close emotional bond—much as Scannell did with his brother Kenneth. And the influence of alcohol is often central to the violence that sufferers display in their later life—because they are unable to modulate or control their emotions, they may treat themselves with drugs or alcohol to dull their emotional suffering, calm down, and eventually sleep. That may seem to work until they overdo it, flip back into the deep-seated abusive triangle of abuser, accomplice, and victim, and act out again the violent thoughts that torment them.

It's impossible to say *which* wartime experiences may have been so damaging to Scannell—huddling in a trench as shells fell around him, watching friends being shot or blown to pieces, or simply the day-to-day hostility and regimentation of army life. 'Gunpowder Plot', published in *A Mortal Pitch* shortly after the family arrived in Limpsfield, describes how the fireworks on Bonfire Night trigger memories of bombs and shelling flooding back:

> The present shifts,
> Allows a ten-year memory to walk
> Unhindered now; and so I'm forced to hear
> The banshee howl of mortar and the talk
> Of men who died; am forced to taste my fear.[38]

Scannell, in fact—like many thousands of ex-servicemen who came home and were distant, cold, hostile. and occasionally violent in the post-war years—was as much a victim of the fighting as if he had lost an arm or a leg. So too, indirectly, were Jo and the other women with whom he shared his life over the next four decades. The huge black cat never returned to the cupboard.

V

One of the more interesting writing commissions that Scannell received around this time was from his old friend and mentor Bonamy Dobrée, who invited him in 1962 to write a critical study of the poet Edward Thomas for the British Council 'Writers and their Work' series, of which Dobrée was general editor. This brief 33-page pamphlet demonstrates how incisive and sensitive Scannell's criticism could be, and shows the esteem in which Dobrée held him, setting him alongside some of the most highly regarded critics of his time. Other pamphlets in the series were written by such figures as Stephen Spender, J. I. M. Stewart, Walter Allen, and G. S. Fraser.[39]

However, one poet writing about another, looking at the areas of his subject's poetry that he finds particularly interesting and significant, is often revealing of aspects of his own work, and the British Council pamphlet *Edward Thomas* provides important clues about Scannell's attitudes towards his own poetry and his own character. He was a lifelong admirer of Thomas's poetry—his diary records the simple assessment that he was 'a fine man and a fine poet'.[40] In his pamphlet, he comments on the irony and unsentimentality of the poems, and notes that Thomas used 'the rhythms of common speech on a flexible metrical leash', that his diction 'favours the simple words of Anglo-Saxon origin', and that in his poetry he shows 'a resolute refusal to inflate the currency of emotion, a sober regard for truth'. All these are observations that could have been made about Scannell's poetry too.

He suggested, too, that changing literary taste was one crucial reason why Thomas's clear, limpid poetry had been unappreciated. There existed, he said:

> a climate in which the poem which offers little or no challenge to the analytical intelligence, the poem whose primary, paraphaseable meaning surrenders itself on one or two careful readings, can scarcely be considered a serious poem at all.[41]

Once more, his analysis applies as much to his own work as to that of Thomas, and reflects again his bitterness about the 'University half-wits' and the academic world in which he still felt so ill at ease.

When he is writing about Thomas the man, the sense of fellow-feeling is even clearer. He was, Scannell says, a man who struggled to find time to write poetry because of the 'hack jobs undertaken grimly for the small sums of money they would yield';[42] he nursed an 'inflexible hostility' for his father; he sought to express, as Scannell later did, 'the feelings of all men who have borne arms in the service of their country'. Thomas was killed in action in 1917, in the war that Scannell remembered respectfully as:

> ... the one called Great
> Which ended in a sepia November
> Four years before my birth.[43]

He focuses on one poem in particular, 'No One So Much As You', in which Thomas laments his 'incapacity for loving', and the way that he can respond to his wife's love:

> With only gratitude
> Instead of love –
> A pine in solitude
> Cradling a dove.[44]

Elsewhere in the pamphlet, Scannell notes that Thomas:

> valued above all other human attributes the capacity for loving, but he believed that it had been denied him.

It is the same gift—'a deep capacity for loving'—that Scannell wished for his new-born daughter, one without which she 'would never know completely joy'. That, he believed, was his own fate:

> I wish I could grow up and show even ordinary sympathies with the tribulations, anxieties and weaknesses of others. The trouble is, I can in theory or with people who are not close to me. But not with those I am supposed to love.[45]

Being able to sympathize 'in theory', of course, is the mark of a poet, but being unable to do so in personal relationships seems to be a sign of some psychiatric imbalance; that icy phrase 'those I am supposed to love' speaks volumes for Scannell's aching awareness of his loss and theirs. Like many victims of post-traumatic stress disorder, he suffered not just from rages of sexual jealousy but from an underlying lack of trust, a pathological inability to give himself emotionally to someone else.

VI

On the surface, however, everything seemed to be going well: Redfern was warmer, more comfortable, than the little cottage in Detillens Lane had been; the two children were a delight; and even for Jo, the behind-closed-doors violence that she suffered did not spoil a time that she remembers as peaceful and fulfilled:

> I think of them as happy days. I was always happy when Vernon was there. I think I just hoped the violence would stop, and pushed it out of my mind most of the time. We got on well, and he was good company.[46]

They were still chronically short of money, but to their neighbours—looking the other way when Jo had bruises on her face—they seemed to be a contented, busy, happy family unit, with friends who thought of them with affection. Bob Ball recalls the girls being driven around the village and, later on, playing with ponies in the fields:

> Jo used to have an old Morris Minor shooting brake, so old that it had moss on the roof, and I can remember her driving the children everywhere in it. I admired Vernon very much. It seemed to me that his vocabulary was extraordinary, although from talking to him you would never have imagined that he could write poetry of the quality he did.[47]

There was a new feeling of optimism, too, about his writing, encouraged by Dobrée's continued regard, by the regular BBC broadcasts, by a new novel, and by the increasing number of commissions he was receiving from newspapers and magazines. He always had a pragmatic and businesslike attitude towards publication, as in this case of 'Song for a Winter Birth':

> It was commissioned by The Sunday Times...they rang up and said, 'Would you do a poem for a Christmas page of poetry by contemporary poets?' I think it was Philip Oakes who rang up. Being a man of integrity and honesty, I said, 'No, I'm not really a Christian.' To which he replied: 'The fee will be £25.' I said, 'It will be in the next post.' I would have written this poem anyway, so although it sounds terribly dishonest, in fact it wasn't.[48]

There was also the appearance of *The Masks of Love* in 1960, a collection which won the prestigious Heinemann Award from the Royal Society for Literature the following year. There is no hint of violence in the poems the book contains—rather, with its verses addressed to Jane and Nancy, and to John and Jean Bourne's first child, it reflects a feeling of domestic content, a look towards the future, and a sense that:

> love's little space
> Has been extended and the harsh
> Destructive seas forced back a pace.[49]

The new novel, however, hammered out on his typewriter in a three-week blast, has a darker feel to it. It was a psychological thriller called *The Shadowed Place*, set in an 'ugly, ungracious' city in northern England that sounds a lot like Leeds, and it gave Scannell a chance to fire off a few darts at some favourite targets—one of its central characters, for instance, gives his views about members of The Movement who had written novels of their own:

> There's not one of them I'd give tuppence for. John Wain hasn't got the first idea how to write a novel. His style's as dull as cold porridge. And [Kingsley] Amis is just as bad...[50]

Snapshots of Scannell's life appear throughout the story—the pub where journalists and university academics meet is clearly drawn from the Pack Horse in Leeds, complete with the boozy old painter, Abraham Karvossky, 'permanently anaesthetized' by alcohol, who might easily have been named Jacob Kramer. But the most unsettling aspect of the book is its central character, Julian Clarke, a literate, civilized and friendly man who turns under the influence of alcohol into a violent maniac who kills women with an expert blow from his hand. After he has been unmasked, the police psychiatrist explains, in words that could almost describe Vernon Scannell rather than Julian Clarke:

> Under certain circumstances he is possessed by a monstrously evil spirit ... His mother was a cold woman, one of those emotional cripples who're quite unable to feel sympathy, affection, love ... puritanical, cold in every way.[51]

The only doubt the psychiatrist has is over whether Julian is aware of his guilt, or whether, in the same way that Jo describes Scannell after his attacks on her, he had simply 'forgotten' what had happened.

Novel writing was never as important to Scannell as his poetry, and *The Shadowed Place* is not a particularly good novel—but consciously or not, it revealed Scannell's own guilt and fear in just the same way as 'A Case of Murder' would do a few years later. At the time, however, its acceptance for publication seemed to open up the possibility of earning more money, even establishing a parallel career as a thriller writer, alongside his teaching and his poetry. Despite the dark secret at home and his private mental turmoil, his prospects were beginning to seem brighter.

But Scannell's fragile emotional well-being was about to take another battering.

VII

In 1960, with the girls aged four and five, Jo found she was pregnant again. This time, she was expecting twins.

As was usual at the time, Scannell was not there for the birth, but telephoned Redhill Hospital from Jo's parents' home in Edenbridge, where he had gone with the two girls. The news was worrying—Jo had given birth to two boys, one of whom was, the nurse said nervously, 'not as well as he should be'. Scannell, she said, should come in and speak to the doctor.

When he got to the hospital, the diagnosis was that the sick baby was suffering from a meningocele, a form of spina bifida in which the meninges, the membranes that cover the brain and the spinal cord, have not properly formed. He had a swelling on the back of his head which would have to be removed—but it was impossible to say how much brain damage might have been caused. It was almost certain that he would never be able to lead a normal life. Jo, still recovering in bed, had been told only that he was weak and had a spinal injury. It was up to Vernon to tell her the whole story.

But Jo had already sensed that the child was in grave danger. They had agreed that the twins were to be called Benjamin and Toby if they were boys, and Benjamin had been christened at once, she told Vernon, because of the danger that he might not survive. They sat together, hand in hand, comforting each other as Vernon spelled out what the doctor had told him. Eventually he looked at the other twin, Toby, who was lying in a cot next to Jo's bed. He, too, was lovely, he agreed. But it was Benjamin, the weak, vulnerable baby he had seen sleeping in an incubator, whose image stayed with him, then and for the rest of his life—'the tiny features...at once exquisitely carved yet tenderly human like the head of one of those babies you see in fifteenth-century Flemish paintings, an idealization of the infant'.[52]

Scannell, like many men of the time, was far from being a 'hands-on' father with babies—but when Jo and the twins came home, he spent much of his time with the sick Benjamin. They had been warned that he would be severely handicapped, that he might never recognize them or communicate with them. 'Vernon adored him. He was very good with him', Jo remembers now.[53] He would feed Benjamin at night, and recalled later that the baby was 'very frail, and on the rare occasions when he cried, his voice was paper-thin, fluttering on silence like the wing of a dying moth'.[54]

Writing *The Tiger and the Rose* eleven years after Benjamin's birth, Vernon told how he was wakened one night when the baby was a few months old, by the sound of his crying—'not his usual dry fluttering cry, but a noise I had never before heard him make, a brief and very soft chirrup and twitter like birds settling in their nests for the night, but heard from a very considerable distance'.[55] His eyes were open, but his face was serene and expressionless—and then, for the first time, he smiled:

> The opening of the lips, the upwards curve of each corner of the mouth and the narrowing of eyes, thrilled me with their sweet and mortal imperfection. The smile lasted for perhaps two or three seconds. Then his eyes closed, the little mask of gravity was resumed, and he slept.[56]

The next day, he died. It is a moving account, and one that was reprinted in *The Times*—but, according to Jo, it was inaccurate in one important particular:

> There are many things in *The Tiger and the Rose* that are both true and totally untrue at the same time, and this is one of them. I hated Benjamin being

exposed and read about like that, but that incident itself was true. The only thing is, it was what *I* experienced, not Vernon. I told him about how he turned and looked at me, and suddenly his face became completely differ-ent—and he told it as if it had happened to him. That did upset me a bit at the time—it was as if he was taking him away somehow.[57]

There could be many reasons for that kind of inaccuracy—perhaps it is just possible that Jo's account affected him so deeply that he genuinely came to think of it as his own experience. Perhaps the same emotional experience happened to him too. It seems more likely, though, that the account was the rearrangement of a writer trying to evoke the intensity of the emotion, and sacrificing literal truth for literary effect. Such single-minded concentration on the writing, the overarching desire to convey the pain and pathos of the baby's death, and the willingness to reorder reality to do so, are surely the hallmarks of a genuine artist. It is a masterful piece of prose—controlled, unsentimental, passionately felt, and almost unbearably sad. But the sleight of hand that transfers the experience from his wife to himself is troubling: the writing may be deeply sensitive, but it is hard to overstate the lack of *personal* sensitivity of a man who would snatch the dying moments of his son away from the child's mother. And for all Jo Scannell's mild protestation that she was 'upset...a bit at the time', the grief and pain of what felt like betrayal clearly burned themselves into her soul. Scannell's diaries record that she was 'furious, regarding it as a kind of obscenity',[58] and more than fifty years later, when I first met her, she still was. This was the first thing that she told me about her memories of Vernon. It makes him perhaps more of an artist, but less of a man.

But none of this lessens the deep emotional scars that the birth and loss of Benjamin caused to Scannell as well as to Jo. 'An Old Lament Renewed', a poem he wrote shortly after the child's death, is a poem about grief, loss, and fear. It focuses on long dead skeletons both seen and imagined, on com-rades who were killed in the war, and on 'the deaths I've died and go on dying'—but the most haunting lines tell how:

> Often some small thing will summon the memory
> Of my small son, Benjamin. A smile is his sweet ghost.
> But behind, in the dark, the white twigs of his bones
> Form a pattern of guilt and waste.[59]

Grief for his son and the thought of that 'sweet ghost' of a smile, whether experienced by him or by Jo, never left him. Asked to read the poem for the

BBC's *Woman's Hour*, he broke down in tears several times during the recording.[60] There was nothing more he could have done for Benjamin, no blame to be attached to the child's sad death—but mingled with the grief, as he says in the poem, was that terrible sense of 'guilt and waste'. Scannell's past, as he saw it, was indeed a dark and frightening place.

VIII

The following year, Jo and Vernon's son John was born, so there were now four children under the age of six in the house. It was not an ideal environment for a writer, especially one who had to snatch what spare time he could for his poetry, when he was not teaching at Hazelwood or in the evening classes that he had started to take. Jo did most of the work with the children, but he loved playing with them, and was easily distracted. He may have been strict at school, but at home he was no disciplinarian:

> Nancy had Anna [a friend from Limpsfield] and her little German friend in, and Jane appeared shortly after I got back. I couldn't do anything except plead with them hopelessly to behave. Toby is the chief work-stopper at present. He is fascinated by the typewriter, and he won't leave me in peace at all. The noise, the clamour, the demands, the limitations of space, the untidiness, lack of routine, interruptions—they all make sustained labour practically impossible... There's not much chance of writing anything half-decent while babies are yelling and crawling over the paper you're trying to write on.[61]

It was the classic writer's dilemma: to earn the money that would provide him with room and peace to write his poetry, he would have to hammer away at commercial projects—'radio scripts, journalism, hastily-written fiction'[62]—and would not have time for poetry anyway. His talent would drain away, and 'I would become a cynical, self-loathing hack.'

In fact, he was still toiling at his novels—another, *The Face of the Enemy*, appeared in 1961, shortly after *The Shadowed Place*. It was a very different book—an attempt at a psychological love story rather than a thriller, but again, with its central character forced to admit that he had faced a court martial for cowardice in Tripoli in 1943, it drew heavily on Scannell's own experience and emotions. Even so, it was not a work into which he poured his soul—it was, he admitted, 'very sloppily written'.[63] But he was also working productively on his poetry—another collection, *A Sense of Danger*, appeared in 1962, and it was shortly after this time that he wrote some of his great poems, such as 'Walking Wounded', 'A Case of Murder', and 'Autumn', his lyrical celebration of the dying year in an everyday, urban setting.

This was also the time when he received an unexpected invitation that would open new doors to him as a poet and as a performer. In early 1961, the young poet Jeremy Robson—later to publish a number of Scannell's books and become one of his closest friends—had begun his series of Poetry and Jazz evenings. Robson's first presentation at Hampstead Town Hall featured Spike Milligan, Dannie Abse, Jon Silkin, Adrian Mitchell, and Robson himself, along with a number of other poets all reading their own poetry, and Lydia Pasternak Slater reading poems by her brother, the Nobel Prize winner Boris Pasternak. It was a sell-out, and after the second Poetry and Jazz evening, at the Royal Festival Hall, the *Daily Herald* wrote, 'The poets went to the Festival Hall yesterday, read their poems...and *three thousand* people gave them the reception normally reserved for the great names of music. I call that a piece of history.'[64]

History or not, it was not, on the face of it, the kind of occasion that would have appealed to Scannell. He found deep and lasting enjoyment in classical music, but little if any in jazz. 'However pleasant jazz may be, it is not the kind of music that either asks for or deserves the sort of attention expected from the audience by the musicians',[65] he wrote dismissively some years later. Putting it together with poetry was, he said, a 'confusion of arts' that did little for either the music or the poems. He had, too, little time for Spike Milligan, who he thought was a comedian rather than a poet, always looking for laughs.[66] And in any case, even though he was a popular reader of his own work, both in person and on the radio, he had a lasting distrust of poetry that was read aloud. Reading poetry, he believed, was essentially a private activity, enjoyed in 'the bedroom, the lavatory, the study, anywhere except in a concert hall or churchy atmosphere'.[67] Later, looking back over hundreds of readings he had carried out during his life, he admitted there was always a temptation to play to the gallery:

> You tend to read only the poems that might make some impact on a single hearing and, in my case, this means reading the jokey ones or those with a clear narrative content which in any case are generally misunderstood. Poems are for reading on the page. I wouldn't cross a narrow road to attend a poetry reading, though I suppose I might have done when I was young.[68]

So when Robson invited him to take part in a Poetry and Jazz evening in Birmingham in September 1962, he might have been expected to have very mixed feelings. But where ordinary poetry readings might attract a dozen or two of the faithful, the Poetry and Jazz sessions, Scannell quickly discovered, had audiences that usually ran into the hundreds. Tickets rapidly sold out for one reading in St Pancras, giving touts an unexpected pay day with 5s. tickets changing hands at £1 a time.[69] Coupled with the persuasive efforts of Robson and of Dannie Abse, whom he also liked and respected, the prospect of selling more books was the clincher.

There were generally four poets at a session, two reading before the break and two after, with interludes of jazz between the different readers. Occasionally, individual poems were read with a jazz accompaniment—exactly the sort of 'confusion of arts' that Scannell instinctively disliked. But Robson was able to tackle his doubts about the poetry head on:

> Poetry readings are an introduction to the written word—or, for those who know the poems, a valuable extension of it—not an end in themselves. Despite the many readings I cannot believe in a 'public' or 'pop' poetry—only in poetry written for the page, in isolation, with the life and discipline and complexity which good poetry has always possessed.[70]

Scannell was convinced, and so began an association with the Poetry and Jazz evenings that would last for some fifteen years. Robson was impressed from the start:

> He was a fantastic reader of his own poetry. It was obvious straight away, although I thought he was a little distant when I first met him, a man it would be difficult to get to know. But that was just the outer cover of a very shy man—one I became extremely fond of.[71]

The readings were a welcome chance to catch up with old friends, like the novelist-turned-poet Alexis Lykiard. Scannell enjoyed meeting other poets, although he was sometimes uneasy with their work—he liked Laurie Lee personally, but found the poetry he read 'a bit too sweet and soft for my taste', while Adrian Mitchell's performance was, like Milligan's, 'more like a top-class comedian than a literary gent's'.[72] But whatever his initial reservations, he clearly began to enjoy the buzz and excitement of the evenings. He particularly appreciated the musical setting for 'Epithets of War' written by the pianist and composer Michael Garrick. The first time he read the poem to the accompaniment of Garrick's jazz quintet, he noted simply, 'I read *Epithets of War* to Michael Garrick's music and everybody seemed to lap it up',[73] but a few weeks later, after a performance at Keele University, he was much more enthusiastic, if perhaps slightly bemused. 'Keele went marvellously well. *Epithets of War* really seems to be enriched by the jazz backing in public performance',[74] he wrote.

It was an ambitious choice for a poetry reading, still more so for a reading against a musical background. The poem, written in 1965, is a five-part meditation on war, and on how the grief and suffering ripple out across whole countries and down through generations. It is not a physically shocking poem—although the image of the ghost of a dead soldier from the desert in a hideous *danse macabre* with a girl at a church hall has its own gruesome, nightmarish horror:

> His terrible kiss will taste of sand
> Gritting on shocked teeth, and his cold cheek
> Will seem to her a stony reprimand.

Essentially, like many of the best poems drawn from Scannell's wartime experiences, it is a poem not about war but about remembering war, a thoughtful and determinedly non-heroic examination of the different types of pain that flowed from the war in which he fought and the one before. It is not a simple poem, but one that demands to be pondered and understood: as in most of his best work, the language is simple but the thought and the emotions are complex. It was not, then, an obvious choice for a reading in which the meaning has to be seized in a single hearing. And with a jazz backing, it would have been easy, as he must have feared, for the music to distract from the poetry.

Even more worryingly perhaps, the music, and its relationship with the poetry, were unpredictable—Michael Garrick, who wrote and directed the jazz for the concerts, explained that no two performances were the same:

> When writing music for a poem, I try to let the words themselves sing me their song. All I then do is write it down in a usable form, so that the jazz musicians can complement the poetic statement. This process is a filling out, an expansion of texture, like adding bass and inner parts to a melody line, thereby throwing it into relief and creating a new range of colours, tensions and resolutions: a kind of aural Cinerama. The words are usually fixed, but the freedom within the jazz composition means that each performance is different—a theme with continual variations.[75]

A recording that survives from Scannell's reading at the 250th Poetry and Jazz evening at London's Queen Elizabeth Hall in June 1969 shows how it worked with 'Epithets of War'. Three mysterious wails of a muted trumpet introduce his opening words to 'August 1914', the first section:

Figure 14. Vernon reading at one of the Poetry and Jazz evenings. The jazz composer and musician Michael Garrick is on the piano. He wrote musical settings for several of Vernon's poems. (Photo: Not known. Jeremy Robson collection)

> The bronze sun blew a long and shimmering call
> Over the waves of Brighton and Southend,
> Over slapped and patted pyramids of sand,
> Paper Union Jacks and cockle stalls...

—a melancholy rather than a military note that placed an ambivalently cheerful pre-War seaside setting in exactly the right ominous context, as the children dig trenches and donkeys charge along the sand. There are the gentle sounds of the saxophone and trumpet in the background, with the calming deep plucked strings of a double bass rumbling beneath. As the imagined scene moves inside, to a girl playing Chopin while her sister sits and sews, the jaunty notes of the piano evoke the homely peace that is soon to be shattered. The first section ends with the return of the wailing trumpet, and a brief rattle of the drums:

> But dead. The end
> Of something never to be lived again.

As the mood of the words changes, so does that of the music—a sharp percussive warning beat of the drum, followed by a brief but thunderous solo of remembered gunfire that dies to an insistent pulse like a hurrying heart-beat behind Scannell's voice as he talks of the guns as unnoticed museum pieces. His voice begins almost imperceptibly to match the insistent beat of the music and, as he starts to speak of the 'spilled thunder' of the guns in the veterans' nightmares, the volume of both voice and music increases. Whether it is the heavy bass behind the lines about casualties, the mock-military tat-too that introduces the section entitled 'War Songs', or the brash music-hall opening of the final section, the music enriches and enlarges upon the sense of the poem.

And Scannell knew it. 'Epithets of War' became a favourite at his appear-ances over the years. The Queen Elizabeth Hall performance was, he said:

> a huge success. The place was packed and my reading of Epithets of War with Michael Garrick's music received an astonishingly lengthy and loud round of applause. Decca recorded the concert and a double LP is to be issued later in the year.[76]

More than anything, he came to believe, the Poetry and Jazz evenings were a way of getting poetry to a wider audience.

> I got to know the jazz composer Michael Garrick and found he was an intel-ligent, sensitive and imaginative man ... If you put on a programme in a pub-lic hall simply of poetry reading, you'd be lucky to get twelve people and a small dog; whereas if you got a well-known jazz group to play, plus the poetry, you're going to get two audiences—the jazz people and the poetry people. I found it quite good because the people who came along to hear the jazz found to their surprise that the poetry wasn't as painful as they'd expected, and they even got interested and bought books.[77]

IX

The mid-sixties, when Scannell's involvement with the Poetry and Jazz evenings was developing, were productive years. When he could get away from Hazelwood, he became a well-known lunchtime visitor to the lounge bar of The George, where BBC producers, poets, and would-be literary figures would congregate, along with the occasional curious academic. It was known unofficially as The Gluepot, because once they were in there, it was very hard to get them out—and, according to one of its habitués, it represented 'the last hurrah of the maverick producers and speakers and poets, before the BBC became conventional'.[78] Scannell was one of those mavericks, a tall, genial figure, always in the same place at one end of the bar, and often deep in conversation with the dapper, pinstriped George MacBeth, already a respected poet and presenter of the BBC's influential *Poet's View* and other poetry programmes. Down at the other end, unspeaking, unsmiling, and barely visible through the thick pall of tobacco smoke, was another— the dark, brooding figure of Louis MacNeice. It was an inward-looking, slightly snobbish, and unwelcoming world compared with Scannell's usual raffish Soho haunts—workers from the 'rag trade', the fashion companies that thronged the surrounding streets were expected to stay in the public bar. 'Vulgar. And Jewish', was a frequent comment among the BBC and literary panjandrums.

It was here in The George that MacBeth had declared that only poets like Scannell, who had seen active service, could write convincingly about war—and it was a little while after that conversation that Scannell sat down to write him a letter that marked a significant turning point in his literary career. He enclosed a new poem, 'Mock Attack', based on his memories of the North Africa campaign:

> I am sending you the poem *Mock Attack* because you are partly responsible for it. When you said you were surprised, or words to that effect, that I didn't write more poems from the experience of war, I began—at first, I think, it was less than consciously—to think about it, and gradually all sorts of memories came back.[79]

MacBeth was presenting a poetry programme on the BBC called *The Poet's Voice*, and the poem Scannell was submitting looked back at the Mareth Line battle, in which Scannell's unit had launched a diversionary attack 'like a boxer's feint',[80] while New Zealand forces made a flanking movement to attack the Germans from behind. It was the start of his sustained interest in his wartime experiences as a subject for poetry. Memories of war would remain central to much of his work.

In 1964, with his reviewing, his radio broadcasts, and his readings, Scannell was starting to make money. He calculated that he made around £1,600[81] during the year—'quite a lot of money by my standards'[82]—on top of another £800[83] pay for his part-time work at Hazelwood. The publication of his collection *Walking Wounded* in 1965 reflected the growing popularity of his poetry in magazines and on the radio, and in the same year there appeared another boxing novel, *The Big Time*. In this book, he revisited his fairground experiences, presenting a boxer who stages fixed fights for the

crowds much as he had, and looks back on his unsuccessful professional
career:

> 'Can't grumble. I'm a professional diver, you might say. I never had it, Bill . . . I
> knew I'd fold up as soon as I got hurt. I've often tried to see what it is that
> makes me like that. I'm a coward I suppose . . .'[84]

No one ever suggested that Scannell lacked courage in the ring—but that
spectre of his supposed cowardice continued to haunt him from his army
days. The point was, however, that his income was growing; and in May
1965, he told the headmaster at Hazelwood that he intended to leave in the
summer. He was going to try once more to earn his living as a full-time
writer. He sounded worryingly unenthusiastic:

> Of late I find there is less and less joy to be found in writing: it becomes more
> and more gruelling, and the end results seem more or less trivial, lacking real
> seriousness. Sometimes I think there's more than enough trivia about without
> my adding to it. If you can't produce the big bang, why bother at all? And yet
> I know I will go on trying to write poems, or be unutterably miserable.[85]

Even before he had left Hazelwood, he was wondering nervously about the
possibilities of finding 'a regular job'[86]—an application to work in the BBC's
radio drama department, for instance, came to nothing—but, with the help
of an Arts Council grant of £1,200,[87] announced the following December,
he just about managed to keep his financial head above water. 'Jo went to
the bank today and found that we are over £50 overdrawn',[88] he wrote in
his diary the day after he heard about the award:

> It's just as well that the Arts Council, like the US Cavalry, have come galloping
> to the rescue. Yet I really feel a bit guilty. There must be umpteen prose writers
> who deserve the money more than I do. Of course there are. Still, I've been
> so often overlooked as a poet that there might be a bit of ironic justice in my
> stroke of luck. We'll be able to pay off all our debts and have quite a bit left
> over.[89]

It was an encouraging start to the new year.

X

Perhaps one problem of the Poetry and Jazz evenings for Scannell was that
he frequently enjoyed them too much. There would be a drink or two

before, and more during the interval, and sometimes he would celebrate so hard that he was barely capable of reading in the second half. The journalist Elizabeth Thomas, one-time literary editor of *Tribune*, remembered 'trying desperately to get Vernon sober enough to get on the platform'[90] at a performance at Hitchin College of Further Education in 1967.

Jeremy Robson recalls similar evenings:

> It was no secret that he liked a drink. That's just the way he was—not aggressive at all, but very jovial and slurry.[91]

Robson remembered one Sunday performance in Cwmbran, South Wales, when Scannell discovered to his horror that local laws meant it was impossible to buy alcohol:

> We were there for the weekend, and he persuaded me to take a train with him into the next county so we could have a drink during the afternoon. When we came back he was in a fairly merry mood, and he really enjoyed the evening. He would have been paid about £20[92] for each performance, and he would certainly have drunk it away by the time he went home.

He kept trying to reduce the amount that he drank, as he frequently did, but he had different standards of sobriety from most people. Six or seven pints of bitter, for instance, counted as a sober evening.[93] And not all the drinking was as jovial and as good-humoured as the Poetry and Jazz binges. Alcohol, of course, was a trigger for the domestic violence, and it was also starting to get him into trouble with the law. So far, he had been very lucky. There had been the £7 fine[94] back in 1952 for attempting to drive away a car when drunk on a three-day bender. Then ten years later, a couple of days after Christmas, a pub crawl that had started in the French pub in Dean Street and woven crazily around Soho ended with him getting into his car to drive home and slamming into the back of another vehicle at Camberwell Green traffic lights. After a night in the cells he came up before a magistrate who sent him to prison overnight while he made up his mind about the sentence. Eventually he got off with a fine again—£50[95] this time, plus one guinea[96] costs.

Now, his luck was running out. It was February 1967, and he had driven to take part in a poetry reading in Guildford with Kingsley Amis and the policeman-poet Edwin Brock. He had a few drinks there, and a few more at the home of a friend nearby where he and Brock went to stay the night afterwards. It was almost dawn before he went to bed, and about midday when he set off home. On the way, he stopped at a pub for a couple more 'hair of the dog' pints, and then turned into a side street to sleep it all off. He was woken by a man living nearby, who called the police—and thirty minutes later Vernon was in the police station. This time, the magistrate had no hesitation—he was sentenced to three months' imprisonment in Brixton.

There had been occasional nights in the cells before, followed by raging hangovers, but this was the first time he had faced a sustained period of imprisonment since the army. The memories of Alexandria came flooding back:

> Already the prison stench was beginning to seep into me, into my clothes, my hair, the pores of my skin. I could taste it sickeningly on palate and in throat. It was an impalpable stew of urine, excrement, disinfectant and something indefinable—unclean bodies and feet, no doubt, but something metaphysical, the odour of misery and hopelessness, the smell of captivity. I sat on the bed, aware of the Judas-hole in the door, and told myself I was getting too old for this kind of lark.[97]

For anyone who had suffered military detention, however, it was a breeze. As a first offender, he was offered the chance to move to an open prison, but when he heard about the supposed advantages—a place in a dormitory rather than a cell of his own, and the chance to play football and watch television—he had no hesitation. 'My God, I thought, I'd rather be sent to Devil's Island.'[98]

For the first couple of weeks, he was put on cleaning duties—a role which included the daily clearing out of the clogged and filthy trough into which the prisoners emptied their slopping out buckets—but then he was moved to the library. It doesn't sound to have been too arduous:

> I have managed to get a selection of Tennyson (edited by Auden), the Eliot selection of Kipling's verse and an anthology of 17th Century Verse edited by dear old Edmund [Blunden][99] and published in Hong Kong! I've also read Conrad's *Under Western Eyes*, and William Sansom's *The Face of Innocence*. Last night I went to the Art class where I did a copy of a Utrillo in chalks. It looks rather as if I've done it blindfolded and with the left hand, but I enjoyed it, which I suppose is the main thing.[100]

To his surprise, he said, he scarcely noticed the enforced lack of alcohol most of the time ('Though I occasionally think, "It's just about time for my appearance in *The Haycutter*"', he added[101])—and, locked away in prison, he had time to think deeply about Jo and the family, as he wrote to her:

I am more grateful than ever I shall be able to say that you have never blamed me or complained about my selfish drinking. My God, I could do with a childish pint right now...I love you more and more, and thank heaven or something for the lucky day we met again in that sleazy coffee bar—or did they call them coffee bars in those days? It's been a long trip since then, but it has got better all the time.[102]

He wrote several poems while in prison, including the tender, affectionate 'No Sense of Direction', which contrasts his own aimless life with the confidence of:

> Those who are sure
> Which turning to take.

However, the poem says, it is this lack of a sense of direction that has led him away from where he might mistakenly have planned to go:

> It made me stray
> To this lucky path
> That ran like a fuse
> And brought me to you
> And love's bright, soundless
> Detonation.[103]

The final oxymoron of the silent explosion reinforces the paradox that it is his lack of purpose that has led him unerringly to his destination, and the shock and revelation of that startling final word are typical of the way Scannell ended his poems. It is an unusually full-hearted and unreserved expression of love and joy, both a confession of his own inadequacy and a celebration of his sheer good fortune. He was typically dismissive later—the poem did not, he said, 'amount to very much'[104]—but it is hard to imagine a more moving message for a man to send from prison to the woman he loves.

Imprisonment reminded him constantly of his time in the Alexandria Barracks—one day, asked for his prison number, he barked out instinctively '2991874', which was the number he had been given when he joined the Argyll and Sutherlands nearly thirty years before.[105] He had an ambivalent attitude towards his sentence—it seemed harsh, he thought, compared with other drink-driving cases, but, on the other hand, he had got away with a lot of drink-related offences, so maybe it was time to even up the score. But the real punishment, he felt, was being imposed on Jo and the children—particularly because Jo was due to have another baby while he was in prison.

It was about a week before he was due to be released when he wrote home:

> This morning—Saturday—I heard the news of the new baby—Marvellous! I hope having it wasn't too hellish and everything went as well as possible . . . The baby—Jake?—is quite big, isn't he? My god, another male Scannell makes me tremble a bit. But thank God he is well and complete.[106]

The thought that the improvident and bohemian Scannells might be having *another* child caused some gossip in the village and among the mainly middle-aged and middle-class students at Vernon's evening classes. He rather enjoyed it: one night, after he had come out of prison, he was approached by some of the students in the bar of The Wheatsheaf after a class:

'MR SCANNELL, I hear your wife is expecting another baby. Will that be your fourth?', asked one.
'Fifth,' he replied, curtly.
'Oh, are you Roman Catholic then?'

Vernon smiled benignly, and raised his voice slightly so that the whole pub could hear: 'No madam. I am a raving sex maniac.'[107]

But there was more for the indefatigable Jo to deal with while her husband was in prison, apart from her pregnancy, apart from the income tax letters that Vernon wanted carefully stored for him, the books he wanted sending, and the messages he wanted passed on to friends and literary contacts. She had a house move to organize. When she had discovered she was pregnant with Jake, they had started looking for a bigger place to live, which they realized would mean moving to a cheaper area. They had looked in East Anglia, and travelled out to see another house in Wiltshire before finally, in January 1967, finding three tiny cottages in the little Dorset village of Nether Compton. With Vernon away, it fell to the heavily pregnant Jo to arrange the sale of Redfern, pack up the house, prepare the children, and arrange for builders to do the work needed to turn the three cottages into one home.

A new baby, a new home, and a husband newly out of prison. It was the start of another phase in their life.

II

Falling Apart

The best games always ended so,
With pain or boredom, screams and jeers;
Were always sure to end in tears.

'It's Sure to End in Tears', from *Walking Wounded* (1965)

I

Vernon need not have worried about how the children would react to his imprisonment—although ten-year-old Nancy came home from school one day asking plaintively what a jailbird was. Her father sent back this wistful reply in one of his weekly letters:

His plumage is dun,
His appetite indiscriminate.
He has no mate.
His nest is built of brick and steel;
He sings at night
A long song, sad and silent.
He cannot fly.[1]

Generally, though, their attitude was one of resignation. For as long as they could remember, they had been used to their father being away from home, either away at readings or out on a bender, and prison seemed just like another, rather more extended, absence. They sent him cards and drawings, which, he said, 'brighten my boudoir considerably'.[2] 'We certainly weren't ashamed, because it wasn't as if he was a murderer or a thief or something', Nancy—then eleven years old—recalls now. 'Drinking and driving seemed very ordinary in those days...I remember the day he came out, I'd got my first violin. I had my dad and I had a violin, and I couldn't decide which was the most exciting thing.'

The weeks following his release were hectic: he had a series of six half-hour radio scripts on war poetry to finish for the BBC, and the rest of the family had to prepare for the move away from Limpsfield. It was early in August when they finally arrived at Folly Cottage—converted now into a single home. There was a garden for the children to play in, and the house was conveniently close to the local pub, the Griffin's Head. It was more remote than Redfern had been, up a rarely used track on the edge of the little village of Nether Compton, midway between Sherborne and Yeovil—deep in Thomas Hardy country, which was a big attraction. More practically, the 7-mile journey to the nearest town would be a problem for a man who had just lost his licence for five years. For Scannell, however, there was one all-important feature of the new house:

> At last I have a room of my own to work in . . . I look out of my study window at Tom Payne's Hill where, so local legend has it, a sheep thief of that name was hanged. No traffic passes Folly Cottage, except for John Hall, my farmer neighbour, with his cows when they come down for milking, for Folly Lane leads nowhere.[3]

Superficially, Scannell appeared to have everything he had wanted. Even his drinking might be less of a threat—after all, in prison, he had managed well with no alcohol at all. Judging from the tender tone of his letters from Brixton, his relationship with Jo was firm and settled; he was happy with his family, particularly now that he had a study into which he could retreat to work.

That was how it seemed when they arrived in Nether Compton. Leaving Limpsfield had completed the daunting move away from the full-time salaried employment that had so distracted him from writing poetry. And now, although he was always short of money, he seemed to be getting enough work to pay his bills. He could not quite see how everything had fallen so neatly into place, but he was also turning over in his mind an idea for an autobiographical book that would eventually become *The Tiger and the Rose*. Now, surely, the poetry would flow. He settled down with a sort of bemused optimism to work out how he should best organize his time:

> Get up early—or not later than the children. Be finished with breakfast and newspaper by 10am. An hour's physical work outside when the weather allows it. From 11 to one, write something creative, i.e. the book or poetry. 2pm to

Figure 15. At Folly Cottage, Vernon had for the first time a separate room in which he could work. (Photo: Andrew Taylor)

> 6pm answer letters and then continue writing. The evening (i.e. after tea) for reading.[4]

It was not, of course, that simple: Vernon's good intentions never were. For a start, the children seemed to spend most of their time in the study, while he sat and tried to work 'among Teddy bears, Lego and Enid Blyton'[5] in the playroom. When he did manage to get to his desk, the mere fact of having a door to open was no barrier to the children when they wanted to come in and disturb him—and, as Jo recalls, Vernon always seemed ready to be disturbed:

> He never ever sent the children away when he was working. I'd say to John 'Go and see Daddy Scannelling'—that's what they called his typewriting—and he'd stop writing and haul him onto his lap, and John would be all over the typewriter. I never heard him say 'Stop doing that', or anything like that.[6]

Alan Millard, headmaster of the local school, recalls that on his first day, he read the children Scannell's poem *Hide and Seek*—'one that I'd always found

Figure 16. Vernon's study looked out onto Tom Payne's Hill. The cows coming down for milking were the only creatures that disturbed the landscape, he said. (Photo: Andrew Taylor)

captured children's imaginations'. At the back of the class, Toby Scannell put up his hand. 'Please sir, my dad wrote that.'

> Of course, I was astonished. Vernon came in later, and read William Blake's *Tiger, Tiger* to the children and talked to them about it. They were spellbound—he really made the poem come alive for them. And for me, too, I have to say.[7]

At other times, Vernon might be less patient:

> Jo is ill in bed; the children have broken up for the Easter holidays and they are all celebrating by wailing, screaming, blubbering and snarling. All I want to do is kick their silly little arses and that is probably what I will do. Thank heaven for strong drink.[8]

There can be few parents who haven't privately felt like that at some time, but the light-hearted reference to his need for a drink masked a more serious problem that quickly became evident. The optimism caused by his teetotal spell in Brixton was short-lived: a couple of drinks would still start him

off on an uncontrollable alcoholic jag. At home, he was a regular in the
Griffin's Head, and on his trips to London he could settle in at The George
or the ML Club in Soho for hours at a time. In January 1968, he spent
another night in the cells in London after 'an insane bender' with BBC
friends following the recording of a piece for the *World of Books* programme.
He paid his £1 fine[9] to the Great Marlborough Street magistrates in the
morning, and then started on the scotch again at lunchtime, finishing the
night with a black eye from a fight that he could not remember. It was three
days before he recovered from the hangover. He knew there was a problem,
but seemed unable to do anything about it. He had to stop drinking.

> Must stop it. *Stop*. It's serious now, more serious than ever before. Not only
> temperamentally can I not stop. I hold it so badly and go so crazy. If I can't
> stop it on my own I'll have to get help of some kind.[10]

He didn't, of course, as he never had and never would. And the craziness that
went with the drink was not confined to drunken brawls in the street. One
night, he brought a drinking companion home from the pub, and then laid
him out with a punch that broke his own hand. But usually, as Nancy—
eleven years old when the family moved to Dorset—recalls, it was Jo who
was the victim:

> He was always fun with us—never got cross with us, never laid a finger on us.
> In fact we ran rings round him. But we were terrified for my mother. He was
> an aggressive drunk, destructive . . . It was always against her, never us. But
> watching it was the worst bit—that and the fear. I can remember lying in bed
> at night knowing he was still in the pub, and I had to stay awake because I
> needed to know whether when he came in he was going to be quiet or
> whether he was going to be horrid.[11]

For all the affectionate words from Brixton, the drunken beatings had carried on. Not surprisingly, perhaps, his relationship with Jo began to fall
apart. Christmas 1969—eighteen month after the move to Dorset—was, he
noted in his diary, 'the worst ever, sheer misery. Nothing else can be said
except—except I've known all this time that J. is occupied elsewhere, and it
is v. painful. Very.'[12] By the summer they were scarcely speaking, and by the
end of the year he was sitting alone late at night, pouring his thoughts about
Jo into his diary again:

> All very dull and dreary. The poor girl needs a more stimulating and stimu-
> lated audience than I can supply and, of course, one that hasn't seen and heard

it all before. I need something too, though I'm not sure what. I have been left to stay up to light the Aga, the only thing I am reckoned able to inflame.[13]

A few days later, there was the same hopelessness:

> Jo and I are on the ropes, there's no doubt about it. Nothing but mistrust, deception, double-shuffles, suspicion and, under it all, a lot of mutual distaste.[14]

His absences in London lasted longer and longer—sometimes he would not come home for a night, sometimes he would stay away for a week or so. Jo had been suspicious before—over a mysterious late-night phone call a couple of years earlier, for instance, as Vernon recalled in his diary. 'A girl whose name I can't remember, wife of one of the Barrow Poets, rang up at about midnight, obviously sloshed', he had written, markedly defensively and with a not-entirely-convincing air of injured innocence:

> I've met her two or three times, the last after the poetry and jazz at Stratford or Romford. I don't remember being more than ordinarily civil to her, but she seemed rather—I'm not sure what the word is—flirtatious, provocative— something like that... I can't think why she should ring me, except on one of those boozy impulses when you feel sorry for yourself or vaguely randy or lonely and ring up the first name you think of. Still, I wish she hadn't, since it must have looked v. odd to J.[15]

By now, in fact, Jo was certain that Vernon was seeing other women, and had been throughout their marriage:

> When he came home, he'd been up in London boozing. That was Vernon's life—he was a womanizer and a boozer. But what is essential to me, and always was, is that he was a poet. That's what I loved about him—everything was related to his poetry.[16]

The older children, Jane and Nancy, had also been aware of other women on the edges of their father's life from as far back as they could remember, as Jane recalls:

> He hated any suggestion of infidelity against him. He would go into rages of jealousy if he thought another man had so much as looked at my mother, but he didn't see it in relation to himself... There were women at Limpsfield, at Detillens Lane—all the way through his life, in fact, though I don't understand exactly what their relationship was. There had always been women—he was fairly casual about being able to move in and out of relationships.[17]

Evidence of the jealousy is there in the diaries, although it appears quieter, more resigned, more desperate than Jane's memories suggest. The diary entries do not reflect the violent rages that Jane and Nancy remember, and that Jo and the other women who came into Scannell's life describe. However, one of the poems he wrote during this period, 'A Simple Need', presents a character tortured and excited at the same time by thoughts of his former wife's probably entirely imaginary infidelity:

> The joke is she got rid of me. Cruelty, she said.
> I can't go near. Not now. They'd jail me if I did.
> But one of these fine nights I'll go,
> I've got to go. Just to see them at it once,
> That's all. Just see the two of them.
> It's only fair.[18]

The poem was included in his new collection, *Epithets of War*, in 1969. Scannell wrote in his diary about its creation:

> There is a kind of plot in the man's boozy maunderings—or perhaps I should say a plot to be deduced from them. The divorce has been largely caused by his jealousy and manic suspicions of his wife's infidelity which, it is implied, conceal a desire for it to happen so that he might enjoy the exquisite thrill of seeing her enjoying and being enjoyed by someone else. A rather nasty poem, I suppose.[19]

There is something unhealthily lascivious about the way the poem leers over memories of the woman's body:

> She's like a plum, a big plum with the smooth
> Bloom on summer skin, a plum of plums,
> The way they halve!

But there is no suggestion that the man's jealousy has any firmer basis than his own fevered imaginings—in his diary, Scannell says the poem presents 'the voyeuristic thrill a divorced man gets from thinking of his (probably quite innocent) ex-wife being fucked by her new lover'. It is, of course, important to avoid facile identifications of the 'I' of this or any of Scannell's poems—but the diaries are scattered with evidence of his own insecurity and jealousy, not just in his relationship with Jo but throughout his life. 'A Simple Need' is a stark, original, and brutally honest poem, and a good example of how Scannell turned the most painful emotions into poetry. But it is surely significant not only that it presents so graphically the cruelly destructive effect of sexual jealousy, but also that Scannell understands that the emotion may have absolutely no foundation in reality. He may have been a terrifying physical bully when drunk, but he was also a damaged, suffering soul. And he knew it.

Earlier in their marriage, back in Limpsfield, Vernon had written a novel, *The Dividing Night*, in which the central character, John Shearman, embarks on a passionate affair with the wife of a neighbour. Although Shearman shares Vernon's name—John—and is the same age as he is, has literary interests and connections through his work as a publisher, lives roughly forty-five minutes' train journey from London, and worries about his marriage, his sexual prowess, and his wife's fidelity, it is important again not simply to place Scannell as a character in his own novel. But the book does reveal some of his thinking about marriage, about fidelity, and about what may encourage a man to betray his wife.

Certainly in John's case, it is more than a bullying, selfish search for sex. He disapproves of the callous way that his brother, Arnold, picks up women and drops them after he has finished with them. 'I thought I could enjoy a simple, unsentimental sexy affair but I can't', John says. 'I have to have something else. Love I suppose, or at least the pretence of it.' Later in the book, he confronts his wife, Irene, with the classic complaint of the errant husband—'You're undersexed, cold, frigid, call it what you like.' So far, so predictable. But what is interesting is Irene's reply:

> There've been lots of times when I've wanted you but you've been tired or you've had a lot to drink or you just haven't noticed ... Then suddenly you decide you'd like a quick bash before going to sleep. And then you call me frigid because I don't enjoy that kind of sex.[20]

Again, the important point is Scannell's emotional intelligence, his understanding of Irene's point of view. Whether he was capable of carrying that understanding into his own life is a different question, but at least he was aware that there was a problem.

The ending of *The Dividing Night* is bleak and hopeless. John is now unsure, and probably always will be, whether Irene has been unfaithful to him as well, but the final scene depicts a telephone call in which she agrees that they should get back together after parting briefly following the revelation of John's affair:

> 'Yes, we'll see each other tomorrow,' and after the click of the line being disconnected, a small and final noise, black like a full stop, the note of resignation and sadness lingered on.[21]

It is not the writing of a man who saw happy endings in relationships. The most John can expect is a lifetime of regretful unfulfilment—not love, but possibly the pretence of it. Perhaps it is not the future Scannell saw for himself, but it is at the very least a possible outcome that he envisaged to problems similar to his own. Taken with the anxiety that he expressed at different times in his diary about his own incapacity for loving, it added up to a bleak and disheartening prospect.

II

None of this is to say that life at Folly Cottage was unrelieved gloom and despair. There were family expeditions to Lyme Regis for jellied eels and cockles by the sea, fishing trips for mackerel with the boys, swimming on various occasions with friends or with the children. During the long stretches when he felt the poetry had dried up within him, the beauty of the countryside outside his door could often stir him into action:

> The sun, very bright but pale like an anaemic yolk, is coming up from behind Tom Payne's hill. There is a thin mist over the fields and the cows move slowly through it as if they are sleepwalking. I expect it will be another fine day, which will make nine or ten on the trot. I think I might try my unpractised hand at a bit of verse.[22]

Nature itself, however, is seldom a subject for his poetry—where Keats's 'season of mists and mellow fruitfulness' is filled with laden apple trees, flowers, and fields of stubble under cloud-barred skies, Scannell's *Autumn* is an exclusively urban poem in which lamps, not apples, 'ripen early in the surprising dusk'. He sees leaves 'mushed to silence in the gutter' and a 'big hotel like an anchored liner'; where Keats hears the song of the robin and the twitter of gathering swallows, Scannell is struck by the swish of tyres on the wet streets.[23] Even so, he delighted in the long walks over the fields to the pub, digging in the vegetable garden at Folly Cottage, and chopping wood for the fire.

For all his grumbles about the occasional interruptions to his work, he was finding unexpected pleasure, too, in being a father—and this time, the pleasure was directly reflected in his writing. In the summer of 1968, the publishers Pergamon asked him to prepare a collection of children's poems, and a couple of months later, he started work on a short novel, also aimed at children, to be called *The Dangerous Ones*. Occasionally, his attitude to this new audience seemed dismissive, even cavalier—on 1 October, he noted that he had 'bashed out a ballad' for the children's poetry collection, and three months later he worked out that he had written 35,000 words of *The Dangerous Ones* in about four weeks:

> Whatever its quality, it shows that I still have the stamina—if nothing else—to turn out great chunks of prose in short periods. I didn't think I could do it these days.[24]

He never wrote so casually about the poetry that he wrote for adults. And yet he seemed to have an instinctive sympathy for a young audience; he had already written several poems *about* his own children for his adult collections, such as 'Poem for Jane' and 'Jane at Play'. It was a small step, particularly with the understanding he had gained first as a teacher and now as a parent, to make poetry that was accessible to children:

> There is no essential difference between the poetry I'd put in these books for younger readers and children, and the kind of poem I normally write; except, I suppose there are certain subjects which would not mean much to younger readers. Also—for children—I would try to get poems which are pretty direct and with a narrative content, something which can be fairly easily understood.[25]

Several of the poems in *Mastering the Craft and Other Poems for Young People* had already appeared in adult anthologies; another, 'Nettles', demonstrates how effectively Scannell managed to combine children's and adult writing. It describes how he cut down a patch of nettles after his son John fell into them and was stung:

> I took my billhook, honed the blade
> And went outside and slashed in fury with it
> Till not a nettle in that fierce parade
> Stood upright any more . . .[26]

The poem is filled with military images of parades, combat, and wounds, and Scannell's comments reveal the serious, adult thinking behind it:

> When this incident happened, about eleven years ago, there was some world crisis—Cuba perhaps—and it seemed there might be another war; I think subconsciously I was very worried about this, about my children being involved in a war; I think that's probably why the military imagery runs through the poem. The poem is really about the continuity of pain, that pain

is part of living, and however much you love and protect your children, you can't avoid the pain.[27]

Many of these new poems sprang from memories of Scannell's own life and childhood—in *The Tiger and the Rose*, for example, he describes stealing apples with a friend on dark autumn evenings in Aylesbury, much like the adventure described in the poem 'The Apple Raid'; another poem, 'Miss Steeples', looks back at his favourite teacher at Nether Street Infants School in Beeston. The short, wistful poem about the jailbird is there, polished and improved from the original rough draft; 'Epitaph for a Bad Soldier', published in his next children's book, rather poignantly includes a direct quote from his old army record:

> On his discharge book
> The seeker may find
> His life summed up
> By the military mind:
> No angry charges
> Of traitor or cad
> But this plain epitaph:
> 'Conduct – Bad.'[28]

Other poems were based either on incidents in his children's lives, like 'Nettles', or on insights that he had gained through watching and listening to them.

Scannell's aim, of course, was to interest and engage his young audience, but he was also just as uncompromising as he had been in the classroom at Hazelwood, just as concerned to instil in them a love of poetry and literature. A teacher at one school he visited told him proudly that he had read his class a poem he had written himself about autumn, along with those of John Keats and John Clare, and then asked them which they preferred:

> Put to the vote, it was his that came out on top, he told me with some complacency. It did not occur to him of course that this was proof, not of his superiority to Keats and Clare, but of his incompetence as a teacher.[29]

He was angered by the thought that children should be sold short by the poetry with which they were presented at school and in children's anthologies. Interviewed by two young teenagers for a book in the mid-1970s, he dismissed the idea that Pop Poetry—'sloppy, sentimental, ill-written'— could provide a stepping-stone from which children could move on to more serious reading:

I simply don't believe that. It's rather like feeding someone on a diet of fish and chips—they will stick to that kind of food and reject more sophisticated foods later. I consider that teachers should never give children anything less than what is considered to be excellent of its kind.[30]

Another diary entry refers to a book of children's verse he has seen—'smelly pap...sloppy, formless, facetious, ingratiating drivel. And this is put before children as poetry.'[31] As an old man, invited by an incautious publisher to offer some poems for a children's anthology, 'the wackier the better', he was practically spitting with rage:

> It is this '"wackiness' that infuriates me...The idea, firmly espoused by the young Fionas who are employed as editors, that children can respond with pleasure only to daft facetiousness in verse, is quite wrong. It wouldn't be quite so galling if they used competently written light verse, but they don't. [They] are almost all totally incompetent purveyors of butter-fingered doggerel or very bad prose disguised typographically as verse.[32]

His own poetry for children, by contrast, was written with as much care for rhyme, metre, and form as his adult verse. It may be comic or occasionally apparently sentimental, but it can also be emotionally and imaginatively demanding, often ending with a shocking twist. 'The Apple Raid', for instance, the title poem of his second children's collection, four years after *Mastering the Craft*, uses rhymed quatrains to tell the story of three boys mischievously stealing apples. It is a straightforward childhood adventure, until the last verse:

> Strange to think that he's fifty years old,
> That tough little boy with scabs on his knees;
> Stranger to think that John Peters lies cold
> In an orchard in France beneath apple trees.[33]

Later collections of Scannell's children's verse included simpler poems aimed at younger children on such subjects as 'My Dog' and 'My Cat'—but even these apparently less demanding poems often come with a surprising change of direction at the end. Sometimes it may be light-hearted and funny—'My Dog', for instance, is a wry, affectionate description of a badly behaved mongrel, which seems to be about to end sentimentally:

> And would I swap him for a dog
> Obedient, clean and good,
> An honest, faithful, lively chap?

But the last line is a reminder that Scannell is seldom interested in sentimentality:

> Oh boy, I would, I would![34]

Even younger children are often given at least the opportunity to take up
an emotional challenge. 'The Horse', for instance, seems to be a short, unex-
ceptionable account of the different breeds of horse, and their interaction
with man. Again, the ending promises to be slightly gooey and childishly
anthropomorphic, right up to the very last word of the penultimate verse:

> Gentle, vegetarian,
> Intelligent and brave,
> The horse for countless centuries
> Has been Man's friend and slave.

That final 'slave' calls into question the whole nature of the relationship
between man and beast. Many young children will miss it, of course, and
read the poem as a simple rhyme about how nice horses are, but for those
who catch the implication—or who have teachers who are sharp enough
to point it out to them—it will start a whole new train of thought.

   Poems for children, Scannell believed, could and should be read every bit
as closely and carefully as those intended for adults.

III

Folly Cottage also gave Scannell, now in his mid-forties, the chance to look
back on his life. In 1969 the writer Joseph Hone, his old companion from
the BBC and The George, now working as literary adviser to the publishers
Hamish Hamilton, wrote to suggest that he should write 'a prose book...a
kind of journal of my life here and elsewhere'.[35] It was not an easy decision
for him: he had first considered the idea himself two years earlier, but even
after the suggestion from Hone, it took him another seven months to sign a
contract. He was thinking of abandoning it in November, when the idea
seemed to have 'gone sour on me',[36] and it was not until January 1970 that
he finally noted in his diary: 'Signed Hamish Hamilton contract to do an
autobiographical book. God help me.'[37]

   It was not primarily lack of time that held him back, although he resented
the way the reviews, radio scripts, and readings kept him from writing

poetry just as relentlessly as teaching had done. None of it was real writing.
'It's a bit like being in the Boys' Brigade, wearing a uniform, blowing a
bugle, marching and drilling, while the real army, the grown men, are fighting the real war',[38] he noted. Frequently—sometimes suffering with a hangover after another long night in the pub, sometimes not—he found it
impossible to get the words down anyway. 'As creative as a dead gelding',[39]
as he memorably put it.

He knew that writing the book would be a struggle—one more obstacle to writing poetry. And although many of his poems drew on specific
incidents from his own past, formal autobiography was a new skill to
learn. He had decided from the start that it should be not a straightforward chronological story of his life, but should alternate between the
present and 'whatever scenes of the past were prompted by the preoccupations of the moment'. That arrangement, he believed, would help to avoid
the self-regarding tedium that he found in many other autobiographies,
and he settled on a working title of *Now and Then*. It would also, of course,
make it easier for him to miss out whatever episodes he chose. There were
several of those—his early marriage to Barbara, for instance, the affair
with Ella and the later bigamy trial. It would be another twenty years
before he could bring himself to confess to his desertion at Wadi Akarit,
or his time in prison at Alexandria; and there was no mention, then or
ever, of the flashes of uncontrollable rage and violence which were blight-
ing his marriage. Those were too painful for him to mention even in his
diary.

In fact, he had foreseen this difficulty from the first:

> The great problem will be what to leave out. My aim must be truth as I know
> it. No falsifying. So certain events and people may have to be left out, to save
> them pain or me a libel action.[40]

Bearing in mind the omissions in the book, however, his lawyerly insistence
in the Introduction to a later edition seems disingenuous. 'It does contain a
truthful record of the earlier part of my life. If there are any untruths in it,
they are not those of fact',[41] he says—but though what is written may, by
and large, be the truth, it is certainly not the whole truth. Did he expect to
be taken at his word? In that same Introduction, he acknowledged that
autobiographies repay close and sceptical reading:

> Even where the writer might consciously or unconsciously be attempting to
> deceive his readers about his true nature, the more perceptive among them

will not be taken in but will learn as much about him from his attempts at concealment or misguidance as they would from a more candid self-portrait.

By the 1980s, contemplating writing *Argument of Kings*, the book that would finally tell the truth, or most of it, about his wartime desertion, he regretted not having been more open to begin with:

> I was not, or so it seemed to me, culpably dishonest with either myself or my reader, although I did change a few names, (on the advice, or rather, the insistence, of the publisher's solicitor) and omitted events which might have caused distress to people involved or to myself. There was no account of my relationship with Ella: this I still believe, was excusable. But the omission of my walkaway at Wadi Akarit and my time in the nick was caused by shame.[42]

But even the challenge of writing an autobiography that he knew would miss out some of the most formative episodes of his life was not the main reason for his unwillingness to commit himself. Rather, it was the idea of raking through the cold ashes of his past for what he called the 'auto-book' at a time when his life with Jo and the family was falling apart. It would be, he knew, a painful process:

> It is weird that one should reach this stage when I am writing the auto-book as a set, middle-aged family man looking back on his unorganised and wild youth. Oh well, it was going to be half-fiction anyway.[43]

There is something deeply sad about Scannell's description of the way he was living as he wrote—the destination at which his story had arrived. *The Tiger and the Rose*, he said in the book, presented:

> the picture ... of a marriage and of a way of life; a marriage that I would not claim as exemplary, but one, as I have said, that has been strong enough to survive sixteen years and a few rough storms which, if not cataclysmic, might still have been turbulent enough to sink a frailer craft.[44]

The marriage would struggle on through the storms for another four years—but Vernon knew, as he wrote those words, that his craft was already foundering.

IV

In June 1969, Vernon made a note in his diary about a day by the sea at Lyme Regis, about an hour's drive away:

> I bought a very nice Milton for fifteen shillings, and got pissed in the Rose
> and Crown [a pub in the nearby village of Trent].[45]

Milton in the bookshop and beer in the pub over the fields pretty well sum
up much of his life at the time. He was drinking a lot, and occasionally worrying about the effect of the booze on his health—at one point, he hung a
heavy punchbag in the garden at Folly Cottage, and used to work himself
into a sweat with it. The poems were coming slowly during this period of
his life, and he was often all too easily distracted from trying to write them,
but he remained passionate about poetry—writing his own when he could,
and lost in books of other people's when he couldn't.

In *The Tiger and the Rose*, he intended to tell the story of his growth as a
poet—the way that 'though I have often appeared to be, and believed myself
to be, lost and blundering around in circles, I have in fact been moving fairly
consistently in a particular direction, towards the fulfilment of my ambition
to be a poet'.[46] It is a thought, incidentally, that adds another layer of meaning to the serendipitous journey he had described in 'No Sense of Direction',
his love poem to Jo from prison. Writing the book was an opportunity not
just to look back on his journey, but also to refine his ideas about poetry in
general and his poetry in particular. Poets, perhaps, are not always the best
commentators on their own work, but years before, back in Hazelwood, he
had written perceptively in his diary about his poetry:

> It seems to me that my poems are chiefly narrative, or they are narrative quin-
> tessences. Often, the essential fictional 'plot' is put down in a kind of short-
> hand. No, that's not what I mean. The poems are tightly-packed essences of
> longer fictions, or the poem might be the climax of a novel with the narrative
> leading to it omitted or, as it were, submerged: ie, there without words, implied
> in the nature of the climax itself.[47]

This has always been true, of course, of most dramatic monologues—think of
Robert Browning's 'My Last Duchess', Tennyson's 'Ulysses', or T. S. Eliot's 'Love
Song of J. Alfred Prufrock'—but Scannell adapted the technique not just to his
longer, obviously narrative poetry but also to such brief, closely observed snapshots as 'Incident in a Saloon Bar', in which a conspicuously ordinary, inoffensive man in a bar is treated with inexplicable hostility by all the other drinkers:

> Not because he was so quiet and unremarkable
> That they suspected that he might be spying
> Did they feel this hostility towards the lonely fellow
> But simply because he was, quite quietly, crying.[48]

As so often with Scannell, the punch of the poem, in this case the explanation of the hostility, comes in the very last word—which is, of course, no explanation at all. But the point here is that in just sixteen lines, Scannell has depicted a scene from an implied story to which the reader has to supply the background, the plot, even the detailed characterizations. The focus is tightly on the single image of the man standing alone in the bar, of implacable dislike directed at a target that might, it transpires, be thought more worthy of sympathy.

The atmosphere of quiet, unexplained menace that infuses the poem might be reminiscent of Graham Greene or W. H. Auden, except that there are no sinister spies, no fugitives on the run from agents of the Fisc—just respectable middle-class people standing stiffly around in a bar. That, too, is the point—Scannell's poetry always sought out significance and resonance in ordinary experience. When he interviewed Philip Larkin for a television programme, he was delighted to find that the more established poet, whom he admired, shared his view:

> He said that in his early attempts at poetry he believed that to produce the stuff you had to jack yourself up to a transcendental mood, and reading Hardy's poetry had shown him that all you had to do was look around you at the ordinary events and furnishings of daily life.[49]

At the readings and broadcast recordings he was doing, he was making lifelong friends with other poets, talking over with them the practice and technicalities of poetry. The poet Christopher Hampton, for instance, recalls:

> Vernon was a man of striking good looks—strong and sensitive, his clarity and eloquence softened by the timbre of his voice. He had a subtle awareness of what he wanted his poems to achieve ... We talked about the formal structure and the music of the poem—how one is always in search of a clarity of line and rhythm, the ways in which words act on each other to give the poem authenticity and conviction and a permanence of its own ... *Difficult*, he thought that.[50]

But poetry, Scannell thought, *should* be difficult—for the poet, that is. The reader should find the literal meaning of a poem lucid rather than opaque, he believed, even though its implications repay concentrated thought and study. As regards the poet, however, he was fond of quoting Yeats's warning against 'the chief temptation of the artist, creation without toil'.[51] It was about not just clear thought and precise expression, but also mastery of the traditional tools of the poet as craftsman—a view that often put him at odds with the literary establishment:

> The tendency among most of the highly-rated younger poets now is to eschew regular metre and rhyme . . . Perhaps I'm being naïve or puritanical or both, but it seems to me that Baudelaire and later Yeats put their fingers on the dead centre when they spoke of, in the first case, 'a passionate taste for the difficult' and in the second of 'the fascination of what's difficult'. And, damn it, strict rhyme patterns, avoiding cliché rhymes, in a complex stanza form are bloody difficult . . . The point about the difficult and restrictive practices of certain formal elements—and rhyme is only one—is that, whatever the readers may feel about the result, the discipline is necessary, to the poet. The more difficult the better.[52]

Occasionally, he worried that his own poetry might be too readily understood—certainly, he believed that the straightforward clarity of his poems led to their being undervalued by many critics. In one late-night conversation, his friend Dannie Abse suggested that Scannell was sometimes too anxious to make the meaning explicit, and that the poems lost impact as a result:

> Maybe, but the trouble with a lot of non-explicit verse is that the poets fail to be explicit because they're not sure themselves what they want to say and, at worst, a smokescreen of pretentiousness is put up with nothing at all behind it.[53]

That is not to say that he valued or approved of facile, undemanding poetry—the Liverpool 'pop poets', he said, 'are not simply inferior poets: what they produce is the direct antithesis of poetry. It is the slackest use of language.'[54] But on the other hand, he dismissed the avant-garde and occasionally baffling work of the Cambridge academic J. H. Prynne as 'nonsensical gibberish'.[55] Poetry, for Scannell, had to say something worthwhile and significant, and it had to be comprehensible.

V

Scannell's poems would generally start with a few jotted thoughts in one of the notebooks that always lay on his desk. There may be first drafts of individual lines, possibly quotes from other poets, odd words or phrases that seem to fit, and maybe an idea or two of how the poem will develop.

A good example is the drafting of one of his last and best poems, 'Missing Things', which starts with a few rudimentary lines:

> I am old and [illegible] and know [crossed out, replaced by 'realize'; 'very' is
>   inserted before 'old']
> that I shall be no more to anyone
> than a sound or fading [crossed out and reinserted before 'sound'] image in the
>   eye [crossed out]
> & of [crossed out] ears of those who knew me. I'll be gone.

It's possible in these rough experimental lines to see Scannell feeling towards the tight, physically realized first line of the poem's final version, and the way it gradually dissolves and recedes from view:

> I'm very old and breathless, tired and lame,
> And soon I'll be no more to anyone
> Than the slowly fading trochee of my name
> And shadow of my presence. I'll be gone.

Beneath the original lines, the first page continues with brief notes of new ideas, false starts, and possible directions the poem might take:

> Might be a ghost haunting places, Soho etc... The things I miss. do miss shall
> miss... my room/ garden/ DOGS/Books/music... Perhaps I'll be a spark...
> One embrace and be... The nothingness of which I'll be a part.

Almost certainly there were more rough jottings, more rejected ideas, between these notes and the almost-finished version on the next two pages of the notebook—but now he is polishing, changing individual words and listening to the sound of each line. He has second thoughts about moving 'very' from 'old' to 'lame' in the first line, and decides that the original version will make the first line flow better; the blunt and simple 'great danger' awaits the troops who sail away, rather than the more scientific and less forceful 'extinction'. 'Devoted' is a better word to describe the care of a scholar for his books than the weaker 'such loving'; it is his own 'small house', and not the 'small town' that he will miss the most. The last line is changed from 'Then why be sad? And, yes, a bit afraid' to 'Then why so sad? And just a bit afraid?' to end the poem with its finely judged note of unease.

'Missing Things' was written only a few months before Scannell died. Before he was ill, he might have hammered out the last version himself, two-finger style, on his battered typewriter, making final changes as he did so. Earlier, his amanuensis and one-time lover Angela Beese might have done a more professional job on his behalf, and given him a typescript to tweak, but now his friend Alan Benson was doing the job for him, and a scrawled two lines underneath remind him of the dates Benson will be away. There is a scribbled list of possible rhymes for another poem, but the date, 5 May '07, marks the fact that this one, except for a few minor changes in typescript, is finished.

Such focus is remarkable in a man already lying in what he knew was his death-bed—but this was generally the pattern of Scannell's composition. An initial idea, maybe a phrase that appealed to him, an imagined situation, a memory, or an observation would be jotted down in rough notes to begin with, and then he would play with both the words and the idea, turning them this way and that, and trying different forms and metres. It might take a few hours or a few days—sometimes, several months elapsed between the different stages—but he never wrote poetry idly or carelessly. If it wasn't difficult to write, it wasn't worth writing at all.

VI

Scannell's acquaintanceship with the poet Dannie Abse dated back to the late forties, when they would both sit in the pubs of Fitzrovia, bit-part players as Dylan Thomas—'the little Welsh Falstaff',[56] Vernon called him—put on another heavy-drinking display in the bar. Their close friendship, however, had begun with Vernon's drink-driving case. Vernon failed to turn up for a reading he was due to give, and Abse—down to read with him—was shocked to hear that he was in prison. He realized that Jo would have no money coming in to feed the family and quietly, without mentioning it to anyone else, he sent Jo his own fee for the reading. It was not a large amount—probably about £10[57]—but it made a big difference to the family, and Vernon never forgot the gesture.

A couple of years later, working as commissioning editor for a series of young people's novels to be published by the Pergamon Press, Scannell signed a contract for Abse to write one about a young medical student. As the book progressed, however, it gradually turned into a more adult story, and eventually Abse asked to be released from the agreement. 'I felt committed to him, but I wrote to ask if he would let me off the hook, and of course he did', says Abse now. When the book, *O. Jones, O. Jones*, finally appeared in 1970, it carried a dedication to Vernon Scannell. The loyalty of Scannell's friends, and the loyalty he showed them in return, suggest a character who inspired genuine respect and regard.[58]

The Nobel Prize-winning poet Seamus Heaney also remembers him with affection from this period:

> At lunchtime in the BBC canteen, Vernon and a few of us contributors were picking up dishes as we went along the counter, but when we got to the dessert section, there were no pies or puddings left, only apples. At which Vernon cried in protest and dismay, 'An apple for bloody duff!' And I suppose it is that 'duff' that gets and keeps him for me—the vernacular word packed with autobiography and attitude—soldier, boxer, freelancer, man at the bar counter—the egalitarian in him, the solidarity with the 'walking wounded' and the usual crowd. I admired the poems not only for their sturdy metrical pace and structure, but for their combination of mordancy and a sense of mortality, what Joseph Brodsky might have called their 'grief and reason', what MacDiarmid might have called 'the poetry of a grown man'.[59]

The poet Ted Walker used to tell a story of drinking with Scannell in a pub in Norfolk while they were teaching together on a creative writing course in 1971. The locals mistook the tall, handsome, well-spoken stranger in the arty donkey jacket and cap for Sir Laurence Olivier. 'He was signing beer mats for them saying "Best wishes, Larry," and then, with twelve pints or so inside him, he started reciting some of the best speeches from *Henry V*', Walker said.[60]

But it was not just the drinking and general bonhomie that Scannell loved with the other poets he met. On the way back from Norfolk, he persuaded Walker to make a detour with him to call on the ageing Edmund Blunden. Scannell had been deeply impressed by him when they had gone on a ten-day poetry reading tour of the Midlands in 1966, and, as his diary makes clear, this visit—just three years before Blunden died—was something of a pilgrimage for him:

> When Claire [Blunden's wife] let us in, Edmund emerged from the shadows behind her, and he said, very quietly, in a faint, hoarse shout, 'Vernon!'... He sat, not saying much, listening, perhaps not, to what we were saying; there was something defiant in the set of his head. He looked very old, much older than his chronological age, but he was still unvanquished. He was tired and battered and perhaps tortured by the years, but he was still very much alive. I was reminded of Yeats's "I spit into the face of Time / That has disfigured me."[61]

They drove away in silence for many miles, Walker said later. 'After a long time, Vernon said, "Nice old chap, old Blunden. A very brave soldier, you know."' Scannell had long admired Blunden's poetry; he liked him as a man, and could sympathize with him as a father who had, like him, gone through the agony of losing a child in infancy;[62] but it was the courage of the man who had seen more front-line service than any of the poets of the First World War that touched his soul.

His liking and respect were warmly reciprocated: Blunden's biographer, Barry Webb, speaks of the 'warm friendship' that grew out of the Midlands tour, which Blunden remembered as one of the happiest times of his life, when the two poets shared 'war memories, poetic enthusiasms, and a taste for beer'.[63] The few years that remained for him after Scannell's visit were clouded by dementia and confusion: Vernon was, says Webb, 'one of the last and most welcome guests'.[64]

Scannell could, and did, value the careful crafting of the old man's clear, plain spoken poetry—two of Blunden's poems were included in the Methuen anthology that had been Scannell's introduction to poetry more than thirty years before. But his regard for the older poet was touched, too, by a kind of wistfully imaginative nostalgia not for his own childhood, but for the simpler, more honest world that was reflected in Blunden's writing. Vernon had barely been in contact with his father since he had left Aylesbury to join the army some three decades earlier—the scars of his childhood were too deep—but he believed that the generation of the First World War had won the right to respect. It was a feeling that he put into words later in his life, writing about his memories of the father of Dannie Abse's wife, Joan.

> What I was thinking about was his eyes. They are blue and clear and candid with a kind of innocence that one rarely sees nowadays in the eyes of anyone over 20 . . . direct, truthful, confiding. And those are the eyes seen—I'm almost sure—only in that generation that went to war in 1914 and looked upon unspeakable horrors, endured physical and spiritual suffering beyond the understanding of succeeding generations. The eyes of the old, of my own lot, may be blue but they are almost always shifty, aggrieved, informed by an undeceivable wariness and potential belligerence.[65]

He was in his eighties when he wrote those words—an old man himself, with, perhaps, an old man's sense of disillusion about the present. In fact— maybe partly as a reaction to his bitterness and rejection of his own father— he showed instinctive respect not only for survivors of the war, but also for former boxers, like 'Peerless Jim Driscoll' in the *Walking Wounded* collection of 1965, or ordinary, ageing men and women, now struggling and physically diminished. They too could 'spit into the face of Time'. Life itself was a combat, and those who survived and did not weaken were worthy of regard: in his forties and even before, Scannell was uncomfortably aware of the inconsolable sadness of age.

But it is his admiration for the veterans of the First World War, with its implied dismissal of his own war and his own contribution, that most clearly reflects the unease that he felt about life, and battle, and the plight of the survivor. Throughout his poetry, from 'Remembrance Day' in *The Masks of Love* in 1960 to 'Behind the Lines' in the collection of the same name published in 2004, 'the war that was called Great',[66] 'the fields sown with poppies, not with mines',[67] and the men who fought in them are a touchstone for sadness and self-sacrifice. There was grief, too, of course, for the dead of his own war, and anger at the waste of life—but these were emotions mixed with survivor's guilt and a nagging sense of his own unworthiness. He himself, he felt, along with his whole generation, had never quite lived up to the standards that had been set for them.

VII

The Tiger and the Rose appeared in September 1971, along with Scannell's first *Selected Poems*—'No omens in the sky, no copies in the Sherborne bookshops, unsurprisingly',[68] he noted sardonically. But they were a double hit which seemed to confirm his status as a serious literary figure. Reviews were encouraging: *The Tiger and the Rose* had 'the clear, shrill ring of truth', said the *Times Literary Supplement*. The book as a whole, said its reviewer, charted Scannell's journey towards becoming a poet and was 'a brilliantly entertaining demonstration of how to master a craft'.[69] There was, too, recognition from a most unexpected source—a letter from the office of the Conservative Prime Minister, Edward Heath, offering him a £300 grant. Scannell was much too pragmatic to allow his hard-edged political views to get in the way.

> The PM had been given a sum of money by an anonymous donor to distribute from time to time to authors or composers, and the PM had chosen me as the recipient of £300 tax free. Would I accept? Would I? I would. I do. I have done. Why work?[70]

In the shops, though, the autobiography was disappointing. Although the *Selected Poems* sold a respectable 1,100 copies in its first six months, the return from *Tiger and the Rose*, even apart from the payment from *The Times* of £120 for the extract about the death of Benjamin that caused Jo such pain, provided him with an income of just £90[71] for the same period. Even though he claimed to view the book dismissively as one of the 'money jobs'[72] that he blamed for keeping him from his poetry, the lack of interest seemed to confirm his feeling that he was out of step with the times. He was dismissed, he grumbled, as 'a representative of the rear-guard bumbling stick-in-the-muds'.[73]

Maybe, but he was still in great demand for readings—Sheffield and Wath-on-Dearne in South Yorkshire, and then off to Sevenoaks; tours of the Midlands, and the West Country; London one night, and then on to Brighton. Then there were television and radio interviews about the auto-biography and the *Selected Poems*, poetry lectures and workshops in schools, recordings of talks and lectures for the BBC, and then more readings. Often, he would be away for a week or more every month—and, of course, subject to all the attendant temptations.

Vernon was never good with temptation. Some of the results are listed in his diary—In September 1971, a course in Brighton ends up with one of Her Majesty's Inspectors for Education sprawled on his back, after unwisely deciding to teach him a lesson; a few days later, Vernon ends up at the Middlesex Hospital after a day and a night and a day on the booze, having stitches above his left eye 'having fallen out of a taxi'.[74] In August 1972, while he was staying in London with one of his greatest friends, the poet Peter Porter, an Irish stranger with whom he had been drinking offered him a lift home.

> Out of the pub we went to where was parked a large yellow Rolls Royce, 1930 vintage. He drove with unwarranted confidence, once the wrong way up a one-way street. But we reached the Porters' in safety. I seem vaguely to remember that he said he was one of the Guinness family.[75]

Drunk or sober, Vernon was a man who attracted stories—although the poet Anne Stevenson, a great friend of Scannell's through the 1970s though never a lover, suggests that booze was a way of life on the poetry circuit.

> I often think that young 'career' poets today have no idea how much many of us drank and depended on drink to get us through 'poetry events' in the 1970s. Some of us were nervous of appearing in public, some of us thought we ought to drink to be sociable, or to conform to some ideal image of a

'poet'; some of us were incipient alcoholics. But as I think of it now, we mainly drank to enjoy ourselves, shock the bourgeoisie, and strengthen links of solidarity or camaraderie between artists. Vernon could absorb a lot more alcohol than most of us; certainly a lot more than I could, although for a while I did my best to keep up![76]

But Vernon's binges were different. Behind many of them lay the dark and ominous shadow of violence that was ever-present in his life. In February 1973, he and Jo went to a party in a village close to Nether Compton that was being given by Field Marshal Lord Harding, one of Montgomery's commanders in North Africa, a former Chief of the Imperial General Staff, and a former Governor of Cyprus. If Vernon felt any embarrassment about their contrasting military records, he did not show it—instead, to Jo's horror, having hammered his host's champagne, he then insisted that Lady Harding should sit on his knee. Jo's fears were unnecessary—far from taking offence, Her Ladyship was consumed with giggles, as was the 77-year-old field marshal. The party was a roaring success, largely thanks to the jovial, laughing Vernon.[77] Then on the way home, he called in at the Griffin's Head. His diary sums up the rest of the evening.

> Gave Jo a black eye. It won't do. I must do something about it all, but God knows what. What I need is a transplant, a spiritual one, that is.[78]

And there was more than that. It was not just readings and broadcasting work that were keeping Vernon away from home.

VIII

Drink and sex were irresistible, and readings and other literary occasions gave Vernon plenty of opportunity to indulge them both: women, it seemed, wanted to show their appreciation of the poet in all sorts of imaginative ways. In the early 1970s, for instance, Scannell was lecturing on one of the Arvon Foundation's regular creative writing courses at Lumb Bank near Hebden Bridge in Yorkshire. It was, he noted afterwards 'fairly disastrous', with the usual obstacles to be negotiated:

> I drank too much and ended up in Halifax Infirmary after taking a nose dive on the rocky path down to the house. I'm still a bit battered looking, but the cuts have cleared up quite well.[79]

In his later life, people would occasionally notice the faint trace of a scar on his nose and assume that it was an old boxing wound. Vernon never admitted that it had been caused by a drunken fall at Lumb Bank—and he certainly said nothing about Carol Bruggen, the young would-be novelist whom he had met there a couple of years before, and whom he was continuing to see whenever he was in Yorkshire.

This time he went to stay with her for a few days at her home in Briercliffe, near Burnley, a 17-mile drive from Hebden Bridge or an 8-mile tramp across the moors. Her son Tom, about twelve years old at the time, was in no doubt about their relationship:

> When he first arrived, the house was in turmoil, and Mum was smoking a pipe. I think he just fell in love with the wildest, craziest character out of the bunch . . . She was madly in love with him, and Vernon loved her as well. They were secret lovers—no-one was supposed to know.[80]

Vernon would drive over to stay for a few days either before or after the Lumb Bank courses, or—even though the courses were meant to be residential, with the tutors staying on site—he would slip away late at night, with Carol driving him back the next morning so no one would know he'd been away. At least once, according to Tom, he brought another tutor from the course to meet one of Carol's friends, the future Poet Laureate Ted Hughes sneaking out of Lumb Bank with him, like two eager fifth-formers bunking off on an adventure at the local girls' school:

> I don't know if Vernon and Ted Hughes were mates, but they were certainly doing this thing with the women. Mum was hooked up with Vernon, and she fixed Ted Hughes up with somebody else as well. Other people, like our neighbours, couldn't believe it when they saw Ted Hughes here—it was like a real celebrity scene. Mum and her friends were regarded as wayward, trippy sixties hippy groupies.[81]

Tom Bruggen remembers how, on other occasions, his mother and Vernon would sit and write together while he did his homework:

> My mum hadn't had anything published then, and hadn't begun to put any poems together. Vernon sparked her writing . . . She had a typewriter on the table, and she would have her glasses on top of her head, and they would sit there drinking and talking and getting drunker and drunker. He used to think in poetry—Mum would say something and he'd say something back, more like jamming or writing a song.

Apart from helping Carol with her writing, Scannell also set about teaching Tom to box, after he had been beaten up in a fight at school:

Mum was in tears when she saw my face after the fight, and Vernon was very upset too. Once the bruising had gone down, he took me into the next room, picked up a cushion and held it to his chest. He said 'Pretend that's my head—go on, punch it', and then I went to punch it and he just slipped to the side very cleverly and threw a punch back at me, into my body. He said, 'That's what you should do—simple as that.' He was a very skilful boxer—not a technical genius by pro standards, but he could slip and counter punch, He was a very powerful guy.[82]

The lessons eventually led Tom to a career as a boxing coach, and in the short term they saved him from any more beatings at school. In the summer of 1975, according to Tom, Vernon's relationship with Carol came to an amicable end, although they exchanged occasional letters and cards for the rest of her life, and he had copies on his shelves of the three novels she wrote in the mid-1980s.

That was one thing that most of Scannell's women had in common—they wanted to learn about writing and literature, and he was always keen to teach them. A few years later, in a slightly different context, he would see this as a weakness that he needed to overcome:

It's this accursed teaching disease—a kind of didactitis—that causes so much trouble. In an odd way, I need pupils as a religion needs converts.[83]

Scannell, in fact, was a loyal and painstaking mentor for male writers as well as women—both Martin Reed, a lifelong friend whom he met in the mid-1970s, and the musical journalist Tully Potter had long and fruitful discussions with him over many years about their own work. So, too, had the young novelist Alexis Lykiard, as he went through the process of establishing himself as a poet. During the early 1980s, Scannell carried on a correspondence with John Neish, a prisoner in Broadmoor Hospital and an aspiring poet. 'I never did quite gather what misfortune brought you into your present unhappy circumstances', he wrote to Neish. 'Whatever it was, you have my real sympathy, since I know only too well what it is like to lose one's freedom.'[84] Scannell had no understanding of the smug concept of the 'deserving' poor: if someone was genuinely interested in poetry and they wanted his advice, then 'deserving' or not, he was there to help them.

His replies to strangers who wrote to him for advice about poetry, and about what to read and how to write, were considered, thoughtful and cogent—always honest and direct, but sympathetic too. He relished the role of mentor. It would be disingenuous to suggest that he wanted women so that he could teach them about poetry—but the urge to pass on what he understood and what he believed in was certainly a genuine and passionate one. It was just that, when the opportunity presented itself, it mixed very conveniently with an exceptionally strong sexual drive. Poetry was sexy—an agreeable discovery that he was neither the first poet nor the last to make.

A new collection in 1973, *The Winter Man*, reflected the pressures and anxieties of his life, and his sense that his relationship with Jo was crumbling away. In one poem ('Charnel House, Rothwell Cemetery'), the speaker imagines placing a human skull on the pillow next to his wife's sleeping head; another imagines lovers falling from their secret hiding place to lie exposed on the ground:

> Without a stitch or feather on
> For the world and his wife to look upon.[85]

In another, a woman who has been robbed of her savings and abandoned by her dishonest and faithless lover admits that for all her suffering, she would return to him despite his treachery:

> again
> To hear his sweet deceitful whisper feign
> A lovelier love than plain and honest fare;
> To feel his hands exploring flesh and hair,
> Re-educating lust until it knew
> How false such categories as false and true.[86]

Deceit and the fragility of love seem to be very much on the poet's mind. For all the defiant claim in this last poem that lust has its own rules and its own morality, this is not the poetry of a happy man.

Jo was aware of Vernon's other flings and affairs, whether or not she knew about Carol specifically. Now, however, she began to realize there was one particular woman, whom he had met at a reading in Oxfordshire, whom he was seeing regularly, and not just on occasional trips to Arvon courses. Her name was Olwen, and she had been living in Oxford.

'Oh, I knew it was going on', Jo says now, sitting at the same kitchen table that she sat at when she told him to leave:

Women were necessary to Vernon. He wanted to be worshipped rather than understood. When he met her, he was probably looking for an escape. I knew it was happening, and it didn't stop. I knew he would leave, and by then I wanted him to go. I wanted to start again. He sat at this table, and I said, 'If you're going, why don't you go?' He said, 'I'll go when I'm ready, honey, I'll go when I'm ready.' I remember those words, because at that moment I could have killed him.[87]

12

A Proper Gentleman

The wounds and scars that ache
the worst, and go on aching,
are from blows delivered by
oneself; there's no mistaking
that sly pain, and, if you cry,
you cannot expect a breath
of sympathy...

'Self-inflicted Wounds', from *The Loving Game* (1975)

I

It was in spring 1974 that Vernon finally packed his car with all the books and belongings that he could fit into it and drove away down the narrow track from Folly Cottage. He would be back—back to visit the children, back to work at his desk with the view of Tom Payne's Hill, back even to live for brief periods—but this was a major turning point in his life. Although he and Jo would never divorce, it felt at that moment as if his marriage of more than twenty years was over. The 'frail craft' he had written about so disingenuously in *The Tiger and the Rose* seemed finally to have sunk.

Vernon was heading to Olwen's home in Rhydyfelin, just outside Pontypridd in South Wales—'out of the matrimonial frying pan, Gawd 'elp me!'[1] as he put it to one correspondent. It was a semi-detached house in a suburban street, very different from the rural idyll he was leaving behind, but he settled down there to work, with occasional trips in to the BBC's Cardiff office to review books—£17 for reviewing Stevie Smith's *Collected Poems* here, £21 for his comments on a new biography of Isaac Rosenberg there[2]— and finishing a critical book about the poetry of the Second World War,

Not Without Glory. He was so busy, in fact, that he turned down an invitation to write an article for *Ambit* on the poet Peter Porter—although the 'absolutely miserable' fee of £8 might also have been a factor.[3] There were frequent trips away for readings and lectures, but little time for writing his own poetry—with the regular cheques he had promised to send back to Jo, he now had two families to support. For a few months, even the regular entries in his diary sputtered to a halt.

Scannell had started writing his diaries on 5 April 1951, with a note about a trip to buy typing paper at the newsagents and see if his latest poem, 'Jairus's Daughter', had been published. His last entry came fifty-five years later, just over eighteen months before his death:

> Jo's birthday. I'm sweating very heavily at 12.40 am. I am also mildly pissed. When I stop sweating I shall go to bed. Isn't that fucking interesting?[4]

By that time, he had a row of thirteen notebooks of different sizes, colours, and degrees of dilapidation—a fourteenth, covering the years 1991–3, had been, he noted, either lost or stolen. In them were notes about the weather; angry rants about women or books or poetry or politics; maudlin late-night drunken scrawls about his need to stop drinking or his lack of recognition as a poet; first drafts of reviews; ideas for poems and novels; and rhapsodic declarations of love for the various women who had shared his life.

He wrote the diaries partly as therapy—like many writers he found that if the poetry wasn't flowing, it was helpful at least to be writing *something*— and partly as a resource to be quarried when he was producing his autobiographical memoirs. It seems likely that he expected them to be read or even published after his death—he even prepared a number of extracts for possible publication under the title *Tightrope Walker—a Poet's Diaries of the Sixties*. In his first entry, back in 1951, he admitted that he planned to omit or change some names 'out of respect for persons' reputations or fear of libel or slander charges',[5] and although he constantly expresses shame over his drinking, the more serious issue of his violence is referred to only rarely and obliquely. One or two pages have been torn out, presumably to prevent anyone from reading them.

The notebooks stayed with him as he moved from flat to flat and house to house. Sometimes, as in Rhydyfelin, there might be gaps of weeks or even months between the entries, but he always came back to the diaries. In the end, they were a way of imposing some sort of much-needed structure on a life that could often be chaotic.

In the spring of 1975, nearly a year after he had left Nether Compton, he started his entries again with an enthusiastic 'I love Olwen. Oh yes, I do, I do, I do!'[6] But he had not been able to walk away from his family without feelings of guilt and regret:

> I live a strange life. A kind of muffled torment goes on, anxiety for the chil-
> dren and Jo, an uneasy feeling that I'm not going to get away with 'it', what-
> ever 'it' is—yet a constant, or almost constant euphoria of sexual excitement
> and fulfilment, a sense never before experienced, of being loved. Olwen is
> about as uncomplicated as anyone could be; could be called, except for her
> beauty, 'ordinary', except that she has immense generosity of spirit and an
> apparently vast capacity for love and steadfastness.'[7]

There is something appealing about this delighted, almost adolescent enthu-siasm for the new woman in his life, even though we've heard it all before. He loved women, and loved the idea of falling in love; he yearned for a stable, lasting, fulfilling relationship, and with each new affair he believed for a time that it was within his grasp. It was the real thing this time—again. 'I have the uneasy feeling of teetering on the edge of something—of real work, of a real life, a real love, a real relationship',[8] he wrote in his diary—a comment that sounds optimistic on the face of it, but also reveals a deep-seated dissatisfaction with his work and his life so far. He was bringing things with Carol Bruggen to a close, or at least a pause, as gently as he could, although occasional phone calls or letters arriving in Rhydyfelin from her seem to have caused some tension—'Olwen is unreasonably vexed',[9] Vernon noted blandly after one such call.

But even as he plunged joyously into his new *grande passion*, he was pri-vately preparing for its collapse. He still had secret fears that he might lack the 'capacity for love' that he had wished for his daughter, and that he believed he had found in Olwen. And some three months later, this rela-tionship, too, would be beginning to fall apart.

III

Shortly before Vernon left Nether Compton, he had heard that he had won the Cholmondeley Award for poetry from the Society of Authors. It was his second major award, and this time it was given to honour the whole body of his work, rather than a single volume. A few months later, after his arrival in Rhydyfelin, the Welsh Arts Council gave him a £500 grant,[10] which he accepted 'with characteristic magnanimity. I'd hate to hurt their feelings by refusing.' The facetious tone of his diary entry is deceptive—it came at a time when he was desperate for money and for reassurance about the value of his work:

> Very broke, not working well in any sustained way, yet not entirely unproduc- tive—bits of verse, some fairly solid reading of two books on prosody... and scatter-brained sketches for three different novels, none of which I expect to get written... [11]

One of those 'scatter-brained sketches', on which he would work on and off for more than a year before abandoning it in despair, started, like many of Scannell's poems, with an idea for the title—*The Getaway Man*. The phrase describes the last man in an army patrol, whose job, Scannell says, was to escape and report back if his comrades were caught in an ambush. The rough outline he noted down sounds very much like another uneasy self-portrait:

> Start in wartime with 18yr old protagonist leaving pregnant (older) girl- friend... End with him on the run again. (Getting up in strange places, no friends, no money, pursued by women and kids—excitedly looking forward to the new day). He is to have depression and setbacks but rarely self-pity; a protective irony and humour preserve him from these. [12]

Vernon knew he was back where he was in the years after the war—on the move, with twenty settled years with Jo irretrievably behind him. For all his enthusiastic declarations of love only three months earlier, the signs of strain in his relationship with Olwen were becoming harder to ignore. He could foresee a return to the shiftless, one-bedsit-to-another lifestyle of the past, and it was not a comforting thought. He would need all the reserves of irony and humour he could find.

In another way, however, he had travelled a long way since those uncomfortable post-war years. Then, he had been a struggling young poet, desperate to see his work in print in any magazine that would take it: now, his old friend Jeremy Robson had just agreed to publish his eighth volume of verse. Many of the poems it contained were quarried from the melancholy experience of his last years with Jo—in the title poem, 'The Loving Game', and in others such as 'Wicket Maiden', 'Where Shall We Go', and 'An Anniversary', he focused on the gulf between what love hopes for and what it achieves, and on the apparently inevitable disappointment that follows in its wake. Some of the poems are wry, some wistful, but the overall mood of the col-

lection is quiet and sombre. It is the poetry of the battered survivor, which
is what Scannell believed he was. Bizarrely but typically, he was unsatisfied
with the book. It was, he declared later, 'the weakest collection I've published since the fifties'.[13] The critics did not agree: *The Loving Game* was
nominated by the Poetry Book Society as its Christmas Choice for 1975—
an important accolade. Like all Scannell's work, its poems are accessible and
subtle and speak with a direct and colloquial voice, but they are also technically highly innovative, as the first verse of 'Enemy Agents' demonstrates:

> Expert in disguise and killing-blows,
> Fluent in all languages required,
> They wrote me ardent letters, but in code.
> My vanity and ignorance combined
> To make me perfect victim for their game:
> I took them at face-value every time.[14]

The final vowel sound of the first line (the 'oh' of 'blows') and the final
consonant of the second (the 'd' of 'required') are brought together in the
final word of the third (code), in a pattern which is repeated throughout the
poem:

> I call it 'triadic rhyme', 'triadic' because, unlike pure rhyme, it requires not two
> but three elements for its composition... My intention is to impose upon
> myself a discipline every bit as exacting as pure rhyme, but the effect of which
> should be less predictable and less obviously euphonious.[15]

It is more than just showing off, being difficult for difficulty's sake. Few, if
any, readers would notice how the effect is achieved if it were not pointed
out to them, but the echoing sounds in each group of three lines bind the
lines together almost subliminally, in a way that gives the poem a diffident,
tentative quality. This perfectly matches its depiction of a man helplessly
bemused by intimacy.

Just as important, though, from Scannell's viewpoint, were the demands
that the technique makes on the poet. It is another example of his consistent
belief in the discipline of difficulty as a crucial part of the poetic craft. Six
years before *The Loving Game*, he had spelt his ideas out explicitly in his
diary:

> An exigent form will force the poet to find ways of saying what he wants to
> say in a more economical and often more vivid way than he would otherwise
> have found. A regular rhyming pattern can suggest ideas, images, locutions
> that in a looser form would have been lost.[16]

In this case, the extra demands of the 'triadic' rhyme impose an even harsher discipline on the poet. It is a reminder that when Scannell inveighed, as he often liked to, against pop poetry, doggerel, and birthday-card rhymes as 'not inferior poetry, but the antithesis of poetry',[17] he was speaking not as some pompous old buffer grumbling about standards in general, but as a crafts-man who delights in the fine detail of his craft. It is the contempt of a mas-ter carpenter for a flat-pack chest of drawers cobbled together out of chipboard and plastic jointing blocks.

IV

Just over a year after his arrival in Rhydyfelin, the offer of a writing fellow-ship from the Southern Arts Association seemed to present Scannell with something of a financial lifeline. The fee was £2,500,[18] and the SAA would provide him with a flat in the village of Berinsfield, some 8 miles outside Oxford. He would live in the village for nine months, spending about fif-teen hours a week organizing poetry readings, talks, and discussions, and giving whatever help he could to local people who wanted to discuss their literary ambitions. For the rest of the time, he would be free to get on with his own writing.

It sounded almost too good to be true—and it was. His initial impres-sions were ominous:

> I drove past a small parade of shops—a supermarket, newsagent and post office, a launderette and ladies' hairdressers. There was a fish and chip shop, a small Co-operative Store and a single pub. The rest of the place reminded me of a large military depot or the married quarters of a prison, and the gaol-like aspect was increased by the huddle of roofs being overlooked by what I sup-pose was a water-tower, but looked like the watch-tower of a prison camp.[19]

The project started badly, with a row over his flat, which many people thought should have gone to a local family, and steadily got worse.

Berinsfield was not the idyllic Oxfordshire village he had imagined, but a newly created community that had been brought together around a few old military huts left behind after the war in an attempt to ease the county's housing problems. Most people there weren't interested in literature and had no desire to have a poet among them—and in the wider area, the few who did write poetry and were glad of the chance of someone to read it to,

seemed at first to have no interest in Scannell's attempts to help them. They
wanted help to get published, not help to write better verse:

> Young poets don't want criticism of the only kind that's of any use at all—
> close reading and weighing of the words on the page, suggestions that cer-
> tain words, especially adjectives and adverbs, are dispensable. They want to
> bask in your silent admiration or perhaps purr softly as you stammer out
> superlatives.[20]

As for getting on with his own writing, that didn't work either. What had
seemed to be an ideal solution to his chronic problem of finding enough
time to write poetry while still managing to earn enough to survive turned
out to be no solution at all.

> The trouble with these jobs (jobs?), fellowships, residences, is that they pro-
> vide me with a rough living to be something—poet, author, artist—Not do.
> They are planned to help you in your art, but they have the reverse effect. I
> have the time, but I spend it boozing, or flying back to Olwen. What I don't
> have here is the ordinary business of living from which, as far as I am con-
> cerned, poems come. It's artificial, fake, dreary.[21]

The real answer to the problem, of course, was that there was no answer.
Like many poets, Scannell needed the frustrations and diversions of daily life
to give him something to write about: it was the same distractions that
made it hard to write poetry which also made it possible to write poetry. In
his first three months in Berinsfield, he calculated later, he wrote one book
review, daily notes in his diaries, scores of letters, and hardly a line of verse.

Right from the start, he felt alienated, under suspicion—left to drink
alone in the pub, with a feeling that he was being watched, covertly and
with barely disguised hostility:

> I felt myself protesting—silently, of course— to the men in the bar: Hell,
> what's wrong with you? I'm not what you think I am, whatever that might
> be. I'm not posh. I'm not one of 'them'. I left school at fourteen, I lived in a
> slum and I know what it's like to go hungry. I never owned a pair of pyjamas
> until I was twenty. I've been in the army, a squaddie, not a bloody officer. I've
> done detention, I've been in the nick, I've done solitary, PD 1—Punishment
> Diet Number One. I don't want to get at you. I don't want converts. I don't
> give a fart if you've never read a line of poetry in your life and don't want to.
> Suits me fine. I'm no different from you.[22]

For a naturally sociable man like Scannell, who had always considered himself one of life's struggling underdogs, it was a disconcerting experience to

be treated as a toff, an outsider—but, being Scannell, he quickly decided to turn it to good account. Within a couple of weeks of arriving in the village, he had decided to keep a detailed diary of his time there, and write it up afterwards as the memoir which would be entitled *A Proper Gentleman*.

Life began to improve after the first few days. A neighbour lent him pots, pans, and cutlery for his grim and sparsely furnished flat, and others gradually became more friendly in the pub. He began to give readings and talks in surrounding towns and villages—one session at Banbury, another at Reading Poetry Society, and others in Pangbourne, Henley, and the towns of the Thames Valley. Whenever he could, he would stay with friends—as he did with the poet Anne Stevenson on one occasion when he was giving a reading at the Old Fire Station Arts Centre in Oxford. Stevenson already knew and liked him—she referred to him among her friends as 'Vernon Scandal'—and had offered to let him sleep at her flat after the reading. He arrived after midnight, 'falling down drunk' and accompanied by a girl whose name he either did not know or had forgotten. Stevenson generously allowed the couple to use her room, and went downstairs to sleep in the bed she had made up for him:

> Who should turn up at 9am but my elegant and rather puritanical mother-in-law, bent on seeing her grandchildren for breakfast. There I was, sound asleep in the front room... and there, coming out of the bathroom behind the kitchen was a large, naked man with a small towel wrapped around his middle, groping blindly around for some means of making coffee. Luckily, the mysterious girl had disappeared—or maybe it was not so lucky, because suspicion naturally fell heavily on me... [23]

Back in Berinsfield, he worked hard to persuade local groups to listen to what he had to say about poetry. There were disappointments—when the friendly neighbour who had lent him the pots and pans suggested that he might speak to the Berinsfield Ladies' Circle, and he replied that he would be happy to talk to them about poetry, the reply was 'I don't think they'd like *that*!' and he heard no more of the proposal. But there were also unexpected successes, such as a group of Rangers—older girl scouts—who seemed completely unmoved by his reading of Hardy, Ben Jonson, Graves, Auden, and Gavin Ewart, but who he heard later had been anxious to hear more. Many of the schools he visited, ranging from the prestigious Radley College to the little village primary school in Cholsey, Oxfordshire, left him exhilarated by the eagerness and enthusiasm of the pupils.

He also received sheaves of poetry through the post, and several visits from people who said they wanted advice, including one woman who—as he told friends later, but avoided saying in *A Proper Gentleman*—ended up in bed with him within ten minutes of walking through his front door. In the Berinsfield Arms, soon after he arrived, he met a local woman who became his permanent girlfriend while he was in the village—his time there was generally split between the pub, the club, his flat, and her flat.[24] The sexual magic of being a poet still worked, and his professed love for Olwen, still back home in Rhydyfelin, seemed to be no obstacle. But for the most part, his role as mentor for would-be poets was a disappointment. None of the people who contacted him measured up to his demanding standards of dedication and hard work. They were in love with the idea of being a poet—the same ambition, in fact, that he had confessed to at the end of *The Tiger and the Rose*. But where he was dedicating himself to hard work and study, several of them admitted to not even reading any poetry other than the verses that they wrote. Some wrote poems in regular rhyme and metre, but with dead, flat, and outdated vocabulary and imagery, 'as lifeless as paper flowers';[25] others wrote formless verse, arbitrarily split into lines, which they proudly called '*vers libre*'. Scannell was fond of quoting T. S. Eliot's pithy dictum,[26] 'No *vers* is *libre* for the man who wants to do a good job', and insisting that to ignore the disciplines of rhyme and metre, it was necessary first to understand them. He told one visitor bluntly:

> A kind of stuttering prose that's broken up into lines of uneven length for no reason that I can follow—people doing that kind of thing simply don't interest me. They're nearly always bores.[27]

For many of the people who came to see him, being a poet meant playing a role rather than writing poems—being the sensitive, misunderstood keeper of the flame of poetry, perhaps, or a tragic roistering figure in the mould of Dylan Thomas. The truth, he knew, was simpler and less narcissistic:

> The *poète maudit*, the tormented, self-destructive bard, is not a romantic invention but among poets of stature, outside fiction, he is to be found in far fewer numbers than the hard-working, abstemious, responsible man.[28]

Those words 'abstemious' and 'responsible' are heavy with self-criticism. On 31 December, sitting alone with his diary, Vernon wrote what started as a depressed and downbeat assessment of *The Loving Game*, which had appeared a few months into his time at Berinsfield, and of his potential as a poet:

I think there are a few good poems in the collection. I hope to Christ that there are, otherwise it's obvious that I'm finished. Most depressing is the thought that I never really started . . .

It doesn't much matter whether I go on writing or not—except to me. I care. After all, I've spent 30 years at the game—I *ought* to be able to produce something worth reading, yet in this mood of profound self-doubt, I am horribly conscious of the fact that many, very many self-deluded folk have struggled all their lives and never produced a line worth a second glance.

But he knew he was in a different class from the self-regarding amateurs who had been visiting him to ask for praise. The diary entry continues with a grim and ironic nod at his besetting problem and a harsh (and inaccurate) assessment of his abilities, and then presents a startlingly clear-sighted view of what he and his poetry have to offer:

There's always drink.

The truth is, I am not very intelligent, I certainly have no originality of thought; I am ill-educated and not even industrious. What then have I to give me reason for going on?

I suppose a certain amount of verbal sensitivity; some (though not a lot) of skill in writing in metre and employing rhymes; perhaps a little gift for producing the image that does illuminate; a kind of scepticism, a sense of the ironic that permeates all human striving and achieving, and an awareness that this irony is ultimately a protective rather than a cruel force; a feeling for the contradictions and antipathies that cohabit in almost every situation. These are the things to work with, to develop, to bring to bear on matters that might yield undetected truths and possibly give pleasure to a reader.

Wring out the old . . . [29]

The entry, and the year, ends with this self-mocking, punning reference to 'In Memoriam',[30] Tennyson's courageous refusal to give way to despair from more than a hundred years before. 'Ring out the old, ring in the new . . . Ring out the false, ring in the true', Tennyson had written. Christmas was seldom a good time for Scannell, and in his dejection, he is unreasonably hard on himself—there was nothing 'false' about the poetry he had written, no doubting his intelligence or his originality, and the education which he had won for himself against all the odds was formidable. Twelve months ago, the prospects for 1975 had seemed good, with the publication of a new collection of poetry and a job that would at last give him both an income and the opportunity to concentrate on his own writing. He had worked through the year on *Not Without Glory*, his study of Second World War poetry, and the book was due to be published in a few months' time. But the reviews of *The Loving Game* had been unenthusiastic, and the job seemed to be turning into a millstone rather than an opportunity. The old worries that his poetry was out of fashion and his talent uncertain had come back to haunt him—but he ended the year on a note of defiance. He was not going to give up.

V

Those late night thoughts make the craft and calling of poetry sound sturdy, determined, even muscular—qualities which he did indeed believe they possessed in abundance. He was fond of reeling off names such as Chaucer, Sidney, Wyatt, Raleigh, Marlowe, Jonson, and Byron—'distinguished soldiers, sailors, men of action', and sometimes, he frequently added, boxers as well:

> Among the prejudices against the art of poetry is the misguided notion that it is a precious activity practised and enjoyed only by highly educated, other-worldly and doubtfully masculine intellectuals. This view of the poet as a cissy, or a zany eccentric, is one which seems to have been born towards the end of the nineteenth century; before that time it would have been incomprehensible.[31]

Berinsfield, however, was not convinced. He returned after Christmas to the same atmosphere of faintly hostile dismissiveness that he had experienced before. 'I feel like a parson',[32] he wrote in his diary—tolerated perhaps, but treated with amused contempt and with a complete lack of interest in what he had to offer. His confidence was not improved by his continuing failure to write any poetry, or by a sudden cold snap, which left him tottering uncertainly on icy pavements:

> I walk like an octogenarian, very slowly, very carefully, as if I've got to concentrate on which foot is the next to go forward . . . I must soon write some poems, or try to, if only as a change from telling other people how to write them.[33]

And with the departure of the snow and ice, things got even worse. A group of teenagers began to gather on the village green in the spring sunshine, laughing and fooling about—and taunting him every time he stepped outside with mocking shouts of 'Poet!' 'Scannell!' and various obscenities. Over the next few days, they began banging on the window of his flat late at night; one morning he found broken bottles carefully pushed under his car tyres, so they would have been slashed to ribbons had he attempted to drive away.

He was told that two of the youngsters had been spotted trying to break into his flat.

The impotent rage with which he responded surprised and shocked him in two contradictory ways. On the one hand, it brought home to him the unwelcome truth that, in his mid-fifties, he was no longer the lean, danger-ous figure he had once been:

> My boxing days were long past. I was no longer young, strong and fit; my reflexes would be slower than once they had been. I drank and smoked heav-ily. In short, I was probably incapable of boxing chocolates.[34]

But at the same time, it frightened him that he should feel so violently towards a gang of badly behaved youngsters. Past it or not, he knew only too well that he could still inflict serious physical damage, and he was well aware of the unpredictability of his temper. If he had ever caught one of the boys, he might have been made to look foolish or he might have behaved like a brute.

In fact he never had the chance—when he was angry enough, he was too slow to get near them, and when he was near them he managed to keep his anger in check. Their mocking taunts and sneers pursued him through his last weeks in Berinsfield, and when he finally packed his possessions into his car for the drive back to Rhydyfelin, he did so with a deep-seated feel-ing of defeat, frustration, and impotence. He had written virtually nothing of value, and he had been little help to the local community. His nine months as a Southern Arts Association writing fellow had been a failure from every point of view, and he knew it.[35]

VI

A couple of months after he left Berinsfield, there was another unexpected offer that might have solved Vernon's chronic money problems at a stroke. He met a wealthy American benefactor, to whom he refers in his diary only as 'Mrs L', who seemed to be willing to sponsor him and support him finan-cially. Once again, it might have seemed that his dream of a life where he might be free to write the poetry he wanted to without having to spend time earning a living might be within his grasp. But he had rejected a simi-lar offer some twenty years before in the embarrassing scene in the Ivy restaurant—now, with the disappointment of Berinsfield behind him, it was even easier:

[She] seems to be willing to rescue me from all financial worries, no strings. I find I'm deeply suspicious and even resentful of the offer. 'I'm not for sale,' I tell her pompously, and added a few insults about rich overfed Americans. Unfair, really, but what the hell?[36]

He had had enough of quick-fix solutions. Instead, he set to work on *A Proper Gentleman*, as an attempt to salvage something from the wreckage of the past nine months—no financial cure-all, perhaps, but a course of self-prescribed therapy designed to get him writing poetry again.

It is good to have a biggish task like *A Proper Gent* on the go. It keeps me in a working frame of mind and the actual physical business of putting words on paper becomes a habit, and from this habit other things might come. I want to get some poems written.[37]

Working on the book also provided some much-needed distraction from life at Rhydyfelin. In March, he had still occasionally been scrawling 'I love Olwen' in his diary late at night, in big drunken letters, but he was apprehensive about whether they had any future together:

Olwen suddenly hostile—the juices dried, perhaps, the acrobatics stale. And what are we left with? Mutual resentment? Well, I don't think I feel much of that. Boredom, yes, but gratitude for the material things, I suppose... the beautifully parcelled gift has a tiny bomb at the centre.[38]

There was at least the appearance of *Not Without Glory* to distract him. In April, he left Berinsfield briefly for a trip to London for the launch party. It began badly, with a late-night drunken drive the wrong way up a one-way street in Soho, smashing a shop window on the way—and got worse. The next day, he and Olwen lunched with his old friends Dannie Abse and Jeremy Robson before the evening launch party, where he met Dennis Enright, Roy Fuller, Alan Ross, much of London's literary set, and also glass after glass of red wine. With Vernon 'helplessly pissed', they made it back to the hotel where they were staying.

Not Without Glory was Scannell's attempt to introduce Second World War poets such as Keith Douglas, Alun Lewis, Roy Fuller, Sidney Keyes, and Charles Causley to a wider audience. When he had mentioned them or presented their poetry at his readings and talks, he had been met by blank stares from his audience: among the reading public, the phrase 'war poetry' called to mind almost exclusively the soldier poets of the First World War. As for his own reputation, Scannell loved to quote a slightly tactless remark from a student during a reading at Keele University. 'I'm surprised to see you here. I thought you were killed during the First World War', the young man had said.

In fact, he said nothing in the book about his own poetry. He had only started to write about the war years after it was over, and it would in any case have been difficult to consider his own writing with the objectivity necessary to prove his point that the Second World War produced 'a body of poetry which is of a very high order indeed and can compare favourably with the best work of the Great War'.[39]

Even so, much of what he had to say about the poets on whom he focused has clear relevance to his own experience in North Africa and Northern Europe. They did not share the disillusionment of Owen or Sassoon, he said, because they had no illusions in the first place; they went to war in a spirit of resigned determination rather than with Rupert Brooke's exuberant thanks to God, 'Who has matched us with His hour'; and they 'reflected the predicament of the civilian in uniform who is struggling to retain something of his sense of identity and individuality, something of his independence and sensitivity'.[40]

The book received mixed reviews, including one particularly scathing one in the *New Statesman* from the Oxford academic and critic John Carey. 'If ever a book were designed to reinforce the impression that World War II yielded no worthwhile poets, this is it',[41] he declared. Scannell was 'dogmatic' and his 'critical sympathy minuscule'; he had only two or three ideas in the book, Carey said, and he applied them 'with mechanical obtuseness'. It was a review to make any author squirm, and Scannell later devoted a page and a half of *A Proper Gentleman* to a rather hurt and angry reply.

VII

The next three years would be played out against a background of alternating passion and disillusion, attempts to put things right at Rhydyfelin and determined plans to move out. One reason, perhaps, was Vernon's continuing sense of guilt, whether about Olwen or about the family he had left behind in Nether Compton.

He made frequent trips back to Nether Compton, including regular stays over Christmas. He was back for Nancy's twenty-first birthday, for trips out with Jacob, and for drinks in the pub with John or Toby. There were sudden panicky appearances when Olwen had lost patience and thrown him out. One letter to a friend early in 1977 is probably typical of several trips home: he is writing from Dorset, he says, 'but will probably return to Wales when the heat is off'.[42] Jo was concerned for him, but phlegmatic: 'Every now and then he'd turn up and there would be about ten cardboard boxes in the house and all his shirts hanging on the rail',[43] she says now. 'I always wanted him to think of this place as his anchor, and I think he did.'

By mid-1977, he was making cryptic little diary notes in Rhydyfelin schoolboy French—hardly an effective code, but maybe a sign that he wanted to keep them secret. In September, for instance, he says, 'Looks like the denouement. Well . . . Je pense que j'allais nord pour vivre douce-ment . . . mais c'est une idée triste et pleine d'ennuie.'[44] In February 1978, he left for a fortnight, which he spent partly back with the loyal and

Figure 17. Whether working with a spade or sitting in the shade with a book, Vernon always found the garden at Folly Cottage a place for relaxation. (Photo: Not known. Scannell family collection)

long-suffering Jo in Nether Compton and partly on a week of poetry readings in Liverpool, Lincoln and the north of England.

It was not a situation that could last, and in July 1978 he was back 'squatting uneasily' at Nether Compton. There is no mistaking the note of satisfaction as he writes:

> Now (7.30 am) am sitting at my desk. The morning is still. A heavy mist, almost as thick as fog, hides Tom Payne's hill completely. The air is full of the trillings and squeaks of invisible birds.[45]

He was working almost manically—not just at his desk, but driving himself physically, with hard digging in the garden, backbreaking labour clearing ditches and streams, and long walks across the fields with his dog, Mick. Dogs would be a part of Vernon's life for years, his relationships with them as turbulent and unpredictable as his relationship with the various women that he knew. Following Mick would be Henry, George, and Robinson, the 'knicker eating monster'.[46] Then there would be Bo'sun, the four-year-old Dalmatian, 'patient, affectionate and well-behaved', according to Angela, his then partner,[47] but rehoused through the RSPCA after he displayed a distressing propensity for vomiting all over the house; and Hetta, the whippet from the Canine Defence League, who stole sausages from a fishmonger's stall and an Easter egg from Vernon's kitchen table. Vernon's initial verdict was that she was 'a fucking nuisance, howling at night and demanding attention during the day, but I think she'll be a good 'un if we can bother to train her properly'.[48] He could almost have been talking about one of his human companions, and when she had to be put down after ten years, it briefly broke his heart.

Finding someone to look after the dogs while he went away on reading tours was a constant challenge, but taking them for walks, wherever he was living, would be an important priority for the next forty years. It was for his own benefit as well as theirs: after his rambles with Mick, he joked that the physical effort 'sweated out a fair amount of malt and hops'. For some time though, he had been feeling his age:

> I have been aware for some years of being less fit than when young, but I always felt that fitness was there within reach. All I would have to do is cut down on the drink, exercise regularly, and I would be able to walk, swim, fuck and fight with the best of 'em. Not now. I am incapable of strenuous exercise—my knee would collapse under me. I am beginning to walk like an old man.[49]

The gardening and the walking were his response—it was as if, reinvigorated and freed from spats, squabbles, and tension, he was starting a new life for himself. Working on *A Proper Gentleman* had not restarted the flow of poetry, as he had hoped: but work was the only cure he knew.

He launched himself into a new round of readings—among other places, at Kidderminster, Taunton, and Exeter, where he had lunch with his friend, Ted Hughes—'in benign mood, it seemed'. An incident at the Taunton reading, however, must have been less welcome to anyone starting to feel uneasy about his age. He was approached during the interval by an elderly man with a beard, who introduced himself as one of his former pupils from Clark's College in Ealing. 'Jesus! I don't fancy the Mr Chips role', Vernon noted ruefully.[50]

He also signed a contract to write another children's book, *A Lonely Game*, telling the story of a teenager who was interested in both boxing and poetry, and who sounded a lot like a young Vernon Scannell. The initial advance of £200[51] on signature of the contract and £200 on publication was, as he put it in his diary 'not much, but better than nowt',[52] and there was hope for more money from royalties—his last effort for children, *The Dangerous Ones*, had been reprinted twice and had made him more money than anything else he had written. And by keeping him writing, the new book might just start him producing poetry again.

He felt relaxed at home—one morning, he picked up Jacob's watercolour paints and a brush and painted his first ever landscape–'Quite pleasing', he noted. 'The luck of the entirely ignorant.'[53]

VIII

But he had no plans to stay at Nether Compton. Reading at Kidderminster College, he had met a teacher, Martin Reed, who would become a lifelong friend and, eventually, Scannell's literary executor. Reed recalls:

> He and I got on well together. A few weeks after the reading, I sent him a poem I'd written, to see if he could help. I got back a very friendly letter with a lot of helpful information in it, and we started a correspondence. It was clear he was in a parlous state, with nowhere to live. He was begging for a floor to sleep on.[54]

Reed, who had a wife called Ruth, two children, and a small house, found him a place in a friend's home nearby, but Vernon was suffering from the old restlessness again: when he had a settled place to live, he found it constricting and stultifying, and when he didn't, he found it inconvenient. After a week in the house in Kidderminster, he seemed content, but still not entirely comfortable.

> The days go well—plenty of work, good work too. The novel is beginning to come to life, asserting its independence and going in directions I hadn't entirely foreseen. The evenings have been—not difficult to cope with but not easy either. After the day of work and light, the dark comes down and with it a sense of being isolated, very much alone.[55]

Martin called round in the morning with fresh eggs from his chickens, and Vernon magically produced 10p pieces out of Ruth's ears and passed them through the wooden table, to the amazement of her daughter Annie.[56] But for all the hospitality he was enjoying, it all felt somehow temporary. He continued with his readings—at one, he teased Reed, a kindly and gentle man, when a member of the audience asked if he himself had actually killed the cat in 'A Case of Murder'. 'No', he said in a stage whisper, and after a suitably dramatic pause he swung round, like a character in a courtroom drama, jabbing his accusing finger directly at Martin, who was sitting nearby. 'He did!'[57]

Once he left Kidderminster, he was moving around again from friend to friend, sofa to sofa, carrying his possessions and as many books as he could manage in his rucksack. In September, at a poetry course at Dyffryn House in Cardiff, 'mainly for middle-aged ladies of doubtful talent and embittered natures',[58] he met a young reporter—'J' in his diaries—with whom he enjoyed a fling of several months. The affair, while it lasted, was as passionate as Scannell's *amours* always were—but it was, perhaps, no coincidence that she, like many others, had a bed and a roof to offer.

There was also his brother Kenneth, now living in Ambleside in the Lake District with his wife Jenny and their three children. Scannell made several trips to stay with them—during one of which, Kenneth mentioned a scruffy old man, looking like a tramp but with a very cultured accent, to whom he had often given a lift on the road to Windermere. Jenny suggested that he might be the man who washed dishes in a nearby hotel, who was often teased about his accent. She thought he was called Short.

Vernon pricked up his ears at that—Short was the name of the mysterious Westmoreland poet whose work he had first come across as a young soldier—the same John Short whose book, *The Oak and the Ash*, had been a gift from Wilfred Childe at Leeds all those years ago. He had searched unsuccessfully for any more information about him and so, the next day, while Kenneth was at work, he and Jenny went and knocked on the door of the tumbledown hut just outside the town where the old man lived:

> I could just see the pale blur of the old face, the watchful, timid eyes peering from the shadows. For what seemed a long time he didn't speak and I was beginning to think our visit was futile when he muttered something I couldn't catch and then opened the door just wide enough for him to slip through and close it behind him. Clearly he didn't want me to see inside his hovel.[59]

He was indeed John Short the poet; thirty years after reading that first poem, Vernon had at last caught up with the author of *The Oak and the Ash*. For several years, he had thought that Short might be dead; he had written to his publishers, but they knew nothing. And now here he was. Vernon wanted to ask him about his life, about his ideas of poetry, and about his work, about why he had published nothing since the 1940s—but now, after the astonishing coincidence that had brought them together, he was finally disappointed.

All Short wanted to talk about, in a mumbling and barely comprehensible voice, was a legal affair in which he believed he had been cheated of an inheritance of land and property. He brushed aside anything to do with his poetry: he was, Vernon concluded, 'helplessly in the grip of his obsession'. Later, in the early 1990s, he heard that Short's death had been announced in a brief notice in the *Westmoreland Gazette*. He continued to read and enjoy the poems for the rest of his life, and to quote from them frequently:

> The riddle of how this trampish little hermit who showed no interest in anything outside his private obsession could be the author of those fine poems remained a mystery... Then I thought that perhaps I should never have embarked on the search, for in a sense I had already found him. The poet, the distillation of what was most valuable in the man, was there on my bookshelf and had been there all the time.[60]

IX

Apart from searching for lost poets, Scannell also had to make a living. He was invited to spend a few days each term as 'visiting poet' at Shrewsbury School, an independent school for thirteen- to eighteen-year-old boys. It was only a few extra pounds to add to his sporadic income from writing and reviewing, and it was hard work—half a dozen sessions of intensive teaching in a day—but it was much more successful than his stay at Berinsfield had been. And, like 'J', it provided him with a bed and somewhere to put his books:

> It's a strange life at Shrewsbury—not a bit like my old public school, Greyfriars. Jesus, these kids are lucky. Their parents are lucky. Someone's paying for it all. I'm not too unlucky either.[61]

Of course, this appointment worked better than Berinsfield partly because he was working there for a much shorter period—a week at a time, rather than nine months. But it was also true that the boys he was dealing with—'very pleasant and in the main intelligent'[62]—were more disciplined, more used to academic work, and more receptive to Scannell's ideas. On the other hand, the role of pedagogue in an English public school jarred slightly with his views on privilege and private education, and there were adjustments to be made on both sides, as David Smith, then an English teacher at the school, recalls:

> At first, he seemed a little inclined to regard us as overprivileged foplings, and he clearly harboured some doubts whether a 'man of the people' like himself should really be swanning around the public school officer-class world... One of the boarding houses is called Churchill's, and he truculently inquired whether it had been named after 'that wicked man'. I reassured him that the building owed its name to the Victorian clergyman who founded it, having nothing to do with 'Winnie'. He then favoured us with a part-militant, part-sentimental and entirely bewitching tirade about the missed opportunity, the golden-age-that-never-quite-was, represented by the Labour government of 1945–50.[63]

It could be an imposing place—the headmaster, Eric Anderson, had previously taught Prince Charles at Gordonstoun, and would later go on to become headmaster at Eton—but Scannell was determined not to be overawed. It was not unusual for him to appear in the staff room looking very red-eyed and hung over, but Simon Funnel, another young teacher at the time, says that on one embarrassing occasion it was noticed that he also had his trousers undone:

> The headmaster's wife, Poppy Anderson, wanted to talk to him, so my colleagues appointed me to be the one to tell him that he needed to do up his flies. This he did, while also beginning his conversation with Poppy.[64]

His stay at the school seemed to be a disaster waiting to happen—there were frequent late-night drinking sessions with the younger teachers, and rumours that Vernon had romanced several of the female members of the catering staff—but it never did. His enthusiasm for poetry and his gift for passing his passion on to the boys that he taught meant that he was invited back several times over the next few years for visits which another former teacher, Richard Field, describes as 'exhilarating and shattering in almost equal measure'.[65]

There were, too, other oases of relative calm during this period of home-lessness—a week at Ripon College of Education, another at Leysland School in Leicestershire, and two weeks teaching creative writing at the Arvon centres in Totleigh Barton in Devon and at Lumb Bank in Yorkshire. For the time being, residential courses offered him the possibility of earning some money and also somewhere to sleep, and he fired off dozens of applications to schools, colleges, regional arts associations, and any other organization he could think of that might offer him a job. Briefly, too, the affair with Olwen sputtered back into life, giving him a bed at Rhydyfelin again. And when that failed, there was always Folly Cottage.

It was, he complained with considerable understatement, 'very difficult to work, because all my books and papers are in chaos and I haven't got a place to write in'[66]—and yet, astonishingly, he began to do just that. Slowly, tenta-tively, he began to write poetry again. In April 1979, for instance, he began work on a poem about a child left alone in a house and searching through his parents' bedroom. He began uncertainly—'a first draft, probably a last one too... I don't quite know what I'm after—something to do with innocence, ignorance'[67]—and picked at it until, ten days later, it was finished. The poem, 'Learning', appeared in his next collection, *Winterlude*, which was published in 1982, but Scannell was in no doubt about its real importance:

> At present I am cautiously pleased with it. It is the first since December—four months—so I hope I shall use it as a lever to release a few more before the big rock rolls back and dams the flow.[68]

There were setbacks and disappointments—rejection notes from two maga-zines sent him briefly into a spiral of despair in which he feared that his life had been wasted, and that he would never produce anything of value.

> The only consolation—if it is consolation—is that there has been nothing I could have turned to and done better. I might not be any great shakes as a writer, but I am horrifically worse at anything else I might have, or actually have, attempted.[69]

But the point was that he *had* started writing again. There was talk about a possible Arts Council grant that would enable the publication of his first *Collected Poems.* The rock had not rolled down again and dammed the flow. And, with an invitation to spend a term as Poet in Residence at The King's School, Canterbury he was about to reach another significant watershed in his life.

13

Young Love

An ugly old man is in love with a woman
who is young enough to be his daughter.
She is beautiful, dark and sensuous.
Can it be possible that she returns
Something of his passionate devotion and desire?

'The Story So Far...', from *A Place to Live* (2007)

I

Scannell had applied for the post at The King's School while he was staying at Folly Cottage in the spring of 1979, with an uncharacteristically formal letter in which he promised to 'encourage students to practise and experiment in various more or less exacting forms', with workshop sessions, critical readings, and one-to-one consultations.

He was lucky to get the job, and he knew it: rumours about his drinking and occasionally erratic behaviour had circulated among many of the organizations that might have employed him, and *A Proper Gentleman*, with its candid description of how things had gone wrong in Berinsfield, had certainly put off some potential employers. Turning down his application for a writing fellowship in Gravesend, the Deputy Literature Director of the Arts Council had told him that 'the shadow of Berinsfield' had done neither him nor the town any good. Staff at The King's School—an upper-crust public school, where the pupils wore black gowns and white wing collars—had let it be known that they were looking for someone 'fairly conventional' and 'not too bizarre', but they had taken a chance on him. He could afford to feel a degree of relief and satisfaction, as he looked about him one Sunday afternoon in the early autumn:

Today I sat in the Cathedral precincts and read Carrington's Life of Kipling and looked every now and then at the flawless blue sky, the grey stone of the buildings, the trim lawns, and the people wandering about. Pleasant.[1]

A few weeks later—presumably swallowing the reservations about privilege and private education that he had expressed so strongly at Shrewsbury—he accepted an invitation to dine with the headmaster at High Table. And, crucially, he now had a guaranteed roof over his head for the next four months, even though it was only a single room in the school's St Augustine's College.

Within a couple of days, he had started on a new poem, with the working title 'In a Town Churchyard'.[2] It was, he noted in his diary, another 'breaking of the dam', and, although it probably also incorporates scenes remembered from Leeds and elsewhere or drawn from his imagination, was clearly sparked by the sombre stonework, the gravestones, and the monuments of his new home and the Cathedral precincts. The poem imagines eternal trumpets proclaiming the resurrection of the dead—in this case, typically for Scannell, the bag lady 'in canvas shoes, Attached to unimaginable legs', the drunk old man asleep 'in methylated peace', and the small mongrel lifting its leg against a gravestone. The promise of eternity, in this poem, is not for harp-playing angels but for:

> Rejuvenated lady, dancing dog,
> The sleeping drinker's dream corporified.[3]

As so often, the last line holds the ironic key to the poem, the Latinate, formal, slightly pompous final 'corporified' echoing some abstruse theological technicality. It is as if Scannell, uneasy at his enjoyment of the grandeur of his surroundings, is returning in verse to his natural world of the defeated and the down-at-heel.

Around the same time, he made a trip to pay his respects to an old friend in the Kent village of Yalding, about 30 miles away. That was where Edmund Blunden, the old man he had admired so much on their Midlands reading tour, had lived as a child. He had died some five years before, and now Scannell was coming to read some of Blunden's poems at the consecration of a memorial window in the village church. The occasion brought flooding back not just his affection for the poet and respect for his poetry, but all his old feelings of nostalgia for a rustic past that lay just beyond his own experience:

> As I was driving there, through the hop fields on a beautiful sunny morning,
> I thought of Edmund enjoying the place and weather, and I was pierced by

the sense of death's inevitability...As I drove back, I passed a horse and cart in one of the country lanes, and for a moment I could have been translated back to when E was a boy.[4]

In between those two journeys, there had been an unexpected and surprisingly low-key meeting. Scannell arrived in the village slightly early for the church service, and went for a pint in The Bull, just opposite the church and close to Blunden Street, named after the poet. He had just ordered his drink when a tall, bespectacled and quietly spoken figure walked in, glanced around and joined him at the bar. Both of them were clearly going to the same service, and they introduced themselves as the newcomer bought his drink. It was John Carey, Merton Professor of English Literature at Oxford University—and author of the lacerating *New Statesman* review which had torn *Not Without Glory* to shreds. 'We talked about Blunden for a while, and as I remember, he did most of the talking', says Carey now. The review was not mentioned, leaving a minor but fascinating mystery hanging in the air. It is inconceivable that Scannell did not connect the name of the genial poetry-lover at the bar with the review that had cut him to the quick—after all, it was barely two years since he had devoted more than a page of *A Proper Gentleman* to his counter-attack. For Carey, always a much more enthusiastic admirer of Scannell's poetry than of his criticism, there was no quarrel to be settled—but did Scannell decide that Blunden's memorial was not the place for an argument? Was he unwilling to confront an adversary as articulate and erudite as Carey? Could he just not be bothered? None of the possible explanations sounds like Scannell. Perhaps it would be sentimental to suppose that a conversation in an English village pub on a warm autumn day just before a memorial service for a poet whom both men respected led to an unspoken declaration of peace by Scannell. But it is as good an explanation of his silence as anything else.

There was no quick and easy end to his fallow period, no sudden release of the dam, no rush of new poetry: instead, there were occasional boosts to his confidence over the next two or three years, individual poems started tentatively and finished triumphantly. In early August 1979, for instance, his friend Martin Bax, the editor of the London-based quarterly *Ambit*, accepted four poems that had previously been turned down by other magazines as not reaching the standard they had hoped for. 'Vintage Scannell', was Bax's response, much to Vernon's relief.[5]

II

In the evenings at The King's School, Scannell would take a book to the
Three Compasses pub nearby, where he would sit reading with a pint of
beer and listening to the Strauss and Chopin that was played there. The
barmaid at the time, a slim, dark, and strikingly pretty twenty-year-old girl
called Angela Beese, still remembers him as a regular visitor:

> He would sit in the same seat by the door, with his feet stretched out and
> crossed over in front of him. He'd have his pint of beer there, his roll-ups on the
> table and he would always be reading. He never spoke to anyone. I was clearing
> the glasses and coming back to the bar and he was at the bar holding the book
> and I asked what he was reading. If you showed the tiniest spark of interest in
> literature or reading, he would never brush you off, and he said, 'I'm reading this
> little book of prose by Ben Jonson. It's seventeenth century.' He opened it and
> said, 'Isn't this absolutely lovely—"A little winter love in a dark corner" '?[6]

Angela quizzed him about his role at the school, and as a poet:

> Vernon was totally self-contained and very easy in himself, which I found
> very attractive. We got chatting, but he was very diffident, and never expected
> anyone to recognize his name. When he told me, I said, 'Oh, I think we read
> some of your poems at school.' I told him which ones, and he said, 'Yeah,
> they're mine.' Just that. So I knew he was a poet from the first time I met
> him.

He spent so many evenings reading in the pub, he told her, because he
missed having music to listen to in his flat. The background classical music
in the Three Compasses was the best he could do. A few days later, having
passed the weekend in London with a woman whom he described in his
diary as 'quite sweet but also fairly mad and also emphatically untrustworthy'—
her name, for obvious reasons, is carefully scratched out—he returned home
to find Angela in his room, installing her record player for him with a selec-
tion of her records.

> He never locked anything and his room was always open, so I did it as a sur-
> prise for him. We talked and talked that evening, and somehow just became
> an item. I moved into his flat—everyone at the school was scandalized, but
> I suppose they just thought, 'Well, he's a poet, and that's what they do.'

Vernon, now fifty-seven, was uneasily aware of the huge disparity in their
ages: when he had been involved with a much younger girl before—'J' in

Wales—he had scribbled bitterly in his diary about her 'lecherous geron-tophilia',[7] and a few months later, propositioned by a precocious sixteen-year-old at a creative writing course, he noted dismissively 'Gerontion rules, Kayo. Silly little cow.'[8] He was not a man who tried to seek out young girls. But apart from her physical attractiveness, Angela was also keen to learn about poetry and anxious to start to write her own poems: at last, it seemed, he might have found someone who could be a pupil as well as a lover, a fresh young intellect to absorb his ideas about art and literature. He could, he told himself, help Angela to grow and develop as a person, even as an artist. She could be his blank slate; he could indulge his 'didactitis' as well as his vanity. She adored him, which helped—and yet . . .

> It is a weird affair. I don't understand it at all. It could end in tears, beers, fears—not, I suspect, in cheers. Disorientating but heady.[9]

For the time being, though, Angela taught him to play the recorder, and he talked to her about the poems that she had written; he took her to spend a weekend with his brother, Kenneth and his wife Jenny; and there was the obligatory Soho pub crawl, starting in The George and including 'last drinks' at the famous 'French pub', where they bumped into Jeffrey Bernard and his two brothers Bruce and Oliver.

Vernon had history with the Bernards—Jeffrey, another former boxer who had metamorphosed into a writer, had once unwisely challenged him to a fight in Tony's Café in Fitzrovia, and lost. A few days later, Bruce had met Vernon in The Wheatsheaf, and tried to take revenge for his brother's dis-comfiture: this time, the fight was in the street outside, but the result was the same—a Bernard sprawled on the floor, nursing bruises to his jaw, his pride, and his reputation. Those days were gone now, though, and 'last drinks' in 'the French' probably went on for a long time. Everyone was older and wiser.

But not much wiser: the next morning, Vernon took Angela to another bar where, according to his diary, he suffered 'a matutinal bombing from the demented Cecily, who lashed out with wild accusations, invective, and wilder haymakers'.[10] Who Cecily was, and what her grievance might have been, are all forgotten—but Angela won his admiration by going back to brave her, after more drinks in the Queen's Elm and The Antelope, when Vernon discovered he had left his car keys behind. Luckily, they avoided the police and the breathalyzer on the way back to Canterbury, where there were a few more drinks in The Chaucer and then wine, cheese, and pickles for supper. 'Very tired', his diary notes, unsurprisingly.

Angela was someone who could keep up with him, or at least make a pretty good fist of trying. A few days later, she joined him while he was getting drunk with a friend called 'Welsh Bob', put on boxing gloves, and laid into Bob enthusiastically, sustaining a black eye for her pains. A few weeks earlier, Vernon had been writing uneasily in his diary about his premonitions of catastrophe:

> I listen to Mozart's Clarinet Quintet, think incessantly of A, and cast shifty glances into the dark corners where I suspect that disaster lurks. Why should not old men be mad? And in love. With a child. Oh Scannell, how did this come about, you silly old bastard?[11]

With drink flowing and fists flying, even with boxing gloves on, it is not hard to see with hindsight where disaster might have been hiding.

But by the end of November—barely two months after they had met—Angela had told her parents that she was leaving Canterbury and going to find somewhere to live with Vernon, and the four of them met for what must have been a fairly tense Sunday lunch at the Beeses' home near the village of Ringwould, some 20 miles from Canterbury. He was a penniless poet in his late fifties who was married, with five children and no income, few apparent prospects, and no home once he left Canterbury in a month's time. A prosperous professional couple cannot have seen him as the most welcome prospect as life's partner for their headstrong twenty-year-old daughter—even without the consideration that she had begun to smoke roll-ups and drink pints of beer since she met him, and seemed to have taken up boxing. But Vernon had put on a jacket and tie, and taken with him a letter he had written 'to reassure them', and the meal went, in his words, 'marvellously and relieffully well'.[12] Angela's father even brought them a box of fresh vegetables from his garden as they left.[13]

There were a couple of sombre telephone calls from Olwen to be negotiated—true to form, Vernon seems not to have managed to end that relationship, or at least not to have made sure that Olwen realized that it was over. 'O phoned today. Sad',[14] was one terse comment in his diary. There was also the first encounter for many years with his father—Vernon's sister, Sylvia, had come back from Australia, where she had moved, and the two of them went to visit the Old Man in Chelmsford just before Christmas. He was, Vernon noted, 'indeed an Old Man. A kind of warning. How can I accept the possibility—the probability—of that?'[15] And then, after a 'fairly grim' Christmas at Nether Compton—Angela going back to

her parents for a few days—the two lovers, young and not-so-young, set
off from Canterbury to start their life together.

III

Vernon had solved the problem of finding a home by answering an advertisement placed in the *Times Literary Supplement* by the poet Selima Hill,
who owned a 'pretty basic'[16] cottage in the Gloucestershire village of
Filkins:

> There was too much to fit inside his car, and so we were rushing round trying
> to find a roof-rack on December 31, which was the last day of his contract.
> When we found one, we couldn't put it together—he was totally cack-
> handed, as he'd say himself—so we got a garage to do it for us and set off next
> day. Half way down the motorway, one of the bags we'd put on top flew off
> and bounced down the motorway. I said 'That's my bag!' and he said, 'There's
> nothing we can do about it now.' That's how we started.[17]

Their arrival at their new home—One Tree Cottage, on the road that ran
through the village—hardly improved matters. It was a picturesque little
cottage with one downstairs room, a single bedroom and an attic—but
since it was let unfurnished, there was only a settee, a mattress, and an unlit
Aga to welcome them.

They shivered through the night on the mattress, under a pile of their
coats and clothes, and then, next day, they bought bedding in Swindon, an
oil stove from 'an Irish horse-thief' in Oxford, and an electric heater from
'a slightly less disreputable junk shop'[18] and struggled to make the place
more comfortable. Vernon was determinedly optimistic despite everything:

> Yesterday we rose late. The car wouldn't start and the village shop was closed.
> All we ate was a cheese sandwich. Evening in the pub. All goes well. Much
> love for A. I hope to be able to work here.[19]

His plan was to renew his contacts with the BBC producers to get some
talks commissioned, and also send round flyers to schools and colleges offering to read for them for a fee—but they needed money immediately to pay
the rent and buy oil for the Aga, and he made a decision then that he regretted for years to come. Long ago, Vernon had refused even his brother
Kenneth when he suggested that he should sell his books to fund their trip
to France. Now he set off to Swindon with Angela, to find a 'bluff, bearded

Figure 18. One Tree Cottage, Filkins, where Vernon and Angela found 'a settee, a mattress and an unlit Aga' to welcome them. (Photo: Angela Beese)

honest con-man' in a second-hand bookshop, and sold some of the precious books that had accompanied him on his wanderings from house to house over more than thirty years. Angela remembers the loss of his treasures:

> It was a horrible occasion. He wouldn't think about going into debt, and he just went around the cottage and picked up the books he thought he could sell. Precious, precious books—there was one set I remember that was a collection of poems in celebration of Shakespeare's birthday, signed by all the poets—Vernon, W. H. Auden, George MacBeth, Dannie Abse, and a lot more. He put that one in too...He took them into Swindon and some shifty little bookseller looked through the box and said 'This is what I'll give you', and that was that. Vernon was never any good at haggling.[20]

Vernon himself was philosophical:

> I was depressed at my treachery, leaving those lovely books in the hands of a
> print-monger. Never mind, I got eighty quid.[21]

It just about covered the outstanding rent. In addition, there was the offer
of a £400 advance[22] for the *Collected Poems* that Jeremy Robson was planning to publish with Arts Council backing, a £40[23] cheque from the BBC,
the invitation to record one of his poems[24] for the radio, and the prospect of
readings at Totleigh Barton and Kidderminster. In February, a dealer in
London offered him £400 for his manuscripts and letters—but, most
importantly, he was continuing to write new poems. 'Some Pictures of the
Thirties' looked back at scenes of his childhood, while 'War Movie Veteran'[25]
took an ironic view of the brash, gung-ho militarism that had characterized
the Vietnam War—both poems giving him a chance to revisit his own past
and put some of the formative experiences of his life in a modern context.

With Angela, he was settling down in the evenings to a survey of English
poetry—'an introduction for A and a reappraisal for me'.[26] It seemed to be,
in many ways, the life he had dreamed of—an all-embracing, sensual affair
with a beautiful woman to whom he could be not only a lover ('A good day,
better night', he noted in his diary lasciviously[27]) but also mentor and
teacher. One night they would sit and read together, another he would listen to Beethoven while Angela sewed, and the next they would go out to
The Lamb, just a few yards from their door, for a drink. 'Jubliate agno
[Rejoice in the Lamb]', Vernon would joke as they entered the bar, and the
landlord, either bored or uncomprehending, would look up stoically and
say, 'Yes, very nice', which amused Vernon even more.[28]

But still, typically, he had a nagging, indefinable sense of foreboding:

> Life is almost terrifyingly good at present. What snipers are beading in on us,
> I wonder?[29]

IV

He knew—he must have known—what the snipers were, what was the
nature of the disaster lurking in dark corners. There are a few brief mentions
in his diary of 'bum-bashing' and rows at home, and of one 'disastrous' night
in London in particular during which 'A sustained multiple abrasions and a

black nose.'[30] Angela, in her diaries, remembers one 'draining and frightening argument', after which she wrote:

> Woke up feeling exhausted, sick and still very scared, apologies half-spoken and life apparently all right. But last night is hard to forget and fear still sits in my stomach ready to kick and wound me ...[31]

It was a confused and volatile relationship: the same day that Angela wrote about her fear, Vernon was noting enthusiastically: 'To have known A for three months is luck enough for anyone. I love her.'[32] They bought a puppy, a seven-week-old black Labrador/spaniel cross which they called Robinson, after the boxer Sugar Ray Robinson; Angela began to introduce herself as Mrs Scannell; she was thrilled when Vernon read her a short story that he was writing and they discussed how it should end; they decided they would like to have a child together. They were lost in each other, living together with the passion of young lovers and the plans of a married couple.

But overshadowing everything was Vernon's uncontrollable jealousy. One Friday night, shortly before setting off for a week's tutoring at the Arvon Centre at Lumb Bank—which Angela referred to bitterly as 'a knocking shop for over-sexed poets'[33]—he found a letter she had written to a boy some years before but never posted:

> He must have gone looking in my bag. I'd sent this boy my love, or said 'I love you' or something like that, and Vernon shouted that I'd said I never said that to anyone but him. That was what started it.[34]

Vernon's account, written more than a week after the event, was still outraged and frenzied:

> Black Friday. Found ancient declaration of love from A to another—unspeakable A. She had told me on at least three occasions that this was something she had never said to anyone else. I was idiotically, disproportionately (I suppose) lacerated, pierced, mauled and sickened by such pain as I have never known. Then insanity. Awfulness.[35]

There is a hideous inevitability about the diary entries as Angela takes up the story. He stormed out to the pub, leaving Angela to go to bed alone:

> I could feel the menace building, building ... I tried to hide in the attic, and then later I heard him come in. I heard him come up the stairs, first to the bedroom, and then right to the top, where I was. I was frightened, but I said, 'Oh hello, how are you?' and then he just punched me in the face. I was sitting

up. He punched me as hard as he could. It was hard, his fist—he knew how to punch. Then I escaped and ran down the stairs and outside.[36]

Angela, blood all over her face, ran to a nearby telephone box from which, crouching down in the shadows in case he came looking for her, she called the police. She was taken to the police station, where she lay on a seat outside the toilets until one of the policemen drove her back home at 5 a.m.:

> He asked if I wanted him to talk to Vernon, but I was so terrified that I just said no. He was asleep upstairs and I crept around hoping he wouldn't wake up. Then he just came down with a monstrous hangover, and nothing more was said.
>
> I had a broken nose and two black eyes, but he didn't even notice he'd hit me...I don't think he knew how it happened, but he knew he had done something so shameful that he couldn't admit it. That's what he did all his life.[37]

The lack of any official response by the police to a serious assault on a defenceless woman is shocking—but that was the way that so-called 'domestics' were frequently treated in the 1980s. It was not only that Angela needed protection, but also that Scannell needed treatment and help. 'This hurts me more than it hurts you', that favourite phrase of brutal Victorian headmasters, would be obscene if applied to an attack like this—there is no equivalence in suffering between the fist and the face—but it would also be simplistic and unthinking to say that Scannell knew what he was doing and should have been punished. There is every sign that he was still suffering from the effects of his childhood and wartime experiences. Angela says that about a month earlier, he had woken at about 3.30 a.m. and tried to suffocate her, terrifying her and severely bruising her nose in the process. She noted in her diary that, the next morning, he 'couldn't remember anything about it...so I had to tell him. He was remorseful and puzzled.'[38]

Like many sufferers from post-traumatic stress disorder, he knew something was wrong, but didn't want to admit what it was—and wouldn't have known where to turn for help if he had. The disaster that had been lurking could be pushed back into the shadows, the snipers' bullets ignored. Within a month, he was writing in his diary:

> Most beautiful day, the sun drenching the village, the grass, the flowers, me. I sit in the garden on the old bench; A reclines nearby on a rug and reads the life of Edward Thomas. I love her. But...
>
> I love her, but I don't think my love is of much value to anybody. I want her as I have never remotely wanted anyone before.

It was as if the uncontrollable flashes of jealousy and the late-night drunken violence had never happened. But later that same day, after he has come back from the pub, riffled through the pages of her schoolgirl Dutch grammar and found another boy's name written there in her childish, rounded seventeen-year-old's hand, his mood changes again:

> All the pain returned. No, not returned. It has always been there, under a bandage of self-deceit and an infantile refusal to face truth. The bandage fell away and there it was, raw and festering. I know in a way I am being idiotically unreasonable. Of course she has had love affairs, of course she has used the words of love to others. Only a complete fool would believe otherwise. Yes, I did believe her when she said on three separate occasions, 'I love you; I have never said that to anyone else.' Now I know those quite gratuitous statements to be lies, I cannot believe anything she says.[39]

The anger and the lack of balance are staggering—but so are the pain and the tentative feeling towards an understanding of his own lack of reason. A short poem he wrote around this time, 'Weaker Sex', puts his feelings into a chilling focus:

> However courteous and tender, man
> Is in the act of love his love's aggressor;
> No matter with what softness he began
> He'll finish as her merciless oppressor...

The lines may be intended ironically, but there is a worrying violence behind them, and a self-justifying claim of powerlessness: whatever the man does, the poem suggests, is not his fault, since he is caught in an inescapable chain of inevitability. He goes on to say that, fortunately, the woman is 'often'—another worrying word—a willing partner, and may even have a stronger sexual appetite than the man. But, he concludes:

> The simple fact remains: she cannot rape him.
> You think he should rejoice that this is true?
> Maybe, but there are worse things she can do.[40]

The poem as a whole may be designed to shock—but the last line is particularly self-pitying and mean-spirited. It is clearly grotesque to compare the woman's experience of rape with any mental torment that she may inflict on the man. But at the same time, the outrageousness of that comparison reflects the way that Scannell saw his own pain. He knew intellectually, as he said in his diary, that his reactions were disproportionate and unreasonable, but that in no way lessened the agony they caused him. There are no excuses for his behaviour, but there are reasons for it, far back in his history; if he was the 'merciless oppressor', he was a battered, suffering oppressor, one of the walking wounded.

V

The night after the violence, Vernon went to the pub alone again as if nothing had happened, and Angela lay in bed, waiting fearfully for him to come home, and writing in her diary:

> He's going to get drunk tonight and he'll hit me again. I can't go on any more, my love is not enough for him. When he is drunk he becomes a monster, insane and irrational . . . I think he might kill me, he is so angry.[41]

In the morning, though, she wrote again:

> Silly girl, that was rather hysterical, wasn't it? V came back sober (almost) and accepted me back. Life continues almost as it was before the bump . . . Reconciliation is complete and I can see love once more in his eyes.[42]

Life really did go on as usual, with Angela accompanying Vernon to readings, on visits to Martin and Ruth Reed and other friends, and to literary parties like the launch of the *Oxford Book of Contemporary Verse 1945–1980*. There, she met the book's editor, D. J. Enright, and other literary figures such as Dannie Abse, Peter Porter, Gavin Ewart, D. J. Enright, and Patricia Beer—while Vernon, predictably, drank too much champagne, resulting in 'a hair-raising journey back to Filkins'.[43] Once again, he managed to avoid the traffic police.

In May, he gave her a pair of sandals and a new Parker pen to celebrate her twenty-first birthday—'She was delightfully and piercingly, almost unendurably beautiful. I love her, but I don't think my love is of much value to anybody', he wrote in his diary.[44] And then, later the same month, they celebrated the arrival in the post of the first copy of Vernon's *New and Collected Poems 1950–1980* with their next-door neighbour and 'quite the largest whisky I've ever been given', followed by so much beer in the pub that Angela's carefully prepared lamb and paprika dinner was left congealing by the sink.

His Introductory Note to the new volume—his first Collected Poems—
shows how important it was to him. The author of such a book, he declared,
'is saying, "This is the best of what I have thought and felt and written from
the time when I first began to write verses until the present"...the author
of a Collected Poems is truly on trial for his life'. The reviewers, he suggested—possibly still thinking of John Carey's savaging of *Not Without
Glory*—'may be licking their lips, sharpening their knives and rehearsing
their deflationary epigrams'.[45]

In fact the reviews, if not ecstatic, were at least quietly appreciative. In
The Observer, Peter Porter hailed Scannell as 'one of the most popular and
widely anthologised poets in Britain',[46] while the *Times Literary Supplement*
said that 'to those who prefer significant communication to self-expression'
the collection demonstrated 'much that is right with the plain presentation
of mood and reflection, linked to incident and episode'.[47]

The four new poems in the collection ('Two Variations on an Old
Theme', 'Old Man in Winter', 'Reformed Drunkard' and 'A Partial View')
presented a bleak and chilly view of the world: at fifty-eight, Scannnell was
uncomfortably aware of approaching age, with death waiting implacably
just over the horizon. In 'Two Variations', for instance—the second part of
which, incidentally, is written in the triadic rhyme that he first used in 'The
Loving Game'—he declares that other people seem to be able to treat the
prospect of extinction with stoicism, even enthusiasm:

> The gaunt religious welcomes it with joy,
> Flings wizened arms ecstatically wide
> And swallow-dives into the awful void...[48]

He, on the other hand, lacks 'the tricks...that could make it seem less terrible'. The pensive melancholy of 'A Partial View' seems to be even more
revealing of his state of mind. The poem starts by presenting an Auden-like
world of bloodthirsty wickedness, in which secret policemen, thugs, and
terrorists delight in causing pain to their victims. Most people are not like
that, he concedes—but humanity and kindness may be fragile qualities, and,
anyway, the decent majority ignore the cruelty and brutality that they know
go on in secret. And then, with a sudden exclamation, comes a break in the
argument:

> God help us, who are we to act the judge
> When fantasies of vengeance warm the blood
> And we are gripped by passions we condemn?[49]

There has been nothing in the poem before to suggest that 'the decent, who deplore such cruelty' actually harbour their own bloodthirsty fantasies—but the lines provide a telling glimpse of the poet's thinking. The message is that we are all guilty, which is both a confession and a denial of personal responsibility. The condemnation of the violent passions that he admits do grip him is a frequent subject of Scannell's diaries, and its appearance in this poem suggests how much the thought troubled him.

The poem goes on to ask how anyone can respond to the violence of the world and our complicity in it. There is almost a despairing shrug of the shoulders in the line 'We live in violent times and always did', and suicide, drink, and religion are rejected in turn as possible refuges. Even music, poetry, and love offer only partial and temporary relief:

> ...When the music fades and meanings blur,
> The hordes remass, you turn again to her
> To whom you might conceivably be true
> As she, against the odds, might be to you.[50]

The end of the poem is a conscious and ironic echo of Matthew Arnold's 'Dover Beach', and Scannell used to enjoy telling people about a letter he received criticizing the specific phrase 'the ocean's long withdrawing roar'—a direct quote from Arnold—as 'weak and imprecise'.[51] But, like 'A Case of Murder', 'A Partial View' is a much more personal poem than it appears to be on first reading. It speaks with the lonely, almost unspeakably sad voice of a man who knows that he deserves condemnation, who has little belief in his own character, and who expects to suffer betrayal and defeat.

But by the time the *Collected Poems* was published, Vernon and Angela had set off on another new beginning together. They had a lot to put behind them, and anyway, One Tree Cottage was a cold and lonely place to live. A couple of months earlier, Vernon had seen a flat advertised in Leeds, close to his old home in Francis Street just after the war, and they had decided to move there:

> Leeds—a different place in some respects, a different me too, I suppose. It is a strange life and it will be a good one if I can extirpate the suppurating mental sores that are no less agonizing for being self-inflicted.
>
> I love her. Of course I love her, and I know that I am miraculously lucky to have her love. Then all should be simple, shouldn't it? Yessir, I shall make it so.[52]

Perhaps it would be an exaggeration to say that Vernon was full of hope and optimism—but he seemed determined to make the relationship work.

VI

The return to Leeds had not been planned—it was only by chance that he had seen the newspaper advertisement—but, even though the city had changed, Scannell found he had a real affection for it:

> Coming back is coming home.
> I have mislaid myself for all these years.
> I know this is, for me, a place to live.[53]

The flat in Spencer Place, rented out by the Leeds and Yorkshire Housing Association, was far from luxurious, but there were shelves for his books and prints of Boswell and Johnson on the wall, and it had the tall windows and imposing doorways of a converted Victorian mansion to give it a feeling of light and spaciousness.

Chapeltown itself was even less salubrious than it had been when Vernon had lived there more than thirty years before, but behind the house was a

Figure 19. Living 'like an affectionate young married couple' at Spencer Place in Leeds. (Photo: Not known. Angela Beese collection)

large lawn bordered by trees and flowers where they could sit in the summer sun and dream about how magnificent it must all have been a century
earlier. As summer gave way to autumn, it became clear that the high ceil-
ings and ill-fitting doors of the flat also gave it a chill against which single
bar electric fires were all but useless, but even so, both Vernon and Angela
grew genuinely fond of the place.

They were living like an affectionate young married couple, with walks
across the moors to the Brontës' home in Haworth, and other expeditions
on Ilkley Moor, or in the Yorkshire Dales around Bolton Abbey. There was
swimming in the River Wharfe and they had days out in York, where
Vernon wrote off the famous Gothic Minster as 'a big, pretty, ancient,
slightly absurd warehouse of state holiness'.[54] They travelled to the Lake
District to see Kenneth and Jenny, and there were even occasional games
of cricket, one bowling at the other, in the park across the road. And yet,
under the surface, the old problems remained. Vernon's jealousy about
Angela's past boyfriends and the imaginary ones of the present, often
sparked by drink, remained uncontrollable. He knew just how destructive
it was:

> There are moments of perfectly clear vision where I can see exactly how
> utterly insane my behaviour is and how incalculably fortunate I am to have
> her love. But then the clouded darkness floods in with the images of bestial
> couplings that parody the act of love. Let me not be mad . . . [55]

A brief snippet of conversation from Angela's diary gives a shocking insight
into the bitterness and malevolence that could suddenly spit like hot fat into
a conversation:

TODAY, THIS IS MY LOVE SPEAKING: 'Unless I've strangled or dumped you.'
ME: 'Why would you do that, darling?'
HIM: 'For the pure pleasure of it. For the pleasure.' Venomously.[56]

After one row, she walked out and fled to Kenneth and Jenny's home in
Ambleside, where Vernon went to find her and spend 'three recuperative
days' in the Lakes, before returning to 'try very hard to be better'.[57]

A short story, In a Dark Corner, which he wrote for the BBC around this
time, describes the jealousy of an older man with a young and attractive
lover. Angela, if she ever read it, would have recognized the lines of Ben
Jonson's prose that the central character reads to his lover, and from which
the story's title is taken—they were the same words about 'a little winter

love in a dark corner' with which Vernon had wooed her in Canterbury. She might have recognized the confessions of jealousy, too, and the unfounded conviction that the young girl has a secret lover—'When you were out, I was creeping around looking for evidence like a mad Sherlock Holmes.' And she would certainly have recognized the violence:

> Maybe I over-reacted. I was wrong. I shouldn't have hit you. It was unforgivable. I was ashamed. You'll never know how sick I felt when I saw what I'd done. That black eye . . .[58]

But she almost certainly never did read it. Although she habitually typed out his manuscripts for him at their flat in Spencer Place, and although this story was carefully and professionally set out, with the title and Vernon's name and address on the cover-sheet, she has no memory of ever seeing this one.

Who actually typed it is unsure. It was as if, just as the violence had never been mentioned to Angela's face, Vernon could only bring himself to talk about it—even apologise for it—through the medium of a story. And even then, he could not bear to let her see what he had written. The story goes on to follow the manic twists of its central character's jealous logic:

> Maybe the black eye—your acceptance of it, I mean—well, couldn't it have been that you knew in your heart it was a just punishment? In a way it eased your guilt . . . You could say that the blow was a kind of proof of my love . . .

So, he is saying, perhaps it was her fault all along that he had hit her. It is the sort of convoluted and self-serving argument that counsellors and women's refuges are used to. But the point, here as in his poem 'A Simple Need', is not to suggest that it reflects Scannell's beliefs about himself—this is a story, after all, a piece of fiction—but that he could see the argument for what it was. In the story, the woman dies in a road accident and the man is consumed by guilt—and the reader is left in no doubt that the man's jealous doubts and the specious defence that he nervously advances for his violence are the products of his own paranoia. This black, bleak story—submitted but never broadcast—was the closest that Vernon got to acknowledging what he had been guilty of.[59]

Much of the time, though, he was affectionate, gentle, and caring. Another of Angela's diary entries refers to the guidance he gave her about writing poetry—'Be less careful—put down anything at first', was one piece of advice he offered, encouraging her to give her ideas complete freedom before trying to rein them in and transform them into poetry. There were his recorder lessons with Angela; at other times he would talk passionately and persuasively about the music and composers that most moved him, or just sit listening to music while she cooked a meal in the kitchen:

> I have just listened to the Elgar cello concerto. I sat, with a glass of dry sherry, my books obediently standing around, always there, eager to give themselves but never sulking or offended if they are not chosen, and A cooking supper in the kitchen and me here, dying. And I was ineffably happy. That 'dying', by the way, is not sentimental, self-dramatising or pitying—it is simply a recognition that mortality is the great bestower of value.[60]

He was hard at work, with Angela as his eager amanuensis, on a book called *How to Enjoy Poetry*, which he had been commissioned to write for a series edited by Melvyn Bragg for Piatkus Books, and which he privately dismissed as 'a bit of a digest, a teach-yourself kind of canter through the history of poetry, prosody, etc'[61]. The book, which was commissioned in July 1980 and finished less than seven months later, is certainly written for those who have little knowledge of poetry, but it is done so seriously and sensitively. And the mere fact of writing about poetry, of picking carefully over some of his personal favourites such as Dylan Thomas's villanelle 'Do Not Go Gentle Into That Good Night', John Donne's 'Batter My Heart', or Edward Thomas's short lyric, 'Thaw', helped to keep his own verse flowing.

There are still moments of uncertainty in the diaries, worries that the poetry has 'dried up' or 'frozen', but he sat at a little table in the sitting room of the flat most mornings, working on new poems. He even stopped drinking for a while—'a kind of jag of sobriety', he called it:

> I revel in soberness like a drunk in his drunkenness...I remember thinking how lucky non-drinkers were. They had so much time to write in; more than that, they had energy and good health. Now I have all of these things. And heightened sensory responses...I must try to write some poetry. Perhaps I am too healthy and happy for that. Eh?[62]

It is a typically downbeat and ironic final comment—but he was starting on one of the most productive periods of his life. And, to encourage him, there was another piece of official recognition:

> The Queen has informed Mrs Thatcher, who has informed her private secretary, who has informed me that I have been awarded a Civil List pension 'for my services to literature'.[63]

As he noted wryly, he would hardly be able to retire on the £700[64] a year of the pension—but Angela's diary probably reveals more about his real response to the honour, which arrived on the same day that she finished typing up *How to Read Poetry* and they packaged up the typescript to send it to the publishers. Vernon—'still teetotal except for wine last night to celebrate, and a pint of beer tonight for his sore throat'—was 'very pleased; slightly pink... There's a happy future. Clink!'[65]

The wine and beer, however, were a bad omen: within a few weeks, the latest 'jag of sobriety' was history, and Vernon's almost manic sexual jealousy and confusion were tormenting him again. 'I must de-louse my mind and count my blessings',[66] he writes, and a few days later, 'I only know I have been horribly hoodwinked. Yet I am not at all sure that A is guilty.'[67]

Perhaps Scannell was right, and he needed the emotional tension, the self-loathing and the loneliness that went with drinking to write his best poetry. Occasional spells on the wagon were interspersed with massive binges, often coinciding with visits from his son John, from his old friend the poet Kit Wright, or from Martin Reed. It was not so much that Vernon fell into bad company, as that he provided the bad company into which other people could fall—and then tortured himself with remorse. But the poems kept coming.

In late April, he completed 'On Leave May 1916', in which he describes the return of a soldier from the First World War, and his welcome by his wife or lover. The poem—explicitly dated in 1916, perhaps to distance it from Scannell's personal experience—shows the soldier listening to his family or friends in another room as he changes out of his uniform:

> the distant, tinkling talk
> Of cups and saucers, spoons, as feminine
> As silver thimbles, those remembered things...[68]

A little later, in the 'disguise' of his civilian clothes, he tries to hide his 'big battering hands', and to speak as softly as everyone else. He knows that this gentle world is now unobtainable for him, and later, as the tension of sexual desire builds, he watches wistfully as the woman plays for him:

> The piano smiles beneath her thoughtful hands,
> Those clever, sad and crushable bones.

For all his attempts to push away the harsh masculinity of army life, he cannot avoid focusing on the vulnerability of her fingers on the keyboard.
Later, alone together as 'the clock tacks down the dark', they finally make
love. And then:

> In deeper dark he lies in one man's land,
> Hears his own voice cry, wounded; far away
> The barrage of big guns begins; the flares
> Illuminate the sky and show, below,
> The crazy scribblings of barbed wire, the fat
> Bulges of stacked sandbags, shattered trees,
> The livid stripped forked branches, tangled hair;
> The rain begins to fall, the dark saps flood;
> Salt stings on her bruised mouth; her tears, and his,
> Are slow, small rain on dust that turns to mud.

The terrifying fascination of the past, of his own 'one man's land', was still
there. Scannell, rightly, cautioned repeatedly against reading his poems as
simple snippets of autobiography, but it is hard to read those lines without
thinking of the recurrent nightmares of wartime that we know he was still
suffering, decades after the war.[69] Is the woman's mouth bruised by passionate kisses, or is there something more sinister going on? We don't know, and
neither, very probably, does Scannell.

It was, he noted later, 'one of the best poems I've written for a long
time'[70]—a poem about the difficulty, even impossibility, of bridging the
emotional gap between men and women, written at a time when he was
veering between confused resentment and passionate love for the woman in
his life; a poem that reflects, if it does not describe, the anguish he was going
through.

As ever, he worried constantly that the writing he was doing for money
was distracting him from his poetry—particularly when a fresh commission
arrived from Melvyn Bragg, who was impressed with the book about poetry
and wanted a similar one on the novel, also for Piatkus. He could not afford
to turn down the £2,000[71] advance, even though he realized guiltily that his
wide knowledge of poetry was not matched by a similar familiarity with a
range of classic novels. 'Perhaps I shall enjoy reading some of the novels that
I've instinctively ducked for ages—Austen, Eliot, Thackeray, Trollope',[72] he
noted optimistically.

But a couple of months into the project, the magnitude of the undertak-
ing was becoming clear:

I grunt and struggle on with the Novel Book, my labours not much sweetened by a sense of fraudulence. I have just been dealing with *Vanity Fair* in tones that are supercilious and admonitory—though I do allow old Thackeray some talent. I have not read *Vanity Fair*.

If this book is satisfactory to M. Bragg and the publishers, I shall feel my vocation has been missed—used car dealer, vendor of gold mines in the Scottish Highlands, card sharper, Gypsy Petulengro. Except I'm working bloody hard.[73]

Over the next few months, the 'novel book' increasingly became a millstone, referred to at various times as 'a hack job', 'a fairly extended confidence trick',[74] and 'the dull book on Novels I Have Never Read'.[75] It did, however, give him and Angela work to do together, as he wrote out each chapter by hand and she typed them out for him. 'Angela and I are moving along very smoothly and in step',[76] he noted with satisfaction, after one such session.

She also went with him on several of his trips away for readings and lectures, including a trip to Cambridge, during which they called on Edmund Blunden's widow, Claire. For Angela, there seemed to be some reassuring parallels:

She is the nicest, easiest woman I have met...When she married Edmund Blunden she was a good deal younger than him. She has grown up daughters now, and Edmund died in 1974. She was obviously very happy with him, and thought I reminded her of her younger self.[77]

Perhaps her relationship with Vernon would prove as durable.

VII

Outside the flat, Leeds was changing even more radically than Vernon had supposed, and in ways that he neither welcomed nor understood. Chapeltown was one of the centres of the riots that ripped through several city centres in England during the summer of 1981, and he looked on aghast as worried shopkeepers hastily boarded up their shop windows. There was an ominous, intimidating atmosphere: when he and Angela walked to the shop, little knots of young men gathered on street corners, muttering aggressively and eyeing the groups of police standing around. Lying in bed, they could hear the occasional shatter and whoosh of petrol bombs:

More violence last night, and much worse. A big garage on Chapeltown Road gutted by fire, scores of shops smashed and looted there and on Harehills Parade. I feel danger in the air and fear... With events as they are, the writing of a book on enjoying novels seems a frivolous thing to be doing—fiddling on one string.[78]

A few months later, there was violence on a much bigger and more organized scale, with a British task force in the South Atlantic starting its operations to recapture the Falkland Islands after the Argentine invasion. Like many writers and intellectuals, Scannell was unequivocally opposed to what he called the 'imprudent and aggressive jingoism' of the war. He was not a pacifist, he said, but he spelled out his opposition with the passion of a man who had heard machine gun fire and felt the bullets:

I cannot help wondering if some of those ferocious Tory backbenchers would be so eager for a military solution if it were they who would have to run the risk of being burned to death or blown to pieces... It will not be seen as a time of glory, as the *Sun* newspaper and too many of our politicians would now have us see it, but as a disgraceful, stupid and squalid consequence of mismanagement, pride and selfishness.[79]

Even without the Falklands, he was disillusioned with politics and politicians. The Labour Party had split with the formation of the Social Democratic Party in March 1981, and Scannell could see no future for left-of-centre thinking:

The Social Democrats are conservative, the Liberal Party is conservative, and half the Labour party is conservative. I can see that we shall end up with a conservative government and a conservative opposition, and a few ineffective rebels. It's a mess. Nearly three million unemployed.[80]

And even away from the rioting, the war, and the politicians, it was not the world he had known: a walk through the city centre took him into WH Smith, which he remembered as a bookstore:

It is a disgusting place, filled with trash, pyramids of commercial excreta— books on the great Falklands victory, that half-baked bovine young woman and her royal offspring, and best-selling fiction by moronic sub-humans. In the poetry section—which took a bit of finding—they offered the works of Leonard Cohen, John Betjeman, William Shakespeare in one volume, Patience Strong and a couple of Oxford anthologies. Rows upon rows of potato crisps. Or is that another Smith?[81]

VIII

And yet, despite being shackled to a book project that he found shaming and frustrating (*How to Enjoy Novels* would not be published until 1984), despite the rioting in the streets, the war, the politics, and even despite Vernon's rage at WH Smith, he and Angela had some intensely happy times. On his sixtieth birthday on 22 January, just after opening his presents—a recorder and a poem to mark the occasion written by Angela—Vernon went for a walk in the park just over the road with their puppy, Bo'sun:

> I thought how good life is. I never experience boredom—or if I do, it is only when circumstances are exceptional and not of my own choosing—waiting in a queue or a railway station, etc. Each day is too small to hold all I would like to fill it with.[82]

A new collection called *Winterlude*—his ninth—appeared in April 1982. One or two of the poems draw on his wartime experiences or look back to his childhood and several, such as 'Sleep Talker', 'Juan in Limbo', and 'Last Attack', seem to comment sadly, affectionately, or ironically on the role of an old man with a young lover. The last one, however, 'Farewell Performance', expresses quite clearly the confused alternation of optimism and despair that he felt about his writing. It starts pessimistically—'I know that I'm squeezed dry...no point in going on', and reviews the pleasures, pains, crimes, and embarrassments of his life. They're all gone, the poem says, and so is poetry:

> I swear I'll write no more. It's all been said.
> I'll down my pen and say goodnight.
> I'm glad there's no one waiting in my bed.
> I'd better douse the light.
> No more parades of syllables – I'm glad –
> At least...no more tonight.[83]

Once again, the poem somersaults in the last three words, turning the confident certainty of 'I swear I'll write no more' into what is virtually a commitment to continue with his work.

And indeed, at around the same time, he began to think, 'very featherily'[84] of another novel, which would be his first for nearly twenty years. It would focus again on boxing—'definitely my last exploration of the subject'— and it would deal with themes he had learned a lot about in the last two

Figure 20. Vernon working on the typescript of *Ring of Truth* at the table in Spencer Place. (Photo: Angela Beese)

years—racial conflict, class, unemployment, and the Falklands War, all set against a northern industrial background.

Ring of Truth, published in 1983 alongside a paperback edition of *The Tiger and the Rose*, was the novel in which Scannell faced his growing reservations about the sport he had so enjoyed as a young man. In those days, boxing had given him a degree of self-reliance and an escape route from the hated dominance of the Old Man; it had helped him to scrape a living when he desperately needed to; he had taught his son, John, to box, and gone to watch him with pride; it had given young Tom Bruggen the ability to protect himself from bullies at school. In his most recent collection, Vernon had compared the dedication required of a boxer with that of a poet.[85] Boxing had given him the strength and technique to survive a dozen pub brawls. And yet for years he had felt ambivalent about it—as far back as 1963, watching the knockout that ended the career of the Welsh middleweight Johnny Gamble,[86] he wondered whether the campaigners to abolish the sport, such as Dr Shirley Summerskill, might not have a point.

> After he hit the canvas, one leg beat an immensely rapid and obviously involuntary tattoo on the floor of the ring. He was out for a good six minutes.

I begin to sympathise with Doctor Summerskill when I see this sort of thing happen.[87]

But the incident that sparked the idea of writing the novel was the death of the bantamweight Johnny Owen following a World Championship fight in September 1980. The hero of the book, Dave Ruddock, is the World Middleweight Champion—his career history, incidentally, including a three-round knock-out of a boxer named Johnny Bain. Like Scannell in his youth, he argues passionately for the purity, the courage, skill, strength, and beauty of boxing, but in the last pages he is battered to death in a fight much like the one in which Owen died. Scannell's description of his final moments looks back to that earlier diary entry about Johnny Gamble's defeat:

> He lay quite still except for his left leg, which beat up and down at tremendous speed, the heel of his boot rapping out a mechanical tattoo on the ring floor. Then, after only a few seconds, it, too, was perfectly still.[88]

It was an unusual book, as Scannell himself stressed. 'It sounds rather conceited, but it's not too unfair to say that only I could write a serious novel about boxing', he said—and the critics liked it. 'One cannot easily exaggerate the brilliance of Mr Scannell's description', said the *Daily Telegraph*,[89] referring to the climactic boxing match and the death of the hero. The *Financial Times*[90] said it was easily the best of his novels, and in the *Yorkshire Post*, Professor Philip Thody declared that it was:

> the best book I have read about boxing since Budd Schulberg's *The Harder They Fall*, and the best novel about professional sport in the north of England since David Storey's *This Sporting Life*.[91]

IX

In the late autumn came another move, away from Leeds.

For several months, Angela had been urging that he should buy a house so they could escape the chilly grandeur of Spencer Place and move to a more salubrious area. Vernon, pleading worries about the disruption to his work, about the money, about the risk, was dragging his heels—but then the Housing Association announced plans to modernize the Spencer Place flat, and warned that they would have to leave for a spell in any case. Anyway, he had just about finished work on the novel, and the last year or so had brought in more money than he had ever had in his life. He was running out of excuses, and in June 1983, already cast down by the post-Falklands tidal wave of support that was sweeping Mrs Thatcher back to power, he admitted defeat. 'I'm going to lose the few bob I've saved, I fear', he noted glumly, scribbling in the margin, 'For few bob, read £5,000.'[92]

Certainly, it had been hard work scraping that money together from the meagre fees he received from readings, the payments from poetry magazines and the royalties on his books—but the real reason for his downbeat response to the prospect of a move was emotional rather than financial. Buying a house would tie him down; it would put his relationship with Angela onto the sort of permanent footing from which he had always shied away ever since he had parted from Jo. It was, at the same time, the stability he had always told himself that he wanted and the commitment that he was scared to make. Returning with Angela from one early viewing of a possible home, he noted with chilly foreboding:

> On the way back she said: 'You will have to be a lot tidier in a little house.' The note of tight-lipped admonishment sent a little ice cube slithering down my spine.[93]

When they found the small terraced stone-built house at 51 North Street, Otley that would be his home for the rest of his life, Angela enthused about its 'lovely kitchen and garden',[94] but Vernon, typically, was less certain of his feelings. 'Shades of the prison house',[95] he wrote dourly, as they prepared to visit a solicitor; and even after the purchase was arranged, he had a vague sense of foreboding:

> The house at Otley looks as if it is to be ours after all. Good—I suppose... hope... wonder.[96]

And then, as they prepared for the actual move, he noted sardonically that they were setting out on 'the Great Adventure'. 'Oh well', he added, probably with no realization of the ironic echo of the 'awfulness' at the house in Filkins, 'At least I shall have a funk hole in the attic.'[97]

In fact, he grew to love the house; more than twenty years later he listed in one of his last poems, the things that he would be sorry to leave behind in death. Chief among them was:

> This small house that I shall miss the most.
> I've been here for so long it seems to be
> A part of what I am...[98]

Figure 21. 'This small house that I have loved so much'—51 North St, Otley, where Vernon lived first with Angela Beese and later with Jo Peters. (Photo: Andrew Taylor)

He loved the little West Riding town of Otley, too, some 10 miles from the city that he had begun to think of as his home:

> It's got that pleasant sort of old-fashioned feel about it. The people are real people who work in the place, they don't commute, and there are small industries—a paper mill on the River Wharfe, and a little stationery factory at the end of my street.
>
> A lot of my friends and fellow writers live in London, and I do see the advantages in getting work, getting readings, getting broadcasting work and so on. On the other hand, there are a great number of distractions about living in a big city which simply don't exist here.[99]

But that mellow affection for the place lay far in the future. For the moment, Scannell—like the characters in many of his poems—had a vague sense of the ominous distant rumble of thunder, of some ill-defined menace waiting just out of sight.

14

Otley

This small house that I shall miss the most.
I've lived here for so long, it seems to be
A part of what I am…

'Missing Things', from *Last Post* (2007)

I

The new house, 'delightful and luxurious'[1] though Angela found it, solved none of their problems. They argued about Angela's intention of finding herself a part-time job, about her desire to carve out an independent life for herself, about Vernon's domineering manner, and about her lack of sympathy. They were both ill during the weeks after the move, each of them complaining of the other's selfishness. They were drifting inexorably apart.

Drawing into himself, Vernon concentrated more and more on his writing. He seldom climbed to his study, the 'funk hole in the attic', but he settled down regularly to work at the kitchen table. Dictionaries, not recipe books, filled the shelves next to him,[2] and the poems began to flow. The idea for 'A Victorian Honeymoon', for instance, had been in his mind for some three years, but he now set about turning it into poetry—'very tight, seven-line stanzas…I hope the form won't be too restrictive'.[3] It is a poem about a bleak and loveless marriage and all the pain that comes with it—but, significantly, its sympathy is entirely with the woman.

The poem is explicitly set in the Victorian age, with the newly married young woman sitting alone and brushing her hair after a long day's sightseeing in some seaside European city. As a child, 'that seraphic girl who died', she had dreamed of marriage as a glittering golden prize, but the reality is one of inescapable disillusion, bitterness and fear:

> Outside, the sea
> Repeats incessant prophecies of waste
> And now its slow, unvaried voice contains
> A salt intelligence which must be faced:
> There is no hope of rescue from these chains.[4]

The setting distances the poem from autobiography, as does the hopeless acceptance by the woman of her fate—but there is an eerie echo of the forlorn state of Scannell's own relationship with Angela. The woman tries to maintain a superficially pleasant manner, but she has no communication with her husband; she feels nothing for him but distaste and fear:

> Her husband soon will come and she must smile;
> She cannot tell him that it hurts…
>   …She smells tobacco smoke.
> It sickens her. She thinks she hears his tread
> Outside the door. She feels self-pity choke,
> A bitter caustic potion: pain and dread
> Compose their plaint, but pride aborts the cry;
> It freezes in the glass; she lifts her head
> And sees reflected eyes, resigned and dry.

Everything is presented from her point of view, with her husband left as little more than a dark, ominous shadow, an unwelcome footstep outside the door. There is no suggestion that he bears any personal blame, no overt accusation of deliberate physical or mental cruelty, beyond a certain insensitivity and a liking for foul-smelling tobacco—he, too, if he only knew it, is caught in the trap of an unhappy marriage that can only bring grief to both of them. But the poem offers no special pleading on his behalf, no reference to any pain or disappointment he may feel; the focus is entirely on the woman's helpless misery.

Such finely judged understanding of the woman's emotional plight would demand a remarkable degree of imaginative sympathy by a male poet at any time but, written as it was at a time when Scannell's relationship with Angela was falling apart, the poem is a work of considerable moral courage and honesty.

Although he was sceptical about the critical reception it might get, he knew that 'A Victorian Honeymoon' was good. It was the sort of success that kept him at work:

I was thinking the other day about those few poems, or perhaps just bits of poems, where you have really produced the goods, something extraordinary, magical and irreducible. Do you feel proud? And the answer is no, because the lines or line come from no-known-where. They are given. But it does seem that you have to hammer out a great deal of the less marvellous, the ordinary, the downright dull, before the miraculous, Pentecostal moment is granted you. So you've earned it, in a way. I shall keep slogging at it.[5]

He was working well—but that didn't absolve him from the need to continue to earn money in any way he could, and it didn't prevent him, in his mid-sixties, from occasionally behaving like a troublesome adolescent. In May, invited by the chocolate firm Cadbury to act as one of the judges of its National Poetry and Arts Competition, he travelled to Manchester for a grand celebration dinner. One of the organizers, Jack Dalglish, a former Inspector of Education and an old friend, recalls what happened:

> There was a lot of drink around—I know he had at least three double whiskies before dinner, and then wine with the meal. I was sitting at the end of the table, and I just looked up to see Vernon suddenly punch the chap next to him—a senior Cadbury's executive. It turned out that he and Vernon had been talking about boxing, and he'd said that he used to be a bit of a boxer once. Vernon apparently nodded, and said, 'Well, try this one then', and just thumped him. Knocked him off his chair.[6]

Dalglish steered him gently off to bed and did his best to smooth things over—but Vernon's own account of the occasion, written in his diary a few days later, gives some indication of how serious the problem had become:

> The next morning, I saw Jack Dalglish, who said, 'I don't think there'll be any legal action.' 'About what?' I asked. 'Your hitting that executive from Cadbury's,' he said. I had, and have, no recollection of this at all.[7]

Another, less violent, occasion shows his drinking in a more genial light. He was giving a talk on 'The Making of Poetry' and reading some of his own work at a writers' conference in Scarborough in 1988, and had greatly impressed everyone with the amount of gin and tonic he could put away before, between, and after his sessions on the platform. One of the writers there, June Emerson, remembers how, on the second night of the conference, Vernon lurched across to her in the bar, leaning heavily on her left shoulder, and the following conversation took place:

VERNON: Do you know about music?
JUNE: Yes.
VERNON: Do you know about Mozart?
JUNE: Yes.

VERNON: Do you know the Clarinet Quintet?
JUNE: Yes.
VERNON: Do you know the slow movement?
JUNE: Yes.
VERNON: Breaks your fucking heart, doesn't it?[8]

He could be an engaging, as well as a violent, drunk. What he could not be, all too often, was sober.

The trouble was that, despite his occasional 'jags of sobriety', he could not resist alcohol when it was offered to him. It was the same when friends came to visit him in Otley: he would embark on massive binges that might last for days, often ending in chaos, broken glass, bruises, and complete amnesia. The poet Kit Wright, for instance—an old friend of Vernon's, from more than twenty years before, when Wright had been a schoolboy occasionally hanging around the Bull in Limpsfield—was a favourite drinking companion. 'Vernon used to get drunker than anyone I've ever known, almost like a stage drunk. Immovable', he says:

> He sometimes complained about his lack of tolerance of alcohol, and I've certainly known people drink a lot more and not get as drunk as he would. It would just happen so quickly—suddenly Vernon would be flailing about, out of control.[9]

Angela Beese remembers times in Otley, both while she was living with him and after, when he would start drinking early in the morning when the pubs opened for the market traders, and carry on until they closed at 11p.m., when he might buy more drink to finish at home with whoever would join him. On one occasion, she found him bleeding and unconscious on the kitchen floor with his nose and glasses broken—and he often had no memory of what had happened. One diary entry records that he was booked for driving without due care and attention one night in June 1984:

> At least I was sober, which is more than I was on the previous Thursday night, when Kit and I both sustained black eyes during a political discussion. What would have happened, asked Angela, had we been on opposing sides? After drinking in pubs from opening time to the death, we took home a litre of vodka and polished that off. Not wise at all.[10]

By this time, Angela was gone but not gone. She had moved out of the house in North Street, but still kept a key, still called in regularly for cups of tea, cleaned his kitchen, filed his papers, typed his manuscripts, and worried about his drinking. For all his earlier grumbling, Vernon was not good on his own: 'I'd make someone a good wife—my cooking is pretty good, if a bit restricted',[11] he claimed, but he was not a natural housekeeper. His daughter Jane, now a social worker, looked around his kitchen on one visit, and told him: 'You, Daddy, would be classified in social welfare terms as "elderly, undomesticated".'[12]

And, as ever, once a relationship was over, he could only look back regretfully on what had gone before. As Angela filed his papers, they discovered old photographs and diaries, first nostalgic memories of their time together, and then of the bad years during the war—records of his time in the psychiatric hospital, entries from his first diary in 1951 describing the daily routine in the Alexandria Military Prison. It was the first time he had talked to anyone in detail about those times, and it both shocked and reassured Angela—shocked her by the description of his mental suffering, but reassured her because the diaries seemed to suggest some psychological reason for the violence that she had found so painful and so inexplicable:

> At the time of writing he was clearly suffering not only from poverty and a hand-to-mouth existence, but also from what were, I suppose, physical effects of the psychological trauma he had suffered during the war. He suffered from nervous rashes and insomnia—he could only sleep when anaesthetised by drink. He had horrible, obscene and violent nightmares—some of horribly distorted faces floating towards him, faces of people he knew. He said he had a dream or dreams of his mother's face like that in his childhood...
>
> He also said in the journal that since his experiences in the detention barracks, when drunk he felt terrible violent and homicidal impulses towards the people with him. This may explain many of the incidents which happened to me when he was drunk.[13]

II

There was a reason for raking over the painful old memories: in early May, a BBC producer, Christopher Warren, came to talk to him about a programme that was being made about military life. 'I spoke with modest self-deprecation about my war experiences', Vernon recorded in his diary. 'Little does he suspect. Or does he? Fuck it.'[14] Warren, now a Church of England vicar, remembers that he seemed to talk very bluntly and openly about his time as a soldier,[15] about his vivid memories of D-Day, about the scores that were settled with unpopular officers in the final hours before the troops embarked, and about his all-consuming hatred of military life. But he said nothing of his desertion at Wadi Akarit or his time in prison in Alexandria.

Over the next few weeks and months, he turned over in his mind the idea of writing a new book that would finally tell the truth about his war-time record, filling in the gaps—or most of the gaps—that had been left by *The Tiger and the Rose*. The book—eventually entitled *Argument of Kings*[16]—was, he said 'a kind of confession',[17] an attempt to confront the sense of shame over his desertion that had been growing over the last forty years. All his old guilty fears about cowardice, 'one of the wrst human weaknesses',[18] came flooding back.

For all Scannell's apparent determination to make the book a confession of the truth, there is, as we have seen, one serious shortcoming in *Argument of Kings*. The book does nothing to correct the clear impression in *The Tiger and the Rose*, written sixteen years earlier, that its author had been involved in the Battle of Alamein and the whole of the Allied push westwards. Perhaps, for whatever reason, that was one confession too far; perhaps, more than forty years on, false memories of battle had persuaded him that he really *was* there. But whatever the reason for that lack of candour, the book remains what he hoped it would be—'something without exact parallel...a book that might come to be seen as necessary, and not just another war bore's blurred reminiscences'.[19]

By writing it in the third person, rather than the first person narrative of *The Tiger and the Rose*, Scannell achieved a certain narrative distance, and also reflected the fact that he felt himself a different person from the young man who had fought in the war. More than just his name had changed with the years. The book is without self-aggrandizement and without self-pity: rather, Scannell studies his earlier self with a cold eye, sympathetically, but also with a degree of scepticism:

> Perhaps the vague dream-like quality of his recollections was a kind of screen erected by his own guilt to protect him from seeing his actions for what they were, the behaviour of a coward...Yet, even if this were true he felt nothing of the guilt that he assumed the coward should, and usually did, experience. He did not *feel* that he was a coward, though this might be because of a deficiency in moral sense.[20]

That searing uncertainty about courage and cowardice that plagued him throughout his life lies at the heart of the book, and its wrenching emotional honesty is remarkable. It is the self-questioning story, perhaps, of the

ordinary civilian who finds himself in khaki uniform—the story of many
more people, in many more wars, than have had the courage to write it. And
it is notable that, among those who have actually experienced the bullets
and the mayhem of combat, there is much less readiness to condemn the
deserter than there may be among more comfortable armchair warriors.[21]

In the summer of 1987, shortly before the publication of *Argument of
Kings*, his tenth collection of poems, *Funeral Games*, appeared. Typically, as he
sent the corrected proofs of the book back to the publisher, he had predicted glumly that it would be panned by the reviewers. 'It's a book for
readers, not for quasi-academic literary journalists whose very last concern
is whether the stuff is likely to give pleasure',[22] he noted. But he was wrong.
It had some of the best reviews he had ever received. In *The Times*, the poet
Robert Nye praised the 'puzzled but embattled tenderness' of 'poetry that
celebrates ordinariness without becoming banal'. He also noted the hard
edge of personal experience that gave many of the poems their characteristic bite:

> He is best when he just accepts, without irony or compassion or any other
> fashionable footwork, the blows of experience that have made him a poet.
> The poetry is in the bruises.[23]

Meanwhile, in the *Times Educational Supplement* another poet, Charles
Causley, declared enthusiastically of *Argument of Kings*:

> His account, quite unvarnished, is that rarity, a voice from the ranks. The mili-
> tary machine is observed, as it were, from the lower depths. The portraits of
> his comrades—their talk, their bearing—have the unmistakable stamp of
> authenticity.[24]

Now sixty-five, and officially a pensioner, Vernon was working more and
earning more than he had ever done in his life.

Argument of Kings was launched with a party in the Imperial War Museum
in London attended by the poets Anthony Thwaite, John Ormond, Kit
Wright, Gavin Ewart, and Roy and John Fuller, as well as, he noted with
pleasure 'my lovely daughters'.[25] However, the *Financial Times* had warned
percipiently that it was 'certain to make blimps see red'—and so it proved.
Kingsley Amis, the archetypal blimp, wrote with characteristic generosity
that it was 'disgraceful' that the book should be celebrated in the Imperial
War Museum. 'This is a case of tolerance and forgiveness gone mad. It's an
insult to the millions who didn't desert',[26] he grumbled. Perhaps he was

thinking of his own arrival on the relatively quiet Normandy beaches three weeks after D-Day—at about the same time that Scannell was being shot in the legs by a Schmeisser machine-pistol. Vernon didn't seem too worried by Amis's bad temper:

> Kingsley Amis would say that, but he wasn't there. I'm not defending what I did. I wrote the book as an attempt at expiation or confession,

he responded mildly in the same article. In his diary, thinking of potential sales, he was positively gleeful: 'Let's hope controversy will rage',[27] he noted.

But writing the book—picking over the memories of more than forty years before—had been a strain. Shortly after the its publication, he was invited to appear on BBC Radio's *Desert Island Discs*—and what happened there may give some idea of how the months of wrestling with these harrowing issues of his past had affected him. He arrived in London the night before the recording to stay with his son John, had a few glasses of Guinness and some cheese and biscuits, and then went to bed fairly early. The next morning, a BBC car arrived to take him to Broadcasting House for the interview with Michael Parkinson:

> After that I remember nothing at all until I was walking around the Portland Place area about three hours later. I remember absolutely nothing of the interview, of Parkinson, or the producer...I must have behaved oddly or looked in a peculiar state. John telephoned the producers of Desert Island Discs, who assured him that I had responded well to the questions—in fact it had been a good interview. It is very peculiar. In fact I still feel tired and a bit woolly-minded.[28]

Even when he listened to the broadcast some six weeks later, he had no memory of what had been said. There was no sign of any hesitation, any distress throughout the forty-minute interview as he talked about his early life, his love of poetry, and, briefly, about his 'unbelieving horror' when he saw the looting of the dead British soldiers at Wadi Akarit and the shame he felt over his desertion. It was a black-out similar to the ones he occasionally suffered after a bout of heavy drinking—but this time, even allowing for a certain flexibility over his idea of 'a few' glasses of Guinness, there is no suggestion that drink caused his problem.

Over the next couple of days, doctors carried out blood tests and suggested a visit to a neurologist, which Scannell refused, so there was never a firm diagnosis. Sir Michael Parkinson said later[29] that he showed no sign of discomfort or of any difficulty in telling his story during their conversation, and Scannell sounds composed and articulate in the recording of the programme.[30] It is possible that he might have suffered a transient ischaemic attack or so-called mini-stroke; or perhaps the disorder was psychiatric in nature, simply the mental blocking out of the stressful and unpleasant experience of raking again over painful memories in public. There were no lasting physical symptoms but, for the rest of his life, he would often be reduced to tears when talking about Wadi Akarit and his desertion.

III

A few statistics from the mid to late eighties give some idea both of the increasing popularity of Scannell's work and of the parlous state of his finances. The total of £444.48[31] that he earned in 1986 in public lending right payments, for example, was hardly enough to retire on, but the figures showed that *Ring of Truth* had been borrowed from public libraries over 16,000 times, the *How to Enjoy* books about 6,000 times, and even *Winterlude* (poetry always being less popular than fiction or other prose works) nearly 1,000.[32] It was enough to encourage the publishers to produce reprints of *Ring of Truth* and *How to Enjoy Poetry*, which meant that, along with *Argument of Kings*, *Funeral Games*, and an anthology of sporting literature that he had edited for the Oxford University Press, he had five different titles in the bookshops. This did not translate into riches now or at any time during his life—Scannell's income tax return for 1988–9, for instance, shows that his total income from royalties, fees, readings, and lectures was just £3,215,[33] or just over £7,000 at today's rates. Poetry, then as now, was not good business: if he had wanted to make money, he would have been better off manning a car park.

Occasional windfalls like a £1,500 grant from the Society of Authors in 1987 made a huge difference. He left a tap running one morning, causing a flood and the collapse of the kitchen ceiling—a feature he was quick to show the representatives from the Royal Literary Fund who came to visit him in Otley, as a demonstration of how poor he was.

He certainly could not afford to turn down jobs teaching poetry or creative writing, even though he was getting sick of would-be novelists who never read novels and poets with no interest in any poetry other than their own. Sometimes it felt as if two mutually incomprehensible worlds were colliding: walking into Wakefield College, for instance, to give a lecture, he met a man whose car was blocked in the car park by another vehicle. 'Gets worse and worse, this parking business', said the irate motorist. Vernon, just appointed as Poet in Residence at the college, and thinking he ought to say something suitably literary, replied: 'Parking is such sweet sorrow'—not a bad joke off the top of his head. 'Aye,' the motorist said, nodding absent-mindedly. 'I'd better find the bloody owner.'[34]

There was a similar incident when a photographer arrived from the local paper to take a picture for a feature on *Argument of Kings*. 'What sort of book is it?' he asked:

> 'An autobiography, I suppose', Vernon replied.
> 'Oh', the photographer said. 'Who's it about then?'[35]

He spent a term at Wakefield College as Writer in Residence, working with A-level and GCSE students. He was quieter, less ebullient, than he had been at Hazelwood, but still managed to gain the rapt attention of his classes, says David Jones, who was then Chief English Lecturer at the college:

> He had a real presence in the classroom, a large, grey-haired, rather venerable and quite famous man, and the kids all felt and respected this. He never had any discipline problems, but only had to raise his eyes to exert authority. There was a twinkle and humour in his classes, and that precise, quiet, slightly upper-class voice of his was an effective classroom tool. The only time he raised his voice was in dramatising poems.[36]

He would also meet individual students for one-to-one discussions about their work, with his dog, Hetta, sitting quietly in a corner of the room. Jones—a respected writer and poet himself under the name David Annwn—became a friend and would go for walks with him around Otley, discussing poetry and listening to Vernon's stories. One favourite was of a visit—almost a pilgrimage—to the ageing Siegfried Sassoon during the 1960s.

Sassoon, for Scannell, was one of the giants of twentieth-century literature, but, despite his respect for the poet, the occasion almost collapsed into farce:

> They turned out to be quite a dour, quiet upper middle-class household who all ate together, mainly in silence, at a long table. During the meal, one of the Sassoons was telling a well-known story about the demise of an aunt; she'd been walking along a raised platform on a sea-front and got blown by heavy winds into a concrete-mixer. No-one saw this as at all funny. The meal

continued in silence and Vernon, who enjoyed deadpan, dark humour, had to stuff his serviette in his mouth to avoid bursting out laughing.[37]

It might have occurred to him as he told the story that the tables were turned now—*he* was the respected elder statesman, and Annwn the promising young poet paying his respects. It wasn't a role with which he was entirely comfortable.

IV

In October 1986, a collection of photographs of poets was published,[38] taken by Christopher Barker, son of the Canadian writer Elizabeth Smart and the poet George Barker. All Scannell's literary friends were there— Dannie Abse, Alan Brownjohn, Anthony Thwaite, Peter Porter, George MacBeth, and the rest. Barker had travelled to Otley to photograph Scannell, and the picture shows the poet in a tweed jacket and checked shirt, wearing a closely cropped grey beard—a confident, upright figure. His own view sounds slightly defensive—'I look a bit prattish I suppose, but not as bad as John Wain and P. J. Kavanagh, both of whom seem to be consciously posing and look monstrously vain.'[39] Maybe—but it was the picture of an elderly man, and he knew it.

A few months later, he shaved off the beard, but that didn't help either: 'I think I hoped for some kind of metamorphosis, but if there was any, it was of a depressing kind. Same old mug, but a bit more wrinkled and sagging.' Even a casual walk with Hetta on Otley Chevin, a ridge of moorland that overlooks the town, depressed him when a woman stopped to chat about their dogs:

> When you're over 60, you're assumed to be out of the sexual lists, neutered by age. No one would think that she might be making 'advances' or for that matter that I could possibly be of the slightest interest to her in that way.[40]

He didn't enjoy being sexually invisible. And there were other, more serious reminders of mortality—Kenneth telephoned in November 1987 with news of the death of their father. Although Vernon had got to know his half-sisters, the Old Man's daughters by his second marriage, he had hardly seen him for nearly fifty years, apart from the one visit with Sylvia a few years earlier. The scars from childhood were too deep for either Vernon or Kenneth even to consider going to his funeral—and yet the news of his death was unsettling:

He was a pretty monstrous fellow yet one feels a kind of sadness, a sense not of loss but of the pointlessness of his existence and perhaps of all human existence . . . There was something childish about him, but it was not an engaging quality. It was the selfishness and cruelty and vanity of an unusually nasty child. I cannot mourn him yet I feel uneasy about not being able to.[41]

And yet one poem in the collection *Funeral Games* suggests that possibly, as his father approached the end of his life, Vernon had more sympathy for him than he chose to admit. It is a short poem, written sometime after that final visit with Sylvia, about an elderly man, a former soldier, like James Bain, who sits nodding in a rocking chair, and remembers his old friends who have already died:

> 'Great days, all gone; dear comrades, all stone dead.'
> He loves them, for the dead do not condemn
> Or mock or boss, or say he's telling lies,
> But smile and whisper from the darkening gloom
> 'You're tired and old. Come in. It's time for bed.'[42]

Perhaps that final instruction, so redolent of childhood, remembers evenings in Beeston, Eccles or Aylesbury; certainly the title, 'Old Man', echoes the name by which the two boys knew the father that they hated. With its sympathy and its quiet understanding, it implies a sadder and more tender feeling towards his father than anything else that Scannell ever wrote.

There was a brief reminder of happier times when he recognized the doctor whom he consulted about a continuous hacking cough: he had been a young medical student at Leeds University boxing club forty years earlier. 'I sparred with him and dumped him on his bum with a left hook. He did not come back to the club after that.'[43] The doctor had forgiven him enough to prescribe steroids and antibiotics, but another visit a month later led to a diagnosis of irreversible emphysema. 'So I shall cough, wheeze, and spit my way to perdition', he noted.[44] It was a typical piece of grim Scannell bravado—but the doctor's diagnosis would eventually prove to be the most serious reminder of all that he was not the man he once was.

V

In October 1986, Scannell received a letter, forwarded by his publishers, from Emma Kilcoyne, a fourteen-year-old schoolgirl in Sunderland, who was asking him about his poetry. She had read one of his poems at school and been so impressed by it that she had ordered his *Collected Poems*. As always, he wrote back thoughtfully and helpfully: yes, he'd been good at English at school; he'd known he wanted to be a writer from the age of nine; yes, he knew most of the writers of his generation, including Ted Hughes, Sylvia Plath, and John Betjeman. It was the sort of reply he gave to dozens of young letter-writers.

This one, though, was different. It marked the start of a correspondence that lasted for some six years, as Emma grew up, went through school, developed her interest in poetry and literature, began to act, and agonized over whether to go on to university or drama college. She sent him gifts at Christmas and Easter, prayed for him when he went into hospital, asked for his advice about the poetry she was writing, and even confided in him about her boyfriends; he dedicated two books of children's poems to her, and was unstinting in his advice about writing, poetry, and life in general. The exchange of letters grew into the affectionate relationship of a young girl and an elderly honorary uncle. She never met him, although they talked on the telephone several times:

> When we spoke on the phone he was lovely. And just what I'd expect. You could tell he was a dad—he absolutely knew how to talk to young people, no problem at all.[45]

She became his 'treasured friend',[46] and he was also very open about his own life and his poetry. His poem 'Nettles' was about an accident that had happened to his son John, he said, while 'Growing Pain' was based on an incident with Toby. In one letter, he confessed that he shared Philip Larkin's famous dislike of travel and sightseeing:

> I haven't travelled much, except with a package tour to the Middle East with the British Army...I'm too lazy to be a real traveller, and I'm not interested in ancient buildings unless they are licensed. I subscribe to the Larkin view that there is plenty to write about at home.[47]

Before a trip to a speaking engagement in Scarborough, he told her:

> I shall be assailed by ladies of a certain age with beady eyes and pursed lips, who will want me to give them the magic password that will get their sadly inept little stories and verses printed in *Woman's Own*, and I shan't be able to help them, and they will hate me.[48]

There are occasional good-humoured grumbles about her grammar, and the teenagerish confusions of 'I' and 'me', but the really interesting parts of his letters are those in which he offers his advice about Emma's poetry, and about the writers she ought to be reading. He may not have had a magic password to offer, but he had sympathy, understanding, encouragement, and ideas.

That's not to say he was a pushover: he praises the 'delightful images and phrases' of one poem, then goes on to suggest that she should treat it as a first draft, and work on the rhyme and metre. A few weeks later, he says it is 'a little improved, but could do with a lot of compressing', and then offers specific suggestions:

> The last stanza would be improved by getting rid of some of the adjectives...cut 'sunny'; 'comfy' is a non-word and 'blowsy' is inappropriate. 'Plentiful', too, seems not quite right—why not simply 'fragrance'? Think about it.[49]

Told that she is working on another poem, he urges her not to settle for easy solutions:

> Don't be satisfied with *approximate* words and phrases. Work away until you get the absolutely 'right' word or words, 'right' in sound, texture, meaning, associations. I don't think anything worth reading has ever been produced without a great deal of hard labour for the writer. Don't believe any of the nonsense about 'spontaneity'.[50]

In those injunctions we can hear the authentic voice of the schoolteacher, the same man who produced such a demanding reading list for the twelve-year-olds at Hazelwood School—but he is also understanding and encouraging: 'Anyway, Emma dear, it's good', he insists, after suggesting 'one or two small revisions' for one of her poems. 'Hope you're not irritated by these carpings. I do think it would be worth polishing.'[51]

He was uncompromising in his recommendations and condemnations. Emma should try the novels of Elizabeth Taylor[52] and William Trevor,[53] he suggested, and also Tony Harrison's 'clever and witty' translation of Molière's *The Misanthrope*;[54] she should not be discouraged by Joyce's *Ulysses*,[55] but should probably put off reading Thomas Mann's *The Magic Mountain* until she is a bit older.[56] John Steinbeck, on the other hand, is 'crude, sentimental and generally third-rate',[57] John Osborne 'rotten with hatred and rancour, a mean-spirited, ugly-minded creature',[58] and D. H. Lawrence 'aggressive, vain, cruel, and very close to madness...on a long rail journey, I would rather read the No Smoking sign than a D. H. Lawrence novel'. Edith Sitwell, he sniffs, is 'a silly, vain old woman, with almost no talent at all',[59] while Stephen Spender is 'a dear old thing, but I don't think any of his poetry is much good. [Ted] Hughes is less dear, less old, and not much better.'[60] Brian Patten is dismissed out of hand as 'a rotten poet—self-indulgent, sentimental and incompetent'.[61]

But it is the personal advice that Scannell offered his young correspondent that best demonstrates the emotional closeness of this long-distance relationship. Late in 1991, when she confided in him her worries about how people thought of her, his reply applied both to her everyday life and to her attempts to write poetry:

> Darling Emma, I do think you worry too much over what you will quickly come to see as rather trivial matters...Be as honest as you can. I don't mean refrain from telling little fibs, though that's not a bad idea either. I mean honest (as far as you can be) about your own responses to others and to experiences of all kinds. Don't *pretend* to a more intense, enthusiastic, disapproving, disgusted reaction than you truly feel. Genuine enthusiasm is fine; bogus, gushing pretence is repellent. [62]

A few months later, she was writing to him about an unrequited love affair; again, he was gentle, sympathetic, thoughtful—and surprisingly self-revealing:

> I'll venture to give you a bit of advice: be patient, if you can. Don't settle for an approximation to what you really want, and above all, be on your guard against self-deception. *I've* been guilty of these things with fairly disastrous results.[63]

Vernon never knew that his young correspondent grew to be a successful professional writer in her own right—scriptwriter for Dawn French and co-author of the BBC television series *Roger and Val Have Just Got In*. But his letters, his advice, and his friendship, she says, were an important part of her development:

> I like to think he would have liked *Roger and Val Have Just Got In*. At least I think he would have seen the ambition in it. He was amazing to talk to or write to about writing, and I think he was a very formative influence on me because he taught me a very important thing. You have to dare to do it, and then show it to someone.
>
> It's an exposing feeling as all writers know, but from 14 or 15, I was picking that up from him. He really bothered because he could absolutely see that I was nuts about literature. He would look at my poems and comment on them, kindly. And always answer the wealth of questions I had for him. I honestly think we were a bit like two poetry nuts gabbling back and forth—and in a way, that's exactly what it was.[64]

So why did a fairly commonplace exchange of letters between a famous poet and a young fan develop into such a close and long-lasting correspondence? Perhaps Emma was a particularly engaging letter-writer—no doubt her obvious enthusiasm for poetry impressed him and awoke the old 'didactitis', the desire to help to form the literary tastes of a young, lively, and impressionable mind. Perhaps he was aware of all that he had missed in the upbringing of his own children—certainly he mentions them frequently in his letters to Emma. Possibly, alone in the little house in Otley when the correspondence began, he was simply lonely. But the letters to Emma reveal a kindly, gentle, concerned, and emotionally generous side of Scannell's character that is sometimes hidden.

VI

He was doing his best to confront his past in the only way he knew how, by writing about it—and, specifically, by writing about his wartime experiences. He told Emma about the new collection that he was working on, with the warning—surely irresistibly tempting to a seventeen-year-old schoolgirl— 'I don't think you'd like the poems (well, certainly not all of them) and I'm sure your teachers wouldn't approve.'[65] In *Soldiering On*, eventually published in March 1989 after nearly two years of work, he was trying to emulate Rudyard Kipling's *Barrack Room Ballads* by giving a voice to the ordinary soldier—but whereas the conventions of the 1890s had meant that Kipling was limited to a 'Punch cartoon Cockney'[66] to represent the daily language of the soldiers, Scannell believed that in a modern age, he could show more successfully 'both the impoverishment and the repetitiveness of barrack room language *and* the power of its invective and humour'.[67]

So, in 'Swearing In', a recalcitrant squaddie on a charge—reminiscent of Private John Bain, one suspects—is complaining about his treatment:

> What a fucking awful mob,
> The Gordon fucking Highlanders.
> That fucking bastard sergeant, I'll
> Smack him in the fucking gob.[68]

The lines certainly demonstrate the impoverishment and repetitiveness of the private's language, and there is humour in the contrast between the obscenities muttered under his breath and the obsequious 'Yes Sarge! Right!

Right away Sarge!' to the NCO's face—but it is hard to see that the poem reveals anything significant about either the soldier or military life in general. The language—'cheeringly accurate barrack room demotic',[69] according to the poet Peter Reading in the *Sunday Times*—is certainly more representative of life in the barracks than Kipling's carefully constructed dropped g's and h's—but it is tempting to ask 'So what?' Impoverished and repetitive language in a barrack room, after all, is impoverished and repetitive language on the page. A more important comparison with *Barrack Room Ballads* perhaps concerns the soldiers' attitudes rather than the way they speak. The ordinary soldier in Kipling's poems is generally, as George Orwell says, 'patriotic, feudal, a ready admirer of his officers and proud to be a soldier of the Queen',[70] while by contrast, in Scannell's 'Swearing In', 'Sanitation Wallah', or 'Twelve Hour Pass', he resents the shouting and bullying of his officers and wants nothing more than to keep his head down out of trouble, preferably with the addition of a few drinks and a cooperative woman or two. It is the poetry of the anti-hero, and a much more accurate reflection of barrack room life. Kipling's primary focus was on the Empire which the soldiers served, Scannell's on the men as individuals. He, unlike Kipling, had actually worn khaki as well as writing about it.

Some months before starting work on the *Soldiering On* poems, Scannell mused in his diary about the unpredictability of poetry. 'The poet is always potentially subversive because he does not know what the truth is until he has voiced it, and it may well turn out to be something that surprises him', he wrote—and the poems of *Soldiering On* provide an excellent example. He set out to achieve realism by using the vulgarity and obscenity of everyday army speech, but it is the pieces in which he speaks with his normal poetic voice that are most telling, most incisive, and most likely to reflect the actual experience of the soldier in wartime.

The sequence 'Troopship', for instance, includes a series of eight finely differentiated letters home to parents, wives, or lovers from, among others, a young subaltern, a senior officer, an army chaplain, and a would-be deserter who has been brought on board in handcuffs. They express fear, bravado, anxiety, disillusionment, or longing: 'Don't look at any man while I'm away,' pleads one; another boasts:

> Me,
> I'm going to stay alive and let the rest
> Get blown to Kingdom Come...

While the chaplain laments wistfully:

> There are ways,
> I now believe, in which I could have served
> Both God and country more effectively
> At home...[71]

The lines *sound* natural, and they subtly reveal the characters of the letter-writers. The quiet desperation just below the surface, like the language itself, is utterly believable. It is this emotional sensitivity and craftsmanship, rather than the self-consciously raucous obscenity of the other poems, that meet Scannell's determined ambition to write poetry that 'could not only be understood but actually enjoyed by simple blokes *and* literary gents'.[72]

Nowhere is this sympathy with the individual more clear, however, than in the softly terrifying 'Casualty—Mental Ward'. The poem is a tightly constructed villanelle—five three-line verses followed by a final verse of four lines, with the first line of the first verse repeated as the sixth, twelfth, and eighteenth lines, and the third line as the ninth, fifteenth, and nineteenth. This repetition—'Something has gone wrong inside my head' and 'I hold long conversations with the dead'—precisely captures the obsessive anxiety of the patient, with his tenuous grip on reality. His deranged image of a bloody world, stabbed by red flares and tracers, booby-trapped and mined, coiled with barbed wire, and with unseen snipers waiting to strike, is a powerful evocation of Wilfred Owen's 'war and the pity of war'.

It's likely that Scannell was right, and that the English teachers at Emma's school would not have felt comfortable putting *Soldiering On*, with its obscenities and vulgarities, in front of their classes. But if so, they would have missed a number of remarkable poems.

15

Last Love

Two children
are laughing as they play with a large black dog
and a pink balloon, while he and she
look down, unseen, from their small balcony.
Behind them, still and cool, the room recalls
Once more a Schubert Trio in B Flat
And, as the Scherzo dances, the black dog bounds
And pounces on the light pink globe
Of air . . .

'Postscript: Andalusian Afternoon', from *Of Love and War* (2002)

I

In the years after Angela's departure, Vernon was sometimes alone, but he seldom had time to be lonely. For a start, he kept himself at work: ever since the
publication of *Argument of Kings* he had thought of writing an account of the
years leading up to his army service to describe his childhood, growing up in
Aylesbury, his fights with the Old Man. It had been a difficult project—at one
point, he abandoned it in disgust and returned the £200[1] advance that Jeremy
Robson had given him—but in 1992 his memoir was finally published as
Drums of Morning, taking its title from A. E. Housman's poem 'Reveille':

> Up lads, up, 'tis late for lying:
> Hear the drums of morning play;
> Hark, the empty highways crying,
> 'Who'll beyond the hills away?'

Following on from *The Tiger and the Rose* and *Argument of Kings*, the book
completed an autobiographical trilogy, but in some ways the memories it

recalled were the hardest of all—the cruelty of his father, the beatings, the coldness, and the lack of love. He had imagined the death of a character very like the Old Man years before, in his poem 'Our Father':

> He lay in sweat
> And silence for nine days,
> Then spoke. 'I'm sorry!' were the last words that he said.[2]

There had been no final apology for Vernon, of course: Kenneth's telephone call telling him about his father's death in 1987 had come some days after the event. It was a few months later that he had started pulling together the ideas that would eventually turn into *Drums of Morning*. He had hardly seen the Old Man for four decades, and his feelings had mellowed over the years. Perhaps he was even beginning to feel more like his father's son—certainly, members of his family commented on how similar they were in appearance, as Vernon grew older. At any rate, he had no wish to cause his father pain: James Bain's death must have made it easier to revisit the old nightmares.

This time, unlike *Argument of Kings*, he wrote the book in the first person, like a traditional memoir. There was nothing like the humiliation of his supposed cowardice or his imprisonment in Alexandria to deal with—incidents in *Drums of Morning* where a reader might expect to find a degree of shame or embarrassment, such as the theft of his father's money, are told with a defiant laddish bravado or, in the case of his marriage and the speedy desertion of his wife and child, simply left out altogether. As his children were growing up, Vernon loved to regale them with horror stories of his own childhood, and now he had the chance to spell it out in all its painful detail. He might look and sound like an officer and a gentleman, but like many old men he wanted to establish his pedigree as an underdog, someone who had struggled against the odds and come through. In the *Sunday Times*, Alan Brownjohn described the book as 'grim, gripping and poignant', and praised Scannell's 'exact and unembellished observation'. *Drums of Morning*, he said, was 'an evocation of a vanished world of which the young George Orwell might have been proud'.[3]

Scannell had also established himself as a radio performer of note—'a very good personal broadcaster in the style of Alistair Cooke', as Alastair Wilson, then Head of Features for the BBC in Manchester says. Brownjohn and Wilson were good friends of Scannell's, and George Orwell and Alistair Cooke are heady comparisons—yet these were not merely flattering compliments, but the sincere and revealing assessments of experienced professionals. Apart from readings of his work on programmes such as *Poetry Please*, Scannell gave radio talks during the early nineties on his time at Hazelwood, on his disappointing search for the Lakeland poet John Short, on life in Soho and Fitzrovia, and, of course, on poetry, poets, and literature. Wilson remembers him as a fast and professional performer:

> He would always rehearse what he had to do before he came in, and then he would turn up, do it, get it right in one take, then have a couple of half pints in the bar and go off back to Otley. Rehearsals in the studio were completely unnecessary.
>
> I can picture him in a corduroy jacket and green polo shirt, with massive square shoulders. He was completely unmoody, more so than anyone I've ever worked with, but he had a rather aristocratic bearing. He would phone up and say, 'Dear boy, I'm in town. Are you around for a natter?' And he was always full of ideas.[4]

This reputation for crisp professionalism, however, doesn't mean that there were never any difficulties with his recordings. Fraser Steel, who used to produce *Poetry Now* for the BBC, recalls one apparently intractable problem when Vernon was reading his poem 'Sentences':

> One day in Manchester, his reading sounded very odd—so odd, in fact, that I asked the studio manager to check out the microphone he was using. It lacked clarity and enunciation, just as if there were some sort of electronic problem. But the studio couldn't solve it and eventually I went in to ask him to read something to me.
>
> He realized at once what the problem was. 'It's my new teeth', he said. 'They don't fit properly.'[5]

More important than either the memoirs or the broadcasting, of course, were the poems. After the publication of *Soldiering On*, he started work in earnest on two books of children's poetry, *Love Shouts and Whispers* and *Travelling Light*, building on the reputation he had established with *The Clever Potato* in 1988. He was still sometimes ambivalent about the poems he wrote for children—one diary entry describes him carelessly rattling one off for the *Travelling Light* collection before and during breakfast:

> Doggerel, of course; I'm not sure I should have been doing these: the ones in *Love Shouts*—well, some of them—were much closer to real poems because my heart was engaged. But poems on transportation! Not really.[6]

But although the poems in the three books are certainly uneven, with one or two, as he said, little more than doggerel, several of them show a startling ability to see the world through the child's eyes. In 'Something in Common', for instance, a love-struck teenage girl feels the understanding and sympathy of a teacher when she meets her in the street, out with her own boyfriend; 'The Little Joke' neatly turns the tables on adults who lecture their children about good manners:

> Cigars replace the chocolate bars,
> Wine or whisky, Coke.
> But the greed's the same as any child's,
> That's the little joke.[7]

In others he presents adult experience and relates it precisely to the child's world. 'Thelma', for instance, identifies the smell of honeysuckle with a young girl that the (possibly adult) speaker knew as a child; 'Waiting for the Call' describes the agony of hope and expected disappointment—the same theme as Scannell's adult poem 'The Spell' from the collection published two years later, *A Time for Fires*. This time, the wait for the ringing phone is seen from a child's point of view:

> He sits and knows the urgent noise
> Probably will not occur:
> There's little hope and, if it does,
> He's sure − almost − it won't be her.[8]

It is as if, in his old age, Scannell was having another go at childhood, and understanding it rather better. The research for *Drums of Morning* had reminded him of the emotional privation of his own young years, and he was guiltily aware of his shortcomings as a largely absent father to his children. But he loved the innocence and limitless potential that he saw in children and in young adults like Emma Kilcoyne. An entry from his diary about a visit to a primary school in Wimborne Minster, Dorset, some years earlier suggests one way that he liked to see himself:

I got out of the car. [The children] swirled around me, reaching out, touching, plucking at my coat tails, my sleeves, scrambling to get close. The one who had first spoken established her claim at once and took a firm grip on my arm. And so I crossed the playground with the little girls dancing around, calling out that they had captured a poet, clinging, reaching, dangling, and so I was ushered along a corridor, feeling like the Pied Piper, and taken to the staff-room door which was opened by an astonished master.[9]

Everyone talked about his empathy with the children at the schools where he gave readings—and in his private life too, he enjoyed being playful, indulgent, and grandfatherly. *Travelling Light*, his book of children's poems about trains, boats, planes, and bicycles, was dedicated to John's son Harry, 'whose journey has just begun', and he was a good friend to another little girl, Rosie, whom he met when he got to know her grandmother later in his life. When Rosie—then aged about two—came to visit, he would amuse her by making coins disappear and laughing as she conducted the music that was playing on the radio—all the tricks that grandfathers have with their grandchildren, in fact. John's children remember how he and they roared with laughter when he drove over an uneven road too quickly, bumped his head on the roof of the car, and let fly with a string of *Soldiering On*-style invective. He was a fun grandfather to have around.[10]

He was still afflicted with the old uncertainty about his work, still resentful of the way he thought he was ignored as old-fashioned by much of the literary establishment—but also, approaching seventy, generally optimistic about the future. There were other poets who respected him—the popular comic writer, Roger Woddis, for instance, paid tribute to him in a verse in the *Radio Times* about boxing. There were few boxers for whom Woddis was prepared to express unmixed regard:

> Yet there are some – not only Ali –
> Whose reach extends beyond the purse:
> Hail Vernon Scannell, one-time boxer
> And writer of enduring verse!

It was hardly the considered critical acclaim that Scannell yearned for, but he certainly welcomed it as 'a handsome compliment'.[11] And all the time, of course, he was concentrating on the poems that would eventually form his next collection, *A Time for Fires*. He was, he noted in his diary, 'working quite well', although he was still unsure of the worth of what he was doing:

> I have the feeling that I am ceasing to exist in the literary world...What does it matter? Not much, I suppose. Anyway, I'm cautiously pleased by my little poem, *Matches,* about an old blind boxer begging at Victoria Station, though I hope it is only a bit of light training, limbering up for something bigger and more formidable.[12]

He had no idea what that 'something bigger and more formidable' might be, or on what terrible personal experiences it would draw. But he was still hopeful.

II

Angela, meanwhile, was getting on with her life, building a new relationship and starting an academic career at Leeds University. She took a degree in psychology followed by a PhD, a lectureship in behavioural sciences, quali-fication as a chartered psychologist, accreditation as a psychotherapist, and a fellowship of the Higher Education Academy. She also continued to look after Vernon—in spring of 1988, for instance, she drove him home after a brief hospital visit: 'A...had done the washing up and tidied the kitchen, and bought flowers to glorify the sitting room. Good A.'[13] Eight years later, a full eleven years after their parting, a note in his diary grumbles that he can't fit the new ribbon he has bought for his typewriter. 'SOS to Angela who promised to do it for me. Good ole Angie.'[14] The poet Anne Stevenson surmised that he deliberately cultivated a reputation as a womanizer, but she wondered if he wasn't essentially looking for 'a motherly woman who would take care of him'.[15] Certainly, if Angela was treating him like a child, he seemed to have no objection.

Vernon was still in touch with Carol Bruggen in Burnley, too; and when-ever he was doing readings or talks in the south-west, he would call in on Jo at Nether Compton—partly so that she could look after his dog for him, but also partly to keep contact with her.

But if Anne Stevenson was right, and he wanted to be seen as a woman-izer, he certainly worked hard at it. For a man comfortably into his sixties, with a wheezy chest and a drink problem, he retained an astonishing capac-ity to attract women. Olwen, now living in Shoreham on the south coast, came back into his life in the summer of 1985, and over the next four years there were occasional visits either in Otley or Shoreham, meetings in London and elsewhere. But by mid 1989 this long-running, on–off rela-tionship was stumbling towards its end.

By this time, in any case, he had delved back even further into his past to revive a relationship from more than thirty years before. While he was teach-ing at Hazelwood back in the 1950s, he had enjoyed something of a fling with Virginia, the niece of the landlady of The Wheatsheaf, near his old home in Limpsfield. She was married now, with a jealous and bombastic Spanish husband, but that did not stop her from embarking on a passionate affair with her old lover.

They had already had several weekends away together by the time she came to spend three days with him in Otley in September 1989. He wrote about her stay with the priapic glee of a teenager, mixed with the more mature circumspection of the 67-year-old that he was:

> It was a delight to have her—well, yes, that too, though I very much doubt if the earth moved for her...I do love her very much. I think.[16]

And apart from his boyish physical excitement, he delighted in her propensity to make sudden, unexpected, expansive, and romantic gestures. About a week after she had left, he drove down to Charterhouse School in Surrey to give a reading, returning the next day after a round trip of nearly 500 miles. He made himself a frugal meal of cheese on toast, and poured a can of tomatoes on top of it:

> Then V walked in, carrying a rose she'd plucked from the flowerbed near the bus station. It was the most astounding, beautiful, bewildering, piercing, mysterious, impossible thing I've ever experienced. She stayed till last Sunday, and I've been aching for her ever since she left.[17]

For a while, he missed her like a teenager. One telephone call was interrupted when her husband walked in and she suddenly changed her tone of voice, talking briskly about a mythical job offer, and after that he didn't hear from her for several days. 'If she doesn't phone today, tonight, I shall suspect that everything is over between us. I have a sense of doom',[18] he noted anxiously one day, before confiding his fears in Angela. The next day:

> Still no news. A has offered to telephone. I'll either take her up on this or ring V myself this evening. I am reminded of her when I make tea—our morning cup—when I boil an egg—our last breakfast; and in the car were those boiled sweets—given to me by V.[19]

Angela did telephone, to discover that Virginia was ill at home, with her husband in the house. A week or so later, she joined Vernon on a trip to see his brother Kenneth in the Lake District, but clouds seemed to be gathering over the relationship—Vernon did not enjoy the deception and the play-acting phone calls, and she seemed uneasy and mistrustful. Even so, it stumbled on for several months, with more surreptitious visits to Otley—'She is very sweet and lovable but a bundle of trouble, I suspect',[20] he noted in April. It was turning into another long-running on-off saga, although, for Virginia if not for Vernon, it was clearly a serious romance.

Some time afterwards, when Vernon's *Collected Poems 1950–1993* appeared, she showed her nephew a copy in which she had marked one poem, 'Second Sight', which she said was based on her idea, and three more which she said had been either about her or inspired by her.[21] Whether that's true or not, it is interesting that all three—'The Spell', 'She Speaks the Words', and 'On the Chevin'—focus on relationships that are in some way threatened. In 'She Speaks the Words', the man's lover tells him that she loves him, but he hears only melancholy and accusation in her voice; in 'The Spell', he prepares through the day for his lover's arrival, repeating to himself the words 'She will not come' in the hope that they will work as a spell to ensure that she does. In the last stanza, instead of hurrying around the house making preparations as he is in the rest of the poem, he sits waiting 'in deepening darkness with closed eyes'. Disappointment would be too simple, too pat, for the poem, which is charged with the tension between hope and despair: the reader is left to wonder whether the final 'She will not come' is actually a simple statement of fact. And in 'On the Chevin', the poet sees two lovers return from a romantic walk, only to get into two different cars:

> Doors slam.
> Both engines snarl. His car moves off, then hers,
> In opposite directions, gathering speed.[22]

It is impossible to say whether Vernon is the man in these three poems. They may or may not relate to his relationship with Virginia, as she believed. But what is sure is that, in their different ways, they present familiar Scannell themes of happiness and fulfilment not quite achieved, of the threat of destruction contained in the moment of joy. He was in no frame of mind to think of settled, rewarding, mutually satisfying relationships.

But then, whether Virginia knew it or not, he seldom was in such a frame of mind at this time of his life. She was hoping for a degree of commitment that he was unable to give and she came to feel bitter, betrayed, and let down more than he realized. Some four years later, he would have to resort to a solicitor to stop the flood of angry and violent letters from her, the pictures of Dachau death camp, the promises to dance on his grave, the ghoulish sketches of skulls, and all the other '*billets aigres*'[23] that landed on his doormat every day for several months.

The names of other women are scattered through his diaries, generally remembered, some more kindly than others, through an alcoholic haze. He met one woman in a hotel in Leeds after an evening pub-crawl—'Pussy for pud', he gloated lasciviously in his diary.[24] Another, known only as Valerie, had a much less successful stay over Christmas 1987.

> She scarcely glanced at my books. She knitted. She either tacitly or directly criticised my housekeeping, and she objected to my 'bad language'... Anyway, I got pissed and stayed pissed for most of the 4 days. Poor woman.[25]

There was Judy S., who came to stay a few months later:

> She became very hostile and ill-tempered, accusing me of sawing her in half and crushing her skull when I attempted a small and gentle caress. I got drunk on the Saturday on champagne, red wine and whisky. The next morning, she had gone.[26]

Then there was Dorothy, who came for tea one weekend in August. The day began quietly, but ended like all the others:

> We started off quite temperately with a cup of tea and even read poems to each other. Then I started on the wine. I saw there were four empty bottles the next morning. I went out to the pub when D left about 9pm... It is madness; self-destructive lunacy, but when I've had four or five drinks it seems I'm quite incapable of stopping.[27]

But everything came disastrously to a head in July 1990, in a late-night drinking session with Maureen, a woman he had known for some time through poetry readings, and who had endeared herself to him by standing up in the audience at a reading given by the Liverpool poet Adrian Henri and telling him, 'You're not fit to lick the boots of Vernon Scannell.' Late one Friday, as Vernon returned from a pub-crawl around Otley, she arrived at his door in a taxi, carrying a curry. He must have eaten the curry but remembered nothing else, except for showing her the spare room as he stumbled off to bed sometime in the small hours.

> I imagine we drank Scotch together. I woke the next morning with a murderous hangover and still quite drunk. I saw a light in the loo and assumed M was in there. I went back to bed. When I got up again a couple of hours later, the light was still on. I tried to get an answer, banging on the door, and finally I smashed the bottom panel in, reached up inside, and drew the bolt. M was on the floor, dead.[28]

He called the police and the ambulance, of course, but it was too late. Maureen had collapsed during the night and died from a heart attack. Angela came round next day to find him sobbing in the kitchen.

> He was sitting slumped at the table. There was that sour, post-alcohol smell in
> the house, and it was chaos in the kitchen—bottles all over the table, and the
> ashtrays full of beer. He'd smashed his hand on the glass when he'd broken
> into the loo, and there was blood all down the wall. He spent the rest of the
> day drinking and crying.[29]

Perhaps it was predictable that something like this would happen—but the
tragedy shattered Vernon. Some weeks later, down in Nether Compton on
one of his visits, he poured out his heart to Jo:

> He was horrified that he had not been able to do anything about it, and also
> about the way she was treated after she died. She'd lived alone in one room,
> and all her books were there, and the council just came and put them all in a
> skip and it was taken off to the dump. To Vernon it was inconceivable that the
> whole of someone's life could just be scooped up and wiped away like that.
> Just left in a skip.[30]

To his friends, it seemed that Maureen's death had shown him how serious
his drink problem was. It was not just savage hangovers, lost days, and gloomy
spells of self-disgust, not only the spark for his occasional violent outbursts
(although he never acknowledged those anyway)—it could actually kill.
The end of Maureen's life, her books hauled away to the dump, was a stark
warning, and for a while he cut back on his drinking. Again. But only for a
while.

III

Certainly, whatever good intentions about drink that he might have had
were ancient history by 4 November 1991, when he was invited to a dinner
party being given in Otley by a woman he knew. One of her friends, a primary school teacher called Jo Peters, would call and pick him up, she said,
so that he wouldn't have to drive. As it turned out, she not only drove him
there, but brought him home as well. And she would be with him until the
day he died.

> When I brought him back, he was so paralytic that he couldn't speak. I
> asked him if he'd like me to make him a cup of tea or coffee or something,
> and he just waved towards a cupboard. I opened it, and there was a bottle of
> whisky. I poured myself quite a large one—I hadn't been drinking all
> evening—and a small one for him, and we sat and drank those, before he
> went to bed and I went home. I knew he wouldn't remember anything the

next day, so I left my name and telephone number on the table—a bit forward of me really, I suppose.[31]

Jo had two children at home, and Vernon had begun to enjoy the independence of living alone, so it was several years before they actually moved in
together.

They each kept their own house, but everyone knew that they were
partners—and the same jealousies that had plagued Vernon's other relationships began to flare up here as well:

> He was quite possessive—he didn't like your attention to be divided. He
> certainly wasn't an easy person—he was very much all-or-nothing, and you
> really had to give him your all. I think there was a degree of insecurity
> there—he could easily feel very undermined, even though most of the peo-
> ple who have been with him have been totally obsessed with him. I know
> I was.[32]

But they suited each other. Vernon would work alone at home, but he
would read over to Jo—who wrote poetry of her own—whatever he had
written. Around the time they met, *A Time for Fires*, was coming out, dedicated to his friend Martin Reed, another person with whom he could discuss his poetry at length. The mood of many of the new poems was
backward-looking, nostalgic, reflecting the way Scannell was feeling when
he met Jo.

'The Party's Over', for instance, introduced in the book as 'A Kind of
Elegy', tells a story he had heard about a gathering at Dannie Abse's home
in Wales, back in the days when Vernon was still with Olwen. The Welsh
poet John Tripp had been invited, and refused to leave when the party finished, seeking out half-empty bottles of wine until they were all finished.
'John was with a very proper local councillor, very much a Tory lady', says
Abse. 'She was horrified when John finally decided everything *was* over,
opened his flies and stood there pissing in the front garden.' Scannell had
been told the story, although he was not at the party, and described the
scene, the poet standing 'as if carved in wood' until:

> The silver glitter of his piss began,
> Rose arching from his centre to descend
> On unaffronted hollyhocks and on
> A world where all the parties had to end.[33]

That was the world Scannell was living in—one where the parties seemed to
have ended and it was time to go. Other poems in the collection, like

'Escapologist' and 'Bobbie', look back to a mythical time of simple working-class generosity, of innocent nights spent dancing and drinking, a time when there was no drunkenness, no fighting:

> The days of sunshine and sweet showers,
> The dancing days of silver saxophones
> And roses.[34]

The poems that do focus on the present, like 'Shadow on the Snow' or 'Old Shaver', tend to consider old age with a wry regret. The tall soldierly shadow cast on the snow, 'Impervious to pain, not aged at all', is a sad contrast to the 'scarecrow body, gaunt and flensed' of reality; the misted mirror in the bathroom, once the Old Shaver has removed his glasses, seems to smooth away his wrinkles and make him look younger. In the end, however he has no choice but to:

> Replace my spectacles to face the day
> And what is there, and always had to be.[35]

The rueful courage of the response, reminiscent of Philip Larkin, does not hide the regret: these are the poems of a man who has known health and strength, and feels his vigour slipping away from him.

A trip to London a few months later reflects a similar sadness: he called in at one of his old haunts, The George, close by the BBC, where he had drunk with Anthony Thwaite, George MacBeth, Louis MacNeice, Joe Hone, and the rest. Alone now, he had a couple of drinks, but the magic had gone: 'I sat in a gloomy corner like a ghost. Too many memories. Too many ghosts.'[36] A meeting a couple of days later with the old boozer Jeffrey Bernard, the man he had once knocked down in a midnight scrap, did nothing to improve his frame of mind:

> That handsome, rather dapper little man is now prematurely aged, white haired, ravaged and unable to walk. His hands shook so violently as he tried to light a cigarette or sip a vodka that he could have been miming a frenzied arpeggio on an invisible piano. He was sad, gloomy, in a lot of pain and discomfort, and almost certainly not long for this world. I felt impotent to help.[37]

Bernard was ten years younger than he was, but perhaps there was an uneasy feeling mixed with Vernon's sympathy that he might just be looking at a vision of his own future. That was the sort of dejection that meeting Jo helped to rescue him from.

She was the grandmother of little Rosie. 'Vernon loved having her about, and he was a natural with young children', Jo says now.

> He did not set out to entertain her—I think he thought that was my role—but he really enjoyed the funny things she said and did, especially when she was about three or four, and so uninhibited and original.[38]

Even so, the relationship with Jo was not always the sort of mellow, peaceful, even restful affair that a man approaching seventy might be assumed to be looking for—Vernon was too complicated a character for any such easy happy ending. The flashes of jealous rage were still there, and the way they had met can have left Jo in no doubt about the kind of hard drinker that she was taking on. It was a volatile, highly charged partnership. Over the years there were, predictably, occasional sudden outbursts of violence, although this time, whether because Jo was ready to stick up for herself, or simply because Vernon was older and less physically dominant, they did not always end the way they had in the past. There were more nights of 'awfulness', with Vernon punching Jo in the face, and bitter insults and recriminations flung between them; one fight ended with Vernon picking shards of a smashed whisky glass out of his head. A couple of times, Jo walked out, apparently for good—but the fact that she came back and stayed with him until his death seems to be a testament to her love, to the strength of their relationship, and to the good qualities in him to which she and all the women with whom he spent his life bear witness:

> He shared his whole life—he would ask me about his poems, and talk to me about anything and everything in his past. He was very easy to be close to—it was very relaxing and nothing was ever a crisis, as long as he wasn't drunk. If he was happy and relaxed, he was an easygoing, pleasant companion. We laughed all the time—he was just a person you were happy to be with.
>
> His drinking was much more under control when I knew him. Reading his diaries from the sixties, it sounds like someone fighting alcohol all the time, but by the time we met, he drank moderately unless he was very happy or very miserable. We both certainly drank far too much in between those times, but that was because we enjoyed it. We drank a lot, but not unhappily.[39]

Vernon poured his heart into his diaries: 'I love her so much and I'm sure that this is really my first experience of wholly committed love for a woman. It is wonderful and terrifying.'[40] This comment may sound familiar—he had presumably forgotten that he had ever said that sort of thing before, and Jo had at that stage no reason to know—but another entry reflects a moment of intense and passionate love. Perhaps the fact that it took place in such an unpromising setting as the refreshment room at Leeds station only re-emphasizes the strength of the emotion:

> Jo sat down at a table with our bag and books, and I queued for coffee. I was waiting at the counter with a few other customers and I looked over at Jo who was looking at the newspaper. It was a curiously epiphanic experience. I felt a sudden piercing sweetness of gratitude and love. She looked so lovely and somehow composed, so utterly what she is and what I love and treasure. I felt blessed.[41]

It was a particularly poignant moment, not just because of that sudden flood of feeling, but also because it came just before a tragedy. Jo was about to help Scannell through one of the most crushing blows of his life.

IV

They were travelling to London for Kit Wright's fiftieth birthday party—at which, Scannell says in passing and quite predictably, 'I got pretty drunk, of course.' The next morning, struggling with the inevitable sore head, he tel-ephoned Angela, who was looking after Hetta back in Otley, to say that they would be home later than arranged:

> She seemed very odd and mysterious—almost as if she had the murderous hangover that I was contending with—and she once or twice asked me if I'd heard from anyone. Naturally I said 'Who?' and she said, 'Anyone from Dorset?' I began to feel uneasy. Then she said, 'Let me speak to Jo.' Jo took the telephone and after a short interchange hung up. Then she gave me the news.[42]

Vernon's son Toby had been killed in a motorcycle accident with his girl-friend, Alison. Written alongside the diary entry about the call is a short, sad, and factual note in very small letters: 'He was thirty-four. Alison was 24.' The memories of the death of Toby's brother, the baby Benjamin, more than three decades earlier, were still strong: now the second of the twin boys was dead.

The funeral was held just over a week later, at the little parish church of St Nicholas in Nether Compton, Vernon standing with his estranged wife Jo and the children as a family again. The church was packed, with more mourners following the service outside, through loudspeakers—the adagio from Max Bruch's violin concerto, Shakespeare's 'Fear no more the heat o' the sun', Dvorak's cello concerto. But there was little comfort to be had:

> The burial service was anguish, terrible. The sun hammered down. There was the sweetness of the scores of wreaths as well as the scents of summer that would have been there anyway. Toby was put in the ground. We all went back to Folly and drank and ate and talked, quite a lot, about Toby and Alison.[43]

There was a day to recover, and then he travelled back to Otley, leaving Jo Scannell and the children, and returning to Jo Peters. She had stayed behind, knowing that this was a time for the family: but now he needed her support as never before:

> Dear Jo had cleaned the house, put fresh garden flowers on the table. That evening she brought food round, salad, milk and fruit. [44]

The only way Vernon knew to respond to grief was to write about it: but in the dark days following Toby's death, he had realized that words, perhaps for the first time in his life, would betray him:

> I can't say anything about Toby. Any attempt to articulate grief and shock must—especially for somebody whose trade is writing—become self-conscious and—God forgive us—begin, despite all efforts to avoid this, to become 'literary'. The only honest expression of grief must be solitary and wordless; maybe a moaning or sobbing, or just a silent huddle of misery.[45]

He wanted to get back to his writing, but all he wanted to write was a poem about his son. 'I don't know whether that is possible but I think I should try.'[46]

It was another three years before he could produce a poem about Toby that he was prepared to see in print. When he did, as he explained powerfully and movingly in his diary, the first raw shock of grief had eased, to be replaced by a deeper, calmer pain:

> Toby will have been dead for 3 years next month…In all that time he has been absent from my thoughts for many days; I feel guilty but not very, I can't really analyse my feelings. Certainly not anger and not the kind of sadness that one feels at fictional, theatrical, operatic deaths. It is more a kind of resigned sickness at the arbitrariness of his death. And, I think, some horror at the fact of mortality.[47]

But the poem that he wrote, 'Good Grief', seems to bear out his original fears that any writing about his son's death might prove to be 'self-conscious and...."literary"'. It opens at with 'the fragrant rites, / The flowers and summer dresses' of the funeral, but, picking up a thought from his diary that 'true mourning, I believe, must be a drab and solitary experience, out of earshot of the Grand Masses, Te Deums, etc', it insists that 'Grief, true grief, is scentless, drab, elsewhere.'

The poem is clever and tightly argued, but its concluding lines, presenting:

> The grief that does not heal or mitigate
> The pain of loss, yet must be understood
> As necessary and will predicate
> Its cauterizing hurt as final good.[48]

seem oddly theoretical, unconvincing and passionless. Scannell is trying to convince himself, and it shows: it is, in fact, a very un-Scannellish description of how grief might work.

But 'Good Grief' was not the first poem he had written about the tragedy. Earlier, less than a month after Toby's death, he had written another poem, which he never published and which, in contrast, provides a dramatic and moving exploration of his own feelings. It is titled simply 'In Memoriam Toby Scannell 1960–1994', and, like the later poem, it opens with the funeral:

> Now all the words, like last year's leaves
> Rustle senseless in the dirt,
> These strings and woodwinds adumbrate
> Something of our grief and hurt.[49]

The rustling of the leaves, with the brutal phrase 'senseless in the dirt' shockingly prefiguring the body in the ground, is contrasted later in the poem with the 'perfect silence' of the grave itself, and with the sound of the music which, as in 'Good Grief', fails to ease his pain. But the anguished insistence that 'Something of him must survive / More than these tears that blur and smart', leads, at its bleakest moment, to a partial resolution:

> Once more I turn to music which,
> Affirming nothing, never lies;
> Transmuting joy and pain it soars
> Beyond terrestrial compromise.
> At last the shimmering echoes fade,
> All hope of solace seems withdrawn;
> And then, through mist, I see him stride
> Towards me, handsome as the dawn.

It is a very limited consolation, drawn, at least partly, from the poet's own need. Toby is seen through mist, not clearly; his appearance is compared to the dawn, which is beautiful but essentially transitory; though he 'strides towards' the poet, there is no suggestion of any mystical reunion. The figure in the mist is vision, not reality. Immediately after writing 'In Memoriam', Scannell was dismissive about it: it was, he said in his diary, 'simple, and I suspect not very effective. Perhaps I shall one day write something more complex and more accurate, but this will have to do for the time being'. But it is the simplicity and directness of the poem, raw and unpolished as Scannell's own grief, that makes the poem so powerful and so moving.

Only a few days before Toby's death, he had been worrying again that his work seemed to be unappreciated—now, at one of the few times in his life when that seemed unimportant, there was a call from the *Sunday Times* to say they wanted to print one of his poems, and another from the poetry magazine *Stand*. Then there was a reassuringly glowing review in the *Irish Independent* of his recently updated *Collected Poems 1950–1993*. The poet Anthony Thwaite, an influential figure in literary circles, had already praised the book in the *Sunday Telegraph*, writing about Scannell's 'unfairly shrouded talent';[50] now, in the *Irish Independent*, the Irish poet, writer, and broadcaster Rory Brennan welcomed it as a 'marvellous' book that should be 'greeted by showers of tickertape'. Scannell was 'scandalously undervalued', he added:

> It is a serious question how our culture can devalue abundant talent and reward the execrable... The combative, wry, wit-riddled work of Vernon Scannell is astonishing in its inventive range and constant virtuosity.[51]

At any other time of his life, Scannell would have been delighted by the praise, and would even have gained a measure of grim satisfaction from the acknowledgement by two other poets of standing that his work deserved more appreciation than it received.

Now, though, none of it mattered.

V

That summer, Vernon and Jo went to Paris for a week—the first of several such trips over the next few years. Strolling around La Musée de l'Orangerie among the Cézannes, Soutines, Matisses, and Renoirs was a calming experience, and then there were the little bookshops of the Boulevarde St Michel—'Bought a nice copy of Maupassant's *Une Vie*'[52]—and the Musée Picasso. There were, too, to judge from Vernon's account of a slightly later trip, less elevated pleasures of Paris to be enjoyed, even if only at a distance:

> Just sitting around in—or rather outside—cafés, sipping Ricard and cold beers and—speaking for myself here—eying the inimitably *roulant* bottoms of French women as they walk. Had some good meals, too.[53]

They came home rested and revived: Otley, it seemed, could be just as relaxing as Paris, if without the *roulant* bottoms:

> Jo and I spend our time doing crosswords, watching a bit of TV, boozing and making love. It is a very agreeable way to pass the time, but if I don't do some work soon, I think guilt will start to nibble.[54]

Such blameless leisure couldn't last, of course—a night out together at a local Chinese restaurant a couple of days later, followed by an unsteady progression home via the Bay Tree and The Swan, to a half-litre bottle of Famous Grouse, culminated in a furious row in which Jo hurled a whiskey glass into the fireplace.

> A horrible night of which I remember little. I don't know how things are going to work out, but I'm apprehensive.[55]

Another three days on, all was peace and love again:

> Jo and I seem to be restored to complete—well, almost complete—harmony. We are wonderfully together I hope.[56]

That was a fairly frequent pattern for Vernon and Jo—spells of mellow affection, interspersed with sudden blazing arguments which vanished, generally, as quickly as they had blown up. At least they could laugh about it: for his birthday the following January, Jo bought him a set of four glass whisky tumblers. They probably needed new ones.

Vernon was also trying manfully to laugh about his declining health. One week his knee was bad, then it was his back—'I am an old wreck. Send for the Inspector of Wrecks!'[57]—then he was off to see 'a new medico who looked about seventeen and was called Peacock'.[58] But there was nothing funny about the breathing problems that he was suffering. For several years his wheezing chest had sounded, as he said, like an old Wurlitzer: the years of heavy smoking had caught up with him:

I have a nasty feeling that I must reconcile myself to becoming one of those poor old crocks I used to feel sorry for as they limped or shuffled or bow-leggedly staggered their way round the streets…

My hand is shaking quite badly. I have difficulty holding the pen and I'm getting this down only with difficulty. Terbutaline seems to help my breathing but causes this nervous trembling and, I suspect, the inability to concentrate. The Tylex tablets help the spinal pain but cause constipation. Choices, choices![59]

There is real fear behind the forced jocularity—a fear that would haunt his remaining years, not so much of death as of weakness, sickness, debility, and age. But despite the pain, the drugs, and the breathing difficulties, he was still writing poems, sitting most mornings at the table in his cluttered and untidy kitchen. By September 1995, his new collection was ready to send to the publisher.

It was called *The Black and White Days*, a name suggested by a question from one of Jo's pupils at the primary school where she taught. She had been talking about her childhood, and one of the pupils had asked her, 'When you were young, Miss, was that the black and white days?'[60] The question suggested to Scannell a way of expressing, affectionately, the distance between memories of his youth and the unfamiliar and not entirely sympathetic world that his readers now inhabited. The title poem recalls not just the musicians in their white tuxedos and black ties, the white 'smooth-as candle flesh' of the singer against her tight black dress, and the black-and-white gangster movies of his youth, but also the journey home at the end of the evening, when along

> The almost silent city street
> > Where all the bars
> And shops were dark and shut, we started back
> Beneath a natural sky, nun's-habit black,
> Sprinkled with salt of stars.[61]

Many of the poems in the collection start from memories of the past: one, for instance, expresses an old soldier's distaste for the formalized and televized remembrance of the fiftieth anniversary of Alamein—grief, after all, whether for a lost son or slaughtered comrades, is an essentially private and instinctive affair. But he finds that he can't scoff:

> Old men, false teeth and medals, pretty toys
> Dangling from their ribbons. Gaunt or stout

Figure 22a–b. Although he had his own 'funk hole in the attic', almost all of Scannell's work was done sitting in the kitchen of the house in North St. (Photo: Jo Peters)

> They wheeze or croak. Fade out. He hears the noise
> Of bugle's rhetoric; then words: *Lest we forget*.
> He snorts; then wonders why his face is wet.[62]

In 'Dirigible', reminiscences of his childhood in Eccles with his father's parents spark thoughts about the crash of the R-101 airship, the shattering of dreams, and the lasting wonder of childhood; 'Magnum Opus', too, considers the arbitrary fragility of hopes and ambitions, recalling drinking sessions in The Victoria in Leeds with the artist Jacob Kramer.

The poem tells of Kramer's plans, sketched in spilled beer on the bar, for a painting that would confound the critics who believe his talent is exhausted, and how, as he described it:

> the barman's damp and grimy cloth
> came swishing down and wiped the lot away.
> 'Drink up now, gents, it's way past time,' he said,
> 'I reckon all of us should be in bed.'[63]

Scannell had told the story before, of course, when he was talking to the BBC about his life in Leeds—but in the poem, he added a telling thought about his own response. For a moment, he said, he could imagine the landscape that was being described and then destroyed:

> I stared and for a spellbound moment glimpsed
> the apocalyptic vision Jacob saw . . .

The thought throws a poignant sidelight on Scannell's anxieties about his own work. Jacob's vision, of course, could refer not just to Kramer's plans for the painting but also to the Old Testament prophet in Genesis, seeing a ladder up to Heaven—the idea of completion, fulfilment. Scannell can see—and, by implication, share—Kramer's conception of a great imaginary work of art, and he could also see it being swept away before it was ever created. That had happened to Kramer's dreams—and Scannell's fear was that it could happen to his own. His fear was that there might after all be no final achievement, no great work to crown his life's efforts.

Even a poem like 'Old Man in Love', which seems to celebrate the good luck and joy of a septuagenarian with a new lover, ends with a shock:

> He capers, sings,
> And all that he can carol, call or cry
> Is love, the rapturous young love that brings
> Him here, to this vertiginously high

> Peak of joy where, arms flung wide like wings,
> Drunk with his luck . . . [64]

So far it seems vibrant, optimistic—but then comes the shock of the final words:

> . . . he swears that he could fly.

The phrase is a delayed-action explosion, that seems at first glance to be a simple, even clichéd, expression of unbridled happiness. It's only a moment later that the reader realizes that, of course, he can't fly, and if he tries, he will crash to the ground. It is a poem about dizzying over-confidence—not a reinvigorated Romeo so much as an elderly Icarus. A poem that appeared initially to be a simple exclamation of delight, the recapturing of youthful passion, collapses at the end in fear and self-doubt. His confidence, whether about his emotions or about his work, was paper-thin.

And yet, Scannell's wit and self-deprecating irony mean that *The Black and White Days* is not, overall, a downbeat or sombre collection. The final short poem, 'Taking a Dive', is an example:

> 'Stand up and be counted!' they said.
> 'Be resolute and strong!'
> There was only one of me
> So the counting wouldn't take long;
> But, all the same, I lacked
> As ever both bottle and clout,
> So I lay down and was counted
> Out.

In another mood, it might be a maudlin lament about loneliness and surrender but as it is, it ends the volume with a wry nod to his fairground boxing-booth past, a half-cheerful, shoulder-shrugging depiction of the poet as Everyman—out but not necessarily down, to reverse the cliché.

Scannell was not optimistic as he sent the poems off to his publisher:

> I'm not at all sure whether the collection hangs together or not. I *think* there are perhaps half a dozen or so good, or goodish, poems. I am very much aware that they speak with an unfashionable cadence, but my hope is that in a couple of decades' time the fashionable will be seen for the tedious garbage it is and at least a few of my things will still offer some kind of pleasure to readers. [65]

But, especially in a man whose health was letting him down so badly, the wry humour of that final poem demonstrated something very close to courage. And that was a quality he was going to need.

VI

Vernon struggled gamely on for the next couple of years, increasingly incapacitated by his failing health. In April 1996 he was prescribed antibiotics and steroids for his wheezing chest. He tried to sound cheerful in a letter to his friend Robert Conquest—'Beginning to feel a bit better, though I don't think Mike Tyson needs to worry too much about my making a comeback'[66]—but then in October he began to suffer intense chest pains— 'squeezing, hard and frightening... It feels like the heart, or like descriptions of heart attacks I've read about.'[67]

A visit for his seventy-fifth birthday from Kenneth, so often a source of reinvigoration, did little to cheer him up: 'I saw him as looking old, hunched, shrivelled and slow moving. I don't like it',[68] he noted in his diary. This time, they didn't even get blind drunk together.

He and Jo were still living in their separate homes, but she was spending more and more time in North Street, caring for him, reading poetry with him in the evenings, and occasionally fighting bitterly with him.

In November 1997, they set off for Nerja in Andalusia, where they planned to escape from the cold and damp of a Yorkshire winter. It was a successful trip, and despite the fact that Vernon was struggling to write much poetry, he began thinking about a completely new venture. It started as a plan for another thriller, set this time on a writing course like the Arvon courses where he had taught so often—but he had hardly begun working on it before he discovered that what he really wanted to write was a satirical novel about contemporary poetry.

The action takes place at a creative writing course at Crackenthorpe Hall, a lightly disguised version of the Arvon foundation's Lumb Bank, and critics had fun identifying the various contemporary writers parodied among the characters—Scannell himself is fairly clearly the hero, Gordon Napier, and the visiting celebrity Zak Fairbrass, with his pronounced Yorkshire accent and his poetic 'explorations of the darker, more destructive forces in nature and in the human psyche' is a dead ringer for Ted Hughes.

Scannell had fun, too, in composing clever pastiches of the various forms of modern poetry that enraged him.

But there was a bitter edge to the humour. His feeling that he was being ignored by the literary establishment was not helped by the appearance of two anthologies of post-war poetry[69] which left him out completely. Anthony Thwaite, at least, was supportive, neatly skewering the assumptions and prejudices that lay behind the selections of poems. He noted that not only Scannell, but also Kingsley Amis, John Wain, Jon Silkin, and Brian Patten had been omitted by the editors of the books. 'Each name I've mentioned is a good deal better than many newer ones in the books', Thwaite wrote. The collections, he said, were 'academic' and 'politically correct', focusing on 'a regiment of younger women; a platoon of vernacular West Indians; and a suave bunch of Borgesian tricksters'.[70] So Scannell was not alone—but he still felt bemused as much as hurt by his omission. He wrote to a friend:

> Apart from a fairly brief period during the sixties and early seventies when I seemed to be quite well thought of, I've been allotted a place in the outer shades with the other minor figures. Maybe that's what I deserve—yet I can't help thinking my stuff is better than, say, McGough, Patten and Wendy Cope to name only a few. Oh well . . .[71]

Perhaps he was particularly sensitive when he wrote that entry, since he had just heard back from the distinguished London publisher Christopher Sinclair-Stevenson, to whom he had sent the typescript of *Feminine Endings*, his Crackenthorpe Hall thriller. Sinclair-Stevenson thought it should be 'more knockabout in the Tom Sharpe mould', which was not what Vernon had in mind:

> I've never read Tom Sharpe, but I've seen the titles on the bookstalls and I've got the impression that they're a kind of literary Carry On movie.[72]

Writing the book had been a struggle, with medications, nebulizers, and frequent visits to the hospital to try and stop his coughing, wheezing, and shortness of breath, and the plan had been to leave for another break in Spain a couple of months after it was finished. However, as he wrote the last chapter, Scannell was also suffering from a sore throat, which the doctor initially diagnosed as thrush—a painful condition, but usually easily treated with antifungal medication. This, though, was more serious:

> The Doctor frowned, more puzzled than alarmed,
> and sent him to a specialist who found

> no thrush had nested snug in his warm throat,
> no feathered flutter, but the hard-clawed crab.[73]

The diagnosis was throat cancer; within five days he was in hospital, and the trip to Spain was cancelled. 'I don't feel very cheerful about all this of course', he noted in his diary with a degree of understatement, 'but there is not much to do except snarl and bear it.' Just a couple of weeks earlier, he had been writing about the death from cancer of Ted Hughes, whom he had known for twenty years; Philip Larkin had died of oesophageal cancer; now, he had every reason to believe, it might be his turn. He started with generous Christmas presents of cash for each of his four children:

> I have a feeling that I'd like to give away as much as I can before I leave these mortal shores—if that's what I shall be doing. I can't help thinking of Philip Larkin, who I think went into hospital for the same kind of thing as I'm going in for.[74]

The diagnosis was quickly confirmed, and the tumour was identified as malignant:

> I'm a bit shaky, I discover, when I pick up my pen. Nerves probably. Am I afraid? Yes, I suppose so. But what I feel is more a grey sadness that I can't go on reading and writing, listening to music, loving my children, Jo, friends. Still, we might lick it yet. Jo is quite wonderful, and I feel a bit guilty at letting her in for all of this.[75]

Later, Scannell would transform those feelings of fear, sadness, and guilt, along with the different experiences of his diagnosis, treatment, and recuperation into a remarkable cycle of poems, *The Year of the Crab*; now, though, he sat down and wrote a hauntingly beautiful villanelle, later published as 'The Ghosts of Love', which casts fascinating sidelights on Scannell's poetry and on his life. The poem was written as an entry for a competition organized by the Keats-Shelley Memorial Association, and its first line, 'In the calm darkness of the moonless nights', comes from Percy Bysshe Shelley's Romantic poem 'Mont Blanc'—a complex and sometimes obscure philosophical reflection which contemplates the human imagination and the awesome, eternal, and potentially destructive power of Nature. Shelley focuses on the River Arve cascading down its Alpine ravine, and fills his poem with overbearing images of strength and power. His frame of reference is vast, from Mont Blanc itself to the mountains piled around its base, from the glaciers creeping downwards to the river rolling finally into the sea.

Scannell, too, considers mankind in the context of eternity and sets human experience against mysterious and irresistible natural forces, but in a far more personal and intimate way. He starts from an idea rather than from any specific event; the powers in his poem are 'the ghosts of love', which remain behind long after the lovers themselves are rendered 'pathetic or absurd'—presumably, like Scannell himself, by illness, age, or some other form of breakdown. Instead of the crash and torrent of the River Arve, 'The Ghosts of Love' describes 'almost silent whisperings', 'sigh and murmured word', and 'calm darkness'. The strict metre and repeated lines of its villanelle form give it an incantatory quality that perfectly catches the semi-religious atmosphere as 'the ghosts of love perform their timeless rites'. It is a calm, quiet, mysterious and—for a man who has just been diagnosed with a painful disease that is likely to kill him—remarkably serene poem:

> Though carnal vases may be smashed, their plight
> beyond all aid, pathetic or absurd,
> in the calm darkness of the moonless nights
> the ghosts of love perform their timeless rites.[76]

Lovers, it says, may be destroyed, but love itself lives on.

It is not just the courage of Scannell's response to his own likely death that is remarkable, but the oblique, thoughtful, and deeply imaginative expression of that courage. It is, above all, the courage of a poet: he is not simply describing his own emotions in the 'Ghosts of Love', but drawing on them to create a poem of universal relevance. Less than three months earlier, he had been complaining in his diary that he was going through a 'sterile period', when he had nothing to write about and no energy to write anyway.[77] These fears that his poetic talent was drying up, along with the recurring doubts about the value of his work, would never leave him, but 'The Ghosts of Love' marked the start of an astonishing outpouring of poetry in the last painful and difficult years of his life.

VII

For now, though, the concentration was on his cancer and treating the tumour that threatened to kill him. At the end of December, he went to Leeds's Cookridge Hospital to have a mask made so that the radiotherapy could be targeted precisely on his throat.

I was x-rayed and clamped down on the table with my head fixed on a kind of execution block. From what the doctor said, the treatment is going to be tough—taste buds destroyed, salivatory glands too, internal and external soreness, no appetite etc. Oh well...[78]

There were several weeks in hospital and repeated doses of radiotherapy. By the beginning of February, its unpleasant effects were beginning to be clear:

My mouth is dry and unpleasantly tasting, and everything I try to eat is slightly bitter but otherwise tasteless. The skin on my neck and jaws is itching and sore. And this is only the beginning of *la saison en enfer*. The future is bleak.[79]

Two days later, he noted that he was eating less and less, and managing only a tiny quantity of liquid:

The effects of the treatment are even worse; when I woke up, my mouth tasted as if I'd been chewing putrescent fish all night.[80]

But all the time he was storing up memories, even struggling to write new poems. In April, the *Times Literary Supplement* published 'On the Oncology Ward'—so quickly that he wondered darkly whether they 'wanted to get it into print before I became a ghost'.[81] Later, those memories of the taste of rotting fish would return in 'The Treatment', another poem in the *Year of the Crab* cycle:

His mouth, a little dungeon, dark and dry
is haunted by the vile, insistent shade
of putrefying fish...[82]

By March, back at home now, there were tiny signs of improvement—a drop of Scotch in his glass of water when Kit Wright came to visit him, or a bit of toast and scrambled egg that 'tasted and felt like old string'.[83] That same month, he was strong enough to slip out of the house to buy Jo a box of chocolates and a card for her birthday. In August, another examination at the hospital brought the welcome news that the tumour was gone, although he remained weak and ill, both from the after-effects of the treatment and from a recurring chest infection:

I weighed under ten stone this morning, and I am beginning to look like an anorexic patient. For the first time in my life I feel really old. Almost with disbelief I see and feel myself doddering across the room, holding onto furniture to keep my balance. I see a frail old man in a story, not fiction alas.[84]

But by the end of the year, he was fit enough to travel with Jo to London for a party being given by the Royal Society of Literature, where he met many of his old friends such as Kit Wright, Peter Porter, Anthony Thwaite, and Dennis Enright. He drank only watered-down wine, and left with Jo before the meal to eat quietly together at a nearby Italian restaurant. A year after his operation, he was still weak and frail, but he was also fit enough, at last, for the long-delayed trip to Andalusia with Jo—the trip he had feared he might never make.

The first poem in the *Year of the Crab* series described the cancellation of their planned trip when the cancer was diagnosed: the final one, 'Postscript: Andalusian Afternoon', focuses on one moment when, the treatment over, they are sitting at last on the balcony of their room in Spain. Schubert is playing in the room behind them, and they are watching two children with a dog and a balloon in the street below. The music, sun, the sound of laughter, and the children playing combine to form an intensely moving image of momentary, fragile happiness. He has survived— for now:

> And this slight incident, without intent,
> is beautiful, this moment in a burnished afternoon
> in a lofty room in southern Spain
> will be remembered with that nimble tune,
> black glossiness of dog and pink balloon,
> and if a whisper of uncertainty is heard
> between the scherzo and the rondo it affords
> a glint of seasoning, a piquancy,
> which makes the mortal moment more their own.[85]

The paradox that the inevitability of Death makes life more precious had haunted Scannell for years. More than twenty years earlier, there was the 1981 diary note about 'mortality . . . the bestower of value', for instance, and in the same year, he had written a sonnet in reply to Donne's famous poem 'Death, be not proud', arguing that Death, 'progenitor of all that is valuable' had actually plenty to be proud about. 'Without that dark majesty, love would lose its potency, indeed everything would become valueless',[86] he argued then. The thought that the ultimate certainty of destruction gives intensity to all the pleasures of life runs like a thread through his poetry, whether it is about a sunny day under the threat of rain ('In Golden Acre Park, Leeds'), children playing ('It's Sure to End in Tears'), or the waxing and waning moon

Figure 23. Vernon in the kitchen at 51 North St with his friend Martin Reed.
(Photo: Not known. Martin Reed collection)

('Lover's Moon'). In 'Andalusian Afternooon' he finally applied the thought
movingly to the possibility of his own imminent death.

As always with Scannell, it's important to be cautious before forcing a
directly autobiographical interpretation onto his poetry—but in this case,
Jo Peters confirms that the poem describes a single, specific event:

> The incident happened exactly as described in the poem. We were staying in
> a small hotel for a few weeks and the room overlooked a quiet street where
> we saw the children and the dog. Even the music is accurate as, hearing it later,
> I would be reminded of that day.[87]

So, unlike 'The Ghosts of Love', this poem starts from a direct personal
experience, but once again, Scannell gives it a universal relevance that
extends to the whole *Year of the Crab* series. It is not simply a description,
but a brief and powerful epiphany, a sudden revelation of the fragility of life,
and of the intensity that awareness gives to the momentary experience. It is
hard to think of a more positive or courageous response to the possibility of
impending death.

'Andalusian Afternoon' focuses on a single afternoon to present a feeling
that had been developing for several months. He had never felt so passionately that emotion was intensified by the prospect of loss as he had since his

diagnosis. Back in September, he had noted a strengthening in his sensitivity to music and poetry:

> I expect it's something to do with my feeling frail and brushed by the wings of mortality but I've noticed that my responses to music and language have sharpened and deepened. Listening to Bruckner's Eighth Symphony and yesterday to Strauss's Alpine Symphony I found myself almost unbearably moved. The same last night, reading *Lycidas* and some of *Paradise Lost*.[88]

A few months later, with the coming of spring, he found the same was true of a simple walk in the fields:

> I have never before enjoyed the late spring flowers and blossom so much. I don't know whether things are especially vivid this year or whether they seem so to me because of old age and the relative proximity of no more springs or any other season. For whatever reason even the simplest and most common flowers have this year entranced me with their freshness and brilliance of colour, flowers like dandelions which I've normally taken for granted, have looked radiant and lovely. The celandines and bluebells in the woods above Wharfedale Park were delicious and along the riverbank the forget-me-nots and speedwell were glorious. Cow parsley, and now the flowering hawthorn have ravished me and buttercups and daisies are seen as if for the first time, golden, white and innocent.[89]

He had also been buoyed during the last few months by the appearance of his novel, *Feminine Endings*, and a new collection, *Views and Distances*, both published by the specialist poetry publisher Enitharmon. And of course there was Jo. In *The Year of the Crab*, he wrote about the love and kindness of her care for him when he was at home:

> Where all his nursing will be done
> by unofficial care which, uncomplaining, works
> on every shift with only gratitude for wage.[90]

His feelings for Jo, though, were much more than gratitude. Again, they were sharpened and deepened by the experience he had been through. One night, left alone in the house in North Street after she had gone to look after her granddaughter Rosie, he noted in his diary:

> It is 8pm now and I find I am lonely without Jo and I think of the many years I spent every night—or almost—on my own without feeling loneliness. I suppose one gets used to the company of one's partner—beloved—and feels the absence acutely after the long time of being together. Apart from the time

I was in hospital I don't think Jo and I have spent more than two or three evenings apart in the nine years we've known each other.[91]

It is an expression of mellow, restrained and affectionate emotion far removed from the exuberant protestations of love that had scattered his diary whenever he took up with a new woman. With Jo he had come through not just the cancer and its treatment, but also through the fights, the anger, and the bitterness to a deeply felt and sincere love.

VIII

None of this is to say that Scannell was preparing to go, in the words of Dylan Thomas, 'gentle into that good night', that the anger had left his soul, and that the cancer had turned him into a quiet, tolerant, inoffensive, and benevolent old pushover—a pussy cat rather than a tom cat.

His taste buds had been destroyed by the radiotherapy for his cancer, and he found it difficult to eat anything that had not been mashed or liquidized—and of course, the painful wheezing with each breath continued. The cancer, perhaps, was beaten: now it was his chest that threatened to kill him. Even so, he could still smile ruefully about his plight: after an eye test which showed that he had cataracts, for instance, he noted:

Going deaf, going blind, can't taste, can't smell, can't fuck, can't breathe. Not much fun.[92]

Worse, the experiences of his childhood and his time in the army still gnawed away at him, the blinding flashes of jealousy still exploded in his brain, and the resentment over what he saw as a lack of appreciation for his work still tortured him. But despite it all, he was fit enough for another trip to Spain early in 2001—and another reminder that the old demons from the past were still there. He spent much of his time in Andalusia reading—Tom Wolfe's *The Bonfire of the Vanities*, for instance, and Shakespeare's sonnets—and writing verse. But his diary tells the story of another tempestuous few days which followed a visit from the poet Ted Walker, the man with whom he had paid that last emotional visit to the ageing Edmund Blunden. He had not liked his old friend chatting to his 'beloved'.

Disastrous evening. Much drink taken. I socked Jo . . . I don't know what will happen. The end of the road, I think.[93]

An anguished and bitter little note in Jo's handwriting adds her perspective: 'Just like old times, wandering around Nerja with a split lip and bruises.' And three days later, he writes in a poignant quotation from George Meredith's poem, 'Love's Grave':

> Here is a fitting spot to dig love's grave,
> Here where the ponderous breakers plunge and strike,
> And dart their hissing tongues high up the sand . . .
> . . . No villain need be! Passion spins the plot:
> We are betrayed by what is false within.[94]

Those two last lines sound like an attempted explanation, an admission that something was 'false within', and always had been. It was a dark and frightening end to the holiday—and yet, as she had done before, Jo stayed. No one was digging love's grave this time—but love and violence, for Vernon, had always been closely aligned, and would continue to be so.

That made it fitting that Jeremy Robson should suggest that he should bring out a collection of some of his earlier poems, entitled *Of Love and War*. Alongside some of the old favourites of his readings, such as 'Walking Wounded', 'The Bombing of the Café de Paris', and 'Casualty—Mental Ward', were a number of new poems, including *The Year of the Crab*—eight poems which together, Scannell said, were 'a kind of celebration of the sustaining power of love'.[95] Apart from the memories of battle and of that other war of love and sex in which Vernon felt he was involved, life had thrown a new and terrible subject at him. *The Year of the Crab*, said Anthony Thwaite in the *Sunday Telegraph*, presented 'annotations and explorations of the pain and humiliation of cancer treatment, done with his usual exactness, decency and wry humour'.[96] It was dedicated, of course, 'To Jo Peters, with love'.

But before the collection was published, there was another huge emotional blow for him to take: one Saturday evening in September 2001, there was a telephone call from his sister-in-law Jenny Bain to say that his brother Kenneth had died from a sudden haemorrhage. Only a few hours before, they had been speaking on the phone, and Kenneth had been saying how well he was feeling. He was the older brother who had protected Vernon as a child, the youngster with whom he appeared before the Aylesbury magistrates after their antics on the fire escape of the Bull's Head, the young man with whom he had signed up for the duration at the beginning of the war—and now he was dead.

For years, they had met only occasionally, but Vernon had made a point of introducing his lovers to Kenneth and Jenny, and Kenneth's roistering weekend visits had been legendary for the amount of drink the two brothers managed to put away, for the occasional violence of their drunken arguments, and for the monumental hangovers when, all the fighting forgotten, the closeness of their affection would reassert itself. Kenneth had never had ambitions as a writer, but he shared Vernon's passion for music and literature. He was, as Vernon described in a letter to a friend:

> that most uncommon species, a 'common reader' who reads as much poetry as prose. I mean he's never written a line in his life, nor felt the slightest wish to, never taught English Literature or anything else for that matter, yet has great knowledge and sound judgement of English poetry.[97]

Scannell did not use words like that lightly: Kenneth was the man he loved and respected above all others. Sylvia had died a few years before: now Vernon, ageing, wheezing, and ill, was the only one left of that unhappy, dysfunctional Aylesbury family of the years before the war.

IX

Vernon retained a sense of humour—albeit a decidedly black one—and a quick wit. A month or so after the news of Kenneth's death, after reading Blake and his rather sickly 'Little Lamb, who made thee?' he wrote his own reply:

> Little Lamb, who ate thee?
> Dost thou know who ate thee?
> Bought thee from the butcher's shop,
> Bit by bit, leg or chop;
> Took thy natural clothing, then
> Fashioned it for use by Men;
> Stunned thee with a little gun,
> Made thy blood in torrents run?
> Little Lamb, who ate thee?
> Dost thou know who ate thee?
>
> Little Lamb, I'll tell thee,
> Little Lamb, I'll tell thee:
> He's the one who claims to care
> For harmless creatures everywhere;

> He's the biped carnivore
> Who swallows little lambs galore,
> Breast or shoulder, bit by bit;
> He's the fleshy hypocrite.
> Little Lamb, God help thee;
> Little lamb, God help thee![98]

Around this time, he was still giving occasional readings—one at Knutsford, for instance, went 'extraordinarily well' although the cancer treatment had left him 'croaking like a raven'. He still had the fighting spirit, too, for another trip to London early in 2002, to meet old friends such as Peter Porter, Fleur Adcock, and Hugo Williams and celebrate the hundredth birthday of the *Times Literary Supplement*—but it was a difficult couple of days:

> God, I was glad to be back. I really can't walk more than a few hundred yards without becoming out of breath and staggery.[99]

A couple of days later he struggled out of bed briefly to welcome Nancy, Jane, and John, his grandson Harry, Angela and her partner Richard, and Martin and Ruth Reed for his eightieth birthday party. It was a happy day, with presents from the family and poems in his honour from Kit Wright and Martin Reed, but it wore him out. Three weeks later, he noted in his diary:

> I'm not well now, but not nearly as bad as I was then. I weigh under ten stone and I'm very weak. I managed to walk into Otley to post a letter a couple of days ago, but I felt as though I had completed and broken all records for a marathon. I feel old and debilitated. No doubt about that. However, I'm able to work.[100]

And work he did, despite his physical weakness and his constant fear that his writing days—possibly all his days—were over. He was regularly reviewing poetry and other books for the *Sunday Telegraph*—including a poignant account of a biography of the little-known poet George Barker, who had an education that was 'in every sense elementary', married his first wife when she was pregnant then deserted her shortly after for another woman, and embarked on 'a long and complicated series of amorous escapades and relationships' before settling down in Norfolk in his old age. Scannell knew Barker personally—'not well, but quite as well as I would have wished' and found him 'conceited and narcissistic'.[101] Even so, he must have found his life story uncomfortably familiar, and there is surely a note of personal defiance in his defence of the shambolic, 'lying and blarneying' Barker:

> All through the year of hectic philandering, travel, economic uncertainty and the decline of his standing as a poet, Barker remained true to his Muse.[102]

Of Love and War appeared in the spring of 2002 to respectful reviews in the newspapers, and Scannell's friend Robert Conquest was also appreciative. He and Vernon referred to the book variously in their letters as *Of Lust and Lunacy* and *Of Sex and Strife*, even once as *Fuckin' and Fightin'*, but there was no doubting Conquest's admiration for the collection.

> How good and unusual piece after piece runs—and *The Year of the Crab*—now as a sequence—an astonishing feat. And much also good to see. I don't think anyone does love as well as you do.[103]

Even so, there was a double-edged feeling about the publication of this latest collection. There were new poems to be proud of, of course, but reissuing his old work seemed to suggest that there might be no more to come. He admired the binding, the jacket, and the typeface of the first copies to arrive in the post, and wondered whether this would be his last book.[104] For several months, he had struggled to put words on paper:

> Perhaps I should hang up the ballpoint and settle for an easy life of enjoying others' work. Yet this isn't enough . . . I suppose one hopes for the little miracle, the divine accident, but the hope is withering at present.[105]

That was from the summer of 2001; the following December, he noted that he had produced no verse for six months; and at the end of February, shortly before the appearance of *Of Love and War*, he wondered again whether he should stop trying:

> Yet I sense that would only prolong the block which can probably only be shifted by positive action. Maybe I'm just written out, emptied.[106]

For all his protestations, he couldn't stop. Still he forced himself to sit at his kitchen table, fighting for breath, and struggling desperately to keep writing. Old, tired, and sick, producing poetry—or trying to—was all he had to live for: he, like George Barker, was remaining true to his Muse.

X

About this time, Angela commissioned a portrait of Vernon by the painter Charlotte Harris, who had recently won first prize in the BP Portrait Award at the National Portrait Gallery. At first sight it shows an old man, gaunt and drawn, gazing stoically into the middle distance, one hand resting idly on a book which seems to lie forgotten on his knee. And yet there is strength in the set of the jaw, a certain defiance in the pose, and above all, perhaps, a sense of acceptance.

That's what Harris sensed, as she sat and talked with him and worked on the drawings, sketches, and photographs from which she would produce the finished portrait:

> He had obviously had a long life and an eventful one, and that comes through in the face. He had very expressive features, especially his eyes, and it struck me how gentle he was with his dogs as he sat there stroking them... There was quite a bit of sadness in his eyes, but a really good sense of humour as well. I wanted to catch something of that—in the picture there's a tiny hint of a half smile, a little wry smile. He was someone who could look back at both good events and bad with a quiet sense of humour.[107]

And the poetry he was writing was good: on Christmas Day 2001, for instance, having had his usual lunch of avocado, banana, and yogurt, he finished a 28-line poem, 'Confiteor', which he said dismissively 'might just be readable',[108] but which seems to have inspired a final effort to produce one more collection. He continued to work over the next few months—still regularly complaining that he was written out, exhausted, finished—and a year later, he began going through all this new work and the unpublished pieces of the last two or three years to put another collection together.

The book that resulted, *Behind the Lines*, appeared in the summer of 2004, a poet's despatch from the cliff-edge of life. It was, he believed, 'my new and last collection'.[109] He was a 'fighting observer, a kind of latter-day Ulysses', said the poetry magazine *Acumen*, demonstrating 'incredible determination and strength in a poet's-eye-view of his life experiences'. Scannell was preparing to die, and writing forcefully, passionately, and without a shred of maudlin self-pity about how it feels to look back on life and forward to extinction.

There is, too, no self-consciously patient resignation—in 'Planning the Occasion', for instance, he returns to the theme of private grief and public display, which had so troubled him at the time of Toby's death. The poet is planning his own funeral—something that Scannell resolutely refused to do—and searching for music 'so lovely it will make them weep / a salt monsoon'. He adds:

> grief of that sort isn't very deep,
> and holds some spice of pleasure: so I swear
> they'll have a ball. That's why I'm not resigned
> to not being there, or anywhere at all.[110]

There is no pious or lily-livered resignation here: Scannell is honest about his resentment of approaching death. The sharp observation of 'Planning the Occasion' and the other poems protects them from sentimentality; so does the humour in a poem such as 'A Serious Bitch', in which an apparently light-hearted poem about his dog, Sally, is the vehicle for a profound thought about the knowledge of impending death. The pun in the title—is the 'serious bitch' Sally, or is it Scannell's grumble?—only becomes clear in the last lines:

> I know, and Sally does not, that she
> will die one day:
> this knowledge seems unfair, but to whom,
> I'm damned if I can say.[111]

But it was the earlier poem, *Confiteor*, that spoke most clearly about Scannell's own state of mind. Most of the trials of age, the poem says, might have been predicted years before:

> Blurred eyes and ears;
> scents visit memory, but not the nose;
> no appetite, except for phantom fare;
> this hunger for lost hungers aches and grows;
> dead voices whisper on the moonlit stair.[112]

But he had not foreseen the guilt and regret that go with approaching death:

> this need to give a full account of all
> the lies and selfish cruelties I know
> I have been guilty of, which now appal.

It was a gentle but moving *mea culpa* for 'those mean treacheries and lusts and greeds' of which he was all too well aware he had been guilty. Vernon had not, to put it mildly, always been an easy man to love; he was not one for expansive gestures or expressions of remorse, but over the next few months he would try to make what amends he could in poetry, the only way he knew.

The reviews for *Behind the Lines* must have delighted him—in particular the comment from the poet Sarah Wardle, in *The Observer*:

> Younger poets could learn from his skilled use of form. Here metre and rhyme are not pointless rules, but harmonies and shapes as necessary as the rhythm of nature.[113]

By now, though, his world was rapidly shrinking still further. A letter to the book's publisher, John Lucas, says that he has had to give up his regular poetry round-ups in the *Sunday Telegraph*:

> I'm unable to concentrate owing to ill-health and the various medications I have to take, one of which contains morphine. I'm afraid I've had to give up giving readings, too—a pity because I used to sell quite a lot of books at those dos.[114]

Figure 24. Vernon with his dog Sally, about whom he wrote in his poem *A Serious Bitch*. Sally was the last of a succession of dogs that Vernon kept for much of his life. (Photo: Jo Peters)

Concentrating or not, he was reading *Hamlet, In Memoriam,* and Baudelaire—
even thinking of trying some translations of some of Baudelaire's later poems—
but his breathing was deteriorating rapidly. Now he was restricted to shuffling
from room to room, oxygen cylinders in each one to connect to his nebulizer
to aid his breathing. By April 2005, even that was becoming too much:

> I have had to give up my short walks (or staggers) around the houses and the
> very slightest effort leaves me gasping for air. Yesterday I couldn't face dressing
> and again, this morning (well, noon) I'm in pyjamas and dressing gown.[115]

The powerful, bulging shoulders were now shrunken and bony, his massive
forearms thin and heavily veined. But, though eating and drinking were a
struggle, and writing and reading increasingly difficult, there was, as he had
noted in his diary some time earlier, still music:

> Listened yesterday to the Schubert String Quartet in C, and I thought then—
> and still think—that music is the chief consolation or pleasure available: well,
> music and chilled Guinness.[116]

Putting the drink in the refrigerator, he added in a letter, was, of course, 'a
great insult to the Guinness',[117] but the thought stayed with him, and four
days later, he had worked on it and turned it into a wistful lament. In 'Small
Mercies', published in the *Times Literary Supplement* and later in *A Place to
Live*, he acknowledges that he is 'waiting for the end', and would rather die
with élan from a bullet in the brain or plunging from a mountaintop:

> Yet you and I both know
> that I must stay marooned
> on this bleak isle of impotence,
> to wait here for the finis,
> grateful for God's providence,
> for Schubert and chilled Guinness.[118]

The diary entry, a clear mark to show where the poem has come from, bears
witness to the honesty of the feeling. In other hands, such a verse on such a
subject might drip with self-pity, but the striking final line, with the almost
jocular finis/Guinness rhyme, end it with a light-hearted defiance. The
gradual shutting down of his world is treated with calm irony. It is the
authentic, courageous and witty Scannell response.

By now, he was almost completely dependent on Jo: she liquidized his
food, chilled his Guinness, helped him to have his bath, and brought him the
writing materials with which he now kept in touch with his friends. The

man who could not even fit his own typewriter ribbon had never mastered computers—telling a friend that the Poetry Archive had recorded him reading some of his poems, he added that the reading would go on their website, 'whatever that means'[119]—and he had never owned a mobile phone, but in his old age, letters had become a fragile lifeline.

He had carried on a regular correspondence with the distinguished historian, writer, and poet Robert Conquest since the mid-nineties, exchanging views on poets and poetry. Their tastes had often coincided—Conquest, for instance, referring to a suggestion that Philip Larkin and Ted Hughes represented two distinct types of poetry, had suggested tartly: 'Yes—Larkin for adults, Hughes for adolescents.'[120] Sometimes Scannell's comments were generous—'Keith Douglas is quite simply the finest poet of the Second World War, and I would say at least as gifted as Wilfred Owen'[121]—and sometimes less so—another poet, he describes as 'a complete arsehole'.[122]

He had been exchanging letters, too, with a retired teacher and academic from Sunderland called John Coggrave on similar subjects for some ten years. Now, though, his writing was spidery, scrawled, and sometimes hard to read. 'I hope you'll be able to excuse the wobbly scribble and the dull brevity of this note: I'm scarcely able to lift the bloody pen these days',[123] he told Coggrave. A letter from Conquest in March 2007, by which time Scannell had been in bed for three months, seems to have an almost valedictory note about it—the two men had become firm friends through their correspondence.

> Yes, we do have different backgrounds, experiences, etc. But none of that seems to matter compared with my feeling for you as a poet and as a thought-producer, if you see what I mean—especially when I come across so much ghastly unpoetry and unthought in general.[124]

Another letter, undated, seems to be saying goodbye to his friend, fellow-poet, and publisher Jeremy Robson:

> I think of you and the good days of jazz and poetry very often. Forgive the scrawl: it's the best I can manage…I just wanted to say how much I valued our friendship and thank you for being such a totally supportive and generous publisher.[125]

The sheer physical effort of dressing, struggling down the stairs, and moving from room to room had defeated him, and he had simply decided to stay in bed for whatever time was left to him. He had no energy for reading or, apparently, for writing either. It seemed that this time, the end really had come.

And yet, once he had abandoned the daily physical struggle, he seemed
to find energy for another 'one last effort'. Working from his bed, he gathered together sixteen poems, some from several years earlier, and a few, such
as 'Small Mercies', written more recently, for a hand-printed collection,
A Place to Live. The book, produced in a numbered limited edition by the
craftsman printing firm The Happy Dragons' Press of Essex, gave him an
opportunity to pay some old debts, to make affectionate final gestures to
two people in particular whose lives he had trampled in the past.

In the first poem in the collection, entitled 'Too Late Again', 'the weary
wanderer' lies awake in the dark, waiting for death, aware now that it is too
late to make amends:

> The last sounds die but then, quite unforeseen,
> he hears the first soft chords from far away:
> the wounded music of what might have been.

The copy which he sent to Jo Scannell has the title underlined in the list of
contents, with a simple note in the weak, uncertain hand that had become
his: 'To Jo'. It was not an apology, not a plea for forgiveness—but it was a
heartfelt recognition of what they had meant to each other.

Another poem, 'The Story So Far', begins:

> An ugly old man is in love with a woman
> who is young enough to be his daughter . . .

Is it possible that this woman, who sounds very much like Angela Beese,
could love him in return, the poem asks. It seems impossible, but in the dark
of the night, half-dreaming, she imagines him, 'straight and handsome' in
her arms:

> And are such seemings, then, enough for them?
> It seems, without a doubt, they are. So far.

Again, there is no apology, no effusive expression of regret, but a simple
acknowledgement of what had been.

XI

And now, surely, the story should be over, and the last book written. But at
the end of June 2007, John Lucas, whose Shoestring Press had published

Behind the Lines three years earlier, received in the post what Scannell admitted was a 'very unlikely' proposal:

> When I became bed-ridden about six months ago, I found to my great surprise that I was writing verse again after a long lay-off. I produced these poems—18 of them—in about five months. I'm pretty sure there are no more to come. It occurred to me that these, or some of them, might make a booklet. *Last Post* might do for the title.[126]

This, if anything, was 'the little miracle, the divine accident' that he had hoped for. Lucas was astounded by the poems that accompanied the letter. Among them were some of the best that Scannell had ever written:

> I knew how ill he was, and I was amazed that someone at death's door could write such lucid, marvellously well-constructed poems. I was bowled over by them. They were so accomplished—not at all the poems you might expect from a sick man.[127]

Lucas worked quickly, and *Last Post*, a slim pamphlet of twenty pages, was published in September. Many of the poems, perhaps inevitably, look back over Scannell's life: 'A Few Words to the Not-So-Old', the last poem in his last collection, describes the gradual fading of memory, but ends with the well-remembered smile of a soldier killed more than sixty years before. In 'War Words', news of fighting in Iraq brings back memories of the D-Day landings.

'A Word', which describes the comfort offered by the single word 'Evensong', suggests that Scannell may have been feeling uncertainly towards some religious consolation—he had always been careful not to describe himself as an atheist. 'If people like Pascal, Newman, Valery, Eliot, Auden, Maritain—none of them numbskulls—can believe in [Christianity], it can't be total nonsense', he had told Robert Conquest in a letter some years earlier.[128] But it was to poetry, and to his memories, not God, that he turned in the last months of his life.

Several of the poems in *Last Post* deal squarely with the experience of growing old and dying. 'Missing Things', for instance, charts the life that the poet is regretfully leaving behind:

> Those Paris streets and bars I can't forget,
> the scent of caporal and wine and piss;
> the pubs in Soho where the poets met;
> the Yorkshire moors and Dorset's pebbly coast,

> black Leeds where I was taught love's alphabet,
> and this small house that I shall miss the most.[129]

The poem is calm, measured and wistful, but without self-pity. After his
death, he says, he will know and feel nothing:

> like the stone of which the house is made,
> I'll feel no more than it does light and air.
> Then why so sad? And just a bit afraid?

'Missing Things', one of the most powerfully moving poems in an extremely
evocative collection, received an enthusiastic response when it first appeared
in *The Spectator* in August 2007. Some of the letters were from friends
Scannell had not seen for years, like Alan Millard, headmaster of the village
school in Nether Compton when the children were growing up; others
from complete strangers who had been touched by the quiet, tragic lyricism
of the poem.

Other poems in this final collection seem, like those in *Behind the Lines*
and *A Place to Live*, to be gestures to individual women he has known.
'Black-Out', for instance, the account of a 'young lad of eighteen years'
meeting his girlfriend early in the war, both of them deaf to the threatening sound of distant gunfire, suggests that he was thinking in those last
months of the long-forgotten Barbara, the deserted mother of his first
child.

But only one of those intimate messages stated plainly and openly what
it was: only the brief, simple, and achingly beautiful lyric 'Last Song, for JP'
contains its dedication in the title. Jo Peters had always loved him, occasionally fought with him, and finally cared for him, and now he offered her this
declaration of love from his dark room in the night:

> Then perfect soundlessness presents
> me with the chance to sing
> one small but heartfelt song for you,
> my love, my everything.
>
> I have no wish to trouble you,
> or make you laugh or weep,
> but just to sing you one last song
> before I go to sleep.[130]

Last Post was a collection of poems that were, too, brief and final love letters.
Vernon saw the book, held it, and admired it—even inscribed copies for a

few close friends. He remained mentally alert and demanding about poetry right to the end—Martin Reed's last telephone conversation with him was a forty-minute lecture about where a semi-colon should go in one of Reed's poems—and he was adamant that he wanted to stay at home, not go into hospital again.

And even with *Last Post,* he had not finished. In October, a note to Hugo Williams, poetry editor of the *Spectator*, thanks him for forwarding 'fan letters' about 'Missing Things', and promises to produce some Christmas poems for the magazine. That was one deadline he couldn't meet, but Scannell's last poem, 'For Those Reliefs', appeared posthumously in *Ambit*. It took one more look back at his days as a soldier: only a man who has actually sat under fire in a slit trench, surely, could have the authority to write a poem about the risks of leaving it to creep out at night:

> with paper and entrenching tools
> to leave our dark deposits in the ground,
> no laxative required beyond pure fear.

Certainly only someone with Scannell's black humour and lack of pomposity could finish these final lines with a friend's verdict:

> A learned chap:
> He read them through with care and then he drew
> A deep breath in, expelled it with a sigh.
> 'Won't do,' he said. 'In fact, a load of crap.'[131]

It wasn't, of course, although it wasn't one of his best poems either. On 23 October , he sent the poem to Martin Bax, editor of *Ambit*, with a note: 'Sorry this is so scribbled—I'm in very poor shape and not likely to be around much longer.' It also said that 'For Those Reliefs' was 'definitely my last effort'. On both counts, this time, he was right.

XII

Since he had been ill, Jo had been sleeping in the attic, and early in the morning of 16 November, she heard the television go on in his room—a sitcom, *As Time Goes By*. She went in to see him, but he was quiet, almost asleep. Through the day he gradually got drowsier, and she gave him painkillers for the pain in his chest. In the afternoon, Angela came in to see him, and Jo telephoned his daughter, Jane. It was clear that there was not long to go.

Jo sat with him all day, holding his warm hand under the bedclothes. She knew when he died by the grey pallor of his face, and the gradual cooling of his hand. There would be no more 'final efforts'. It was over.

16

Afterword

Then why so sad?

'Missing Things', from *Last Post* (2007)

Successful poets are not always—maybe not often—successful people.

That's true, of course, in the crude, materialistic sense: writing poetry is seldom a good way to make a living. Vernon Scannell was almost always short of money, struggling to find a balance between the teaching, reviewing, or journalism that would pay the bills, and the poetry that he knew would ultimately define his life.

More importantly, though, it's also true of personal relationships: faithful devotion to poetry above all else may not sit easily with the duties of a lover, a husband, or a father. Poets may be entertaining companions, even easy people to fall in love with, but they are not necessarily a good bet as a lifelong partner. In fact, relationships were always, perhaps, going to be a problem for Scannell. His brutalized, loveless childhood might almost be a textbook example of the way that, as Philip Larkin said, 'They fuck you up, your mum and dad'—although Alan Bennett has pointed out that a writer should not complain too bitterly about that:

> If your parents do fuck you up and you're going to write, that's fine because then you've got something to write about. But if they don't fuck you up, then you've got nothing to write about, so then they've fucked you up good and proper.[1]

The various partners of Scannell's life might have argued with that breezy logic, but he would have understood. For him, poetry always came first, and the bleak years in Ballaghaderreen, Beeston, Eccles, and Aylesbury provided him with an inexhaustible wellspring of emotional experience on which his poetry could draw.

So too, of course, did the various exquisite miseries of his time in the army. Like most people who put on a uniform, he was no hero but a young man who wanted neither to kill nor to be killed, who struggled through as best he could, sometimes frightened, often confused, frequently insubordinate, and generally resentful. Scannell, without doubt, was seriously damaged by the war—the jealous rages, the drunkenness, the violence, and the nightmares are all common enough symptoms of the post-traumatic stress disorder that is the forgotten legacy of combat for many thousands of old soldiers. It was the women he loved who suffered the bruises, the blood, and the tears—but it would be a harsh judge who ruled that Scannell himself was not a victim as well. The scars of war cut deep, and can often be hidden from view.

Scannell freely admitted that he had not been a good soldier, but the war also left him with the lifelong conviction that he had proved himself to be a coward. The vast majority of people in today's generations, never having been under fire, are probably not qualified to have an opinion about that, although we may wonder whether a journey across the D-Day beach and three weeks' fighting in the Normandy hedgerows should not be thrown into the balance. In any case, we have moved on from the days when boys were shot for running away in the trenches, or handed white feathers in the street for not joining up. We like to think we understand more about the way people may behave under the pressure of combat and active service.

And there is, anyway, a different sort of courage to be found in a man who leaves school at fourteen and then educates himself to the degree that Scannell achieved, sitting alone and charting his own course through English literature. If nothing else, his determination deserves to be treated with respect by those who have made the seamless and painless transition from sixth form to university. There is courage, too, in old age: Scannell's resilience in his grim final years as a painful and debilitating disease made its remorseless advance would surely be enough to acquit him of the charge of personal cowardice.

But most of all, what greater courage can be asked of a poet than the courage to keep writing, honestly and truthfully, in the face of approaching death? It may be hard not to smile at the repetitive confidence with which he insisted in his diary, little-boy-crying-wolf-like, that each of four successive books was definitely his last—but his determination to keep writing as his world gradually closed in was remarkable. Often when a terminally ill patient decides to take to his bed, the next step is to abandon hope, turn to the wall, and wait to die—but in Scannell's case, it marked the start of another energetic spurt of writing and, astonishingly, the production of some of his finest work. If poets can be heroes, then that was heroism. Scannell had his petty vanities, of course—which of us does not?—but he never entertained any doubt about what was important to him. This was the last thing that Jo Scannell, the wife he loved, left, but never divorced, told me as I finished writing this book:

> "What an enigma he was! He was the cloth cap and the plummy voice, the Labour Party card and the longed-for middle-class characteristics. The Harris tweed jackets—but he made sure you knew they came from the Oxfam shop. He never really came to terms with his outward attitudes and, if faced with it, he'd just say, 'So what? All I am is in my verse.'

And how will that verse, the whole body of Scannell's work over the sixty years or so of his writing career, survive? The short answer, of course, just a few years after his death, is that it is too soon to say. Reputations come and go. Scannell's collected poems—or at least those written before 1993—remain in print. His work is regularly anthologized, a favourite in books of children's poetry, and featured in various serious collections of the poetry of the twentieth century. He even appears on examination papers—a dubious honour that might have amused him.

Scannell wrote on the big themes—'Death, courage, art, sex. C'est tout!' he once suggested sardonically [2]—but he found them, above all, in everyday life and the experiences of disregarded, forgotten people. He not only understood but instinctively shared the plight of, for example, the jealous husband in 'A Simple Need', the despised stranger in 'Incident in a Saloon Bar', or the miserable bride in 'A Victorian Honeymoon'. The great triumph of the verse he wrote for children and young people is the way that he entered into their emotions and took them seriously. A teenage romance, for Scannell, could be as moving as the greatest of *grandes passions*; he shared with awe in the uncomprehended pain of unrequited love which his five-year-old son describes in 'Growing Pain'.

He had a sharp eye for the significance of the unregarded detail: Proust famously recalled the taste of a *madeleine*, but with Scannell it was the mingled smell of tobacco, wine, and piss in a sleazy Paris bar.[3] Like the child in his poem 'The Gift', he would rather weave his imagination around a collection of clothes pegs than play with a box of finely painted toy soldiers, with all their weapons and equipment; in 'Apple Poem', he sees the orchards hiding within the single fruit.

He never lost his sympathy for the underdog: the resurrection he fore-sees in 'In a City Churchyard' is of a bag-lady, a sleeping drunk, and a little dog that pisses against the gravestones. Like several other poets, he wrote a rejoinder to Frances Cornford's singularly objectionable poem, 'To a Fat Lady Seen from the Train'. He called it 'To a Georgian Lady Poet':

> O Poetry lady who travels first class
> Watching the meadows and trees as they pass
> Why do you sneer, in your silly pink hat
> At the woman in gloves? Because she is fat?
> Or because she wears gloves? I do not see why
> Either could possibly justify
> Your scorn and judgmental, superior pose.
> You've no right at all to talk down your nose:
> There might have been medical reasons for
> Her avoirdupois and the gloves that she wore.
> But there's no excuse for your lofty disdain
> Or the drivel you write as you ride on the train.[4]

It's a squib, scribbled in an idle hour or so in his diary, not a piece of great poetry, but it does give a sense of the flashing contempt with which Scannell responded to an assumption of social, moral, or emotional superiority like Cornford's.

He also demanded the highest standards of those who dare to call them-selves poets. For him, the word was less a job description, more an accolade that should be earned hard and bestowed sparingly. If it sounds like faint praise today to say that he was a master-craftsman, a poet who understood and valued the technical framework of poetry, the demands of metre and the subtleties of rhyme and near-rhyme, it's only in the last few decades that that would have been so. Scannell took the craft of poetry seriously; he believed in the discipline of difficulty, which makes the poet search for the precise word or phrase that he needs, and keeps him honest. Poetry, he believed, should be hard—for the poet.

The one thing that angered him more than slipshod writing or construc-tion was needless obscurity: for the reader, a poem should be clear and lucid. That's not the same as simplistic—Scannell's poems can be read and reread, extra depths of meaning winnowed out of them and the most delicate shades of feeling revealed—but it means that for a newcomer to poetry, it's hard to think of a better place to start.

He had, like most people, a complex mix of faults and virtues—violent bully, loyal friend, scholar, drunk, inspiring teacher, sexual predator, and passionate lover. To love him was never easy—a telling phrase he used in one of his deceptively light-hearted poems.[5] Lives and relationships are complicated, few more so than Scannell's—but that a man should be so long and loyally loved by those whom he has hurt surely says much about him, and about them as well. He could be romantic, generous, kind, cruel, deceitful, and bitingly honest, both in his life and in his poetry.

Several years after his death, Angela Beese summed up the one passion that ran consistently through his life from his earliest days:

> Poetry was Vernon's religion, his faith if you like, secure and permanent, even in his darkest moments. Whether he could make it or not, it was always there in the books on his shelves, the books that were always with him, and still with him when he died—the books in *Last Post*.
>
> Nothing, no human, mattered to him as much. Poetry was his wife, his mistress, his mother, his father—any female or indeed male role you can think of.[6]

He knew it. 'I want to be a poet,' he told the court martial trying him for desertion. In his diary, he scribbled, 'I'm no novelist. Or anything else, I suppose, except, just possibly, a poet. Once in a while.'[7] At other times, drunk and depressed in the bleak hours of the early morning, he would scrawl in his diary that he would never achieve that aim, that he was giving up—but he never did.

All he was was in his verse. First, last, and always, he was a poet. He had earned the accolade.

Notes

CHAPTER 1

1. 'A Note for Biographers', from *Walking Wounded*.
2. *Drums of Morning*, p. 9.
3. Conversation with Jenny Bain.
4. *Diaries*, 12 January 1954.
5. *Diaries*, 12 January 1954.
6. *Drums of Morning*, pp. 8–9.
7. Conversation with Jenny Bain.
8. Conversation with Jenny Bain.
9. 'A Small Hunger', from *Behind the Lines*.
10. *The Tiger and the Rose*, p. 68.
11. *The Tiger and the Rose*, p. 22.
12. *The Tiger and the Rose*, p. 22; also see 'Miss Steeples', from *Of Love and War*.
13. *The Tiger and the Rose*, p. 22. 'Miss Steeples', by then Mrs Ella Reeves, wrote to Scannell after reading about herself in *The Tiger and the Rose*, and they carried on a friendly correspondence for some ten years.
14. Published in the collection *The Clever Potato*.
15. *Drums of Morning*, pp. 11–12.
16. *The Tiger and the Rose*, p. 69.
17. *The Tiger and the Rose*, p. 73. James Bain went to work with a firm of seaside photographers owned by his wife's cousin. The company still exists, now named Wrates Scholastic Photographers Ltd, and run by the fifth generation of the Wrate family.
18. *The Tiger and the Rose*, p. 74.
19. *The Tiger and the Rose*, p. 74.
20. Undated letter, Leeds University Archive.
21. From *Grandpa Bain*, undated, unpublished poem, Leeds University archive.
22. *Vernon Scannell—a Writer in Otley*, privately produced video interview by Martin Reed.
23. *The Tiger and the Rose*, p. 77.

CHAPTER 2

1. 'The Child Contemplates God', from *Graves and Resurrections*.
2. *Drums of Morning*, p. 13.

3. *Drums of Morning*, p. 28.

4. *Drums of Morning*, p. 24.

5. *Drums of Morning*, pp. 14–17.

6. *Drums of Morning*, p. 27.

7. *Diaries*, 22 May 1986.

8. *Drums of Morning*, p. 26.

9. *Vernon Scannell—a Writer in Otley*, privately produced video interview by Martin Reed.

10. Perhaps the Old Man was not alone. More than seventy years later, in 2005, the Ministry of Defence issued an order requiring members of the Armed Forces to wear underpants when going for fittings for their uniforms. 'It's always been the macho thing not to wear underpants', commented one senior officer.

11. *Drums of Morning*, p. 29.

12. *Drums of Morning*, p. 22.

13. *Drums of Morning*, p. 33.

14. *Diaries*, 10 April 1951.

15. *Drums of Morning*, p. 34.

16. *Drums of Morning*, p. 109.

17. In 'Knockout', for instance, in *Behind the Lines*.

18. Interview with Jim Greenhalf, published in the *Bradford Telegraph and Argus*, 25 August 1987. Mills, who died in 1965, fought the American Lesnevich twice for the world title. In the first bout, in May 1946, he was knocked down four times before the fight was stopped, but he won the second two years later, knocking Lesnevich down twice and winning the fight on points.

19. 'Mastering the Craft', from *Winterlude*.

20. 'Comeback', from *The Winter Man*.

21. 'Last Attack', from *Winterlude*.

22. *Diaries*, 18 February 1985.

23. *Diaries*, 20 November 1971.

24. *Diaries*, 10 April 1951.

25. *Argument of Kings*, p. 82.

26. *Argument of Kings*, p. 83.

27. *Drums of Morning*, p. 32.

28. *Diaries*, 28 January 1952.

29. *Diaries*, 20 May 1980. Raphael did use the quote, but it comes originally from a 1920s detective story, *The Copper Bottle*, by E. J. Millward.

30. Conversation with Jenny Bain.

31. Letter from Elsie Bain to VS, May 1975, Leeds University Archive.

32. Conversations with Pat Cornford, Tina Daubney.

33. 'Dockery and Son'.

34. *The Tiger and the Rose*, p. 78.

35. *Drums of Morning*, pp. 74–5.

36. *Coming to Life in Leeds*, BBC Radio broadcast, repr. *The Listener*, 22 August 1963.

37. Quoted in *Drums of Morning*, p. 75.
38. *Drums of Morning*, p. 46. Most people grow out of Brooke, and later, in his diaries, Scannell returned more acidly to his boyhood hero: 'Was Brooke really *always* laughing? It occurred to me that laughter is really one of the nastiest of human noises—the laughter of the mindless yobs, the studio audiences, the Yuppies, the "county families, baying for broken glass". My bet is that Brooke did laugh a lot, and loudly, as many humourless people do' (*Diaries*, 16 July 1988).
39. *Drums of Morning*, p. 61.
40. 75 p, or about £41 at today's rates.
41. For comparison, a farm labourer in 1937 would have earned about £1 15s. (£1.75) for a fifty-hour week.
42. Just over £11.
43. *The Tiger and the Rose*, p. 80.
44. *Drums of Morning*, p. 75.
45. 'The Old Books', from *Walking Wounded*.
46. *Drums of Morning*, p. 77.
47. Lawrence was another writer, like Brooke, with whom Scannell fell out of love later in his life. In *Drums of Morning* (p. 77) he says that as a sixteen-year-old boy, he thought Lawrence 'a great writer, a poet, a prophet, a sage', but in his mid-sixties he described him as 'aggressive, vain, cruel and very close to madness . . . he does grossly over-write and his attitudes are intolerable' (Letter from VS to Emma Kilcoyne, 21 June 1988).

CHAPTER 3

1. *The Tiger and the Rose*, p. 22. Later in his life, Scannell was mortified to have to call Barbara as a witness in a court case, and it seems likely that he changed her name in the books in order to avoid further embarrassment for her.
2. 'Black-Out', from *Last Post*.
3. 'Black-Out', from *Last Post*.
4. £1.25, or just over £66 at today's rates.
5. *Bucks Herald*, Friday 5 April 1940.
6. *Drums of Morning*, p. 132.
7. *Drums of Morning*, pp. 134–5. That is the way Scannell chose to remember the interview, with himself in control. A diary entry years later, on 29 December 1961, suggests that the conversation may have been more one-sided: 'Worked as a junior clerk for a firm of accountants. Fired in 1940.'
8. *Drums of Morning*, p. 151.
9. *Drums of Morning*, p. 141.
10. *Drums of Morning*, p. 140.
11. *Drums of Morning*, p. 154.
12. *Drums of Morning*, p. 171.

13. *Drums of Morning*, p. 174.
14. *Drums of Morning*, p. 174.
15. *Drums of Morning*, p. 159.
16. *Bucks Herald*, 4 October 1940.
17. £1.75, or about £90 at today's rates.
18. £1.05, or about £53 at today's rates.
19. Letter from VS to Rayner Heppenstall, BBC producer, 18 February 1967, BBC archive.
20. In *Drums of Morning*, pp. 178 ff.
21. About £20,000 at today's values.
22. *Drums of Morning*, p. 186.
23. Around £1,900 at today's rates.
24. Kenneth's signing up papers give the same birth-date as Vernon. The deception didn't work: Kenneth's pre-war experience with a photographer meant he was swiftly transferred to a photographic interpretation unit in an Army Field Survey Company. The two brothers did not see each other again until after the war.

CHAPTER 4

1. The novels were *The Fight* (1953), *The Wound and the Scar* (1953), *The Big Chance* (1960), *The Shadowed Place* (1961), and *The Face of the Enemy* (1961), and the poetry books *Graves and Resurrections* (1948), *A Mortal Pitch* (1957), and *The Masks of Love* (1960). The collection *A Sense of Danger* appeared in 1962.
2. VS to George MacBeth, 8 March 1962, BBC archive.
3. 29 December 1962: *Tightrope Walker—a poet's diaries of the sixties*, unpublished typescript by VS. 'Glass-house' was a slang term for a military prison, taken originally from the Detention Barracks in Aldershot, which had a glazed roof.
4. *Vernon Scannell—a Writer in Otley*, privately produced video interview by Martin Reed.
5. Information from Ms Annie Scott, Aberdeenshire Cultural Co-ordinator at Duff House.
6. 'Perimeter Guard', from *Soldiering On*.
7. *Argument of Kings*, p. 17.
8. Information from Mrs Isobel Alexander of Banff.
9. *Argument of Kings*, p. 18.
10. 'Bayonet Practice', from *Soldiering On*.
11. 'John Short, the Lost Poet', *The London Magazine*, 34(11) (February 1995).
12. *Coming to Life in Leeds*, BBC Radio broadcast, repr. *The Listener*, 22 August 1963.
13. *Argument of Kings*, p. 112.
14. *Vernon Scannell—a Writer in Otley*, privately produced video interview by Martin Reed.
15. *Diaries*, 17 October 1998. The book in question was *A Pacifist's War*, by Frances Partridge.

16. The phrase 'take a powder', common in 1920s American gangster films, meant to run away. It referred originally to women leaving a group to powder their noses.

17. Bierman and Smith, *Alamein: War Without Hate*, p. 222.

18. Churchill had reminded the Canadian Parliament in 1941 that the defeated French generals had warned that Britain, fighting alone against the Nazis, would have its neck wrung like a chicken. 'Some chicken, some neck', he scoffed.

19. Cecil Woolf and Moorcroft Wilson, *Authors Take Sides on the Falklands*, p. 99.

20. Conversation with Jo Peters.

21. *Diaries*, 16 April 1951. Also included in what he entitled 'A Hymn of Hate' were The Gordon Highlanders and 'the one-time sergeant-major of 55 Military Prison and Detention Barracks (whose name I forget)', alongside such varied characters and institutions as the writers Hannen Swaffer and Beverley Nichols, Richard Dimbleby, Erroll Flynn, and 'Ivor Novello, the Boy Scouts, and Uncle James Agate and all'. Scannell could be a good hater, with catholic tastes and a long memory.

22. Barker, *Gordon Highlanders in North Africa and Sicily*, p. 6.

23. War diaries of Field Marshall Viscount Alanbrooke, 4 February 1943, published in Bryant, *The Turn of the Tide*, p. 577.

24. Miles, *Life of a Regiment*, p. 155.

25. *The Tiger and the Rose*, p. 84.

26. 'War Graves at El Alamein', from *Soldiering On*.

27. 'Remembering El Alamein', from *Soldiering On*.

28. Quoted in Bierman and Smith, *Alamein, War Without Hate*, p. 63. The book mistakenly sources this quote in *Argument of Kings*. Bierman, who carried out the interviews with Scannell, is dead, but the tone and style of the quote make clear that it originates in a conversation rather than from any written source.

29. Douglas's wounds kept him out of action for nearly four months, and mark the end of his memoir *Alamein to ZemZem*. He died in Normandy on 9 June 1944.

30. *The Tiger and the Rose*, p. 85.

31. Letter from John Bierman to VS, 20 May 1999. Bierman, a highly respected journalist and former Royal Marine, died in January 2006.

32. Letter from VS to John Bierman, 20 May 1999.

33. *Argument of Kings*, p. 13.

34. Information from Martin Reed.

35. *Diaries*, 3 April 1968.

36. 'The Spandaus opened up, and casualties were increasing. The Battalion pressed on. Piper McIntyre of Blair-Imrie's company was hit three times as he played; he played as he lay dying on the ground; when he was found the next morning, the bag was still in his oxter and his fingers upon the chanter; he was not yet 20 years of age.' Fergusson, *The Black Watch and the King's Enemies*, pp. 128–9.

37. Fergusson, *The Black Watch and the King's Enemies*, p. 161.

38. *Diaries*, 4 January 1953.

39. *The Tiger and the Rose*, p. 3.

40. *A Terrible Rain*, ed. Brian Gardner (London: Methuen, 1966).

41. *The Guardian*, January 1998.

42. Official Army Statement of Services, John Vernon Bain (Form B200b).

43. The story that Scannell used to like to tell of marching into Tripoli on his twenty-first birthday seems to be another minor inaccuracy. He could not possibly have been in North Africa for the fall of the city—and in any case, Wilfrid Miles in *The Life of a Regiment*, says that his battalion, the 5/7 Gordons, didn't arrive in the outskirts of Tripoli until 24 January, the day *after* Scannell's birthday. It was the 1st Gordons, riding on the tanks of 40th Royal Tank Regiment, who entered the city on 23 January.

44. *5/7 Gordons' War Diaries*, 14 February 1943, Public Record Office.

45. *5/7 Gordons' War Diaries*, 25 February 1943, Public Record Office.

46. *Argument of Kings*, p. 40.

47. He would leave Africa for the last time on 9 March. Eighteen months later, falsely implicated in the plot on Hitler's life, he took the option of suicide rather than facing trial and execution.

48. Fergusson, *The Black Watch and the King's Enemies*, p. 161.

49. *The Tiger and the Rose* p. 88.

50. 'Mock Attack', from *Mastering the Craft*.

51. Conversation with Jo Peters.

52. *The Tiger and the Rose*, p. 90.

53. Barker, *Gordon Highlanders in North Africa and Sicily*, p. 15.

54. Miles, *Life of a Regiment*.

55. Barker, *Gordon Highlanders in North Africa and Sicily*, p. 16.

56. Information from Tom Bruggen.

57. Douglas, *Alamein to Zem Zem*, p. 7.

58. *Not Without Glory*, p. 43.

59. *Not Without Glory*, p. 51.

60. 'Casualty—Mental Ward', from *Soldiering On*.

61. 'A Few Words to the Not-So-Old', from *Last Post*.

62. *Argument of Kings*, p. 14.

63. *Argument of Kings*, p. 9.

64. *Argument of Kings*, pp. 20–1.

65. *Argument of Kings*, p. 119.

66. *Soldiers, A History of Men in Battle*, BBC Television, 1985.

67. *Argument of Kings*, p. 8.

68. 'The Bombing of the Café de Paris, 1941', from *Winterlude*.

69. *Diaries*, 30 August 1987. The letter was published in the *Telegraph and Argus* on 28 August 1987, signed by William Handley, of Fagley, Bradford. It says that Anderson's mother was told in a letter: 'He had only a notebook which was completely

destroyed when he was killed.' Handley also quotes a comrade of Anderson's as saying that he saw his body after the battle: 'The only wound was a single shot through his left thigh, below the hem of his shorts. There was no blood.'

70. *The Face of the Enemy*, p. 202.
71. *Argument of Kings*, p. 90.
72. *Diaries*, 10 April 1951.
73. *Diaries*, 14 May 1985.
74. *Not Without Glory*, p. 40.
75. *Not Without Glory*, p. 24.

CHAPTER 5

1. *Argument of Kings*, p. 23.
2. *Argument of Kings*, pp. 25–30.
3. *Argument of Kings*, p. 34.
4. *Argument of Kings*, p. 40.
5. *Argument of Kings*, p. 41.
6. *Army Records Society*, quoted in Bierman and Smith, *Alamein: War without Hate*, p. 395.
7. *The Wound and the Scar*, p. 161.
8. Mark Connelly and Walter Miller, 'British Courts Martial in North Africa 1940–1943', *20th Century History*, 15(3) (2004).
9. Connelly and Miller (n. 8 above)..
10. Speech at Tripoli, 3 February 1943.
11. *Argument of Kings*, p. 50.
12. *Argument of Kings*, p. 66.
13. *Argument of Kings*, p. 86.
14. *Diaries*, 25 July 1985.
15. *Diaries*, 7 August 1986.
16. 'Family Secret', from *The Black and White Days*.
17. *Diaries*, 13 May 1988.
18. *Argument of Kings*, p. 97.
19. *Argument of Kings*, p. 103.

CHAPTER 6

1. *Diaries*, 17 April 1951.
2. 'On Leave: May 1916', from *Winterlude*.
3. *Argument of Kings*, p. 116.
4. 'On Leave: May 1916', from *Winterlude*.
5. *Argument of Kings*, p. 116.
6. Quoted in Hastings, *Overlord*. The general was probably disappointed with the parcels he received each month for the rest of the war—instead of the silk

stockings and lipsticks he had in mind, his mother sent him men's long socks and Vaseline sticks to prevent chapped lips.

7. Fergusson, *The Black Watch and the King's Enemies*, p. 262.
8. Miles, *Life of a Regiment*, pp. 248 ff.
9. *The Tiger and the Rose*, pp. 91–2.
10. *The Tiger and the Rose*, p. 90.
11. *Argument of Kings*, pp. 125–6.
12. Thomas, *An Underworld at War*, p. 190.
13. 'War Words', from *Last Post*.
14. Borthwick, *Battalion*, p. 131.
15. *Argument of Kings*, p. 139.
16. Miles, *Life of a Regiment*, p. 252.
17. 'Missing Things', from *Last Post*.
18. See Miles, *Life of a Regiment*, pp. 252 ff
19. *Argument of Kings*, p. 146.
20. *Argument of Kings*, p. 148.
21. Cramer, *Gone for a Soldier*, p. 66.
22. 'Cows in Red Pasture', from *A Sense of Danger*.
23. *Argument of Kings*, p. 151.
24. *The Tiger and the Rose*, p. 93.
25. *Argument of Kings*, pp. 151–2.
26. *Argument of Kings*, p. 156.
27. *Diaries*, 6 June 1994.
28. Salmond, *History of the 51st Highland Division*, pp. 144–5.
29. Major Peter Griffin, 1st Canadian Parachute Battalion, National Archives of Canada/Archives Nationales du Canada, quoted in Beevor, *D Day*, p. 187.
30. Letter from Montgomery to Field Marshal Sir Alan Brooke, 15 July 1944, National Archives, Kew, quoted in Beevor, *D Day*, pp. 278–9.
31. Morale rapidly improved under the new commander, and the 51st Highland Division went on to fight its way across France and into northern Germany. By the time the Germans surrendered in May 1945, it had suffered a total of nearly 20,000 battle casualties.
32. Scannell's poem 'Robbie', from *Mastering the Craft*, describes the death of a young soldier who 'Sucked on his rifle muzzle like a straw| And somehow managed to blow away his head.'
33. *The Tiger and the Rose*, p. 97.
34. *Argument of Kings*, p. 166.
35. These are the casualty figures given in the Gordons' regimental history. In *Argument of Kings*, Scannell says that six soldiers died and sixteen were sent back to the Casualty Clearing Station.
36. 'Walking Wounded', from *Walking Wounded*.
37. Interview with Hilary Smith for the Recorded Sound Department of the British Council, 9 September 1963, British Library Sound Archive.

38. *Diaries*, 20 November 1962.

39. Information from Martin Reed.

40. *The Tiger and the Rose*, p. 99.

41. *Argument of Kings*, p. 165.

42. *Argument of Kings*, p. 170.

43. Undated typescript, Leeds University Archive.

44. *Coming to Life in Leeds*, BBC Radio broadcast, repr. *The Listener*, 22 August 1963.

45. 'Grannie', from *Love Shouts and Whispers*. Jo Peters, VS's partner in his later years, is in no doubt that the poem refers to an actual hospital visit from his grandmother.

46. 'Grannie', from *Love Shouts and Whispers*.

47. *Argument of Kings*, p. 180.

48. Renamed Manchester Piccadilly in 1960.

49. *Argument of Kings*, p. 182.

50. *Argument of Kings*, p. 200.

51. *Argument of Kings*, p. 223.

52. *Argument of Kings*, p. 253.

53. *The Tiger and the Rose*, p. 5.

54. *The Tiger and the Rose*, p. 7.

55. *The Tiger and the Rose*, p. 8.

56. Penal Servitude.

57. Max Hastings, in *All Hell Let Loose*, gives a figure of 382,700 for British war dead.

CHAPTER 7

1. *The Tiger and the Rose*, p. 11; conversation with Cliff Holden.

2. Conversation with Cliff Holden.

3. Letter from VS to Peter Stephenson, BBC producer, 16 August 1954 (BBC archive).

4. He later went to teach English at Cairo University.

5. *The Tiger and the Rose*, p. 15.

6. *The Tiger and the Rose*, p. 105.

7. Conversation with Cliff Holden.

8. 12.5 p, or about £4.07 at today's rates.

9. Letter from VS to Emma Kilcoyne, 14 August 1989.

10. 'Missing Things', from *Last Post*.

11. Fothergill, *The Last Lamplighter*, Willetts, *Fear and Loathing in Fitzrovia*. Later, when the name of the *York Minster* was formally changed to *The French House*, the regulars insisted on calling it the *York Minster*.

12. VS, interviewed on *Calendar Carousel*, Yorkshire Television, 16 July 1981.

13. About £130 at today's rates.

14. Conversation with Cliff Holden.
15. *The Tiger and the Rose*, p. 24.
16. Conversation with Cliff Holden.
17. About £20 in today's money.
18. *The Tiger and the Rose*, p. 26.
19. *The Tiger and the Rose*, p. 27.
20. *The Tiger and the Rose*, p. 29.
21. *Diaries*, 10 April 1951.
22. *Diaries*, 10 April 1951.
23. Something over £150 in today's money.
24. Conversation with Elizabeth Whitmore, Ella's cousin.
25. A description of the encounter which may be closer to the truth occurs in Scannell's novel *The Wound and the Scar*, pp. 83–92, where the central character, Jeff, is persuaded by Ruth, a woman he has met in a pub, to go and live in the imaginary northern city of Texton.
26. *The Tiger and the Rose*, p. 34.
27. *The Tiger and the Rose*, p. 23.
28. Conversation with Angela Beese.
29. *Coming to Life in Leeds*, BBC Radio broadcast, repr. *The Listener*, 22 August 1963.
30. 50 p, or about £16.00 at today's rates.
31. Jean Stead, who later became Scannell's girlfriend, recalls that when she first met him in Leeds, he was distraught because his wife was undergoing an unspecified gynaecological operation, so it is possible that Ella was telling the truth. But after the first few months, Scannell never believed it.
32. 'A Place to Live', read on *Calendar Carousel*, Yorkshire Television, 16 July 1981. Confusingly, another poem with the same name appears in Scannell's collection, *A Place to Live*.
33. 37.5 p, or nearly £12 at today's rates.
34. *Diaries*, 28 May 1981.
35. 'Birthday Poem (for E.A.C.)', from *Graves and Resurrections*. Ella's middle name was Ann.
36. *Coming to Life in Leeds*, BBC Radio broadcast, repr. *The Listener*, 22 August 1963.
37. 'Belle Isle', from *Graves and Resurrections*.
38. *Coming to Life in Leeds*, BBC Radio broadcast, repr. *The Listener*, 22 August 1963.
39. VS, interviewed on *Calendar Carousel*. He recalled this incident later in a poem, 'Magnum Opus, in Memorian Jacob Kramer 1892–1962', from *The Black and White Days*.
40. 'Magnum Opus, in Memorian Jacob Kramer 1892–1962', from *The Black and White Days*.
41. *A Proper Gentleman*, p. 130. Dobrée's obituary in *The Times*, on 4 September 1974, said: 'He saw his duty, perhaps too clearly, as turning raw lads into something like the *homme de lettres* he had been.'

42. 'John Short, the Lost Poet', in *The London Magazine*, 34(11) (February 1995).
43. *Diaries*, 31 October 1986.
44. *Diaries*, 17 April 1956.
45. Anand, *Conversations in Bloomsbury*.
46. *Coming to Life in Leeds*, BBC Radio broadcast, repr. *The Listener*, 22 August 1963.
47. *The Tiger and the Rose*, p. 40.
48. *The Tiger and the Rose*, p. 39.
49. 'One Who Died', from *Graves and Resurrections*.

CHAPTER 8

1. *The Tiger and the Rose*, p. 46.
2. *The Tiger and the Rose*, p. 46.
3. *The Tiger and the Rose*, p. 53.
4. VS, interviewed on *Calendar Carousel*, Yorkshire Television, 16 July 1981.
5. Thomas, *An Underworld at War*, p. 359.
6. *The Tiger and the Rose*, p. 58.
7. *The Tiger and the Rose*, p. 59.
8. About £1,800 at today's rates.
9. *Yorkshire Evening Post*, 19 February 1948.
10. Undated draft of letter to Peter Redgrove, Falmouth College of Art, Leeds University Archive.
11. Conversation with Jean Stead.
12. *The Tiger and the Rose*, p. 105.
13. Draft of letter from VS to unknown correspondent, 3 October 1966, Leeds University Archive.
14. About £240 at today's rates.
15. Slightly over £1,300 at today's rates.
16. Conversation with Jean Stead.
17. Later, Jean married, and in 1960 Scannell wrote a poem, 'First Child', dedicated to her and her husband, celebrating the birth of their first child.
18. *The Tiger and the Rose*, pp. 100–1.
19. *Diaries*, 5 May 1951.
20. *Diaries*, 17 July 1981.
21. *Diaries*, 25 October 1963. He is quoting John Wilmot, Earl of Rochester's song, 'Love a woman? You're an ass'.
22. *Diaries*, 15 October 1963. *Agenbite of inwit* (*'Remorse of conscience'*) is a four-teenth-century treatise on religious morality. James Joyce uses the phrase several times in *Ulysses*.
23. *The Tiger and the Rose*, p. 119.
24. Nearly £270 at today's rates.
25. Just over £130 at today's rates.

26. *The Tiger and the Rose*, p. 131.
27. G. Wilson Knight to VS, 28 November 1949, Special Collections, Archives and Special Collections, Libraries and Cultural Resources, University of Calgary.
28. About £160 at today's rates.
29. *The Tiger and the Rose*, p. 136.
30. 'The Four Roys', from *A Time for Fires*.
31. Conversation with Natalie Bartington.
32. *The Tiger and the Rose*, p. 142.
33. *Diaries*, May 1952.
34. Conversation with Natalie Bartington.
35. The £300 grant came in 1971, part of a gift which an anonymous donor had asked the Prime Minister to distribute to authors and composers. Scannell's response to the letter was enthusiastic. The Civil List pension 'for services to literature' was awarded in 1981.
36. *Diaries*, 28 October 1970.
37. *Diaries*, 15 October 1982.
38. *Diaries*, 11 October 1990.
39. 'The Visitation', from *A Mortal Pitch*, originally published in *Poetry Quarterly* (Spring 1951).
40. *Diaries*, 8 April 1951.
41. Diaries, 5 April 1951.
42. *Diaries*, 8 April 1951.
43. Letter from Bonamy Dobrée, Leeds University Archive.
44. *Diaries*, 9 March 1952.
45. *Diaries*, 17 January 1952.
46. *Diaries*, 10 March 1952.
47. *The Tiger and the Rose*, p. 147; conversation with Don Brown, former Clark's pupil.
48. The equivalent of about £1,150 today.

CHAPTER 9

1. *Diaries*, 2 January 1953.
2. *The Tiger and the Rose*, p. 151.
3. *The Tiger and the Rose*, pp. 151–2.
4. *Diaries*, 1 May 1951.
5. *Diaries*, 31 March 1954.
6. BBC Archive, 5 April 1953. Wain chose 'Two Lessons in Grammar' and 'Posthumous Autobiography', both of which later appeared in *A Mortal Pitch*.
7. BBC Written Archives Centre, Scannell Vernon, RCONT1 Scriptwriter File 1, 25 September 1953. Newby went on to become Managing Director of BBC Radio.
8. £12.50, or about £265 at today's rates.

9. *Diaries*, 5 October 1953.
10. *Diaries*, 18 September 1953.
11. *Diaries*, 14 October 1953.
12. *Diaries*, 20 October 1953.
13. *Diaries*, 14 October 1953.
14. *Diaries*, 26 January 1954.
15. *Diaries*, 26 November 1953.
16. Conversation with Jo Scannell.
17. *The Tiger and the Rose*, p. 158.
18. About £530 at today's rates.
19. He described Spender later, in *The Tiger and the Rose*, p. 164, as 'a man of great kindness, intelligence and integrity'—an odd contrast to the view expressed earlier in his diaries, before he received Spender's letter, that he was 'really rather an old maid. There is something girlishly immature about his beefing over "personal relationships", his oh-so-sensitive sensitivity. He's a lousy poet too' (*Diaries*, 10 March 1952).
20. *Diaries*, 18 September 1953.
21. *Diaries*, 26 November 1953.
22. *The Tiger and the Rose*, p. 161.
23. *The Tiger and the Rose*, p. 161.
24. *The Tiger and the Rose*, p. 169.
25. Conversation with Jo Scannell.
26. Note from VS to RE Keen, 24 June 1954, BBC Archive.
27. Note from VS to Paul Stephenson, 16 August 1954, BBC Archive.
28. Broomin-White is described in Keith Jeffery's *MI6, The History of the Secret Intelligence Service* as 'a very well regarded officer who had been an exceptional head of station in Istanbul for a year before being brought back to Head Office to be Deputy Chief Controller Mediterranean'. Philip Knightley, in '*Philby: The Spy Who Betrayed a Generation*' portrays a dashing figure who was a master horseman and expert pistol shot, and who carried out several of his secret missions in the Middle East and elsewhere in disguise.
29. Letter from VS to R. E. Keen, 1 February 1955, BBC Archive.
30. *The Tiger and the Rose*, p. 175.
31. About £9,600 at today's rates.
32. *The Tiger and the Rose*, p. 179.
33. Letter from VS to George MacBeth, 17 August 1955, BBC Archive.
34. 'First Child', from *The Masks of Love*.
35. 'Poem for Jane', from *The Masks of Love*.
36. *The Tiger and the Rose*, p. 179.
37. Conversation with Jane Scannell.
38. Conversation with Jane Scannell.
39. Introduction to *A Choice of De La Mare's Verse*.
40. 'Apple Poem', from *Funeral Games*.

CHAPTER 10

1. *The Tiger and the Rose*, p. 180
2. Conversation with Jo Scannell.
3. *The Tiger and the Rose*, pp. 182–3.
4. *The Government Inspector* was written by Nikolai Gogol, not Tolstoy. Treffry believes that the slip is a schoolboy copying error of his own.
5. Conversation with Dudley Treffry.
6. *The Guardian*, 27 September 2007.
7. Letter to author from Mike Jordan.
8. Letter from Dudley Treffry to VS, 12 December 1987, Leeds University Archive.
9. Conversation with Dudley Treffry.
10. Letter from VS to Dudley Treffry, 11 January 1988, Leeds University Archive.
11. *The Tiger and the Rose*, p. 182.
12. Letter from GWK to VS, 28 November 1949, University of Calgary collection.
13. Nearly £5.5 million at today's rates.
14. Conversation with Robert Crick.
15. Donald Davie, 'Towards a New Poetic Diction', in *Prospect* (Summer 1949).
16. John Lehmann, *New Soundings*, BBC Radio, 24 September 1952, quoted in Morrison, *The Movement*.
17. Dannie Abse, Introduction to Abse and Sergeant (eds.), *Mavericks*. The other *Mavericks* poets included Michael Hamburger, John Silkin, J. C. Hall, and Abse himself.
18. Howard Sergeant, Introduction to Abse and Sergeant (eds.), *Mavericks*.
19. *Diaries*, 9 February 1969.
20. *Diaries*, 13 June 1956.
21. *Diaries*, 21 June 1956.
22. *Diaries*, 22 June 1956. The quotation is from a sonnet addressed to Robert Bridges by Gerard Manley Hopkins.
23. *Diaries*, 6 February 1963.
24. *Diaries*, 6 January 1956. The title of the collection is taken from Shakespeare's Sonnet CLXXXVI, in which the poet asks whether his lover has been tempted away by another, more skilful, poet: 'Was it his spirit, by spirits taught to write / Above a mortal pitch, that struck me dead?'
25. 'The Unsuccessful Poet', from *A Mortal Pitch*. The other poems from the collection previously published in *Mavericks* were 'Schoolroom on a Wet Afternoon', 'How to Fill in a Crossword Puzzle', 'Gunpowder Plot, and 'The Word of Love'.
26. Church, *The Voyage Home*.
27. Conversation with Jo Scannell.
28. From *Walking Wounded*.

29. Letter to VS from Virginia Browne-Wilkinson, 26 October 1966, BBC Written Archives Centre, Scannell Vernon, RCONT 12 Talks File 2, 26 October 1966.

30. 'Outcry as pupils taught "cat-killing" poem', *The Scotsman*, 24 January 2009.

31. *How to Enjoy Poetry*, p. 25.

32. *How to Enjoy Poetry*, p. 25.

33. *Drums of Morning*.

34. *Let the Poet Choose*, ed. James Gibson (London: Harrap, 1973). This was the book used in school by his future partner Angela Beese, shortly before she met Scannell.

35. Conversation with Bob and Inge Ball.

36. Conversation with Felicity de Zulueta.

37. 'My Father's Face', from *A Sense of Danger*.

38. 'Gunpowder Plot', from *A Mortal Pitch*.

39. Later, in his Introduction to a collection of poems in celebration of Thomas's life (*Elected Friends*, ed. Anne Harvey (Enitharmon Press, 1991)) Scannell said he had first suggested writing the pamphlet in the late 1950s, but Dobrée had thought at that time that Thomas lacked sufficient academic standing or interest. It is hard to think of any response that would have been more of a spur to Scannell's efforts.

40. *Diaries*, 14 April 1963.

41. *Edward Thomas*, p. 6.

42. *Edward Thomas*, p. 7.

43. 'The Great War', from *A Sense of Danger*.

44. Edward Thomas, 'No One So Much As You'.

45. *Diaries*, 23 August 1971.

46. Conversation with Jo Scannell.

47. Conversation with Bob Ball.

48. Badham-Thornhill, *Three Poets, Two Children*, p. 54. £25 would be about £420 at today's rates. 'Song for a Winter Birth' was included in *The Winter Man*.

49. 'First Child', from *The Masks of Love*.

50. *The Shadowed Place*, p. 19.

51. *The Shadowed Place*, p. 184.

52. *The Tiger and the Rose*, p. 191.

53. Conversation with Jo Scannell.

54. *The Tiger and the Rose*, p. 192.

55. *The Tiger and the Rose*, p. 194.

56. *The Tiger and the Rose*, p. 195.

57. Conversation with Jo Scannell.

58. *Diaries*, 9 September 1971.

59. 'An Old Lament Renewed', from *A Sense of Danger*.

60. Information from Martin Reed.

61. *Diaries*, 7 December and 28 December 1962.

62. *Diaries*, 28 December 1962.

63. Letter from VS to Alexis Lykiard, 28 January 1974.

64. *Daily Herald*, 11 June 1961, quoted by Robson in *Poems from Poetry and Jazz in Concert*.

65. *Diaries*, 20 November 1986.

66. Conversation with Jeremy Robson.

67. *Diaries*, 2 September 1965.

68. *Diaries*, 19 February 1971.

69. Conversation with Jeremy Robson. About £17.50 at today's rates.

70. Robson, Introduction, *Poems from Poetry and Jazz in Concert*, p. 13.

71. Conversation with Jeremy Robson.

72. *Diaries*, 10 December 1962.

73. *Diaries*, 12 March 1968.

74. *Diaries*, 20 May 1968.

75. Michael Garrick, quoted in sleeve notes to the 1963 double-LP record, *Poetry and Jazz in Concert* (ARGO ZDA 26/27).

76. *Diaries*, 30 June 1969. The comment, from the edited version of Scannell's diary, seems to represent a later reminiscence. The manuscript entry for 30 June 1969 reads simply: 'Sunday, we rehearsed in the afternoon at the Queen Elizabeth Hall and performed in the evening. The place was packed and the concert was very successful.'

77. Badham-Thornhill, *Three Poets, Two Children*, pp. 41–2.

78. Conversation with Joe Hone.

79. Letter from VS to George MacBeth, 4 March 1963, BBC Archive.

80. 'Mock Attack', from *Mastering the Craft*.

81. About £26,600 at today's rates.

82. *Diaries*, 26 April 1966. During the 1980s, Scannell prepared an edited version of his diaries from the 1960s, which he hoped to publish under the title 'Tightrope Walker'. It never appeared, but the typescript is included in the Leeds University Vernon Scannell archive. This passage was inserted into the edited version, and does not appear in the manuscript diaries.

83. About £13,300 at today's rates.

84. *The Big Time*, p. 207.

85. *Diaries*, 11 May 1965.

86. *Diaries*, 29 January 1966. Inserted into the later edited version of the diary.

87. About £17,000 at today's rates.

88. About £710 at today's rates.

89. *Diaries*, 23 December 1966. Inserted into the later edited version of the diary. The manuscript has no entry for 23 December 1966.

90. Letter from Elizabeth Thomas to Jeremy Robson, July 1997.

91. Conversation with Jeremy Robson.

92. About £280 today.

93. 'Last night, for instance, was really my first sober evening in a week, and even then I suppose I drank six or seven pints of bitter', *Diaries*, 26 June 1964.

94. About £160 today.

95. About £820.

96. About £18.

97. *A Proper Gentleman*, p. 21.

98. *A Proper Gentleman*, p. 22.

99. In April 1966, Scannell had been on a ten-day Arts Council poetry reading tour with Blunden, for whom he developed great affection. 'He was modest, gentle and often funny. You'd never have guessed that this little, quiet, scholarly old man had seen more service on the front line in France than any of the other war poets of the 1914–18 conflict.'

100. Letter from VS to Jo Scannell 9 March 1967, the Archives and Special Collections Department at the McFarlin Library, University of Tulsa.

101. Letter from VS to Jo Scannell 9 March 1967, the Archives and Special Collections Department at the McFarlin Library, University of Tulsa. The Haycutter is a pub in Oxted, near Limpsfield.

102. Letter from VS to Jo Scannell, March 1967, the Archives and Special Collections Department at the McFarlin Library, University of Tulsa.

103. 'No Sense of Direction', from *Epithets of War*.

104. *Diaries*, 7 July 1967.

105. *Diaries*, 7 November 1967.

106. Letter from VS to Jo Scannell, 23 March 1967, the Archives and Special Collections Department at the McFarlin Library, University of Tulsa.

107. Conversation with Robert Crick, son of the landlord of The Wheatsheaf.

CHAPTER 11

1. Letter from VS to Jo Scannell, 16 March 1967, the Archives and Special Collections Department at the McFarlin Library, University of Tulsa. The poem was later published in *Mastering the Craft*.

2. Letter from VS to Jo Scannell 23 March 1967, the Archives and Special Collections Department at the McFarlin Library, University of Tulsa.

3. *Diaries*, 14–18 August 1967. The references to Tom Payne's Hill, his neighbour, and the cows are all inserted into the later, edited version of the diary. The manuscript entry is more downbeat: 'I still have the feeling that I am on holiday here and will soon return to a more familiar world . . . There doesn't seem to be a library or bookshop worth a damn anywhere near and my not being able to drive [He had lost his licence over the drink-driving conviction] is a hell of a tie.'

4. *Diaries*, 9 November 1967.

5. Letter from VS to Jeremy Robson, 29 August 1967 (private collection).

6. Conversation with Jo Scannell.

7. Conversation with Alan Millard.

8. *Diaries*, 3 April 1968.

9. Just over £14 at today's rates.

10. *Diaries*, 13 January 1968.

11. Conversation with Nancy Scannell.

12. *Diaries*, 31 December 1969.

13. *Diaries*, 8 December 1970.

14. *Diaries*, 22 December 1970.

15. *Diaries*, 29 December 1967.

16. Conversation with Jo Scannell.

17. Conversation with Jane Scannell.

18. 'A Simple Need' from *Epithets of War*.

19. *Diaries*, 13 January 1968. This discussion of the poem is inserted into the later edited version of the diary, and is not included in the manuscript entry for 13 January 1968.

20. *The Dividing Night*, p. 196.

21. *The Dividing Night*, p. 207.

22. *Diaries*, 21 May 1971.

23. 'Autumn', from *Walking Wounded*.

24. *Diaries*, 8 January 1969.

25. Badham-Thomas, *Three Poets, Two Children*, p. 53.

26. 'Nettles', from *Mastering the Craft*.

27. Badham-Thomas, *Three Poets, Two Children*, pp. 52–3.

28. 'Epitaph for a Bad Soldier', from *The Apple Raid and Other Poems*.

29. *Diaries*, 11 June 1969. This story is inserted into the later edited version of the diary, and does not appear in the manuscript entry for 11 June 1969.

30. Badham-Thomas, *Three Poets, Two Children*, p. 40.

31. *Diaries*, 1 September 1986.

32. *Diaries*, 3 May 2000.

33. 'The Apple Raid', from *The Apple Raid*.

34. 'My Dog', from *The Very Best of Vernon Scannell* (2001).

35. *Diaries*, 19 May 1969.

36. *Diaries*, 10 November 1969.

37. *Diaries*, 18 January 1970.

38. *Diaries*, 5 November 1968.

39. *Diaries*, 2 May 1968.

40. *Diaries*, 23 February 1967.

41. *The Tiger and the Rose*, Introduction to the 1983 edition.

42. *Diaries*, 14 May 1985.

43. *Diaries*, 30 November 1970.

44. *The Tiger and the Rose*, p. 172.

45. *Diaries*, 3 June 1969.

46. *The Tiger and the Rose*, p. 197.

47. *Diaries*, 23 December 1963.

48. 'Incident in a Saloon Bar', from *A Sense of Danger*.

49. *Diaries*, 20 May 1968. This account is inserted into the later edited version of the diary, and does not appear in the manuscript entry for 20 May 1968.

50. Letter to the author from Christopher Hampton.

51. *The Collected Works of WB Yeats*, vol. 3: *Autobiographies*, ed. Richard J. Finnerah and George Mills Harper, London, Simon and Schuster, 2010.

52. *Diaries*, 5 June 1963.

53. *Diaries*, 20 November 1967.

54. *Diaries*, 24 March 1970.

55. *Diaries*, 20 April 2004.

56. *A Proper Gentleman*, p. 39.

57. About £150 at today's rates.

58. Conversation with Dannie Abse.

59. Letter to the author from Seamus Heaney.

60. Ted Walker, National Poetry Centre, Sixtieth Birthday Celebration for Vernon Scannell, 2 November 1982, British Library Sound Archive.

61. *Diaries*, 8 June 1971. The actual quotation, from Yeats's 'Lamentation of the Old Pensioner', is 'I spit into the face of time / That has transfigured me'. Later, after Blunden's death, Scannell remained in touch with his widow.

62. Blunden's daughter, Joy, died in 1919 when she was forty days old.

63. Webb, *Edmund Blunden: A Biography*, p. 317. Blunden died in 1974.

64. Webb, *Edmund Blunden: A Biography*, p. 323.

65. *Diaries*, 30 March 1985.

66. 'The Great War', from *A Sense of Danger*.

67. 'Behind the Lines', from *Behind the Lines*.

68. *Diaries*, 9 September 1971.

69. *Times Literary Supplement*, 17 September 1971

70. *Diaries*, 16 December 1971. £300 would be worth slightly over £3,500 today.

71. Just over £1,000 at today's rates.

72. *Diaries*, 22 February 1971.

73. *Diaries*, 2 May 1972.

74. *Diaries*, 29 September 1971.

75. *Diaries*, 8 August 1972.

76. Letter from Anne Stevenson.

77. Conversation with Jo Scannell.

78. *Diaries*, 16 February 1973.

79. *Diaries*, 9 May 1975.

80. Conversation with Tom Bruggen.

81. Conversation with Tom Bruggen.

82. Conversation with Tom Buggen.

83. *Diaries*, 30 January 1979.

84. Letter from VS to John Neish, 14 April 1980, Leeds University Archive.

85. 'Love Nest', from *The Winter Man*.

86. 'The Defrauded Woman Speaks', from *The Winter Man*.

87. Conversation with Jo Scannell.

CHAPTER 12

1. Letter from VS to Martin Bax 24 June 1975, Pennsylvania State University Archive.
2. Details from the BBC Archive. £20 is worth about £165 at today's rates.
3. Letter from VS to Martin Bax 26 June 1975 (Pennsylvania State University Archive). £8 would be about £65 at today's rates.
4. *Diaries*, 5 April 2006.
5. *Diaries*, 5 April 1951.
6. *Diaries*, 30 March or 1 April 1975.
7. *Diaries*, 14 April 1975.
8. *Diaries*, 12 June 1975.
9. *Diaries*, 28 October 1976.
10. Nearly £3,500 at today's rates.
11. *Diaries*, 2 July 1975.
12. *Diaries*, 2 July 1975.
13. Letter from VS to Alexis Lykiard, 22 September 1977.
14. 'Enemy Agents', from *The Loving Game*.
15. From *Poetry Society Bulletin*, Christmas 1975.
16. *Diaries*, 10 February 1969.
17. *Diaries*, 11 March 1987.
18. About £16,500 at today's rates.
19. *A Proper Gentleman*, pp. 6–7.
20. *Diaries*, 12 December 1975.
21. *Diaries*, 23 February 1976.
22. *A Proper Gentleman*, p. 15
23. Private letter to author.
24. Conversation with Mark Hiles, Berinsfield.
25. *A Proper Gentleman*, p. 139.
26. From his Introduction to *Selected Poems of Ezra Pound* (1928).
27. *A Proper Gentleman*, p. 94.
28. *A Proper Gentleman*, p. 39.
29. *Diaries*, 31 December 1975.
30. Ring out the old, ring in the new,
    Ring, happy bells, across the snow:
    The year is going, let him go;
    Ring out the false, ring in the true   [*In Memoriam*, CVI]
31. *How to Enjoy Poetry*, p. 16.
32. *Diaries*, 2 February 1976.
33. *Diaries*, 3 February 1976.
34. *A Perfect Gentleman*, p. 151.
35. In fact, there was one major achievement that he might not have expected. According to local historian Mark Hiles, who was a teenager when Scannell

was in Berinsfield and is now a local councillor, one of the reasons for his appointment was the desire of the local authority to develop a sense of community in the village. 'It had been a very divided place before, but things certainly improved after his visit', he says. 'At last there was something the village was united about. Everyone hated him.'

36. *Diaries*, 12 December 1976.
37. *Diaries*, 12 September 1976.
38. *Diaries*, 20 March 1976.
39. *Not Without Glory*, p. 17.
40. *Not Without Glory*, p. 19.
41. *New Statesman*, 28 May 1976.
42. Letter from VS to Alexis Lykiard, 18 February 1977.
43. Conversation with Jo Scannell.
44. *Diaries*, 21 September 1977. 'Ms Welon is very difficult, almost impossible . . . I think that I went [Clearly Scannell has got his tense wrong here] north to live quietly, but it's a sad idea, and full of aggravation [*ennui* should not have the extra *e*].'.
45. *Diaries*, 13 July 1978.
46. Diaries, 4 August 1980.
47. Angela Beese's diaries, 1 November 1981.
48. *Diaries*, 24 June 1984.
49. *Diaries*, 13 April 1977.
50. *Diaries*, 27 July 1978.
51. About £980 at today's rates.
52. *Diaries*, 27 July 1978.
53. *Diaries*, 31 July 1978.
54. Conversation with Martin Reed.
55. *Diaries*, 15 August 1978.
56. Ruth Reed's diary, 6 August 1978.
57. Conversation with Martin Reed.
58. *Diaries*, 10 November 1978.
59. 'John Short, the Lost Poet', in *The London Magazine*, 34(11) (February 1995).
60. 'John Short, the Lost Poet' (n. 66 above).
61. *Diaries*, 27 February 1979.
62. *Diaries*, 27 February 1979.
63. Letter from David Smith to author.
64. Letter from Simon Funnell to author.
65. Letter from Richard Field to author.
66. *Diaries*, 17 May 1979.
67. *Diaries*, 7 April 1979.
68. *Diaries*, 17 April 1979.
69. *Diaries*, 27 June 1979.

CHAPTER 13

1. *Diaries*, 16 September 1979.
2. Retitled 'In a City Churchyard' in *Winterlude*.
3. 'In a City Churchyard', from *Winterlude*.
4. *Diaries*, 30 September 1979.
5. The four poems, 'Last Attack', 'Simplicities', 'Of Love and Poetry', and 'Love Poet', appeared in *Ambit* (Autumn 1979) 80. The first three also appeared in *Winterlude*.
6. Conversation with Angela Beese. The Ben Jonson quote is from *Timber, or Discoveries Made Upon Men and Matter*.
7. *Diaries*, 22 November 1978.
8. *Diaries*, 25 April 1980.
9. *Diaries*, 9 October 1979.
10. *Diaries*, 2 November 1979.
11. *Diaries*, 2 November 1979. Mozart's Clarinet Quintet in A Major, K.581, was the piece of music Scannell had recommended to a writing student at a conference in Scarborough.
12. *Diaries*, 10 December 1979.
13. Angela Beese's diaries.
14. *Diaries*, 5 December 1979.
15. 20 December 1979.
16. Letter from Selima Hill.
17. Conversation with Angela Beese.
18. *Diaries*, 4 January 1980.
19. *Diaries*, 4 January 1980.
20. Conversation with Angela Beese.
21. *Diaries*, 22 January 1980. £80 would be worth around £320 today—but a copy of the three-volume *Poems for Shakespeare* alone, published by the Globe Playhouse Trust and signed by all the poets, was for sale recently at £700.
22. About £1,600.
23. About £120.
24. 'In a City Churchyard' from *Winterlude*.
25. Both poems were published in *Winterlude*.
26. *Diaries*, 18 January 1980.
27. *Diaries*, 26 January 1980.
28. Conversation with Angela Beese.
29. *Diaries*, 18 January 1980.
30. *Diaries*, 11 February 1980.
31. Angela Beese's diary, 7 January 1980.
32. *Diaries*, 7 January 1980.
33. Angela Beese's diary, 2 March 1980.
34. Conversation with Angela Beese.
35. *Diaries*, 25 April 1980.

36. Conversation with Angela Beese.
37. Conversation with Angela Beese.
38. Angela Beese's diary, 4 February 1980.
39. *Diaries*, 13 May 1980.
40. 'Weaker Sex', from *Winterlude*.
41. Angela Beese's diary, 11 April 1980.
42. Angela Beese's diary, 12 April 1980.
43. Angela Beese's diary, 2 June 1980.
44. *Diaries*, 9 May 1980.
45. Introduction to *New and Collected Poems 1950–1980*.
46. *The Observer*, 27 July 1980.
47. *Times Literary Supplement*, 1 August 1980.
48. 'Two Variations on an Old Theme', from *New and Collected Poems 1950–1980*.
49. 'A Partial View' from *New and Collected Poems, 1950–1980*.
50. 'A Partial View' from *New and Collected Poems, 1950–1980*.
51. Letter from VS to Sandy Brownjohn, 6 April 1979.
52. *Diaries*, 1 August 1980.
53. 'A Place to Live', read on Yorkshire Television's *Carousel*, 16 July 1981. Another poem with the same title is included in *A Place to Live*.
54. *Diaries*, 27 September 1980.
55. *Diaries*, 3 October 1980.
56. Angela Beese's diary, 15 December 1980.
57. *Diaries*, 2 August 1981.
58. 'In a Dark Corner', typescript in Leeds University Archive, 1981.
59. Angela Beese suggests that Vernon may have typed it himself while she was away visiting her parents. She says: 'Psychologically it's possible that I suppressed the knowledge of the story (it's amazing what the mind can do) but I think it's unlikely, as it is exactly the acknowledgement of the horror of it all that I had hoped, even yearned, for until I gave up around the year 2000.'
60. Diaries, 15 September 1981.
61. *Diaries*, 5 February 1981.
62. *Diaries*, 9 February 1981.
63. *Diaries*, 15 February 1981.
64. About £2,350 at today's rates.
65. Angela Beese's diary, 15 February 1981.
66. *Diaries*, 31 March 1981.
67. *Diaries*, 4 April 1981.
68. 'On Leave May 1916', from *Winterlude*.
69. Information from Jo Scannell, Angela Beese, and Jo Peters.
70. *Diaries*, 30 December 1985.
71. About £6,750 at today's rates.
72. *Diaries*, 24 May 1981.
73. *Diaries*, 6 August 1981.

74. *Diaries*, 2 July 1981.

75. *Diaries*, 4 January 1982. The typescript of *How to Enjoy Novels* was completed on 31 March 1982, but not published until 1984.

76. *Diaries*, 29 January 1982.

77. Angela Beese's diary, 7 June 1981.

78. *Diaries*, 13 July 1981.

79. Woolf and Wilson, *Authors Take Sides on the Falklands*, p. 98.

80. *Diaries*, 7 January 1982. Official unemployment figures reached three million for the first time since the 1930s on 26 January.

81. *Diaries*, 16 September 1982.

82. *Diaries*, 24 January 1982.

83. 'Farewell Performance', from *Winterlude*.

84. *Diaries*, 6 June 1982.

85. 'Mastering the Craft', from *Winterlude*.

86. The Welsh middleweight Johnny Gamble had to retire after a brain scan following a knock-down defeat in February 1963. He died in 2008 after a long coaching career.

87. *Diaries*, 13 February 1963.

88. *Ring of Truth*, p. 327.

89. *Daily Telegraph*, 11 November 1983.

90. *Financial Times*, 29 October 1983.

91. *Yorkshire Post*, 10 November 1983.

92. *Diaries*, 9 June 1983. £5,000 would be nearly £14,000 at today's rates.

93. *Diaries*, 17 October 1982.

94. Angela Beese's diary, 24 June 1983.

95. *Diaries*, 25 September 1983.

96. *Diaries*, 6 August 1983.

97. *Diaries*, 10 November 1983.

98. '*Missing Things*', from *Last Post*.

99. *Vernon Scannell—a Writer in Otley*, privately produced video interview by Martin Reed.

CHAPTER 14

1. Angela Beese's diaries, 8 December 1983.

2. *Letter from Otley*, BBC Radio 4, 13 September 1991.

3. *Diaries*, 19 January 1984.

4. 'A Victorian Honeymoon', from *Funeral Games*.

5. *Diaries*, 23 January 1984.

6. Conversation with Jack Dalglish.

7. *Diaries*, 8 May 1984.

8. Conversation with June Emerson.

9. Conversation with Kit Wright.

10. *Diaries*, 22 June 1984.
11. *Diaries*, 28 July 1985.
12. Quoted in *Letter from Otley*, broadcast on BBC Radio 4, 13 September 1991.
13. Angela Beese's diary, 24 November 1985.
14. *Diaries*, 1 May 1985.
15. Conversation with Christopher Warren.
16. The title comes from an inscription on a cannon from the army of the French king Louis XIV to the effect that guns are 'Ultima ratio regum', the final argument of kings.
17. Introduction, *Argument of Kings*.
18. *Diaries*, 14 May 1985.
19. *Diaries*, 18 September 1986.
20. *Argument of Kings*, p. 71.
21. I am thinking in particular of two professional soldiers, both veterans of the Falklands War and both decorated for their bravery in action. One of them, crippled for life by a bullet, just nodded understandingly when told about Scannell's experience at Wadi Akarit, while the other, told about the looting of corpses after the battle, simply said, 'Yes, that tends not to get into the history books.'
22. *Diaries*, 13 December 1986.
23. *The Times*, 23 July 1987.
24. *Times Educational Supplement*, 16 October 1987.
25. *Diaries*, 6 October 1987.
26. 'Londoner's Diary', in the *Evening Standard*, 22 September 1987.
27. *Diaries*, 26 September 1987.
28. *Diaries*, 9 October 1987.
29. Desert Island Discs archive: <http://www.bbc.co.uk/radio4/features/desert-island-discs/castaway/0fe4d232#p009ml4q>
30. Private letter to author.
31. Just over £1,000 at today's rates.
32. Public Lending Right statement, 1986, Leeds University Archive.
33. Income tax statement 1988–9, Leeds University Archive.
34. *Diaries*, 8 January 1987.
35. *Diaries*, 26 November 1987.
36. Conversation with David Jones.
37. Conversation with David Jones.
38. Christopher Barker, *Portraits of Poets* (Manchester: Carcanet, 1986).
39. *Diaries*, 12 October 1986.
40. *Diaries*, 18 May 1986.
41. *Diaries*, 26 November 1987.
42. 'Old Man', from *Funeral Games*.
43. *Diaries*, 28 May 1987.
44. *Diaries*, 16 June 1987.

45. Letter from Emma Kilcoyne to author.
46. VS to Emma Kilcoyne, 7 April 1988.
47. VS to Emma Kilcoyne, 11 May 1988.
48. VS to Emma Kilcoyne, 7 April 1988. This was the Scarborough weekend at which he drunkenly recommended Mozart's Clarinet Quintet to one of the participants.
49. VS to Emma Kilcoyne, 5 December 1987 and 19 February 1988.
50. VS to Emma Kilcoyne, 7 April 1988.
51. VS to Emma Kilcoyne, 3 January 1989.
52. VS to Emma Kilcoyne, 18 April 1987.
53. VS to Emma Kilcoyne, 27 May 1987.
54. VS to Emma Kilcoyne, 3 January 1989.
55. VS to Emma Kilcoyne, 2 March 1989.
56. VS to Emma Kilcoyne, 28 April 1989.
57. VS to Emma Kilcoyne, 27 April 1987.
58. VS to Emma Kilcoyne, 16 December 1991.
59. VS to Emma Kilcoyne, 2 October 1988.
60. VS to Emma Kilcoyne, 2 October 1988.
61. VS to Emma Kilcoyne, 2 March 1989.
62. VS to Emma Kilcoyne, 7 December 1991.
63. VS to Emma Kilcoyne, 16 June 1992.
64. Letter from Emma Kilcoyne to author.
65. VS to Emma Kilcoyne, 27 October 1988.
66. VS interviewed by Michael Parkinson for *Desert Island Discs*, BBC Radio, broadcast on 29 November 1987.
67. *Diaries*, 27 June 1987.
68. 'Swearing In', from *Soldiering On*.
69. *Sunday Times*, 9 April 1989.
70. 'Rudyard Kipling', in *George Orwell: The Collected Essays, Journalism and Letters*, vol. 2: *My Country, Right or Left, 1940-43*, ed. George Orwell, Sonia Orwell, Ian Angus, London, Penguin Books Ltd, 1970.
71. 'Letters Home from Troopship', from *Soldiering On*.
72. *Diaries*, 30 June 1987.

CHAPTER 15

1. About £420 today.
2. 'Our Father', from *The Loving Game*.
3. *Sunday Times*, 3 May 1992.
4. Conversation with Alastair Wilson.
5. Conversation with Fraser Steel.
6. *Diaries*, 14 April 1990.
7. 'The Little Joke', from *The Clever Potato*.

8. 'Waiting for the Call', from *Love Shouts and Whispers*.

9. *Diaries*, 11 April 1985.

10. Conversations with Jo Peters and John Scannell.

11. *Diaries*, 30 September 1989.

12. *Diaries*, 28 February 1990. 'Matches' was published in *A Time for Fires*.

13. *Diaries*, 13 May 1988.

14. *Diaries*, 27 February 1996. There was also a bleaker aftermath to Angela's relationship with Vernon—a serious mental breakdown followed by hospital treatment in 1997. 'Certainly my experiences with Vernon played a large part in that', she says now. 'There is no blame implicit in that statement—it's just the way it was, and part of taking risks in life.'

15. Private correspondence with author.

16. *Diaries*, 5 September 1989.

17. *Diaries*, 15 September 1989.

18. *Diaries*, 15 November 1989.

19. *Diaries*, 16 November 1989.

20. *Diaries*, 30 April 1990.

21. Conversation with Robert Crick.

22. 'On the Chevin', from *A Time for Fires*.

23. 'Billets Aigres' is the title of a poem in Scannell's collection *Views and Distances*, in which he describes the daily arrival of the cards:

Each more violent and obscene,
and on the backs of all were scrawled
in a spiky hand he recognised
variations on one bleak theme,
short and soundless yelps of rage
and hatred . . .

24. *Diaries*, 28 February 1985.

25. *Diaries*, 31 December 1987.

26. *Diaries*, 5 April 1988.

27. *Diaries*, 13 August 1988.

28. *Diaries*, 12 July 1990.

29. Conversation with Angela Beese.

30. Conversation with Jo Scannell.

31. Conversation with Jo Peters.

32. Conversation with Jo Peters.

33. 'The Party's Over', from *A Time for Fires*.

34. 'Bobbie', from *A Time for Fires*.

35. 'Old Shaver', from *A Time for Fires*.

36. *Diaries*, 12 September 1993.

37. *Diaries*, 14 September 1993.

38. Private communication with author.

39. Conversation with Jo Peters.

40. *Diaries*, 24 November 1993.

41. *Diaries*, 24 June 1994.

42. *Diaries*, 21 June 1994.

43. *Diaries*, 21 June 1994.

44. *Diaries*, 1 July 1994.

45. *Diaries*, 24 June 1994.

46. *Diaries*, 1 July 1994.

47. 'Good Grief', from *Views and Distances*.

48. 'In Memoriam Toby Scannell 1960–1994', Leeds University Archive.

49. *Sunday Telegraph*, 17 April 1994.

50. *Irish Independent*, 26 June 1994.

51. *Diaries*, 4 August 1994. It is a tribute to Scannell's self-taught, if sometimes erratic, French that he was, as Martin Reed confirms, quite comfortable reading French novels and newspapers.

52. Letter from VS to Robert Conquest, 10 August 1996, Leeds University Archive.

53. *Diaries*, 25 August 1994.

54. *Diaries*, 28 August 1994.

55. *Diaries*, 31 August 1994.

56. *Diaries*, 23 September 1994.

57. *Diaries*, 26 September 1994.

58. *Diaries*, 9 March and 27 March 1995.

59. Conversation with Jo Peters.

60. 'The Black and White Days', from *The Black and White Days*.

61. 'El Alamein: 50th Anniversary, October 1992', from *The Black and White Days*.

62. 'Magnum Opus', from *The Black and White Days*.

63. 'Old Man in Love', from *The Black and White Days*.

64. *Diaries*, 20 September 1995.

65. VS to Robert Conquest, 27 September 1996, Leeds University Archive.

66. Diaries, 3 October 1996.

67. Diaries, 20 January 1997.

68. The Firebox: Poetry from Britain and Ireland After 1945, ed. Sean O'Brien and The Penguin Book of Poetry from Britain and Ireland Since 1945, ed. Simon Armitage and Robert Cranford.

69. Sunday Telegraph, 15 November 1998.

70. Letter from VS to John Coggrave, 18 November 1998.

71. Letter from VS to Robert Conquest, 14 October 1998.

72. 'Intimations of Mortality', from The Year of the Crab, in Of Love and War.

73. Diaries, 26 November 1998. Larkin died in December 1985, just under six months after surgery for oesophageal cancer.

74. Diaries, 2 December 1998.

75. 'The Ghosts of Love', from Views and Distances.

76. *Diaries*, 26 October 1988.

77. *Diaries*, 31 December 1998.

78. *Diaries*, 8 February 1999.

79. *Diaries*, 10 February 1999.

80. Letter from VS to John Coggrave, 26 April 1999.

81. 'The Treatment', from *Of Love and War*.

82. *Diaries*, 29 March 1999.

83. *Diaries*, 3 September 1999.

84. 'Postscript: Andalusian Afternoon', from *Of Love and War*.

85. *Diaries*, 30 April 1981.

86. Private communication with author.

87. *Diaries*, 19 September 1999.

88. *Diaries*, 26 May 2000.

89. 'Going Home', from *The Year of the Crab*, in *Of Love and War*.

90. *Diaries*, 20 December 2000.

91. *Diaries*, 8 August 2000.

92. *Diaries*, 14 March 2001.

93. *Diaries*, 17 March 2001. The quotation from Meredith should read, 'Passions spin the plot.'

94. Introduction to *Of Love and War*.

95. *Sunday Telegraph*, 21 April 2002.

96. VS to Robert Conquest, 27 September 1996, Leeds University Archive.

97. The poem was not published but was included in a letter to John Coggrave dated 22 October 2001.

98. *Diaries*, 20 January 2002.

99. *Diaries*, 14 February 2002.

100. Letter from VS to John Coggrave, 5 April 2002.

101. *The Sunday Telegraph*, 3 February 2002. The biography is Robert Fraser, *The Chameleon Poet: A Life of George Barker* (Jonathan Cape, 2002).

102. Letter from Robert Conquest to VS, 6 May 2002, Leeds University Archive.

103. *Diaries*, 25 March 2002.

104. *Diaries*, 24 July 2001.

105. *Diaries*, 26 February 2002.

106. Conversation with Charlotte Harris. Angela still has the portrait. 'There were no good photographs of him at the time, and I thought it was important for the future that people should get a sense of what he was really like', she says now.

107. *Diaries*, 25 December 2001.

108. *Diaries*, 17 November 2004.

109. 'Planning the Occasion', from *Behind the Lines*.

110. 'A Serious Bitch', from *Behind the Lines*. Sally, a chocolate mongrel bitch, was bought from the Canine Defence League shortly after the death of Vernon's old friend Hetta, who died in 1994.

111. 'Confiteor', from *Behind the Lines*.

112. *The Observer*, 5 September 2004.

113. Letter from VS to John Lucas, 7 October 2004.

114. *Diaries*, 18 April 2005.

115. *Diaries*, 17 April 2004.

116. Letter from VS to John Lucas, undated.

117. 'Small Mercies', from *A Place to Live*.

118. Letter from VS to John Coggrave, 22 May 2001.

119. Letter from Robert Conquest to VS, 10 December 1998, Leeds University Archive.

120. Letter from VS to Robert Conquest, 12 April 1998, Leeds University Archive.

121. Letter from VS to Robert Conquest, 20 March 1997, Leeds University Archive.

122. Letter from VS to John Coggrave, 22 November 2005, Leeds University Archive.

123. Letter from Robert Conquest to VS, 22 March 2007, Leeds University Archive.

124. Letter from VS to Jeremy Robson, private collection.

125. Letter from VS to John Lucas, 24 June 2007.

126. Conversation with John Lucas.

127. Letter from VS to Robert Conquest, 10 April 1997.

128. 'Missing Things', from *Last Post*.

129. 'Last Song, for JP', from *Last Post*.

130. 'For Those Reliefs', *Ambit* 192 (Spring 2008).

CHAPTER 16

1. *Poetry in Motion*, Alan Bennett, Channel 4, June 1990.

2. *Diaries*, 2 July 1965.

3. In 'Missing Things', from *Last Post*.

4. *Diaries*, 3 September 1987. G. K. Chesterton ('Why do you rush through the field in trains?') and A. E. Housman ('O why do you walk through the fields in boots?') were among other poets to be stirred into action by the poem.

5. 'A Note for Biographers', from *Walking Wounded*.

6. Conversation with Angela Beese.

7. *Diaries*, 28 December 1966.

Appendix

Some Vernon Scannell Poems

These poems are discussed in detail in the text. Most are not easily available elsewhere, and two have not been previously published in book form.

Birthday Poem, (For E.A.C.) from *Graves and Resurrections* (1948)

And so, as unseen snow prepares to change
Your close horizon, grace immediacy
Of personal foreground with tiny diamonds
In the soft white lawn, I watch the living page
Turn over,
Filled by the hand of what unknown author?

The twenty-fifth page confused with records,
Illuminated illustrations,
Stained with ghosts of fallen tears
Shed for your Autumn whose death was a symbol
Of something
Elusive, something suffering,

Is turned revealing a page as white
As the imminent snow of your December;
I bring you a birthday gift of knowledge:
No anonymous author will fill this page.
Take courage my darling, accept me ever,
Your permanent collaborator.

Walking Wounded, from *Walking Wounded* (1965)

A mammoth morning moved grey flanks and groaned.
In the rusty hedges pale rags of mist hung;

The gruel of mud and leaves in the mauled lane
Smelled sweet, like blood. Birds had died or flown,
Their green and silent attics sprouting now
With branches of leafed steel, hiding round eyes
And ripe grenades ready to drop or burst.
In the ditch at the cross roads the fallen rider lay
Hugging his dead machine and did not stir
At crunch of mortar, tantrum of a Bren
Answering a Spandau's manic jabber.
Then into sight the ambulances came,
Stumbling and churning past the broken farm,
The amputated signpost and smashed trees,
Slow wagonloads of bandaged cries, square trucks
That rolled on ominous wheels, vehicles
Made mythopoeic by their mortal freight
And crimson crosses on the dirty white.
This grave procession passed, though, for a while,
The grinding of their engines could be heard,
A dark noise on the pallor of the morning,
Dark as dried blood; and then it faded, died.
The road was empty, but it seemed to wait −
Like a stage which knows the cast is in the wings −
Wait for a different traffic to appear.
The mist still hung in snags from dripping thorns;
Absent-minded guns still sighed and thumped.
And then they came, the walking wounded,
Straggling the road like convicts loosely chained,
Dragging at ankles exhaustion and despair.
Their heads were weighted down by last night's lead,
And eyes still drank the dark. They trailed the night
Along the morning road. Some limped on sticks;
Others wore rough dressings, splints and slings;
A few had turbanned heads, the dirty cloth
Brown-badged with blood. A humble brotherhood,
Not one was suffering from a lethal hurt,
They were not magnified by noble wounds,
There was no splendour in that company.
And yet, remembering after eighteen years,
In the heart's throat a sour sadness stirs;
Imagination pauses and returns
To see them walking still, but multiplied
In thousands now. And when heroic corpses
Turn slowly in their decorated sleep
And every ambulance has disappeared

The walking wounded still trudge down that land,
And when recalled they must bear arms again.

A Case of Murder, from *Walking Wounded* (1965)

They should not have left him there alone,
Alone that is, except for the cat.
He was only nine, not old enough
To be left alone in a basement flat,
Alone, that is, except for the cat.
A dog would have been a different thing,
A big gruff dog with slashing jaws,
But a cat with round eyes mad as gold,
Plump as a cushion with tucked-in paws –
Better have left him with a fair-sized rat!
But what they did was leave him with a cat.
He hated that cat; he watched it sit,
A buzzing machine of soft black stuff,
He sat and watched and he hated it,
Snug in its fur, hot blood in a muff,
And its mad gold stare, and the way it sat
Crooning dark warmth: he loathed all that.
So he took Daddy's stick and he hit the cat.
Then quick as a sudden crack in glass
It hissed, black flash, to a hiding place
In the dust and dark beneath the couch,
And he followed the grin on his new-made face,
A wide-eyed, frightened snarl of a grin,
And he took the stick and he thrust it in,
Hard and quick in the furry dark.
The black fur squealed and he felt his skin
Prickle with sparks of dry delight.
Then the cat again came into sight,
Shot for the door that wasn't quite shut,
But the boy, quick too, slammed fast the door:
The cat, half through, was cracked like a nut
And the soft black thud was dumped on the floor.
Then the boy was suddenly terrified
And he bit his knuckles and cried and cried;
But he had to do something with the dead thing there.
His eyes squeezed beads of salty prayer
But the wound of fear gaped wide and raw;
He dared not touch the thing with his hands,
So he fetched a spade and shovelled it

And dumped the load of heavy fur
In the spidery cupboard under the stair
Where it's been for years, and though it died
It's grown in that cupboard and its hot low purr
Grows slowly louder year by year:
There'll not be a corner for the boy to hide
When the cupboard swells and all sides split
And the huge black cat pads out of it.

Autumn, from *Walking Wounded* (1965)

It is the football season once more
And the back pages of the Sunday newspapers
Again show the blurred anguish of goalkeepers.
In Maida Vale, Golders Green and Hampstead
Lamps ripen early in the surprising dusk;
They are furred like stale rinds with a fuzz of mist.
The pavements of Kensington are greasy;
The wind smells of burnt porridge in Bayswater,
And the leaves are mushed to silence in the gutter.
The big hotel like an anchored liner
Rides near the park; lit windows hammer the sky.
Like the slow swish of surf the tyres of taxis sigh.
On Ealing Broadway the cinema glows
Warm behind glass while mellow the church clock chimes
As the waiting girls stir in their delicate chains.
Their eyes are polished by the wind,
But the gleam is dumb, empty of joy or anger.
Though the lovers are long in coming the girls still linger.
We are nearing the end of the year.
Under the sombre sleeve the blood ticks faster
And in the dark ear of Autumn quick voices whisper.
It is a time of year that's to my taste,
Full of spiced rumours, sharp and velutinous flavours,
Dim with the mist that softens the cruel surfaces,
Makes mirrors vague. It is the mist that I most favour.

In Memoriam Toby Scannell 1960–1994 (unpublished, 1994)

Now all the words, like last year's leaves
Rustle senseless in the dirt
These strings and woodwinds adumbrate
Something of our grief and hurt

But even Bach and Mozart seem
To lack the power to mitigate
The mauling misery which art
And nature fail to palliate
I cannot live with,or without
The knifing sweetness of this sound
Inscribed on what he has become,
That perfect silence in the ground.
Where such illimitable hopes
And possibilities shone bright
The thrown switch left a starless sky,
A cold and everlasting night.
Yet something of him must survive
More than these tears that blur and smart,
The lingering image in the mind
And noiseless keening in the heart.
Once more I turn to music which,
Affirming nothing, never lies;
Transmuting joy and pain it soars
Beyond terrestrial compromise.
At last the shimmering echoes fade
All hope of solace seems withdrawn
And then, through mist, I see him stride
Towards me, handsome as the dawn.

Good Grief, from *Views and Distances* (2000)

It is not here, among the fragrant rites,
The flowers and summer dresses in the cool
Twilight of the nave where slanting lights
From clerestory and gilded oriel fall,
Gleaming softly on the polished box
Which, to our puzzled eyes, seems far too small
To hold his broken body and which mocks
Our shattered notions of the brave and tall;
Nor can the muted music's wiliest arts –
His favourite Dvorák, Beethoven and Brahms –
Coax it to the chill vault of our hearts
Or hold us safe in reassuring arms
Though those diminished sevenths seem to float
The scent of all June's flowers made audible,
And loop a noose of honey round the throat,
We find their blandishments implausible.

Some facile tears expressed, a sob or two,
But grief, true grief, is scentless, drab, elsewhere,
And that elsewhere, which waits for me and you,
Beyond the cypress, marble crosses, square
White or lichened tablets of carved stone,
Is silent, cold, and it will not permit
Entry save to those who are alone;
And this is where we must contend with it,
The grief that does not heal or mitigate
The pain of loss, yet must be understood
As necessary and will predicate
Its cauterizing hurt as final good.

The Ghosts of Love, from *Views and Distances* (2000)

In the calm darkness of the moonless nights
those almost silent whisperings are heard:
the ghosts of love perform their timeless rites
Not lovers' ghosts but shades of love's delights
return to haunt, with sigh or murmured word,
in the calm darkness of the moonless nights.
A disembodied voice of air recites
its litany of loss and, disinterred,
the ghosts of love perform their timeless rites.
The icy call of owl and star invites
the jilted lover t make up a third
in the calm darkness of the moonless nights.
Each place where passion flowered and rose in flights
of petals will remember this occurred:
the ghosts of love perform their timeless rites.
Though carnal vases may be smashed, their plight
beyond all aid, pathetic or absurd,
in the calm darkness of the moonless nights
the ghosts of love perform their timeless rites.

Postscript: Andalusian Afternoon, from *Of Love and War* (2002)

In the narrow street between the tall
white buildings with jet iron traceries
and whispered secrecies of glass,
which tell you nothing though they hint
at sensuous possibilities, dark shadows slant

and splash on wall and paving-stone. Two children
are laughing as they play with a large black dog
and a pink balloon, while he and she
look down, unseen, from their small balcony.
Behind them, still and cool, the room recalls
once more a Schubert Trio in B Flat
and, as the Scherzo dances, the black dog bounds
and pounces on the light pink globe
of air held tight in shining weightless skin
which quite astounds by bouncing free,
unpunctured by the canine claws,
and, teasing, settles only feet away.
Delighted squeals float up like small balloons.
And this slight incident, without intent,
is beautiful, this moment in a burnished afternoon
in a lofty room in Southern Spain
will be remembered with that nimble tune,
black glossiness of dog and pink balloon,
and if a whisper of uncertainty is heard
between the scherzo and the rondo it affords
a glint of seasoning, a piquancy,
which makes the mortal moment more their own.

Planning the Occasion, from *Behind the Lines* (2004)

Music and just one poem, not too long,
but something that will pierce right to the bone
and linger in the head. It would be wrong,
I think, to choose a work that's too well-known
or anything too slick and up-to-date:
something by Herbert, or a Shakespeare song,
should strike a note to charm and resonate.
The music, though, is harder still to choose:
it must be something easy on the ear,
yet serious stuff. Not New Orleans blues,
that trails a haze of sex and smoke and beer,
nor anything austere, like late Baroque;
and yet the smooth and richly sensuous ooze
of Suk or Gluck might come across as schlock.
That's not the thing we want, so I must find
a work so lovely it will make them weep
a salt monsoon; don't think I'm being unkind,
for grief of that sort isn't very deep

and holds some spice of pleasure; so I swear
they'll have a ball. That's why I'm not resigned
to not being there, or anywhere at all.

Confiteor, *from Behind the Lines* (2004)

I saw the warnings in my middle years
of penalties survival would impose;
it's paying-up time now – blurred eyes and ears;
scents visit memory but not the nose;
no appetite, except for phantom fare;
this hunger for lost hungers aches and grows;
dead voices whisper on the moonlit stair.
I think I could have prophesied the lot
a quarter of a century ago,
except for this one item I could not
have guessed would shake me like a body-blow,
this need to give a full account of all
the lies and selfish cruelties I know
I have been guilty of, which now appal.
If I could find a way of balancing
the scales with memories of virtuous deeds,
I'd feel less miserable, but rummaging
through those mean treacheries and lusts and greeds
I find no selfless act of charity
or bravery shines there and intercedes,
redressing the account's disparity.
And further searchings turn up nothing more
than flimsy moral negatives to weigh
against the debit side – a dismal score
of unkicked dogs and cats, a dim display
of unbruised babies, unraped girls and boys;
so 'mea culpa' as they used to say,
who prayed that God would mend his damaged toys.

Last Song, for JP, from *Last Post* (2007)

Another day relinquishes
last memory of sun,
and nightfall prowls the lamplit streets
as silent as a nun.
I lock the door against the threats
that populate the dark,

and in my attic room I hear
a lost dog's distant bark.
Then perfect soundlessness presents
me with the chance to sing
one small but heartfelt song for you,
my love, my everything.
I have no wish to trouble you,
to make you laugh or weep,
but just to sing you one last song
before I go to sleep.

Black-Out, from *Last Post* (2007)

An evening in late autumn, unprepared
to yield completely to the icy steel
of winter's infantry and, in the air,
slight ghost of garden bonfire-smoke still there,
though muffling folds of darkness now conceal
all details of the street in which he waits,
for this is nineteen-forty and a time
when spilling light at night is serious crime,
as German bombers would release their load
of carnage if a splash of glitter showed.
And still he waits, this lad of eighteen years,
and still she does not come. A car slides past,
its headlamps masked, so just the merest smear
of pallid yellow trickles on the road;
and then, as his anxiety swells, he hears
the distant clicking of her heels at last.
This sound is thrilling, more so as she nears.
And now she's here! Her fragrance claims the air;
their lips connect; her closeness sweetly stuns,
although, from far away, deep growl of guns
begins its low and unrelenting threat,
which neither he nor she can hear, as yet.

Missing Things, from *Last Post* (2007)

I'm very old and breathless, tired and lame,
and soon I'll be no more to anyone
than the slowly fading trochee of my name
and shadow of my presence: I'll be gone.
Already I begin to miss the things

I'll leave behind, like this calm evening sun
which seems to smile at how the blackbird sings.
There's something valedictory in the way
my books gaze down on me from where they stand
in disciplined disorder and display
the same goodwill that wellwishers on land
convey to troops who sail away to where
great danger waits. These books will miss the hand
that turned the pages with devoted care
And there are also places that I miss:
those Paris streets and bars I can't forget,
the scent of caporal and wine and piss;
the pubs in Soho where the poets met;
the Yorkshire moors and Dorset's pebbly coast,
black Leeds, where I was taught love's alphabet,
and this small house that I shall miss the most.
I've lived here for so long it seems to be
a part of what I am, yet I'm aware
that when I've gone it won't remember me
and I, of course, will neither know nor care
since, like the stone of which the house is made,
I'll feel no more than it does light and air.
Then why so sad? And just a bit afraid?

A Few Words for the Not-So-Old, from *Last Post* (2007)

About old age, here's something you might find
worth knowing when senescence's embrace
begins to squeeze you tight:
your inability to call to mind
from long ago some once familiar face
seems perfectly all right.
It's the things of days, or even hours ago,
of which you have no memory at all
that cause you some distress;
a splendid poem I thought I'd got to know
by heart would disappear beyond recall
within a week or less.
Dates and numbers, names of quite close friends,
even simple words, all fade away
before they can embed.
I start a tale, but mislay where it ends.

the lively music I could sing or play
lies dead inside my head.
But certain memories will never die:
Tom Fenton's smile, part naughty urchin's grin
yet just a little sad,
before the bomb blew it and him star-high
at Mareth when the Company moved in
and the universe went mad.

For Those Reliefs . . ., published in *Ambit* (Spring 2008)

An early memory: the Infant School
in Beeston's Nether Street, where Iris White
raised high one hand and called out loudly, 'Miss!
Bernard Scannell shit hisself, so who'll
clean up the mess miss?' (Although no fool
she never seemed to get my first name right).
I can't recall what happened after this.
I know that shame was burning on my face
and I could see there was no hope of flight
or any hiding place from deep disgrace.
I may have been responsible for more
childhood lapses such as Iris saw;
if this is so, I've buried them away
with multitudes of best-forgotten deeds,
but what I'm sure will always stay with me
are later memories from time of war,
not images of carnage, but the way
we lived for months in holes in mud or sand,
and had to wait for dark to ease our needs
as even Iris White might understand.
To leave slit trench in the daylight's glare
would be an act of certain suicide
and so, in frequent torture, we stayed there
until, when dark descended, we defied
the snipers' bullets and machine-gun fire,
crept out with paper and entrenching tools
to leave our dark deposits in the ground,
no laxative required beyond pure fear.
There could have been few areas free from stools
interred by frightened squaddies in that year.
I showed these lines to someone who I knew

would judge their merit, giving reasons why
he thought them good or bad, a learned chap.
He read them through with care and then he drew
a deep breath in, expelled it with a sigh.
'Won't do,' he said. 'In fact, a load of crap.'

WALKING WOUNDED

Also by the author
God's Fugitive: The Life of C. M. Doughty
The World of Gerard Mercator
Travelling the Sands
A Plum in Your Mouth
Burning the Suit
The Rise and Fall of the Great Empires
Books That Changed the World
Poets and Poetry
Random Acts of Politeness